MIRA___

WEIRD AND WONDERFUL STORIES OF ANCIENT GREECE AND ROME

PAUL CHRYSTAL

REAKTION BOOKS

For Anne, Rachael, Michael and Rebecca

Published by
Reaktion Books Ltd
Unit 32, Waterside
44–48 Wharf Road
London N1 7UX, UK
www.reaktionbooks.co.uk

First published 2025
Copyright © Paul Chrystal 2025

EU GPSR Authorised Representative
LOGOS EUROPE, 9 rue Nicolas Poussin, 17000, La Rochelle, France
email: contact@logoseurope.eu

Printed and bound in Great Britain by Bell & Bain, Glasgow

A catalogue record for this book is available from the British Library

ISBN 978 1 83639 049 7

MIRACULA

CONTENTS

SEX AND SEXUALITY

SOCIAL SCIENCES

HISTORY AND ETHNOGRAPHY

'Life without celebration is a long road without an inn.'
DEMOCRITUS (*c.*460–*c.*370 BC), frg. 230

'Learning never exhausts the mind.'
MARCUS TERENTIUS VARRO (116 BC–27 BC)

'Baths, wine, and sex corrupt our bodies; but the baths, wine and sex are what we live for.'
Epitaph for TIBERIUS CLAUDIUS, *Corpus Inscriptionum Latinarum* (*CIL*) VI.15258, Rome, first century AD

'The Ethiopians are old by the age of thirty because their bodies are exposed to excessive heat . . . whereas the Britons live for 120 years because their country is so cold.'
PSEUDO-PLUTARCH, *On the Opinion of Philosophers* 911b

Pliny's caveats, caveats that this author shares . . .

'For the most part, I cannot guarantee that any of this is actually true; whether it is true or not is down to the authors quoted.'
PLINY, *Natural History* 7, 8

'Some of these facts will seem astonishing and, indeed, incredible to many. Who, for example, could ever believe that the Ethiopians existed if they had not actually seen them?'
PLINY, *Natural History* 7, 1

Foreword by Philip Matyszak

Paul Chrystal and I first met on the Internet through a mutual interest in one of the more arcane aspects of the ancient world – the practice of magic and witchcraft in antiquity. We discussed the topic over several months, both of us taking approaches most suitable to our characters and each enriching the other's perspective through our different viewpoints.

The upshot of these discussions was – in my case – the book *Ancient Magic*, though I was aware at the time that Paul intended a more academic and comprehensive review of the known material. I am delighted to see that he has also expanded this survey into a wider study of the strange (and often very strange indeed) views held by some in the ancient world.

One of the strengths of this book is that Paul is not only well-informed about the ancient world in general, but he has an astonishing knowledge of texts that were probably obscure and recondite even at the time they were published hundreds or thousands of years ago. Much of this material is often dry, poorly written and, frankly, boring. However, it also contains unexpected passages that cause us to gasp, guffaw or simply shake our heads in wonder. The joy of this book is that Paul has done for you the hard work of extracting the gems from the sludge. He presents his results here in page after page of incidents, anecdotes and opinions which are sometimes amusing, sometimes *outré* or horrifying and sometimes nuts.

It is interesting to note that had this book been around 2,000 years ago, it would also have been in demand back then. The Greeks and Romans used dinner parties as a major form of social interaction. Where you sat (or reclined), what food and wine you were offered and how much attention you received from your host were all keenly observed as markers of personal status. It helped immensely if you were yourself an interesting and amusing character, and part of so being was to have a useful stock of anecdotes and *bon mots* to draw upon for every occasion. Needless to say Paulus Chrysostom would have been the star guest at such events.

Of course, like his modern counterpart Paul Chrystal, our ancient dinner guest had a stock of books that he could read up beforehand for juicy stories, and indeed sometimes these are the same books, for ancient collections of dinner-party anecdotes have survived. Two examples are the *Saturnalia* tales from ancient Rome and the *Deipnosophistae* from Hellenistic Greece. However, an abundance of gems are also to be gleaned from Pliny the Elder, Aristotle the philosopher, Herodotus the historian and dozens of others.

Remember, though, that these are reports of the offbeat and bizarre from the ancient world rather than accounts of everyday experience. For these occasions were not for accounts of the mundane lived experience of the ancients. Our writers would much rather tell us of the day the sky turned green than inform us that most days it was blue (or grey, if they lived in Britannia). The audience – then and now – could accept these stories with a greater or lesser degree of incredulity. Some tales might be obviously fiction, such as those told by explorers who reckoned that if one travelled far enough north one eventually reached a point where the sea turned into solid ice. As if!

The tales of magic and witchcraft – and these accounts I would reckon as still being the strongest part of this book – were more readily accepted by an audience that pretty much took the existence of these things for granted. So if you are looking for evil witches, love potions or horrible curses, you have come to the right place.

Again though, snicker ye not too much at those superstitious ancients, or do so only if you have never touched wood, looked at healing stones on offer on the Internet or informed people that you don't believe in magic because you are a Taurus, and people with your sign are too down-to-earth for such nonsense. Remember when people would solemnly inform you that putting a razor blade under a little pyramid at home would keep the blade miraculously sharp? (If you are Gen Z or later, google it!)

Humans are suckers for tales of the supernatural and always have been, whether their imaginations took them to the walls of Troy or the dormitories of Hogwarts. We love stories of uncanny healing, of spells that make light work of difficult endeavours and of malignant powers that sabotage the way to success because they tell of the world not as it is but as we somehow persist in thinking it should be, even as science changes our lives on an almost daily basis. Actually, come to think of it in any case, a lot of modern science is only magic that is better understood.

So, whether you are looking for something to dip into quickly to enliven a commute to the office, or planning on snuggling down on the sofa for a long read in the evenings, you'll find plenty in this book to meet your needs. You might even find some good anecdotes for a dinner party. Paul Chrystal is as much editor as he is author, and if it's ghost stories you are looking for, how about the voices of people dead for 2,000 years whispering directly into your ear from these pages? The ghosts of historians, satirists, poets and philosophers are all here, telling those stories that were *mirabilia* to them then and every bit as strange and wonderful to us today.

Preface

The title of this book is a bit of a mouthful, perhaps making it sound somewhat daunting; it is anything but, however – far from it. Taken from Palaephatus' paradoxographical work *On Incredible Things* (late fourth century BC), it could just as easily have been borrowed from Antigonus of Carystus' *Collection of Wonderful Tales*, or the *Mirabilia* of Apollonius Paradoxographus (*fl.* third century BC), the pseudo-Aristotelian *On Marvellous Things Heard* (*c.* 250 BC), the *Wonderful Things* of Callimachus (third century BC), Phlegon of Tralles' wonderful *Book of Marvels* (second century AD) or, bringing us full circle, even Heraclitus the Paradoxographer's *On Incredible Things* (second century AD).

Anyway, enough of all that serious stuff: this book is humorous, full of astonishing stories (well over one hundred in all), many of which have rarely, if ever, seen the light of day in English; it is sometimes shocking but always fascinating – it is about 'the incredible', the barely believable, as given to us by the paradoxographers mentioned above. But there is much, much more to it. Cicero, for example, was never just writing about (sometimes) dry-as-dust legal niceties and complex law cases; Pliny was not only immersed in plants, medicinal herbs and rolling rocks – at other times, he regales us with strange drugs and stranger sex. Indeed, many of the canonical authors known to us had their sensationalist, tabloid side, failing to resist the temptation to jazz up and embroider their work with the fantastic and the funny, the outrageous and the *outré*. This book has it all: it could be titled *Sex, Drugs and Rolling Rocks in Antiquity* but that would be to miss out lots of other subjects. The qualification for inclusion has quite simply been that the pieces are absorbing and enchanting, curious, unbelievable, comical, astonishing and sometimes just plain daft. Indeed, some have called it a kind of Horrible Histories for adults.

But, for all that, we can always learn something from these oddities. Some are, by our moral standards, disturbing and distressing: for example, the treatment of slaves, foreigners and immigrants; attitudes to people with disabilities; misogyny; sexual violence in war, torture, public displays of gratuitous cruelty, social immobility, poverty, pandemics and (often avoidable) disease, social injustice, religious intolerance, gluttony, xenophobia and genital mutilation. I have made efforts not to make this gratuitous, sensational or tabloid-esque, adding, wherever possible, references for such abominations in the literature, from archaeology and inscriptions, in an attempt to apply context and veracity – historical, religious and social.

Paradoxically (there's a theme here), those two paragons of civilization, Greece and Rome, were, by any standards, actually *un*civilized in some of their so-called civilizing activities. Alongside educating and entertaining, this book also shows us how far we still have to go in order to eradicate the dark, evil things that continue to stain our own contemporary societies, because even 2,000 years later, few of the repellent things included here have been completely eliminated: readers will recognize many as ever-present facets of contemporary life. The aim of this book of paradoxes exposed by paradoxographers, then, is itself paradoxical: it is surely to educate, amuse and entertain, but at the same time, it looks to startle us into action. If we take away from it a sharper sense of what is right and still wrong in the modern world – and what needs working on to improve those societies – then it will have achieved part of its aim.

The chapters open with an introduction briefly describing each topic or event as it was received in the ancient world with an assessment of Greek and Roman attitudes to those topics: what was the ancients' stance on torture or slavery, for example, and what were the societal norms and values relating to them?

As stated, for the content of the book I have obsessively mined a vast range of literary, and some archaeological, sources. Herodotus' *Histories*, Virgil's *Aeneid* and Homer's *Odyssey*, for example, may be familiar but who really knows these jewels of obscurity that have also helped: *On the Nature of the Non-Existent; The Type of Women Who Ought to be Taken as Wives; On Moles* (dermatologically speaking); *About the Barren Woman; On Semen* and *Forty Marvellous Things about Water*?

As an example of the book's research credentials, here are some examples of how we take the urine:

- A child should be washed in the urine of someone who has been living on a diet of cabbage.
- Before the days of safe-to-use tooth whitener, Catullus, the love poet, put a rival's dazzling smile down to the Spanish custom of brushing one's teeth with urine from the *latrinae publicae* – a product usually reserved for public laundry.
- You can remove those ill-advised and regrettable tattoos by smearing on them a mixture of very sharp vinegar and the stuff that sticks to the insides of a chamber pot.

Before we proceed, here are eight important questions for which you really do need to know the answer:

- Why is the rectum so called?
- Why are lions scared of hens, especially white ones?
- How do you catch a monkey up a tree?
- Why if a female partridge stands downwind from a male does it get fertilized?
- What are the thirteen different types of animal dung used in medicine?
- Can you name the seven efficacious uses of water cress in medicine?
- Why do all animals have an even number of feet?
- What do you do when stung by a scorpion? (I'll give you the answer to the last one: *you should sit on a donkey, facing backwards towards the tail, because this transfers the pain to the donkey and makes it fart.*)

All the above are supported by full references to help with further research. Please remember that they were all written by men.

Introduction

The extant literature of Greece and Rome is awash with wondrous tales, astounding facts, odd and miraculous events that never cease to astonish and to stretch credulity to its limits. Some are well known, many others less so, recorded for us by obscure authors or left to languish in the darker corners of works by more familiar writers. While many of the stories emanate from works of history, geography, science, medicine or philosophy, others are the product of a genre devoted specially to *mirabilia* – wonders and marvels.

Paradoxography is the name for this genre recording the miraculous; it flourished in both Greece and Rome, providing a vehicle for the unnatural, the perverse, the unexpected and the decidedly odd. Paradoxographical material also featured in more 'conventional' works such as the fifth-century BC *Histories* of Herodotus, the fourth-century BC philosophical works of Aristotle and Plato, Strabo's (*c.* 64 BC–*c.* AD 25) *Geography* and Pausanias' second-century AD *Description of Greece*; and then there is Pliny the Elder's encyclopaedic *Natural History* (AD 77–9), Suetonius' *Lives of the Twelve Caesars* (AD 121), the *Annals* of Tacitus (*c.* 55 BC–*c.* AD 120) and the work of Gaius Licinius Mucianus (*fl.* first century AD), whose natural history and geography of the East was an important source for Pliny the Elder when foraging for things miraculous to include in his *Natural History*.

Aulus Gellius (AD *c.* 125–180), a Roman author and grammarian, conveniently gives us a real-life instance of paradoxography, not to say serendipity, which neatly defines the genre and leaves us thirsting for more:

When I was returning from Greece to Italy and had reached Brundisium, I got off the boat and was ambling about in that famous port ... There I saw some bundles of books for sale, and I eagerly hurried over to them. Now, they were all in Greek, filled with marvellous tales, things unheard of, incredible; the writers were ancient and authoritative: Aristeas of Proconnesus, Isigonus of Nicaea, Ctesias and Onesicritus, Philostephanus and Hegesias. The volumes themselves, however, were dirty from long neglect, in bad condition and dog-eared. Nevertheless, I went up and asked their price; then, taken in by their extraordinary and unexpected cheapness, I bought lots of them for a small amount, and quickly read through all of them over the next two nights ...

This is the sort of stuff contained in those books: the most remote of the Scythians, who live in the far north, eat human flesh and subsist on the nourishment of that food, are called 'cannibals'. Also there are men in the same region having one eye in the middle of the forehead and called Arimaspi, who look like what the poets call Cyclopes. There are also in the same part of the world other men, of marvellous swiftness, whose feet are turned backwards and do not point forward, as in the rest of mankind. Further, tradition has it that in a distant land called Albania men are born whose hair turns white in childhood and who see better by night than during the day. It was absolutely certain that the Sauromatae, who dwell far away beyond the river Borysthenes, take food only every other day and fast on the intervening day. (AULUS GELLIUS, *Attic Nights* 9, 4)

Paradoxography itself flourished in its own right from the Hellenistic age (323–30 BC), with perhaps the first work, *Marvellous Things* (Θαυμάσια, or *Thaumasia*) by Callimachus, describing wonders of the known world: natural phenomena and miraculous rivers, springs, stones, animal, plants and the like. Callimachus' sources were many and included Aristotle, Megasthenes, Theophrastus,

Theopompus and Timaeus. Others followed, although all survive only in a fragmentary form: Philostephanus (*On Marvellous Rivers*), Antigonus of Carystus (*Collection of Wonderful Tales*, a paradoxographical work chiefly extracted from *On Marvellous Things Heard*, attributed to Aristotle), Polemon of Ilium, Isigonus of Nicaea, Απιστα (*Incredible Things*), Alexander of Mindus, Sotion and Mucianus. Phlegon of Tralles, whose second-century AD *Book of Marvels* is concerned with the supernatural as well as astonishing aspects of the natural world, and covers ghost stories, the discovery of giant bones, congenital malformations, centaurs, hermaphrodites and gender transition, men giving birth and women giving birth to animals. His *On Long-Lived People* (περὶ μακροβίων) deals with persons in ascending order of longevity from 100 to 1,000 years of age. Then there is the geographer Solinus from the mid-third century AD, author of *De mirabilibus mundi* (The Wonders of the World), also published under the title *Collectanea rerum memorabilium* (Collection of Curiosities), and *Polyhistor* (Polymath), much of which is sourced from Pliny's *Natural History* and the *Geography* of Pomponius Mela.

More familiar to us are Cicero (106–43 BC), who wrote a non-extant paradoxographical *Admiranda*, as cited twice by Pliny and by Columella in relation to aquatic curiosities, zoological and human wonders, and Varro (116–27 BC), whose paradoxographical work has survived only in a very fragmentary form. The title was possibly *Gallus Fundanius de admirandis* (On Wonders by Gallus Fundanius), and the book comprised various marvels in zoology, botany, medicine, aquatics and human achievements. Pliny the Elder adds spice to his *Natural History* when he marks out paradoxographical sections and provides us with mini-*thaumasia* in his table of contents by designations such as *miraculae terrae motus* (II.86, the wonders of earthquakes and precautions), *mirae magnitudines serpentium* (VIII.14, huge snakes) and *de fabulosis avibus* (X.70, fabulous birds). Books VII (human biology), VII–XI (zoology) and XXXI (many water marvels) are particularly full of paradoxographical material.

Other authors whose works we plunder include well-known figures, from the fifth-century BC Thucydides to Virgil (70–19 BC),

Ovid (43 BC– AD 17), Livy (c. 64 BC–AD 17), Statius (fl. late first century AD), Lucan (39–65), Juvenal (c. 55–127), Martial (c. 40–104) and Dio Cassius (c. 150–235) – as well as intractable priapism in the *Priapeia* (a collection of eighty anonymous short Latin poems composed in various metres on subjects pertaining to the phallic god Priapus) – and the less well known, such as the early third century BC Egyptian priest Manetho, the first-century AD Valerius Maximus (*Memorable Deeds and Sayings*) and Phaedrus (*Fables*), the second-century works of Arrian (*Indica*), Soranus (*Gynaecology*), Galen, Aulus Gellius (*Attic Nights*), Lucian and Aelian, the fourth-century Archbishop of Constantinople John Chrysostom (*The Type of Women Who Ought to Be Taken as Wives*), Byzantine historian Procopius (*Secret History*) and many, many more.

This book mines many of these works for the fascinating and astonishing; it features scores of outrageous, sensational and unexpected tales – some anecdotal, some historical and others that land somewhere in the middle. It includes legendary and actual peoples and eccentric characters and many aspects of what may qualify as the darker side of life: war; monsters;

Ivory statuette of Lakshmi, 1st century CE, the Hindu goddess of wealth, fortune, power, beauty, fertility and prosperity, discovered in the ruins of Pompeii c.1930–38. It is a good example of Rome's global reach in relation to Eastern trade and cultural assimilation.

cannibalism; barbarians; child exposure; voodoo dolls, deformity and disability; all manner of sexual deviancy; war crimes and atrocities; misogyny, the madness of Roman emperor Caligula (r. 37–41); the incest and necrophilia of Nero (r. 54–68); persecution and torture of the Christians and others; the cruelty of the games, xenophobia and not to mention zoophilia. And then there is abortion; contraception; castration and female genital mutilation (FGM); unconventional scientific beliefs; strange, exotic and fabulous animals; natural (and unnatural) phenomena; magic and exotic religion; science fiction and space travel and alpha-male Julius Caesar as an effeminate homosexual.

Throughout the chapters, veracity and verisimilitude are by no means guaranteed – ask Pliny the Elder, with his caveats quoted at the opening of this book – but everything in here can claim to be exceedingly interesting, marvellous, magical, mysterious, maddening or mad, and hopefully, instructive to the modern world. So, if you want to know . . .

- how to sober up a drunk person with radishes and vinegar;
- how to punish an adulterer with a strategically inserted radish;
- all about interplanetary space flight in the first century AD;
- what the three forms of human being are: male, female and . . .;
- why it is that people can't tickle themselves;
- about the Spartan Stasi;
- how death was guaranteed in the arena by someone with a red-hot poker and another man with a sledgehammer;
- how Pomponia took Philologus, the freedman who betrayed Cicero, and ordered him to cut off strips of his own flesh, cook them and eat them;
- how Porcia, the constant wife of conspirator Brutus, committed suicide by swallowing hot coals when Brutus was killed

. . . then proceed with this collection.

Beware the woodpecker! They say that 'the peony should be dug up at night, for, if a man does it in daytime and is observed by a woodpecker while he is gathering the seeds, he risks the loss of his eyesight; and, if he is cutting the root at the time, he gets a prolapsed anus.'

Look at this random selection of wonderful advice, instructions and anecdotal observations:

- Sexual intercourse has never done anyone any good, and we should be thankful if it does us no harm. (EPICURUS, frg. 62)
- People have died of too much pleasure before now. (GALEN, *Semen* 4, 588k)
- Your hand serves as the mistress of your pleasure. (MARTIAL, *Epigram* 33)
- The people of Miletus are not stupid; they just do the sort of things stupid people do. (ARISTOTLE, *Nicomachean Ethics* 1151a)
- Why do all animals have an even number of feet? (PSEUDO-ARISTOTLE, *Problems* 893b)
- There is also a type of mullet called the grayfish which feeds on its own slime; and the octopus sits through the winter devouring himself. (PLUTARCH, *On the Cleverness of Animals* 965a)
- Anyone who is stung by a scorpion should sit on a donkey, facing backwards towards the tail. For this transfers the pain to the donkey and makes it fart. (ANON., *Geoponica* 13, 9)
- Lions are scared of hens – especially white ones. (As in a number of Aesop's *Fables*)
- I have heard that there is a tribe in Ethiopia that is ruled by a dog. (AELIAN, *On Animals* 7, 40)
- Cress juice when poured in through the ears cures toothache. (ANON., (Byzantine), *Farm Work*)
- When Alcibiades asked his teacher for a copy of the *Iliad*, the teacher replied that he had no Homer. Alcibiades punched him. (PLUTARCH, *Sayings of Kings and Commanders* 186d)

- They say that camels in Arabia do not mate with the females and will not do so even if force is used. A story is told that once when no stallion was available the man in charge surreptitiously introduced a colt. The colt completed the mating but soon after bit the camel driver to death. (PSEUDO-ARISTOTLE, *On Marvellous Things Heard* 2)
- Baths, wine, and sex corrupt our bodies; but the baths, wine, and sex are what we live for. (Epitaph for TIBERIUS CLAUDIUS SECUNDUS, *CIL* VI.15258)
- Weasels give birth through their ears, though some say through their mouths. (TIMOTHEUS OF GAZA, *On Animals* 39)
- You can remove tattoos by smearing on them a mixture of very sharp vinegar and the stuff that sticks to the insides of a chamber pot. (PAUL OF AEGINA, *Medical Compendium* 4.7)
- [Coming to the end:] men ejaculate when they die. (CASSIUS IATROSOPHISTA, *Problems* 47)

Within this volume, we also answer that famous question: what are the benefits of a small penis? The relatively small size of the penises possessed by gods and heroes as reflected on Greek statues has exercised – obsessed, even – classics and fine art scholars and visitors to museums for centuries.

And you can forget about chickens and eggs; this book finally answers the eternal question revealed by an elderly visionary man of impaired vision: who gets the greater pleasure out of sex, men or women?

If any of this appeals, then this is certainly the book for you.

I

Strangely Strange and
Oddly Normal

'*barbara barbaribus barbarant barbara barbis.*'
A hexameter line of untranslatable gibberish graffiti scratched
in Pompeii playing on the word *barbarus*, Latin for 'barbarian'
(*Select Latin Inscriptions* 351)

In Libya there is a city called Dionysopolis that can never be
located twice by the same person.

(STRABO, *Geography* 7, 3, 6)

This chapter is indicative of the innate xenophobia of the Greeks
and Romans and speaks of their shared fascination for the
incredible, the absurd and the miraculous.

One odd habit of the ancient world was the quoting of dates
of the consuls as an effective and oft-used way of giving a date, for
example on a letter or in a history. The following missive was giving
nothing away, thanks to the absence of crucial specifics: 'Written
in the consulship of the current consuls' (*Oxyrhynchus Papyrus* 1121).
Names would help. It was in fact written in AD 295.

Herodotus tells us about some decidedly odd foreigners and
places that it may be best to avoid; the hairstyles may be familiar to
us, though:

West of the Triton river and next to the Aseans begins the
country of Libyans who till the land the soil and live in
houses; they are called Maxyes; they wear their hair long
on the right side of their heads and shave the left, and they
paint their bodies scarlet ... For the eastern region of Libya,

which the nomads inhabit, is low-lying and sandy as far as the Triton river; but the land west of this, where the farmers live, is exceedingly mountainous and wooded and full of wild beasts . . . In that country are huge snakes and the lions, and the elephants and bears and asps, the horned asses, the dog-headed and the headless men that have their eyes in their chests, as the Libyans say, and the wild men and women. (4, 191)

Human Monsters

Pliny (*Natural History* 7, 15) adds to our knowledge of these varied types of monsters, as equally feared as they were subjects of awe.

Cynocephali

The Cynocephali were dog-headed men. Roman lore apart they can be found in the mythology and legends of ancient Egypt, India, Greece and China. What's more the Greeks and Romans called a species of apes 'cynocephalus', probably baboons with the face of a dog.

The fifth-century BC Greek physician Ctesias expatiated on the existence of cynocephali in India, while Greek traveller and ethnographer Megasthenes (*c.* 350–290 BC) was also aware of dog-headed mountain people in India – where he was sent as an ambassador to the court of Sandracottus in around 303 BC – who communicated through barking, wore the skins of wild animals and lived by hunting. Aelian (AD 175–235) references the dog-headed tribes in India, confirming that they are of human shape and clothed in animal skins. He also added that although they have no speech and howled to communicate, they could nevertheless understand the Indian language (*Characteristics of Animals* 4.46). Herodotus (4, 91) reported that such creatures inhabit the east of their lands, as well as headless men and various other hybrids.

There was a battle between the Argonauts and the cynocephali in what is now northern Serbia or southern Hungary. The cynocephali were emblematic of the magical nature and brutality characteristic of bizarre people at the ends of the earth. St Augustine of Hippo (AD 354–430) mentioned the cynocephali in *The City of God* (16, 8), in the context of discussing whether such beings were descendants of Adam. In the Eastern Orthodox Church, some icons covertly identify St Christopher with the head of a dog. Muslims in the French medieval epic *The Song of Roland* (*c.* 1140–70) yelped like dogs (3526–7), and there was depicted the dog-headed Muslim army in *Kyng Alisaunder* (*c.* 1275) 'whose men could neither speak nor shout/ But only bark and rage like hounds' (1934–6).

Monopods

Monopods were one-legged dwarfish men with a large foot who moved speedily and on hot days lay on their backs using their foot as a parasol. Also known as sciapods, monopods appear in Aristophanes' play *The Birds*, first performed in 414 BC. St Augustine mentions the 'Skiopodes' in *The City of God* in the same section as the cynocephali, entitled 'Whether Certain Monstrous Races of Men Are Derived from the Stock of Adam or Noah's Sons'. C. S. Lewis features monopods in *The Voyage of the Dawn Treader* (1952), the third novel in the fantasy series *The Chronicles of Narnia*.

Machyles

The Machyles were a Libyan tribe of hermaphrodites or androgynes whose bodies were male on one side and female on the other. An unphased, matter-of-fact Herodotus (4, 180) says:

> The Makhlyes wear their hair long behind, the Auseans in front. They celebrate an annual festival of Athena, where their maidens are separated into two bands and fight each other with stones and sticks, thus, they say, honouring in the way of their ancestors that native goddess whom we call Athena. Maidens who die of their wounds are called false virgins.
>
> The warlike practices of the young women and long-hair of the men probably gave rise to the legend of androgyny. The name perhaps derives from the Greek words makhlês and makhlos meaning 'lewd' or 'lustful'.

Miniature showing a headless man with face on chest (Blemmyes), one-footed sciapod on his back and a cyclops bearing a club and buckler, from Marco Polo, *Le Livre des merveilles*, 1400–1420.

Blemmyae

The Blemmyae have heads, but their faces are set in their chests. Pomponius Mela (*fl.* AD 43) was the first to name the 'Blemyae' of Africa as being headless with their face buried in their chest. Likewise, Pliny in the *Natural History* records the Blemmyae tribe of North Africa as '[having] no heads, their mouths and eyes being seated in their breasts'.

Scholars have suggested the headlessness among Blemmyes may be due to their characteristic combat pose of keeping their heads pressed close to the chest, while half-squatting with one knee to the ground. Solinus adds that they were believed to be born with their head partly dismembered, their mouth and eyes deposited on the breast.

St Augustine swears he saw men with one eye in the middle of their foreheads in lower Aethiopia.

The Phoenix

The sober-minded and serious historian Tacitus reports all manner
of *miracula* – sea monsters and 'ambiguous humans' – seen by prisoners of war in Germany and Britain (*Annals* 2, 24, 4); he also believes
firmly in the existence of the phoenix:

> During the consulship of Paulus Fabius and Lucius Vitellius,
> the bird called the phœnix, after many, many years, appeared
> in Egypt and furnished the most learned men of that coun-
> try and of Greece with abundant matter for the discussion of
> the marvellous phenomenon. It is my wish to make known
> all on which they agree with several things, questionable
> enough indeed, but not too absurd to be noticed.
>
> That it is a creature sacred to the sun, differing from all
> other birds in its beak and in the tints of its plumage, is held
> unanimously by those who have described its nature. As to
> the number of years it lives, there are various accounts. The
> general tradition says five hundred years. Some maintain
> that it is seen at intervals of fourteen hundred and sixty-one
> years, and that the former birds flew into the city called
> Heliopolis successively in the reigns of Sesostris, Amasis,
> and Ptolemy, the third king of the Macedonian dynasty, with
> a multitude of companion birds marvelling at the novelty of
> the appearance. But all antiquity is of course obscure. From
> Ptolemy to Tiberius was a period of less than five hundred
> years. Consequently some have supposed that this was a
> spurious phœnix, not from the regions of Arabia, and with
> none of the instincts which ancient tradition has attributed
> to the bird. For when the number of years is completed and
> death is near, the phœnix, it is said, builds a nest in the land
> of its birth and infuses into it a germ of life from which an
> offspring arises, whose first care, when fledged, is to bury its
> father. This is not rashly done, but taking up a load of myrrh
> and having tried its strength by a long flight, as soon as it is
> equal to the burden and to the journey, it carries its father's

body, bears it to the altar of the Sun, and leaves it to the flames. All this is full of doubt and legendary exaggeration. Still, there is no question that the bird is occasionally seen in Egypt. (*Annals* 6, 28)

The Polyphagus

Your personal cannibal? Such was Nero's reputation for brutality depicted in the stories that surrounded his cruelty, that a mythical monster was born – an embodiment of all that was vile about the emperor. Suetonius reports on the Polyphagus, an all-consuming monster of a man from Alexandria that ripped apart and ate the raw flesh of those condemned to die (*Nero* 37, 2). The Chronology of 354 (*Chron. Min. sv Nero*) confirms this, adding his name, Arprocras, and what he routinely ate each day: 'A cooked boar, a live hen complete with feathers, 100 eggs, 100 pine nuts, hobnails, broken glass, the brush from a broomstick, four table napkins, a bay suckling pig and a handful of hay – after which it was still hungry.' Nero's plan was to turn him into a cannibal for his own perverted, voyeuristic pleasure.

The Magnetism of Eryx

Eryx, on the west coast of Sicily, is built on the summit of Mount Erice, some 750 metres (2,460 ft) above sea level. Today it boasts two castles: the Saracen Pepoli Castle and the Norman Venus Castle; the latter is built on the ancient Temple of Venus and, according to legend, was founded by Aeneas. In his *On the Nature of Animals*, Aelian records that animals selected for sacrifice would walk up to the temple altar of their own volition to be slain.

African Pygmies

Carthaginian Hanno the Navigator describes meeting the African pygmies:

African pygmies probably reached Europe during the Stone Age, and were certainly frequent visitors at the courts of the Pharaohs. At present they are all denizens of the woodlands, everywhere keeping to the shelter of the Welle, Ituri

Ruwenzori, Congo, and Ogoway forests within the tropics [around modern Sierra Leone]. This may be due to the fact that they are not black but of a yellowish colour with reddish-brown woolly heads, a somewhat hairy body, and extremely low stature ranging from 3 ft. to perhaps 4 ft. 6 in. at most.

Gorillas

Hanno noted in the fifth century BC the hirsuteness and dwarfish size of the pygmies, but it is also to him that we owe the term 'gorilla' (*gorillae*), applied 'to certain hairy little people seen by him on the west coast – probably the ancestors of the dwarfs still surviving in the Ogoway district'. He then 'encountered some very hairy and barbarous females who were incorrigibly savage and totally uncivilised. So, he killed them and took their skins home. He called them gorillas' (*A Carthaginian Exploration of the West African Coast*).

THE
SCIENCES

2

Agriculture

Agriculture in the Greek city-states was obviously small scale and goes some way to explain the existentialist need to colonize and exploit trade connections with states that had more plentiful resources in and around the Mediterranean.

Rome, in common with its central Italian tribal neighbours, started life as an agricultural state in which the vast majority of its citizens lived on, and off, the land. However, by the Late Republic (133–31 BC), agronomy and urbanization developed to levels not seen again until the eighteenth century. Land, and all things relating to the land, were under the control of the elite while most Romans were dependent labourers. Private ownership of land came into being by the end of the sixth century BC; two hundred years later, Rome was a state of citizen smallholders. This is significant because these citizens became a large and convenient recruiting ground from which emerged a conscript army of smallholders who could afford to arm themselves (*assidui*) and formed the nucleus of the Roman army, ever ready to conquer its neighbours and so acquire more land, on which more *assidui* were created to fight in the army to overrun more neighbours – and so it goes throughout Roman Republic history. Agriculture to the early Romans, then, was hugely important – existentially important even – and, along with military conquest and trade, allowed the Romans to expand into what became the Roman Empire, a major force in known-world civilization. The Roman Empire was a major trading nation with overseas commerce. For Rome, trade, like war, was a necessity: the Romans needed to go to war to occupy new territories in order to exploit minerals, spices and incense, for example, and to compensate for their own resource-poor archipelago, but they also needed to trade to pay for the upkeep of legions using trade surpluses. By the time of Augustus, international commerce was well established.

The massive significance of agriculture is reflected in the way agriculture and country living are depicted in Roman religion, literature and society. The early Greek poet Hesiod had stipulated two essentials for a farmer setting out to work the land: the first is an ox for ploughing; the second is a woman, not to marry but to help with the ploughing and keep the house neat, tidy and organized (HESIOD, *Works and Days* ll. 405–6). An early example of the innate sexism of Greek and Roman men. (See also women as fortune-hunters, an idea that penetrated all of society: 'Do not let a flaunting woman coax and trick and deceive you: she is after your barn. The man who trusts women trusts those who deceive' (HESIOD, *Works and Days* l. 373).)

The following quote shows the inextricable link between agriculture and superstition:

> The sixth day of the month is no good for plants but it is fine for the birth of boys; it does not favour either the birth or the marriage of girls. But gelding of kids and lambs hurts less then ... On the eighth of the month geld the boar and bawling – bellowing bull, but geld hard-working mules on the twelfth. (HESIOD, *Works and Days* 782)

A late Roman harvesting machine seen on a limestone funerary relief from Neumagen (Trier).

The *Geoponica* – a twenty-book encyclopaedia of agricultural lore, compiled in the tenth century in Constantinople for the Byzantine emperor Constantine vii Porphyrogenitus – is a treasure trove of all things agricultural. It draws on Pliny the Elder, various lost Hellenistic and Roman-period agriculture and veterinary authors, the Carthaginian agronomist Mago and works by the Persian prophet Zoroaster. It embraces celestial and terrestrial omens, viticulture, oleoculture, apiculture, pest control, horses, donkeys and camels, breeding of cattle and sheep, dogs, hares, deer, pigs, salting of meat, veterinary medicine, medicinal wines, thunder divination (brontoscopy), how to build a fishpond and lots more.

A century or so before, Cicero had some cautionary news for farmers: 'If both oxen in a team defecated at the same time while yoked, it was seen as a bad omen' (*On Divination* 2, 77).

Cato the Elder (239–149 BC), arch conservative that he was, gave no slack to the farm manager, or to his housekeeper. On the duties of the farm manager:

[You] the manager should be responsible for the duties of the housekeeper. If the master has given her to you for a wife, you should be happy with her, and she should respect you. Make sure she doesn't waste her time; that she does not gossip with the neighbours and with other women. She should not receive visitors either in the kitchen or in her own quarters. She should not go out to parties, and she should not gad about. (*De agri cultura* 143)

Columella (Lucius Junius Moderatus) of Gades (Cadiz) died around AD 70. As a young man he moved to Italy, where he owned farms near Rome. His *On Agriculture* (*De re rustica*) is the most comprehensive, systematic and detailed of Roman agricultural works. Book i covers choice of farming site, water supply, buildings and staff; Book ii: ploughing, fertilizing and care of crops; Books iii, iv and v: the cultivation, grafting and pruning of fruit trees, vines and olives; Book vi: the acquisition, breeding and rearing of oxen, horses and mules, as well as veterinary medicine; Book vii: sheep, goats, pigs and dogs; Book VIII: poultry and fishponds; Book IX: beekeeping; Book X (in hexameter poetry): gardening; Book XI: duties of the overseer of a farm, the calendar for farm work and more on gardening; and Book XII: duties of the overseer's wife, the manufacture of wines, pickling and preserving. There is also a separate treatise, *De arboribus*, on vines and olives and various trees, perhaps part of an otherwise lost work written before *On Agriculture*.

One of his less cerebral pieces of advice concerns the naming of farm dogs: 'Dogs should be called by names which are not very long, so that each may obey more quickly when he is called, but they should not have shorter names than those which are pronounced in two syllables.' More importantly buying a dog should be 'among the first things which a farmer does, because [a dog] is the guardian of the farm, its produce, the household and the cattle' (*On Agriculture* VII, II, I). It should have a loud bark and be big, the former to intimidate the intruder when it is heard and the latter to scare them when it is seen. Colour too is important. An all-white dog is recommended for the shepherd to avoid mistaking it for a wolf in the half-light of dawn or dusk, and an all-black guard dog for the farm to terrify thieves in the daytime and be less visible to trespassers at night.

3

The Climate and Natural Disaster

Ammianus Marcellinus records the cataclysmic tsunami that engulfed much of the Mediterranean on 21 July 365: 'Dreadful terrors suddenly stalked the earth, the like of which neither myth nor history records for us' (26, 10).

Lightning almost never strikes twice; the one and only time it did, as reported by Callimachus (PLINY, *Natural History* 7, 152), was when two different statues of Euthymus the boxer were struck simultaneously: one of the statues was in Locri (the boxer's hometown in Reggio Calabria), the other miles away in Olympia. Decision: double knockout.

SOMETIME BETWEEN 1700 and 1500 BC, the Mediterranean was well and truly shaken by the Minoan eruption of Thera (Santorini), one of the greatest volcanic events on the planet in recorded history. The eruption destroyed Thera, blanketing it in pumice, including the Minoan settlement at Akrotiri, as well as laying waste to communities and farmland on nearby islands and on the coast of Crete through a 12-metre-high (40 ft) tsunami four times greater than that which overwhelmed Krakatoa in 1883. On Thera, a timely evacuation saved most of the inhabitants, but the explosion still killed up to 40,000 people in just a few hours, deposited volcanic ash across Asia, triggered a drop in global temperatures and created weird-coloured sunsets for three years. The blast was heard some 4,800 kilometres (3,000 mi.) away. Its energy was tantamount to several hundred atomic bombs exploding simultaneously in a fraction of a second. Its impact was recorded across the world.

According to the fourth-century BC Chinese chronicle the *Bamboo Annals* (*Zhushu Jinian*), the collapse of the Xia dynasty and the rise of the Shang dynasty, approximately dated to 1618 BC, were accompanied by something like a nuclear winter: 'yellow fog, a dim sun, then three suns, frost in July, famine, and the withering of all five cereals'.

An inscribed stele erected at Egyptian Thebes by Ahmose, the first pharaoh of the 18th Dynasty, describes a highly destructive storm accompanied by flooding during his reign (mid-sixteenth century BC).

Hesiod's description in the *Theogony* of the battle between the gods is believed to derive from the eruption. For example, Zeus's thunderbolts could be inspired by volcanic lightning, the boiling earth and sea as a breach of the magma chamber, massive flame and heat as evidence of phreatic explosions:

Zeus no longer held back his might; but his heart was filled with fury and he demonstrated all his strength. From Heaven and from Olympus he came forth, hurling his lightning: the bold flew thick and fast from his strong hand together with thunder and lightning, whirling an awesome flame. The life-giving earth crashed around in burning, and the vast wood crackled loud with fire all about. All the land seethed, and Ocean's streams and the unfruitful sea. The hot vapour lapped round the earthborn Titans: ineffable flame rose to the bright upper air: the flashing glare of the thunder-stone and lightning blinded their eyes. Astounding heat seized Chaos: and to see with eyes and to hear the sound with ears it seemed even as if Earth and wide Heaven above collided; for such a mighty crash would have arisen if Earth were being hurled to ruin, and Heaven from on high were hurling her down; so great a crash was there while the gods were clashing. Also the winds brought a rumbling earthquake and dust storm, thunder and lightning and the lurid thunderbolt – the shafts of great Zeus. (683–712, adapted from the 1914 translation by Hugh G. Evelyn-White)

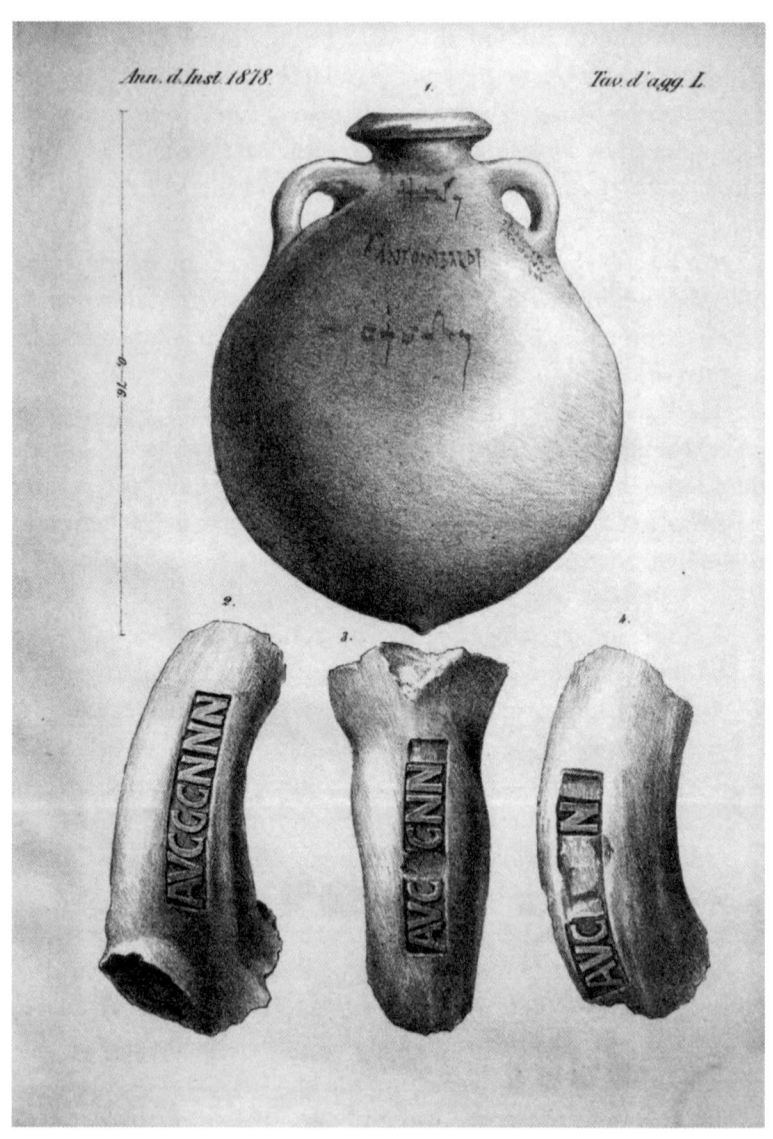

Dressel 20 amphora with examples of *tituli picti* and potters' stamps found at Monte Testaccio in Rome.

4

Roman Waste

H ave you ever wondered how green the Romans were? Well, if Monte Testaccio is anything to go by, they were well ahead of the game when it came to landfill sites. Monte Testaccio (or Monte dei Cocci, 'Mount of Shards') is a huge artificial mound – a kind of ceramics slag heap – in Rome composed almost entirely of *testae*, shards of broken, mostly discarded *amphorae*, some of which were helpfully labelled with *tituli picti*. These are painted or stamped inscriptions that record information such as the weight of the oil contained in the vessel, the names of the people who weighed and documented the oil and the name of the district where the oil was originally bottled. Archaeologists can thus establish whether the oil in the vessels was imported under state authority and earmarked for the *annona urbis* or the *annona militaris*, the civil and military corn doles.

The eminent archaeologist Amanda Claridge (1949–2022), a professor of Roman archaeology at Royal Holloway, University of London, added more detail in her *Rome: An Oxford Archaeological Guide* (1998), stating that Monte Testaccio is one of the largest spoil heaps found anywhere in the ancient world, covering an area of nearly 2 hectares (5 ac) at its base and with a volume of approximately 580,000 cubic metres. It is estimated by Bryan Ward-Perkins, a classical architectural historian and archaeologist, and author of *The Fall of Rome and the End of Civilization* (2005), that it contains the remains of 53 million olive oil amphorae, in which some 1.3 billion imperial gallons (6 million litres) of oil had been imported. The mountain boasted a circumference of nearly 1 kilometre ($^3/_5$ mi.), standing 35 metres (115 ft) high, though it was surely much higher in ancient times.

The heap indirectly sheds important light on the immense scale of the olive oil industry to Rome: Julian Bennett, former excavations director for English Heritage, tells us that

> Studies of the hill's composition suggest that Rome's imports of olive oil reached a peak towards the end of the second century AD, when as many as 130,000 amphorae were being deposited on the site each year. The vast majority of those vessels had a capacity of some 15 imperial gallons [68 L]; from this it has been estimated that Rome was importing at least 1.6 million imperial gallons [7 million L] of olive oil annually. As the vessels found at Monte Testaccio appear to represent mainly state-sponsored olive oil imports, it is very likely that considerable additional quantities of olive oil were also imported privately.

The slag heap that was Monte Testaccio was hugely important in and around the city of Rome. However, waste management was alive and well throughout the empire over many centuries. Chloë Duckworth's *Recycling and Reuse in the Roman Economy* (2020) is a fascinating account of recycling of a number of materials – including textiles, papyrus, statuary, amphorae (of course), copper-alloys, Roman silver coinage, elements, isotopes and glass – showing just how prevalent it all was. Sites examined include Spolverino in Tuscany, Roman villas and recycling points of Roman Britain.

5

Astronomy and Space Travel

The sciences in general provided fertile ground for the career paradoxographer and for encyclopaedists such as Pliny the Elder. What we learn from them is an exciting blend of the proven and rational with the fantastic, highly speculative and contrived – which is just bad science. The following veers to the last of these, but is all the more interesting and entertaining for it.

Astronomy

For the Greeks and Romans, astronomy was one of the many sciences in which both civilizations excelled and in which significant discoveries were made that have helped shape astronomy to this day. To the Greeks, astronomy was a branch of mathematics; beginning with the Pythagoreans in the sixth century BC, astronomers strived to create geometrical models that could imitate celestial motions. For them, astronomy was among the four mathematical arts, along with arithmetic, geometry and music. Plato, Aristarchus and Hipparchus have all left their mark. In the Roman period, Ptolemy contributed much to our early knowledge of astronomy. His *Almagest* is one of the most influential books in the history of Western astronomy.

The Antikythera mechanism, which consists of a complex system of thirty wheels and plates with inscriptions relating to signs of the zodiac, months, eclipses and pan-Hellenic games, was a kind of astrolabe. Derek J. de Solla Price, a physicist and historian, was the first to suggest that the apparatus calculates the solar and lunar calendar, an ingenious machine to determine the time based on the

242244222422423242342222222224242222222222

movements of the Sun and Moon, their relationship (eclipses) and the motions of other stars and planets known in that period.

The device was probably built by a mechanical engineer of the school of Posidonius in Rhodes. Cicero, who visited the island in 79/78 BC, reported that such devices were indeed designed by the Stoic philosopher Posidonius of Apamea. The design of the Antikythera mechanism appears to follow the tradition of Archimedes' planetarium and may be related to sundials. His modus operandi is based on the use of gears. The machine is dated around 89 BC and comes from the wreck found off the island of Antikythera.

Plutarch in his *Table Talk* treats us to some of the most intractable questions known to man, and justifies them as a means to deflect the evils of inebriation at *symposia*: is it more plausible that

The Antikythera mechanism, 150–100 BC, an analogue computer designed to calculate the positions of astronomical objects.

the total number of stars is an even rather than odd number? (9.12); why is alpha first in the alphabet? (9.2); and that old chestnut: which came first – the chicken or the egg? (2.3).

On the side of eccentricity the *Greek Anthology* – a vast collection of epigrams and songs, compiled over centuries by various editors – gives us the wonderful 'man as sundial': 'If you point your nose towards the sun and open your mouth wide, you will be able to tell the time to passers-by' (11, 418).

Philolaus confirms that there is (of course there is!) life on the Moon, and that the grass is definitely greener, and a lot cleaner – our first encounter with ecology: 'The moon is like the earth in that its surface is inhabited. However, the animals and plants there are bigger and more attractive than those here; animals there are fifteen times bigger and do not defecate' (frg. 20). No litter or methane gases to worry about there then.

Flat-earth-Pliny the Elder would seem not to agree – astronomy is a complete waste of time: 'It is madness to trouble the mind, as some have done, with attempts to measure the world . . . or to argue . . . that there are many other worlds' (*Natural History* 2, 1).

In Lucian's *Icaromenippus*, Menippus contemplates early space flight: 'Let me see, now. First stage, Earth to Moon, 350 miles [563 km]. Second stage, up to the Sun, 1,500 miles [2,415 km]. Then the third, to the actual Heaven and Zeus's citadel, might be put at a day's non-stop eagle flight' (1–5). The eagle was a bit of a red herring as Menippus had his own wings for propulsion, taking his inspiration from multi-skilled polymath Daedalus, father of Icarus – that hubristic young man, our first aeroplane, who flew too close to the Sun.

Lucian's work is, in fact, a hybrid of Menippus and Icarus.

From his great altitude, Menippus, our first drone, is all-seeing, and what he bears witness to seems very much like the shenanigans in a modern TV soap opera, or a page in a tabloid newspaper:

I had no sooner flapped the wing than a flood of light enveloped me, and things that I had not even been aware of before became perfectly clear. I looked down towards earth, and could easily see cities, men, and everything that was going on down there, not just in the open, but inside the supposed privacy of houses. There was Ptolemy in his sister's arms, the son of Lysimachus plotting against his father, Seleucus's son Antiochus making signs to his step-mother Stratonice, Alexander of Pherae being murdered by his wife, Antigonus corrupting his daughter-in-law, the son of Attalus putting the poison in his cup; Arsaces was in the act of slaying his mistress, while the eunuch Arbaces drew his sword on him; the guards were dragging Spatinus the Mede out from the banquet by the foot, with the lump on his brow from the golden cup. Similar sights could be seen in the palaces of Libya and Scythia and Thrace – adulteries, murders, treasons, robberies, perjuries, suspicions, and monstrous betrayals. (LUCIAN, *Icaromenippus* 1–5)

The circumference of the Earth in fact measures about 40,000 kilometres (24,900 mi.). In the third century BC, Eratosthenes put it at 39,750 kilometres (24,700 mi.) – not bad. However, it was Claudius Ptolemy of Alexandria (AD 90–168) who was considered the key opinion leader in cartography and astronomy, but his estimate was way out, at 28,645 kilometres (17,800 mi.). The error was partly to blame later when Christopher Columbus (1451–1506) placed the Caribbean where India actually is – hence the West Indies.

Menippus also tackles the vexed existentialist question *is there a god*? Or is everything science?

For some of them God is a number; some swear by dogs and geese and plane-trees. Some again banish all other Gods, and attribute the control of the universe to a single one; I got rather depressed on learning how small the supply of divinity was. But I was comforted by the lavish souls who not only make many, but classify; there was a First God, and second and third classes of divinity. Yet again, some regard the divine nature as unsubstantial and without form, while others conceive it as a substance. Then they were not all disposed to recognize a Providence; some relieve the Gods of all care, as we relieve the superannuated of their civic duties; in fact, they treat them exactly like supernumeraries on the stage. The last step is also taken, of saying that Gods do not exist at all, and leaving the world to drift along without a master or a guiding hand. (*Icaromenippus* 9)

The Romans were aware of seven celestial bodies that they could observe with the naked eye: the Sun, the Moon and five planets: Mercury, Venus, Mars, Saturn and Jupiter. The planets were given the names of Roman gods, as were later discoveries (Neptune and so on).

Thrasyllus of Mendes

We know from Tacitus (*Annals* 6:22) and Suetonius that Thrasyllus of Mendes, astrologer and grammarian, was a freedman friend of Tiberius – a risky job at any time. He was also an ally of Caligula, Tiberius' great-nephew, who was having an affair with his granddaughter, Ennia Thrasylla. Riskier still.

MEDICINE

6

Medicine and the Medical Arts

Pliny: was he ahead of his time or just stating the obvious?

Many aspects of treatment in antiquity were very stressful and unsophisticated. (PLINY, *Natural History* 26, 16)

Asclepius, the son of Apollo, was taught his medicine by the Centaur Chiron. Athena gave him the blood that flowed from the veins of the Gorgons and with it he healed lots of people. He used the blood from veins on the left side to kill people, and that from the veins on the right to cure them. It is said that he even restored people to life in this way. (ZENOBIUS, *Proverbs* 1, 18)

Aelian provided us with a template and business model for the NHS:

When the tragedian Aristarchus of Tegea contracted a disease, Asclepius cured him and told him to make an offering to the god in thanks . . . but the gods would never accept payment for providing health . . . they provide us free of charge. (frg. 101)

The Romans knew this 2,000 years ago: 'We rely so much on medicine because our modern lifestyle is so indulgent and extravagant' (AMMIANUS MARCELLINUS, *History of Rome* 22, 18). And the Greeks were aware that 'People who lisp are prone to extended bouts of diarrhoea' (HIPPOCRATES, *Aphorisms* 6, 32).

Men, a word of advice: check yourself regularly, for 'It is a fatal sign if the right testicle is retracted and cold' (HIPPOCRATES, *On Sevens* 51). Scribonius Largus, apart from accompanying Claudius (r. AD 41–54) on his invasion of Britannia, has a shocking cure for gout:

> Stand on the sea shore, at the water's edge, and stand on a black electric eel. You should do this until you feel a numbness in the foot and up the leg as far as the knee. The shocks not only stop the pain from this episode but prevents it from recurring in future. (*Prescriptions* 162)

Some illnesses were more than just a sore head: 'Theophrastus tells how he once saw flames shooting out from a person's eyes and Megethius, the doctor from Alexandria, told me that he had seen a flame coming out of the hip of someone with sciatica and burning the bed sheets' (SIMPLICIUS, Commentary on Aristotle's *About the Heavens* 7).

How about an emergency de-intoxification?

> Someone who is so drunk that he loses his voice gets better if he becomes febrile straightaway; if he does not, he dies on the third day. If you come across a patient in this condition wash him in lots of warm water . . . then peel onions and stuff them in his nostrils. (HIPPOCRATES, *Diseases* 22)

This sounds a bit suspicious: 'Experts say that it is vital that a poultice for an abscess should be applied by a naked virgin after both she and the patient have been fasting' (PLINY, *Natural History* 26, 93).

The *asclepeion* at Epidaurus was the most famous centre of healing in the classical world, the place where ill people went in the hope of being cured. To find out the right cure for their ailments, the pilgrims spent a night in the *enkoimeteria*, a huge dormitory that served as a clinical guest house with 160 guestrooms. In their dreams, Asclepius himself would advise them what they had to do to regain their health. Nearby mineral springs may have been used in healing, while there were also other options: 'A dog cured a boy

from Aegina with a growth on his neck . . . the dog licked him
and made him well' (EPIDAURUS, *Inscriptions* stele B6). However:
'In my father's time and my grandfather's no doctor ever prescribed
hellebore. If anyone did actually prescribe it he ordered the patient
to make his will first . . . most patients choked to death on hellebore'
(CTESIAS (*c.* 400 BC), *Indica* frg. 68).

Bedside Manner

Bedside manner is the way in which a doctor communicates face to
face with a patient at the bedside and includes issues like diagnosis,
treatment plans and procedures, outcomes and prognosis. Breaking
bad news is a key constituent in any doctor's bedside manner, and some
physicians are more direct and blunt than others: 'If a patient suffering from consumption (TB) is losing his hair, and has in fact already
gone nearly bald, and if his sputum smells when he spits on hot coals,
you should tell him that he is going to die soon, and that diarrhoea is
what will kill him' (HIPPOCRATES, *Diseases* 2, 48). Pliny says,

> A tick from a dog's left ear, worn as an amulet, will allay all
> kinds of pains. They predict, too, from it on matters of life
> and death; for if the patient, they say, gives an answer to a
> person who has a tick about him, and, standing at the foot
> of the bed, asks how he is, it is an infallible sign that he will
> survive; while, on the other hand, if he makes no answer, he
> will be sure to die. They add, also, that the dog from whose
> left ear the tick is taken, must be entirely black. Nigidius has
> stated in his writings that dogs will avoid the presence all
> day of a person who has taken a tick from off a pig. (*Natural
> History* 30, 24, 10)

In a case of stereotyping gone mad, the physician Adamantius
stated:

> If the distance from the lowest part of a patient's chest
> to his navel is greater than that to where his neck starts,

he is greedy and gluttonous. Praise a large and firm chest. A chest that is thin and weak indicates a weakling and a coward; a fleshy chest indicates ignorance and clumsiness. Anyone with a chest that is flabby and wobbly is a lech and a drunkard. (*Physiognomonica* 2, 15)

No doubt Adamantius is adamant that the following too is all based on empirical evidence (*Physiognomonica* 2, 29):

Big ears = insensitivity
Small ears = criminal tendencies
Very small ears = stupidity
Good-sized square ears = sensitivity and bravery
Hollowed-out ears = intelligence and sharp wits

Assumptions were ubiquitous: 'People who gamble have short arms, they like weasels, and they like dancing. Scrawny buttocks indicate a bad character, as with apes. Red-haired people are very devious, like foxes' (PSEUDO-ARISTOTLE, *Physiognomonica* 808a; 810b; 812a).

Very Bad Dreams

Jungian scholars have suggested the dream-healing therapy practised at Epidaurus and elsewhere represents the early forerunner of modern psychoanalysis and psychotherapy.

Arata, a Spartan, suffered from swelling. Her mother slept in the sanctuary on her behalf while she stayed in Sparta. She believed that the god cut off her daughter's head and hung her body up with the neck downwards. After lots of fluids had flowed out, the god released the body and put the head back on her neck. After this dream she returned to Sparta and found that her daughter had recovered and had had the same dream. (EPIDAURUS, *Inscriptions* stele 21)

Sexually Transmitted Infections

A certain amount of confusion persisted with gonorrhoea and semen:

Gonorrhoea is not, indeed, a deadly affection, but one that is disagreeable and disgusting even to hear of. For if impotence and paralysis possess both the fluids and genital organs, the semen runs as if through dead parts, nor can it be stopped even in sleep; for whether asleep or awake the discharge is unrestrainable, and there is an unconscious flow of semen. Women also have this disease, but their semen is discharged with titillation of the parts, and with pleasure, and from immodest desires of connection with men. But men have not the same prurient feelings; the discharge which runs off being thin, cold, colourless, and unfruitful. For how could nature, when congealed, evacuate vivifying semen?

And even young people, when they suffer from this affection, necessarily become old, torpid, relaxed, spiritless, timid, stupid, enfeebled, shriveled, inactive, pale, whitish, effeminate, loathe their food, and become frigid; they have heaviness in their limbs, torpidity of the legs, are without strength, and incapable of all exertion. In many cases, this disease is the way to paralysis; for how could the nervous power not suffer when nature has become frigid in regard to the generation of life? For it is the semen, when possessed of vitality, which makes us men, hot, well braced in limbs, hairy, well voiced, spirited, strong to think and to act, as the characteristics of men prove. For when the semen is without vitality, people shrivel up, have a high tone of voice, lose their hair and their beard, and become effeminate, as the characteristics of eunuchs prove. But if any man ejaculates his semen well, he is bold, daring, and strong as wild beasts. (ARETAEUS, *On the Causes and Symptoms of Acute Diseases* 2, 5, 1)

It follows that sexually transmitted infections (STIs) would have plagued both men and women alike, particularly in a society that endorsed men freely consorting with prostitutes, male and female, and with slaves. We hear of the characteristic discharges and ulcers, but reporting on infection or contagion is scarce. The Campanians, apparently, had a predilection for oral sex, resulting in a high incidence of *campanus morbus* – a facial skin condition, probably a STI. The Hippocratics, using findings from a dissected inflamed urethra, Celsus and Galen all describe the symptoms of gonorrhoea, referring to it as 'strangury' (painful urination) caused by the 'pleasures of Venus'. Martial and Galen write of anal warts and piles, Celsus and Galen genital warts, and the Hippocratics and Galen describe oral sores that present during menstruation – possibly *herpes zoster* (CELSUS 4, 28; GALEN *Diseases of Women* 109; *Epid.* 3, 7).

Phytomedicine

Theophrastus warns of the dangers lurking unseen in some medicinal plants. Beware the peony . . .

> The properties of these plants are hurtful; they take hold, it is said, like fire and burn; for hellebore too soon makes the head heavy, and men cannot go on digging it up for very long and that's why they first eat garlic and take a draught of neat wine. On the other hand the following ideas may be considered far-fetched and irrelevant; for instance they say that the peony, which some call glykyside, should be dug up at night, for, if a man does it in day-time and is observed by a woodpecker while he is gathering the fruit, he risks the loss of his eyesight; and, if he is cutting the root at the time, he gets a prolapsed anus. (*History of Plants* 9, 8)

Diagnosis for Dummies

Be very careful when you're born, because if

> Mars and Saturn are in opposition to each other you'll vomit
> blood. Mars in Scorpio, Capricorn, Pisces, or Cancer, if he
> is in opposition to the Moon, brings on impetigo, leprosy,
> and jaundice. If Saturn is in opposition to the Moon, when
> she is not in her own house or in the house of Saturn, this
> will make haemorrhoids or boils ... If Mars, Venus, and the
> Moon are in tropical signs and in opposition to each other,
> and Saturn aspects them by night from Leo, Taurus, Pisces,
> or Sagittarius, this will produce gout; if by day, elephantiasis.
> If the Moon is found in Taurus and Saturn in Scorpio or vice
> versa, with no planet in aspect to the Moon, local people will
> suffer from elephantiasis. If Mercury in Virgo or Pisces is
> exactly on the ascendant, and Saturn and Mars are in square
> aspect to him, they will produce madmen. Mars and Saturn
> on the anaphora of the ascendant or in the eighth house
> will cause a flow of blood from the nose, mouth, or anus.
> (FIRMICUS MATERNUS, *Astrology* 7, 20, 11–13)

An Early Appreciation of Music Therapy

We may think of music therapy as a relatively recent medical
advance but these quotations show that it was prevalent in ancient
Greece and Rome:

> I came across the statement very recently in the book of
> Theophrastus *On Inspiration* that many men have believed
> and put their belief on record, that when gouty pains in the
> hips are most severe, they are relieved if a flute-player plays
> soothing notes. That snake-bites are cured by the music of
> the flute, when played skilfully and melodiously, is also stated
> in a book of Democritus, entitled *On Deadly Infections*, in

which he shows that the music of the flute is therapy for many illnesses. (AULUS GELLIUS, *Attic Nights* 4, 13)

Theophrastus (frg. 88) adds that music helps with fainting, panic attacks and chronic depression. Pipe music cures seizures and sciatica. Censorinus (*The Birthday Book* 12) tells how Asclepiades advocated music therapy in psychiatric patients; Herophilus was an advocate too. Perhaps Asclepiades was going too far when he tried to cure the profoundly hard of hearing with trumpet blasts (MARTIANUS CAPELLA, *The Marriage of Philosophy and Mercury* 9, 926).

High Blood Pressure

Learning that his son [Demetrius] was sick, Antigonus went to see him, and met a beautiful women at his door; he went in, nevertheless, sat down by his son, and felt his pulse. 'The fever has left me now,' said Demetrius. 'No doubt, my boy,' said Antigonus, 'I met it just now at the door as it was leaving.' (PLUTARCH, *Life of Demetrius* 19)

Life Expectancy

Life expectancy was generally around the 25 years mark; Pliny, however, could point to plenty of centenarians, one of whom reached 140 (*Natural History* 7, 164).

Dung Therapy

Various types of dung had myriad beneficial medical uses; here are just a few, as recorded by Dioscorides (*Medical Material* 2, 80):

Cow: prolapsed uterus
Goat: menstrual flow
Sheep: warts
Wild pig: vomiting blood

Donkey: scorpion sting
Dove: carbuncles
Chicken: mushroom poisoning
Stork: seizures
Vulture: abortifacient
Mouse: baldness
Dog: tonsillitis
Human: wound inflammation
Crocodile: cosmetics for women's faces

To Dioscorides, beaver testicles were a silver bullet – they were efficacious against a whole range of conditions: poor menstrual flow; flatulence; colic; hiccups; deadly poisons; varicoceles; lethargy; trembling; convulsions; depression and anxiety; and they act as an abortifacient (*Medical Material* 2, 24).

Infection Control

Moreover, dirt is good for you too: 'The scum scraped from the walls of the public baths is good for anal fissures. Knuckle tumours benefit from the dust and grime from the wrestling ground while the grime from statues and the gymnasium wall help cure old sores' (DIOSCORIDES, *Medical Material* 1, 30).

Anatomy

Herophilus (335–280 BC) produced nine medical books (all lost) including a *Maiotikon* – a midwifery text; he pioneered human dissection and founded the medical school in Alexandria, a centre of excellence that was particularly important around the Mediterranean because the dissection of cadavers was illegal in Rome, banned on religious grounds. This obviously had implications on the understanding of the deep structures and workings of internal organs; only Alexandria had special dispensation to dissect.

To get round this inconvenience, Galen (AD 129–c. 200) encouraged medical students to go to Egypt and learn their anatomy from bodies flushed out of their graves by rain or washed up on the banks of the Nile, or from the skeleton of a highwayman slain by his victim (*On Anatomical Procedures* 1, 2).

This set of exam questions and answers for anatomy students from the third or fourth centuries AD was found in Roman Egypt, written in Greek (*Lund Papyri* 1, 7):

Q. Why is the rectum so called?
A. Because it is in a straight line (*recta linea*) whereas the other intestines are twisted in a spiral.

Q. Where is the sphincter situated?
A. At the end of the rectum.

Q. What is it made of?
A. It is neurocartilaginous.

You can't look without strong feelings of disgust at the features that go together to make up a human being – blood, flesh, bones, veins and so on . . . (ARISTOTLE, *Parts of Animals*, 645a). With the use of human cadavers illegal in Mediterranean cities other than Alexandria in Egypt it was necessary to use other primates: 'Apes for use in dissection should be drowned, to avoid damage caused to the organs of the neck by strangulation' (GALEN, *Anatomical Procedures* 2, 423k).

Breast is best: 'Men and women both have thick veins in both breasts that make the greatest contribution to a person's intelligence' (HIPPOCRATES, *Epidemics* 2, 6, 19).

Keeping an Eye on Your Diet

Pliny has wise words: 'I think there is a vein linking the eyes to the stomach – no one has ever taken a blow to the eye without then vomiting' (*Natural History* 11, 148).

Toxic Teeth

'Human teeth contain some kind of poison: baring your teeth to a mirror causes it to go dull and kills baby pigeons' (PLINY, *Natural History* 11, 170).

Gluttony Explained – and the Meaning of Life

Those who were creating mankind were aware of our lack of restraint when it came to food and drink, and how, because of our greed, we would consume far more than what was moderate and necessary. So, to prevent disease bringing mankind to a complete end, the Gods made the stomach serve as a receptacle for holding the superfluous meat and drink; and round about they coiled the intestines, to prevent the food from passing through quickly and thereby compelling the body to demand more food so soon, and causing an insatiable appetite, whereby because of its gluttony the human race would be rendered devoid of philosophy and of culture. (PLATO, *Timaeus* 72e)

Cardiology

The post-mortem on the hero Aristomenes of Messenia revealed his heart to be full of hairs (VALERIUS MAXIMUS, *Memorable Deeds and Sayings* 1.8.ext.15). Swallowing a swallow was an innovative solution to refractory angina: 'Eating a baby swallow ensures against angina for a whole year' (CELSUS, *On Medicine* 4,7).

Care of the Elderly

The Indians and Aethiopians know something we clearly do not: Ctesias says that Indians don't get headaches, eye problems, toothache, mouth ulcers or any kind of abscess; some live up to two hundred years (PHOTIUS, *The Library* 72, 47a). A view not shared by all: 'The Ethiopians are old by the age of thirty because their bodies are exposed to excessive heat ... whereas the Britons live for 120 years because their country is so cold' (PSEUDO-PLUTARCH, *On the Opinion of Philosophers* 911b).

Life in the Fast Lane

Krateros, brother of King Antigonos, knew someone who, in just seven years, was a child, a youth, a man and an elderly man and had married and had children before he died age seven. (PHLEGON OF TRALLES, *Marvels* 32).

Child Abuse as Child Health

The arch conservative Cato the Elder recommended that a child be washed in the urine of someone who has been living on a diet of cabbage; this ensures the good health and strength of the child (*On Farming* 157. 10). The real expert on the role of cabbage in medicine was Mnesitheus of Cyzicus, a fourth-century BC Greek physician who belonged to the Dogmatic School of Medicine and was celebrated for his work on the classification of diseases and *On Diet*. The tenet of the Dogmatic school was that a physician had to be familiar with the hidden causes of diseases, as well as the more obvious reasons, and to know how the natural actions and different functions of the human body take place, which necessarily assumes a knowledge of anatomy and physiology.

Dermatology and Trichology

Apparently, 'If a man has a mole close to his nose and a ruddy complexion, he will be sexually insatiable' (PSEUDO-MELAMPUS, *On Moles* 3).

Ever wanted to remove that ill-advised tattoo? You can do so 'by smearing on them a mixture of very sharp vinegar and the stuff that sticks to the insides of a chamber pot' (PAUL OF AEGINA, *Medical Compendium* 4.7). Excrement and urine – of human and other animals alike – comes in handy in other ways: 'Rubbing the patient's hair with bull's urine cures dandruff' (GALEN, *The Composition of Drugs According to Places* 12, 476k). For those without a head of hair, there's still a silver lining: 'Bald people tend not to suffer from varicose veins. If a bald person does develop varicose veins, his hair grows again' (HIPPOCRATES, *Aphorisms* 6, 34).

Epilepsy

Anecdotally, epileptics think that drinking the blood of gladiators is the most effective cure for their condition – to take in the warm blood while the gladiator is still breathing, thus drawing out his living soul (PLINY, *Natural History* 28, 4).

According to Pliny, 'Only quails and humans are afflicted by epileptic seizures' (*Natural History* 10, 69). Epilepsy is marginally more common in men than in women, but it has implications for women in reproductive health – fertility, puberty, menstruation, for example – so would have had potentially serious social as well as medical consequences when diagnosed in premenopausal women. Caelius is scathing towards those practitioners who prescribe for epileptics the binding of limbs or a diet of weasel, smoked brain of camel or the testicles of a beaver – even tickling the patient while a flame is placed close to his or her eyes. Pliny recommends as a cure the touch of a young girl with her right thumb, the meat of an animal that has never mated, mare's milk or a horse's chestnut in sweetened vinegar (*Natural History* 28, 43).

Gastroenterology

The Greek king, statesman and commander Pyrrhus (d. 272 BC) claimed that he could cure his ailments of the spleen by touching his stomach with the big toe of his right foot. When he died and was cremated, his big toe refused to burn and it was preserved in a casket in a temple (PLINY, *Natural History* 7, 20). If you're not that flexible, 'Swallowing a lead pill helps many patients suffering from intestinal blockage because its weight pushes against and thrusts out whatever is causing the obstruction' (CAELIUS AURELIANUS, *Acute Diseases* 3, 17, 160).

Liver disease has a long history, and many myths: 'Patients whose liver expands become delirious, hallucinating about snakes and armed soldiers fighting them. This disease usually afflicts people when they are travelling abroad, going along a lonely road, although it does strike at other times as well.' (HIPPOCRATES, *Critical Days* 3)

Seneca describes the messy death of Claudius (in parody):

He was listening to a troupe of comedians when he died . . . The last words he was heard to speak in this world were these when he had made a great noise with that part of him which talked easiest, he cried out, 'Oh dear, oh dear! I think I have made a mess of myself.' Whether he did or not, I cannot say, but certain it is that he always did make a mess of everything else. (*Apocolocyntosis* 4)

Such a death is not a laughing matter: 'They say that Vespasian always looked constipated. When the emperor dared someone to say something funny at his expense, one wag replied, "I will, as soon as you've finished relieving yourself"' (SUETONIUS, *Life of Vespasian* 20).

Women's Health

The *Hippocratic Corpus* is a cornerstone of ancient Greek medicine, indeed, of Western medicine; it is a collection of medical treatises dating mainly from the fifth and fourth centuries BC that are the work of twenty or so authors covering sixty or so medical subjects. Gynaecology, obstetrics and women's health generally are reasonably well represented, with eleven gynaecological subjects covered, over 18 per cent of the total of the corpus. Some of the eleven are: *Semen* or *Generation* or *Intercourse*; the *Nature of the Child or Pregnancy*; the *Diseases of Women*; *Sterile Women*; the *Diseases of Young Women or Girls*; *Superfoetation*; the *Nature of Woman*; and *Excision of the Foetus*. This may be accounted for by the anxiety felt by Greek men to ensure the biological function of women remained in good working order to produce those vital male heirs to sustain the armies and the *oikos* (household). Numerous other works of obstetrics and gynaecology were to follow down the years from various physicians, mainly Greek in origin.

Crucially Aristotle taught that men were more perfect than women; women were incomplete, deformed men because women were less capable than men of generating the heat that was vital for generation of the species due to the debilitating effect of menstruation.

Hippocrates gives us some intriguing gynaecological case studies: a woman from Pheres suffered from idiopathic headaches that persisted even after her skull was drained; while on her period, the headache was less severe. The headaches stopped when she became pregnant. A woman from Larissa suffered pain during intercourse when she reached sixty; she felt what she thought were severe labour pains after eating lots of leeks. When she stood up, she felt something uncomfortable in her vagina and fainted; a woman nearby pulled out what appeared to be the whorl of a spindle from her vagina. 'She worked the wool': *Lanam fecit* indeed! Hippocrates records that the patient made a full recovery; one wonders if the other woman ever did.

Breast Is Still Best and *Caritas romana*

The breast was considered first and foremost a symbol of nurture and of motherhood. Breast-shaped drinking cups and representations of breasts have been found among the votive offerings at sanctuaries of Diana and Hercules, some dedicated by wet nurses. Breast milk was sometimes drunk by the elderly, or by those on the point of death. An Etruscan tradition has the goddess Juno offer her breast to Hercules so that he may become immortal.

A wall painting shows Pero offering breast milk to Cimon, her elderly father, who had been imprisoned and sentenced to death by starvation; it bears the legend: 'in sadness is the meeting of modesty and piety'. In this *caritas romana* (Roman charity),

Pero is discovered by a jailer, but her piety was so impressive that she and her father were allowed to go free (VALERIUS MAXIMUS, *Memorable Deeds and Sayings* 5, 5,4,7). The legend originates from earlier Hellenistic sources and was often depicted in Roman frescos. A painting in the Temple of Piety reportedly is the source: wall paintings and terracotta statues from the first century, excavated in Pompeii, suggest that the visual representations of Pero and Cimon might have been common in ancient Rome. The theme echoes that Etruscan myth cited above.

Pliny has a similar story in which a plebeian woman is jailed and nursed by her daughter. A twentieth-century fictional version of Roman charity can be found in John Steinbeck's novel *The Grapes of Wrath* (1939), in which Rosasharn (Rose of Sharon Joad) nurses a sick and starving man in the corner of a barn.

Women Who Smoke

Some areas of women's medicine involved remedies made up from various concoctions and potions. Some of these were applied topically via salves and plasters; others were administered internally as fumigants, nasal clysters, enemas or pessaries. Fumigation involved the burning of agents such as human hair, medicinal herbs and bitumen in a pot; a lead tube from this was introduced into the woman's vagina. This, of course, was not without its hazards, if Soranus' warning about the dangers of burning the vagina is anything to go by (*Gynaecology* 4, 14–150). Hippocrates had recommended procedures that involved squatting over an open fire, with similar risks of localized singeing:

> If a woman fails to conceive and you want to find out if she ever will, wrap her in blankets and fumigate her lower body. If it looks like the smoke passes up through her whole body and exits through her nose and mouth, you can be sure that she is not infertile. (*Aphorisms* 5, 59)

Sex: Faking It, Enemas and the Role of Women

Puppy love: to encourage conception, Hippocrates recommends eating 'fat little puppy pies, well boiled, and cuttle fish boiled in very sweet wine' (*Women's Diseases* 217). The Hippocratics contended that whenever a woman became pregnant, she had enjoyed the sex during which she conceived; Soranus believed that a woman could only conceive if she was sexually excited, which led him into a difficult corner where he was forced to accept that if a woman became pregnant after being raped then she had, subconsciously at least, enjoyed the violation (*Gynaecology* i. 37). Lucretius argued that sex provided mutual pleasure for man and woman – *est communis voluptas* – and that any children conceived would take after the mother whenever the woman took the dominant role during sex. The Greek philosopher Empedocles (*fl.* fifth century BC) believed that 'children are shaped by what the woman was thinking at the time of conception, and it often happens that a child is born looking like a statue or picture which its mother really liked' (PSEUDO-PLUTARCH, *On the Opinions of Philosophers* 906e).

The king of the Cypriots would have agreed:

> While they were having intercourse some women saw monkeys and produced children who looked like monkeys. Because he was deformed, the king of the Cypriots made his wife look at very handsome statues during intercourse and he fathered good-looking children. Horse trainers make pedigree stallions stand in front of mares that are being mated. A woman should be sober during intercourse so that the child conceived is not born ugly. (SORANUS, *Gynaecology* i, 39)

Faking it: women, Lucretius says, do not always fake sexual excitement – sometimes it is for real. Ovid, in his turn-of-the-millennium *Joy of Sex*, the *Ars amatoria*, methodically runs through the various sexual positions a woman should adopt to achieve mutual orgasm with her partner, or if she wants to show off her looks and body to best effect; he also gives handy tips on how to conceal unsightly stretch marks. Women who cannot climax are encouraged to fake it, convincingly though – with much flailing about, gasping and rolling of eyes (3, 769ff).

Both Pliny and Dioscorides list various agents that will determine or alter the sex of a foetus: Pliny recommends thistle, hare's testicles, rennet or uterus or a cock's testes for generating male babies (*Natural History* 27, 23).

Enemas were introduced for disorders of the bladder, rectum, vagina and uterus – vaginal douches via vaginal clysters were often deployed. Pessaries were inserted for a wide range of conditions including menstruation, inflammation of the womb, expelling dead foetuses and relieving hysteria. Pessaries were also used in cases of prolapsed uterus, while stents were administered to staunch uterine haemorrhage and suppurating wombs. Stents in a medical context are cylinders, usually absorbent, introduced into an artery or sinus to dilate it.

A swollen vulva can be treated by smearing it with a mixture of oil and the dung of a wild boar or a domestic pig. The powder of the dried dung is even more effective sprinkled on a drink and can be administered to pregnant women and nursing mothers. (PLINY, *Natural History* 28, 249)

Women's bodies could kindle and set alight: 'Those who perform cremations maintain that they burn one woman for every ten men because women's bodies contain a resinous and fatty substance that acts as an accelerant' (PLUTARCH, *Table Talk* 651b).

The Mysteries of Menstruation

Amenorrhoea (the absence of menstruation) was a cause of numerous physical and psychological issues, with virgins especially vulnerable. That virgins were particularly prone went some way to explain their tendency to hang themselves or jump down wells to their deaths – so great was the shame thy suffered when their condition stood in the way of their quest to to find a husband.

The ancient Egyptians and Greeks were practical when it came to tampons: the former used softened papyrus as rudimentary tampons while Hippocrates observed that the Greeks used lint wrapped around wood. Aristophanes' word for the cloths women used was 'a pigpen'; a sixth-century AD philosopher and mathematician stored her used ones up to put off an unwanted admirer. One alternative to cloths was simply to bleed into one's clothes, as described by Pliny (*Natural History* 7, 33; 36; 51; 30; 23).

Menstruation was responsible for much anxiety among Greek males and there was a lot of male superstition and speculation regarding the mysterious, and alarming, qualities of menses, named after the Latin for 'month'. Some of this reached back to the *Talmud* in which men were advised to keep their distance from a menstruating woman because if one walked between two men, one of the men would surely die. It was forbidden for menstruating Persian women to speak to men or to sit in water during menstruation. Hesiod warned men against washing in water that women had already used – just in case it was polluted by menstrual blood.

Menstrual stimulants were many and various: Dioscorides knows of over a hundred agents, while Pliny the Elder lists over ninety. Pliny describes the astonishing powers of menstruation: 'it would be hard to find anything that produces as many amazing effects (*magis monstrificium*) as menstrual discharge.' According to him, having a period during a solar or lunar eclipse led to disaster for the woman, and for any man who copulated with her then. If a man with suicidal tendencies had sex with a menstruating woman, it would tip him over the edge, and he would certainly go on to commit suicide. Most extraordinarily, if a woman, during her period, should walk naked through a field buzzing with pests, those pests would die as she walked past; Metrodorus of Scepsis is Pliny's source: he says this is exactly what happened in Cappadocia during a plague of cantharid beetle and explains why women there still walk in the fields with their dresses hitched up. Ironically, cantharidin was to become a popular aphrodisiac in the nineteenth century.

The ashes of menstrual blood acted as a bleach when sprinkled onto clothing and spoilt them and spoilt expensive purple dyes.

A menstruating woman was also not welcome in the kitchen or the garden: she would turn grape juice sour, make seeds sterile when touched by her, cause grafts to wither away, dry up garden plants and cause fruit to fall prematurely from the tree. When she looked in a mirror her reflection would cloud it over (ARISTOTLE, *On Dreams* 469b); she would blunt a blade of steel and dull the sheen of ivory. When she looked at a swarm of bees, they would all drop down dead; brass and iron would instantly go rusty, and smell offensive; dogs that licked the discharge went mad, and their bite then became poisonous and incurable. Josephus, a Romano-Jewish historian (AD 37–*c.* 100), reveals the heavy-duty industrial qualities of menstrual fluid: 'When they have filled the boats with bitumen, it is no easy task to decant their cargo, which owing to its tenacious and glutinous character, clings to the boat – until it is loosened by the monthly secretions of women and urine, to which it alone yields.'

Looking on the bright side, for women in ancient Greece and Rome, the monthly period may have come as something of a relief, offering respite from the serial intercourse to produce endless babies, and a sign that she was not yet again pregnant.

Megasthenes, the third-century BC Greek geographer, says in his *Indica* (now lost) that women in Pandaia in India gave birth when they were six years old (PHLEGON OF TRALLES, *Marvels* 33).

Birth Control

The ancient Greeks had some interesting, if not worrying, methods of contraception. Soranus prescribed water recycled from blacksmiths that had been used to cool iron. For Soranus again, just as unromantically, his contraception of choice was stale olive oil, honey or the sap from a balsam or cedar tree applied to the vulva – on its own or (alarmingly) mixed with white lead and bunged up with wool. It apparently works because of its coagulating and cooling effect that causes the vagina to close before sex and thus acts as a barrier to the sperm. An alternative method, just as inelegant, involves the woman holding her breath when her partner ejaculates, pulling away so that his semen does not penetrate too deeply, then getting up straight away and squatting and sneezing before wiping her vulva clean.

Dioscorides knew of 24 contraceptive potions, three of which involved magic, including an amulet made of asparagus. Others were the application to the genitals of peppermint, honey, cedar gum, axe weed and alum in various concoctions. He also recommended using vinegar, olive oil, ground pomegranate peel and the ground flesh of dried figs as vaginal suppositories.

Olive oil was still being advocated by the Marie Stopes Clinic as recently as 1931, along with other effective spermicides like lemon, alum and vinegar. Douches of vinegar, alum or lemon juice were still used by the working classes in New York in 1947, and lemons were still in use in 1970s Glasgow.

The author of this innovative method likes to think that he has the monopoly on contraceptives; considerable pre-preparation is required if the spontaneity of the moment is not to be lost:

A contraceptive, this is the only one in the world: Take as many bittervetch seeds as you want for the number of years you wish to remain sterile. Steep them in the menses of a menstruating woman. Let them steep in her own genitals. And take a frog that is alive and throw the bittervetch seeds into its mouth so that the frog swallows them, and release the frog alive at the place where you captured him. And take a seed of henbane, steep it in mare's milk; and take the snot of a cow, with grains of barley put these into a [piece of] leather skin made from a fawn and on the outside bind it up with mule skin, and attach it as a mulch during the waning of the moon ... Mix in also with the barley grains cerumen from the ear of a mule. (*Greek Magical Papyri* 36, 320)

First, catch your donkey. Why? 'The testicles of castrated mules, roasted and then mixed with the juice of the willow tree boiled in water, act as a contraceptive' (AËTIUS, *On Medicine* 16, 17).

Contraception generally, then, was often toxic and somewhat makeshift. Pliny the Elder, quoting Caecilius, recommends the use of a special amulet which had to be made from the worms that crawl around in the large head of the hairy spider; if the woman attached it with deer skin and wore it before dawn, she would prevent conception for up to one year (*Natural History* 20,99, 263; 25, 54,97; 30,43,123; 25,18,39).

Aristotle advocated smearing cedar oil, white lead or frankincense on the female genitals. The *Hippocratic Corpus* swore by drinking *misy*, diluted copper sulphate (ARISTOTLE, *Historia Animalium* 583A; HIPPOCRATES *Natura Mulierum* 98; *Muliebria* 1, 76). Lucretius taught that women should, after their partner ejaculates, wriggle their hips to divert the semen – but by no means all women; certainly not respectable *matronae*, just common prostitutes (*De rerum natura* 4, 1269–78). In the third century BC, Manetho in his *Aegyptiaca* (4, 312) advocated breast relief, thrusting the penis between a woman's breasts to ejaculate.

The Egyptians were the first to develop the first diagnostic pregnancy test based on the isolation of a unique substance in the urine of both women and domesticated animals. This is called the germination test: it requires the woman to urinate onto bags of wheat and barley. According to the *Berlin Medical Papyrus*, 'if the barley grows, it indicates a male child. If the wheat grows, it means a female child. If both do not grow, she will not give birth at all.'

The *Berlin Medical Papyrus* also recommends that a woman should have her nipples and skin examined for unusual pigmentation, or that she should drink milk from a woman who has had a son: if she vomits, she is pregnant. The *Kahun Medical Papyrus* suggests placing a woman in the daylight, where pregnancy can be confirmed or not by the colour of her skin. Another test was grasping a woman's fingers and gripping her arm: if the veins in her arms pound against your hand, then she is pregnant. Several of these rudimentary pregnancy tests resurface in the *Hippocratic Corpus* under 'About the Barren Woman'.

The prolific writer on medical science in antiquity, John Scarborough, tells us that Soranus of Ephesus had set out a list of common contraceptives and abortifacients, and many of the ingredients employed in second-century Rome appear in the multi-ingredient compounds recorded by Aetius four hundred years later. Soranus, however, gives many 'simples', whereas Aetius usually sets out complicated formulas requiring careful preparation, demonstrating that Byzantine pharmacy had improved upon both formulation and application. For example, Soranus recommends 'grinding up the inner layers of a pomegranate peel and applying it [into the vagina]' as a contraceptive suppository, as contrasted with Aetius who replicates the 'fresh pomegranate rind,' but adds, 'grind up two parts of the inner peel of the pomegranate rind along with one part of oak gall, and fashion them [into] acorn-like vaginal suppositories, and use them, inserting the suppositories [to prevent pregnancies] after the menstruals have ended'. An even more complicated formula follows: 'take two drachmas of pomegranate flower calices, two drachmas of oak gall, one drachma of wormwood, compound these with cedar oil, and fashion vaginal suppositories the size of barley kernels, and insert them for two days, after the menstruals have ceased; take them out, and, once removed, a woman can have sex without fear of pregnancy' . . . Pointedly, the physician adds, 'This is always reliable, since this [formula/method] has been used for many years.'

Abortion and the Embryo Slayer

The ancients were familiar with surgical abortion, although, due to lack of anaesthetics and antibiotics, it was a highly dangerous and exceedingly painful procedure. Celsus (*c.* 25 BC–AD 50) provides the most complete account of the dilatation and curettage (D&C) operation: it required placing one, sometimes two, hands into the uterus to straighten the foetus and then extracting the foetus with a hook. Hippocratic texts such as *Diseases of Women, Superfetation,* and *On the Excision of the Foetus* refer to a surgical tool called an *embruosphaktes*, 'embryo-slayer': in order to save the mother it was deployed when manipulation failed to effect an embryotomy to evacuate the foetus as soon it was presumed dead. Hooked knives were used to dismember the foetus and thus ease delivery; likewise, decapitating instruments enabled the head to be delivered first (CELSUS, *On Medicine* 7, 29, 7).

Soranus recommended amputating parts of the foetus as they presented, rather than internally, to avoid cutting the vagina with the blade (*Gynaecology* 4, 2). Unusually large foetal heads were crushed with a cranioclast (a bowed forceps with teeth) or split with an embryotome; both instruments are still in use today. Traction hooks were also part of the instrumentation; samples have been found in Pompeii. Their use is described in Hippocrates (and was practised until the times of Paul of Aegina (seventh century AD)), and by Celsus and Soranus (SORANUS, *Gynaecology* 4, 12). The Hippocratic Corpus' *Diseases of Women* tells 'that prolonged and unsuccessful labour usually means a difficult presentation, stillbirth, or multiple birth. Suggestions include vigorous shaking to stimulate delivery, and drugs to speed labour (*ōkytokia*); if all else fails, the doctor may resort to embryotomy, the extraction by instruments of a foetus which is stillborn or impossible to deliver alive.'

Ovid was passionately opposed to abortion: 'The woman who first set about ripping out her tender foetus deserves to die midst the carnage she started' (*Amores* 2, 13). He questions how a woman can tear out her stomach with sharp instruments or administer *dira venena* (terrible poisons) to her unborn child. To him these evil toxins are reminiscent of the poisons used by witches and that conjure up an association between abortion and nefarious activity.

Sterility

Sterility may be due to the man, not just the woman, or to both ... for example, if a man looks like a eunuch and has only a small penis, he cannot ejaculate far into the vagina. Obesity can also be the cause of the problem: fat men are prevented from ejaculating deep into the vagina, presumably because their distended stomachs get in the way. Aetius of Amida (AD 502–575) was a Byzantine Greek physician and medical writer, who wrote of diseases of the brain and discussed mental illnesses such as *phrenitis*, *melancholia* or *mania*. Book 16 of Aetius' gynaecological *Tetrabiblion* demonstrates his detailed knowledge of contraceptives, abortifacients and surgical procedures.

Infectious Diseases: Mosquitoes and Child Burial

Malaria was endemic in much of Italy and other parts of the southern Roman empire, despite attempts to improve drainage of marshlands and river plains. Maureen Carroll in *Infancy and Earliest Childhood in the Roman World* (2018) discusses Lugnano, 'where the skeletons of forty-seven premature infants, neonates, and post-neonatal children were excavated in five rooms of a Roman villa no longer in use when it was reused for burials in the mid-fifth century AD'. The foetuses were from miscarriages, particularly from *primigravidae* mothers, caused by the immune suppression brought on by malaria, and common in women in the final two trimesters of pregnancy.

The female anopheles mosquito was thought to be attracted to certain chemical receptors found in the placenta of pregnant women. Empedocles blocked off a gorge in Acragas, Sicily, because it was acting as a conduit for a southerly wind bringing in mosquitoes that introduced placental malaria. Pliny quotes Icatidas, a Greek doctor who taught that malaria in men is cured by having sex with a woman just starting her period.

If you needed to spot an infected person in a crowd, you could notice that 'A person suffering from typhus takes on a pale, washed out and sallow complexion, rather like a bag full of urine' (HIPPOCRATES, *Internal Affections* 43).

Little did he know it, but the cerebral Marcus Aurelius was one of history's most prolific serial killers. He can put his hand up to 6 million deaths brought about by his inadvertent introduction of smallpox into the Mediterranean population, imported after a campaign in AD 165 in the East. The pandemic raged for 25 years, and Marcus Aurelius succumbed himself, along with 10 per cent of the population of the empire: poetic justice?

A mass plague grave was opened just outside Rome in 1876 containing an estimated 24,000 corpses from the early imperial period. Even after all those years, the stench was insufferable.

Alexander of Tralles wrote an encyclopaedia of medicine in the sixth century AD; he was the author of the first textbook on parasitology, *Letter on Intestinal Worms*, and made progress in the diagnosis of angina and in ophthalmology.

Rabies and Tetanus

The opportunities for cuts, grazes, bites and other trauma were many and numerous in Roman cities and in the countryside so it is not surprising that cases of tetanus and rabies were correspondingly high.

Novel Diseases

Plutarch in his *Table Talk* (733a) identified some terrible new conditions that, one could argue, might make for a wonderfully weird icebreaker or the jumping-off point for an after-dinner conversation. Who could resist responding to the following: 'An Athenian called Ephebus ejaculated, along with a load of semen, a fast moving hairy creature with many feet'? Or: 'A person who suffered for a long time with urine retention voided a knotted barley stalk.'

According to Agatharchides, speaking of strange and unheard diseases, in an outbreak of pestilence near the Red Sea symptoms included little snakes that ate their way out of a person's arms and legs; if the snakes were touched, they reacted by retreating and caused insufferable inflammations by wrapping themselves around the victim's muscles. Eat your heart out John Hurt, or should that be chest?

Minor Injuries

To ease or avoid saddle-soreness, Cato recommended sticking a sprig of wormwood into the rectum (*On Farming* 159). For snake bites, 'Hippopotamus testicles dried, ground and mixed with wine are an antidote' (DIOSCORIDES, *Medical Material* 2, 23).

Celsus was an expert on the safe extraction of missiles, be they arrows (poison or otherwise), spears, lead balls or rocks. Totally unconnected, but no less painful, is his description of reverse circumcision (*On Medicine* 7, 5; 7, 25).

'Anyone dragged along by a chariot or mangled in its wheels or just bruised should apply wild boar's dung that has been collected in the spring and dried. Fresh dung smeared on the wound is just as good' (PLINY, *Natural History* 28, 237): a handy tip for those daily bumps and scrapes.

The philosopher Anaxarchus of Abdera bit off his own tongue – he won't have been contributing much to Valerius' collection (*Memorable Deeds and Sayings* 3.3.ext.4):

> Anaxarchus made an enemy of Nicocreon, tyrant of Cyprus. Once at a banquet, when asked by Alexander the Great how he liked the feast, he is said to have answered, 'Everything, O king, is magnificent; there is only one thing lacking, that the head of some satrap should be served up at table.' This was a slur on Nicocreon, who never forgot it, and when after the king's death Anaxarchus was forced against his will to land in Cyprus, he seized him and, putting him in a mortar, ordered him to be pounded to death with iron pestles. But he, making light of the punishment, made that well-known speech, 'Pound, pound the pouch containing Anaxarchus; ye pound not Anaxarchus.' And when Nicocreon commanded his tongue to be cut out, they say he bit it off and spat it at him. (DIOGENES LAERTIUS, *Lives of Eminent Philosophers* 10)

Galen says that toe injuries can be cured by urine – a seeming cure-all – by wrapping a pad round the bad toe and making sure to urinate on it every time you relieve yourself (*The Mixture and Properties of Simple Medicines* 12, 286k).

Obesity

In some parts of the Greek world, child obesity was apparently a problem, particularly in Xenophon's time (d. 354 BC):

> And when the Greeks . . . were among the friendly Mossynoecians, they would show them the fattened children of the wealthy inhabitants; these children had been fed on boiled nuts and were extraordinarily soft and white, and more or less as broad as they were tall. Their backs were adorned with many colours and their fronts all tattooed with flower patterns. (XENOPHON, *Anabasis* 5, 4, 32)

Galen has sound advice that still pertains today: 'We can think ourselves thin, but combine this with a modicum of exercise and we get a healthy body and a sharp mind' (*On Exercise with a Small Ball* 5, 904). But the following, unsurprisingly, has never caught on: 'Dew is a natural corrosive. We know this because it makes fat people thinner. Fat women soak up dew on their clothes or on soft tufts of wool and think that this causes excess flesh to melt away' (PLUTARCH, *Natural Phenomena* 913f).

Overweight or obese women were thought to have difficulty conceiving because their fat blocked the entrance to the womb. Another myth says that a pregnant woman with a blooming complexion will deliver a male baby; poor colour brought with it the threat of a girl. Lucius Apronius Caesianus (consul with Caligula in AD 39) was so fat he was unable to move. He was relieved of his immense bulk by an early liposuction procedure (PLINY, *Natural History* 11, 213). Note the insinuation that baby girls are not a good thing.

A timely warning, then as now: 'Magas of Cyrene was choked to death by his own fat' (ATHENAEUS, *Philosophers at Dinner* 549a) To avoid this fate, weight loss can be achieved through:

Bathing in hot water especially if it is salty; by bathing on an empty stomach; by a scorching sun; by heat of all kinds; by worry; by late nights; by too little or too much sleep; by sleeping on a hard bed throughout the summer; by running or fast walking or any vigorous exercise; by vomiting; by purging; by only having one meal a day; by drinking wine (not too cold) on an empty stomach. (CELSUS, *On Medicine* I, 3)

Obstetrics

Gorgias of Epirus (*c.* 485 BC–*c.* 380 BC), later to become a Sophist philosopher and teacher of Greek, was born, and nearly buried alive, at his mother's own funeral (VALERIUS MAXIMUS, *Memorable Deeds and Sayings* 1.8.ext.5). Fortunately, pallbearers heard a baby crying from his mother's coffin.

Here is Soranus expatiating on childbirth; no mention of pain, or relief thereof. But advice on how to deal with abnormalities and exposure thereof. For normal childbirth Soranus advises the following sympathetic, patient-centred procedures: oil for injections and cleansing, hot water for washing, hot compresses to relieve labour pains, woollens to cover the mother and bandages to swaddle the baby in, citruses to help the mother regain her strength. The midwife should wash her hands in oil and, when the mouth of the womb opens, she should insert the trimmed forefinger of her left hand and rearrange the opening so that the amniotic sac falls forward . . . three women should be in attendance to reassure the mother, even if they have no experience of childbirth; the midwife should then sit lower down and opposite the mother holding her thighs apart; she should tell the woman behind to hold the mother's anus with a cloth lest it be pushed out with the straining. If the amniotic sac fails to open the midwife should break it with her nails, insert her finger and widen it gradually, taking care that the baby does not drop out. On delivery the midwife cuts the umbilical cord and the infant is placed on the floor symbolizing contact with Mother Earth; it is encouraged to cry, lifted up, then cleaned and wrapped up and presented to the mother. A grandmother or maternal aunt would then massage the baby's forehead and lips with a finger covered in lustral saliva, a gesture designed to ward off the evil eye.

It is at this point that the father would perform the heart-stopping ritual of lifting up the baby, giving his decision as to whether it lives or dies. Those accepted into the family were named, girls on the eighth day, boys on the ninth – after the critical period for infant death had passed. Unwanted babies might be abandoned at the Temple of Pietas or the Columna Lactaria; those with serious abnormalities would be drowned or suffocated (SORANUS, *Gynaecology* 1, 60, 4; 1, 61, 1–3; 1, 64, 1–2, 1, 65, 1–7).

Pliny recommends a way of concluding a protracted labour; what it lacks in expediency and medical science it more than makes up for in creativity. Get a stone or similar projectile that had killed three living things – human, bear, wild boar, say – in three blows and throw it over the roof of the house where the woman is in confinement; she will then give birth immediately (*Natural History* 28, 33).

The doctor Dorotheos reports in his *Reminiscences* that in Alexandria, a male, who was homosexual, gave birth and the newborn was embalmed and preserved for posterity in a jar (PHLEGON OF TRALLES, *Marvels* 26). Less conveniently, perhaps, a male slave to a soldier under the command of Titus Curtilius Mancias gave birth while serving in Germany (*Marvels* 27).

Multiple births: Alexandria was the setting for a woman who gave birth to twenty children in four deliveries; most survived (*Marvels* 28). Equally productive was another Alexandrian woman who gave birth to five babies at once – three male and two female; Trajan was so impressed that he had them brought up at his own expense. Perhaps seeing that she was on to a good thing here, the following year, the woman gave birth to another three (*Marvels* 29).

Also in Egypt, Hippostratos in his *Minos* records that Aigyptos fathered fifty sons with the same wife, Euryrrhoe (*Marvels* 30).

Danos likewise had fifty daughters from the same wife, Europe (*Marvels* 31).

Antigonus the paradoxographer adds: '[110(1)] A woman gives birth to five at a time at most; though one is memorable because from four births, she had twenty children and reared most of them. [2] If a woman uses an over-abundance of salt while pregnant, the children are born without nails.'

'Nicasiboula, a Messenian, slept in the sanctuary [at Epidauros] in order to have children and saw a dream. The god seemed to come to her carrying a snake that approached her; she had intercourse with the snake. After this she bore two boys within the year' (EPIDAURUS, *Inscriptions* stele 40).

Soranus cautions against upsetting the patient's genitalia: 'The midwife should take care not to look too intently at the genitals of the woman in labour for fear that her body might contract through embarrassment' (*Gynaecology* 2, 6).

Pliny advises to have a mouse handy for cases of perinatal breast engorgement: 'In childbirth, if a woman's breasts swell they can be brought back to their normal size by a drink of mouse droppings in rainwater' (*Natural History* 30, 124).

Ophthalmology

Seeing is definitely *not* believing:

An old woman suffering from an eye problem called a doctor who charged a specified fee. She told him that if he cured her, she would pay him that fee, but if no cure then no fee. The doctor began the treatment, visiting the woman every day. He would smear an ointment on her eyes which prevented her from seeing; then he would steal some object from her house. He did the same thing day after day; by the time she was cured, all her household goods were gone. The doctor asked her for the agreed fee, since she was now able to see clearly, and he summoned witnesses to their agreement. The woman protested, 'I can't see a thing! Even when

MEMPHI   GLEGORI

Roman ophthalmologist conducting an ocular examination, 3rd century AD, from a sarcophagus.

my eyes were ailing, I was able to see everything I had in my home. Now, you claim I am cured, but I can't see anything!' (AESOP, *Fables* 57)

(Anti)Social Psychiatry

Women presenting with mental health problems were 'treated' in much the same 'sensitive' way as men with the same affliction: they were shunned, taunted and often spat at in public. Spitting was thought to prevent the spread of disease and madness; Pliny records how it was customary to spit at epileptics when they are fitting in a bid to throw back the contagion. Spitting was also a weapon against witches, and spitting at anyone lame in their right leg dispelled bad luck. Spitting as therapy was clearly an accepted first line treatment: see Pliny, *Natural History* 28, 36; Plautus, *Captivi*

547–55; and Apuleius *Metamorphoses* 44, where an epileptic is spat at and ostracized by his family, among many other references in the ancient literature.

Alexander of Tralles leaves us the case of the woman who habitually bandaged up her finger; she believed that if she bent it, the world would end (*Therapeutics* 1, 605). From Galen, we know of

- the man who thought he was an earthenware pot and was terrified in case he shattered;
- the man who was terrified of being crushed because he was a snail;
- the man who thought he was a chicken and crowed and flapped accordingly;
- men who thought they were carrying the world on their shoulders, just like Atlas, fearing they may drop it and destroy the world. (*The Affected Places* 8, 190k)

According to Caelius, the causes of mental illness were many and various, and included persistent inebriation, excess of love, grief, anxiety, the removal of haemorrhoids or amenorrhea. His therapies were largely empathetic: he recommended massage and rest in a calm environment. For the woman who believed she had swallowed a snake and was in pain if she did not eat lots of food, he prescribed an emetic, surreptitiously placing a snake in her bowl for her to see. He recommended that the depressed go and watch a comedy, the manic a tragedy – good signs of an early attempt at understanding bipolar disorder? He was also quite pragmatic, recommending that phrenitis (acute inflammation of the brain) sufferers be kept in rooms with high windows, since they were inclined to jump out of them to their deaths.

Elsewhere, Celsus advocated the use of torture and shackles in what was routine bestial treatment of the mentally ill, a practice that persisted in Europe right up to the nineteenth century when Philippe Pinel introduced humane reforms at La Bicêtre in Paris in 1792 and the Quaker Tuke family did likewise at the ground-breaking and enlightened Retreat in York in 1796 (*On Medicine* 3, 18–19).

Sexual Medicine in Ancient Greece

Sexual medicine all started with Hesiod in the eighth century BC. What happened before then to ensure the world had a population was something of a *miracula*. He cited a folk tradition that held that men suffered more than women from the effects of heat, diminishing their sexual performance and the production of semen from its sources, the head and knees: 'in the draining heat, when goats are plumpest and wine is finest, and women are on heat but men are weak' (*Works and Days* 582–8).

Sexual intercourse is a virtual panacea: 'uninhibited fornication cures dysentery' (HIPPOCRATES, *Epidemics* 7, 122). And according to Pliny, it is good for low back pain, diminishing eyesight, dementia and depression (*Natural History* 28, 58). He also recommends the application of tree moss from Gaul as therapy for gynaecological infections, and bramble berries are excellent for gums, tonsils and genitals. If aconite comes into contact with female genitalia, the woman dies the same day. A good aphrodisiac is produced by rubbing the genitalia with a donkey's penis plunged seven times into hot oil (he omits to say if the penis should still be attached to the donkey or not). He describes the use of calcinated lead in ophthalmic medicines, especially in the treatment of proptosis (bulging eyes), itself often a sign of hyperthyroidism and Graves' disease, and in the treatment of ulcers, haemorrhoids and anal fissures – even though he knows that the fumes are harmful to dogs. Other aphrodisiacs involve wearing an amulet made from the right part of a vulture's lung in a crane's skin; drinking the yolk of five duck eggs mixed with pig fat and honey; and an amulet made from a cockerel's right testicle wrapped up in ram's skin. A lizard drowned in a man's urine had the opposite effect as does the enticing cocktail that is snails and pigeon droppings mixed with olive oil and wine (*Natural History* 30, 141ff).

In the days before sildenafil (Viagra) . . . look out all you lizards, you're just the thing for erectile dysfunction: 'If you catch two lizards copulating and cut off the male's penis and dry it and then give it to a woman as a powder, she will be strongly attracted to

you . . . Wearing a lizard's tail as an amulet guarantees an erection'
(*Kyranides* 2, 14).

Salamanders too may have been in great demand, because 'If a
woman wears one attached to her knee, she will not conceive nor
have a period' (*Kyranides* 2, 36). Soranus teaches that successful
conception is all down to timing. 'The end of menstruation, when
the urge and desire for sex is present, when the body is not full
nor the partner drunk, after light exercise and a light snack, when
the mood is right' – these are the most promising conditions for
making babies.

Paul of Aegina recommends

> for those with no enthusiasm for sex and are depressed about
> it to burn a gecko and grind the ashes to a fine powder, pour
> on some olive oil, smear the big toe of your right foot with
> the mixture, and then have intercourse. If you want to stop,
> wash the mixture off your toe. (*Medical Compendium* 3, 58)

Sports Medicine

It seems that Galen had little time for athletes: 'Athletes live just
the way pigs do, except that pigs do not over exert or force feed
themselves' (*Exhortation to Study the Arts* 1, 28k). He goes further:

> If a man is not interested in having children, but is keen on
> winning victory crowns at the games or is engaged in some
> other pursuit to which he appreciates that sexual intercourse
> is detrimental then nothing would be of greater benefit
> to him than castration. It is time, therefore, to cut off the
> testicles of Olympic Athletes. (*Semen* 4, 571k)

Galen adds that athletes and singers tend to have shrivelled
penises anyway, just like old men (*Affected Places* 8, 451k). He once
saw a coach putting lead sheets under an athlete to stop him having
wet dreams (*Matters of Health* 6, 446k). This would have done
nothing for his personal best, though.

Surgery

Apart from being something of an expert in toxicology, Mithridates VI of Pontus liked to try his hand at a spot of surgery. In what must be the ultimate act of obsequiousness, subjects actually volunteered as patients to go under his knife (PLUTARCH, *How to Tell a Flatterer from a Friend* 14). Some years later, the emperor Commodus (r. AD 180–92) took up the scalpel and made a profession of killing his patients (*Historia Augusta, Commodus* 10).

The various practitioners of surgery in the ancient world acquired idiosyncratic techniques to cure their patients:

A doctor performing trephination [a surgical procedure in which a circular piece of bone is drilled and excised, most commonly from the human skull] should take the saw out frequently and dip it in cold water, to prevent the bone from heating up. (HIPPOCRATES, *Head Wounds* 21)

The entrails sometimes roll out as the result of a stomach wound . . . when he puts the entrails back in, the surgeon must always reverse the sequence in which they fell out. When the entrails are all in again the patient is to be shaken gently, so that each coil may return of its own accord to its proper position and settle there. (CELSUS, *On Medicine* 7, 16)

Patently, a patient undergoing surgery in the ancient world would have faced a terrifying experience. But 'a surgeon . . . has to perform his task as if the patient's screams had no effect on him' (CELSUS, *On Medicine* Preface 7). What's more, 'In cases of skull fracture . . . if the patient is in distress, we use fetters during surgery . . . the patient's ears should be blocked with wool, to prevent him from being alarmed by the noise of the bone being chipped away' (ORIBASIUS, *Medical Compilations* 46, 11).

Those hoping to train in surgical procedures had to start somewhere: 'Anyone who wants to practice surgery should go on campaign with an army of mercenaries. (HIPPOCRATES, *The Physician* 14)

It's difficult to know which is the more painful: the piles themselves or the surgical procedure:

> Having laid the patient on his back, and placed a pillow below, force out the anus as much as possible with your fingers, and make the irons red-hot, and burn the pile until it be dried up, and none are left unburnt. You will easily recognize the haemorrhoids, for they project on the inside of the gut like dark-coloured grapes, and when the anus is forced out they spurt blood. When the cautery is applied the patient's head and hands should be held so that he cannot move; let him scream, for this will make the rectum protrude all the more. (HIPPOCRATES, *Haemorrhoids* 2)

ENT *Surgery*

'If a polyp develops in the nose swelling out sideways from the nostril, you remove it by dragging it with a noose from the nose through into the mouth' (HIPPOCRATES, *Affections* 5).

Trauma Surgery

Cutilas was struck in the middle of the head by a javelin, but he kept on running with the javelin still embedded in his head. And after the rout had taken place, he rode into the city at about sunset together with the other survivors, the javelin in his head waving about, a most extraordinary sight.

During the same encounter Arzes, one of the guards of Belisarius, was hit by one of the Gothic archers between the nose and the right eye. The point of the arrow penetrated as far as the neck behind, but it did not leave an exit wound, and the rest of the shaft projected from his face and shook as the man rode ... And when everyone had returned to the city, they attended to the wounded men.

Now in the case of Arzes, though the physicians wished to draw the weapon out of his face, they were for some time reluctant to do so, not so much on account of the eye, which they supposed could not possibly be saved, but for fear lest, by the cutting of membranes and tissues such as are very numerous in that region, they should cause the death of a man who was one of the best of the household of Belisarius. But afterwards one of the physicians, Theoctistus, pressed on the back of his neck and asked whether he felt much pain. And when the man said that he did feel pain, he said, 'Then both you yourself will be saved and your sight will not be injured.' And he made this declaration because he inferred that the barb of the weapon had penetrated to a point not far from the skin. Accordingly he cut off that part of the shaft which showed on the outside and threw it away, and cutting open the skin at the back of the head, at the place where the man felt the most pain, he easily drew toward him the barb, which with its three sharp points now stuck out behind and brought with it the remaining portion of the weapon. Thus Arzes remained entirely free from serious harm, and not even a scar was left on his face. But as for Cutilas, when the javelin was drawn rather violently from his head (for it was very deeply embedded), he passed out. And since the membranes about the wound began to be inflamed, he fell a victim to inflammation of the brain and died soon afterwards. (PROCOPIUS, *On the Wars* 6, 2)

Being a politician with a predilection for prodigious violence, Marius (157–86 BC) was apparently the first man to endure surgery without being tied down (never mind the absence of any anesthetic!). The procedure was to remove varicose veins from one leg; he declined a further operation on his other leg, saying that it wasn't worth the pain (CICERO, *Tusculan Disputations* 2, 22; PLUTARCH, *Life of Marius* 6).

DIY Surgery

This is surely taking self-harm to extremes:

> Hegesistratus of Elis was . . . condemned to die by the Spartans for the great harm he had done them. Being in such dire straits, as he was in peril of his life and was likely to be tortured before his death, he did something which was almost beyond belief. Trapped in iron-bound stocks, he got an iron saw which was smuggled into his prison, and straightaway conceived a plan of such courage as we have never known: he sawed off his own foot at the instep. He then tunnelled through the wall beyond the guards who kept watch over him, and so escaped to Tegea. All night he journeyed, and all day he hid and lay concealed in the woods, till on the third night he came to Tegea, while all the people of Sparta were out looking for him: they were amazed when they saw half of his foot which had been cut off and lying there but were unable to find the man himself . . . After he was healed and had made himself a wooden foot . . . the Spartans caught him at prayer in Zacynthus and killed him.
> (HERODOTUS, *Histories* 9, 37)

Bleeding from fractured skulls was stemmed by the use of cobwebs; brain haemorrhages by goose or duck fat and blood (PLINY, *Natural History* 29, 114).

Intestinal Worms

Miraculous head transplants had amazing results for not-so-obvious complaints:

> Aristagora of Troezen had a tapeworm in her stomach; she slept in the sanctuary of Asclepius in Troezen and had a dream. The god (Asclepius) was not there, but away in Epidaurus. So, his three sons cut off her head, but when they

were unable to put it back again they sent a messenger to get Asclepius to come. Meanwhile, when daylight dawned the priest saw her head removed from her body. The next night Aristagora had another dream. The god came from Epidaurus and replaced her head on her neck; then he cut open her stomach and took out the tapeworm and sewed her up again, and after this she was cured. (EPIDAURUS, *Inscriptions* stele B3)

Ad-hoc stomach surgery works wonders on the worms:

Sostrata of Pherae was pregnant with worms. When she was too weak to walk, she was brought into the sanctuary and slept there. When she did not have a dream, she went back home again. After that Cornoi … her escort, a distinguished-looking man, inquired about her misfortune; he told them to put down the litter on which they were carrying Sostrata. Then he cut open her stomach and removed a large multitude of worms, two washbasins full. Then he sewed up her stomach, and once he had cured her, Asclepius showed that it was he who had appeared, and ordered her to send votive offerings to Epidaurus. (EPIDAURUS, *Inscriptions* stele 25)

Toxicology

Mithridates was not the only amateur toxicologist who caused Rome a lot of trouble; the elegantly late Cleopatra VII was both an amateur toxicologist and an in vivo human and animal experimenter.

Plutarch records that a prescient Cleopatra carried out toxicological research to establish the least painful, efficacious and elegant way to commit suicide. This involved experimentation with various toxic herbs (*pharmaka*) that were cruelly tested on human guinea pigs: namely, condemned prisoners of war and slaves. When this failed to produce a solution, she resorted to intensive animal experimentation, pitting venomous creatures against each other and observing the results. This is how the Egyptian ruler hit upon the famous asp:

> she found that the bite of the asp alone induced a sleepy torpor and sinking, where there was no spasm or groan, but a gentle perspiration on the face, while the faculties were relaxed and dimmed, and resisted all attempts to rouse and restore, as is the case with those who are sound asleep. (*Life of Antony* 71)

Urology, Castration and Circumcision

Ever wondered why male statuary in museums and art galleries is rarely endowed with large penises?

The Benefits of a Small Penis

The relatively small size of the penis possessed by gods and heroes as reflected on Greek and Roman statues has for centuries exercised – obsessed, even – classics and fine art scholars and visitors to museums. In what sounds suspiciously like art *not* reflecting life, it turns out that the usual uncircumcised, little penis was a badge of nobility and cultural superiority; big penises were vulgar and outside the cultural norm, something sported by the barbarians of the world. The small penis was consonant with Greek ideals of male beauty; it was an emblem of the highest culture, a paradigm of civilization. Conversely, large organs and prosthetic phalluses were an object of fun and humour: on the comic stage, any actor playing the 'fool' was immediately recognized by his prodigious phallus – the emblem of stupidity, more of a beast than a man. *Pace* all you satyrs.

As noted, the repellent, rapacious satyr was recognized by his ever-erect penis. The penis was never a badge of virility or manliness in ancient Greece, as it was in other cultures; potency came from the intellect needed to power man's responsibility to father children, prolong the family line and the *oikos* and sustain the *polis*. Anyway, a small penis meant a shorter distance for the sperm to travel on its journey of impregnation. So why crave one? Ask Zeus: he had 45 children all tooled using a decidedly unspectacular penis.

A good example of the modest member can be seen on a bronze statue fished out of the Adriatic Sea near Fano, Italy, in 1964 of a victorious athlete touching the olive wreath on his brow. It was intended as a thoroughly serious piece of art, reflecting not just the pinnacle of Greek sculpture but a male in perfect physical shape, and a highly successful male at that. Zeus of Cape Artemision hurling his thunderbolt – the epitome of male physique – is similarly less well endowed, as is the Hermes from Atalante.

This is where it gets technical: indifference to what we (well, some men) now consider a badge of manliness extends into Greek views regarding public nudity, particularly in athletics, where the ideal male body in action was clear for all to see. However, only barbarians and slaves appeared in the nude, so a *kynodesme* was worn. A *kynodesme* (κυνοδέσμη, or 'dog leash') was 'a thin leather thong wound around the *akroposthion* that pulled the penis upward and was tied in a bow, tied around the waist, or secured by some other means' and worn by some athletes to conceal the penis. It was tied tightly around the *akroposthion*, the part of the foreskin that extends beyond the glans. It could either be attached to a waist band to expose the scrotum or tied to the base of the penis so that the penis appeared to curl upwards. The public exposure of the penis head was regarded by the Greeks as immodest, dishonourable and shameless – again, something only seen in slaves and barbarians.

Coming to the end: 'men ejaculate when they die' (CASSIUS IATROSOPHISTA, *Problems* 47).

Castration and Attis

We have ample evidence of divine castration, genital mutilation, eunuchs and impregnation by nuts. According to Pausanias in his *Description of Greece* (7, 17, 8), Attis was a Phrygian vegetation god, the consort of the great Mother Cybele, who compelled him to castrate himself in a mad frenzy as punishment for his infidelity. Initiates into the resulting eunuch priesthood were called the Gallai, those who re-enacted the myth with their ritual self-castration.

Attis' mother was Nana, a woman impregnated by an almond from the tree that grew from the severed genitals of Agdistis, himself born of Gaia after she was accidentally impregnated by the sleeping sky-god Zeus:

> The gods, fearing Agdistis, cut off his penis from which grew an almond-tree with its fruit ripe; a daughter of the river Saggarios they say, took the fruit and laid it in her breast; it immediately disappeared leaving her pregnant. A boy [Attis] was born, and exposed, but was brought up by a he-goat. (*Description of Greece* 7, 17, 8)

Attis himself was so extraordinarily beautiful that a deity fell in love with him. But his family wanted him to marry the daughter of the king of Pessinus.

> But at the moment when the wedding song had begun, Agdistis appeared, and Attis was seized by a fit of madness, in which he castrated himself; the king who had given him his daughter followed suit. Agdistis now regretted her deed, and obtained from Zeus the promise that the body of Attis should not decompose or rot away. (*Description of Greece* 7, 17, 5)

Circumcision and Reverse Circumcision

To the Neoplatonic philosopher Sallustius, in his fourth-century AD *On the Gods and the World*, circumcision smacked of cannibalism and incest; he associated the snip with the Massagetae who 'eat their fathers' and the Persians who 'preserve their nobility by begetting children by their mothers'.

If the thought of circumcision was loathsome to the Romans, it would be intriguing to know what they thought of the procedure to reverse circumcision. Some Jews resorted to a surgical procedure (epispasm) to restore the foreskin, or prepuce, and cover the glans 'for the sake of decorum' and to make themselves less conspicuous at the baths or during athletics. Celsus (*On Medicine* 7, 25) describes how to raise the prepuce from the penis with a scalpel (and a steady hand), stitching the foreskin to its rightful place with a threaded needle. Apparently, it was neither painful nor accompanied by much bleeding!

If you were an actor, the worst thing that could happen to you would be losing your voice. So, very desperate measures were taken to prevent this: 'A fibula is a little ring that tragic and comic actors have inserted into their penis, to prevent them from having sex, fearing that this might make them lose their voice' (SCHOLION TO JUVENAL, *Satires* 6, 379).

Some believed that the *kynodesme* had a valuable spin-off use: in Greek and Roman medicine, involuntary ejaculation was disapproved of and thought to compromise men's virility; it was also believed to affect the quality of the masculine voice – particularly important in a culture in which oratory was a paramount skill. This form of non-surgical infibulation was used by singers to preserve the voice. Others, according to historian Frederick M. Hodges, in his aptly titled article 'The Ideal Prepuce in Ancient Greece and Rome' (2001), thought that 'tethering the *akroposthion* with the *kynodesme* is frequently confused with preputial infibulation, which had different objectives and was achieved by surgically piercing the prepuce and using the holes so created for the insertion of a metal clasp (fibula) in order to fasten the prepuce shut.'

The foreskin was particularly important: it can be impressively long, representing more than three-quarters of the length of the penis. Indeed, these are the proportions we sometimes see on vase paintings. Probably the best-known such image is an Attic red-figure vase painting attributed to the Sosias painter, in which Achilles bandages the wounded arm of Patroclus. Patroclus' penis is there for all to see, resplendent with extensive foreskin.

The long foreskin is celebrated in literature, too, notably in Lucian's *Lexiphanes* (12): '"Surely," I said, "you don't mean that notable Dion, that lusty, low-scrotumed, cuntish, and mastic-chewing youth who masturbates and gropes whenever he sees someone with a large penis [πεωδη] and a long prepuce [ποσθωνα]?"'

A long prepuce was just as erotic as any big penis. This is evident from the *Thesmophoriazusae* of Aristophanes, where the randy father-in-law buries his face in a garment owned and worn by the young and handsome poet Agathon; he exclaims: 'By Aphrodite, this has a pleasant smell of a prepuce [ποσθη]!' (254).

Circumcision, then, was deplored, as were those barbarian countries who routinely practised circumcision for cultural or religious reasons. The only exception was the surgical management of serious cases of penile gangrene. Celsus says:

> Sometimes through such an ulceration the penis is so eaten away underneath the foreskin that the glans falls off; in which case the foreskin itself must be cut away all round. It is the rule, whenever the glans or any part of the penis has fallen off, or has been cut away, that the foreskin should not be preserved, lest it come into contact, and adhere to the ulceration, so that afterwards it cannot be drawn back, and further perhaps may choke the urethra. (6, 18, 3b)

Herodotus is our earliest Greek source for circumcision: he ascribes circumcision to the Colchians, Ethiopians, Phoenicians, Syrians and Macrones, as well as to Egyptian priests. On the plus side, in their role as great civilizers, the Greeks persuaded the Phoenicians to abandon circumcision. Circumcision is also one of the things the contrary and annoying Egyptians did that was the opposite to everyone else:

> Everywhere else in the world, priests have long hair, but in Egypt they shave their heads ... other people, unless they have been influenced by the Egyptians, leave their genitals in their natural state, but the Egyptians practise circumcision. Their concern for cleanliness also explains why they practise circumcision, since they value cleanliness more than comeliness. (HERODOTUS 2, 104)

One cannot help sympathizing with Herodotus when he marvels that the same people who set such store by genital cleanliness routinely handle dung and prepare food with their bare feet.

As an example of the Greek preference, a fifth-century BC Attic red-figure *pelike* by the artist known as the Pan painter depicts Heracles overthrowing Busiris, a mythological priest-king of Egypt. The Egyptians are shown with fat, ugly, wrinkled, circumcised penises and bulbous externalized glandes, in sharp contrast to Heracles' tidy penis with its elegantly long and tapered prepuce.

Later Greek writers such as Strabo and Diodorus Siculus observed what must have been sickening and horrific accounts of the genital mutilation practised by various, sometimes cave-dwelling, tribes living around the Red Sea, as well as the Hebrews and Egyptians (STRABO, *Geography* 16, 2, 37; DIODORUS SICULUS, 1, 28). Some of these people, it was reported, might cut off just the foreskin (STRABO, *Geography* 16, 4, 5) and others amputated the entire penis (DIODORUS SICULUS 3, 32).

According to Strabo in his description of the Hebrews and the descendants of Moses,

> in the first place, superstitious men were appointed to the priesthood, and then tyrannical people; and from superstition arose abstinence from flesh, from which it is their custom to abstain even to-day, and circumcisions and excisions [of females] and other observances of the kind.
> (*Geography* 16, 2, 37)

Apart from barbarians, primitiveness, backwardness, superstition, a tendency for vegetarianism and oppression, in the Greek mind the circumcised penis is also associated with slavery, as evidenced by a sixth-century Corinthian painted clay tablet showing four slaves hard at work in a mine. One slave is clearly circumcised: his prodigious penis swings between his legs, the glans exposed.

If we need further evidence of the anathema ancient Greeks felt towards the Hebrew practice of circumcision, we need go no further than Antiochus Epiphanes, a descendent of one of Alexander the Great's greatest generals; he, somewhat fanatically, ruled that the rabbis who performed circumcision should be 'stoned or fed to wild dogs. Mothers who permitted their sons to be circumcised should be garrotted, their strangled infants strung about their necks, and then hanged upon crosses as terrible warnings to others.'

In the ancient world generally, the penis was king, and masturbation was evidence of that regality. Ancient Iraqi poetry from the third millennium BC shows that the seminal creative force of the world was Enki, or, more precisely, Enki's penis. His penis dug the world's first irrigation ditches, created rivers and introduced human sexual reproduction. After he fathered the first human baby, Enki exulted: 'Now let my penis be praised!' The ancient Egyptian god Atum jubilantly announced: 'I created on my own every being. My fist became my spouse. I copulated with my hand.' Atum's penis created all life, divine and mortal, through this gesture of sacred masturbation. In ancient Egypt, the penis was so powerful that it conquered death. Osiris flaunted his virility in the underworld as king, declaring in the *Book of the Dead*: 'I am Osiris of the stiff penis, I am mightier than the Lord Terror; I copulate and I have power over myriads.'

The Penis, Linguistically Speaking

The penis is blessed with a whole host of Latin words describing it and its functions; there are no fewer than 120 or so. Pride of place for the obscene use of the word is *mentula* – a term that Martial uses 48 times, while Catullus deploys it 8 times, most notoriously as a nickname of sorts for Mamurra (that is, 'dick-head'). Not surprisingly, it appears 26 times in the *Priapea*, 18 times in graffiti from Pompeii and 3 in the Graffiti del Palatino. *Verpa* was a more offensive phrase, denoting an erect penis with foreskin drawn back, fresh from vigorous sexual activity. *Verpa* is used once each by Catullus and Martial, and in the *Priapea*. *Virga* too, meaning branch, rod, stake or beam, and *vomer*, plough, were both used in a metaphorical sense, as were *vena* (vein), *penis* and *cauda* (tail) and *nervus* (tendon).

7

Physiology

Aristophanes was recorded by Plato (*Symposium*, 190c) as believing that there were three types of human: male, female and androgynous. People were originally pear-shaped, with their back and sides forming a circle. They had four hands, four feet, one head with two faces, four ears and, usefully, two sets of genitalia. They could speed along on their eight legs, were multi-dexterous, excellent listeners, versatile when it came to sex and were practised in the art of duplicitous two-facedness. The plan of a paranoid Zeus was to keep the human race going, but to weaken it by cutting humans in half in order to reduce their rebelliousness. The upside of this was that there would be more of them to offer themselves up as human sacrifices. If man still refused to settle down, then he was intent on splitting them again so that they would be forced to hop about on one leg.

Demolishing the cliché that size matters: according to someone from Aristotle's school, 'People with small heads are more thoughtful than people with large heads' (PSEUDO-ARISTOTLE, *Problems* 955b).

In terms of eternal questions, we've all surely wondered, *why is it that people can't tickle themselves?* Aristotle's acolytes did (PSEUDO-ARISTOTLE, *Problems* 965a). The answer for all those honest enough to admit to being intrigued is given in a *Scientific American* article of 29 January 2007 by University College London researchers:

> The answer lies at the back of the brain in an area called the cerebellum, which is involved in monitoring movements. Our studies . . . have shown that the cerebellum

can predict sensations when your own movement causes them but not when someone else does. When you try to tickle yourself, the cerebellum predicts the sensation and this prediction is used to cancel the response of other brain areas to the tickle.

Pliny, as we know only too well as the author of a fact-filled encyclopaedia – and a polymath to boot – never lost, it seems, the ability to surprise his readers with a dose of mythic fantasy. He actually believed in the existence of the merman, and this is what he had to say on the matter, to the astonishment, no doubt, of his many readers:

A deputation from Olisipo [Lisbon] brought word to the Emperor Tiberius [r. AD 14–37] that a triton [or merman] had been both seen and heard in a certain cavern, blowing a conch-shell, and looking just like they are usually look. Nor yet is the figure generally attributed to the nereids [mermaids] at all a fiction; only in them, the part of the body that resembles the human figure is still rough all over with scales. For one of these creatures was seen on the same shores, and as it died, its plaintive murmurs were heard even by the inhabitants some distance away ... The legatus of Gaul, too, wrote to the late Emperor Augustus that a considerable number of nereids had been found dead on the sea-shore. I have, too, some distinguished informants of equestrian rank [and thus well-educated], who say that they themselves once saw in the ocean of Gades a sea-man [or merman] which bore in every part of his body a perfect resemblance to a human being, and that during the night he would climb up into ships; upon which the side of the vessel where he seated himself would instantly sink downward, and if he remained there any considerable time, even go under water. (*Natural History* 9, 4; see also JUVENAL 14)

The coast of Gaul washed up quite a lot of sea monsters, it seems:

In the reign of the Emperor Tiberius, a subsidence of the ocean left exposed on the shores of an island which faces the province of Lugdunum [Gaul] as many as three hundred animals or more, all at once, quite marvellous for their varied shapes and enormous size, and no less a number upon the shores of the Santones [a Gallic tribe]; among the rest there were elephants and rams, which last, however, had only a white spot to represent horns. Turranius has also left accounts of several nereids, and he speaks of a monster that was thrown up on the shore at Gades, the distance between the two fins at the end of the tail of which was sixteen cubits [233 ft], and its teeth one hundred and twenty in number; the largest being nine, and the smallest six inches in length.

M. Scaurus, in his ædileship, exhibited at Rome, among other wonderful things, the bones of the monster to which Andromeda was said to have been exposed, and which he had brought from Joppa, a city of Judæa. These bones exceeded forty feet [12 m] in length, and the ribs were higher than those of the Indian elephant, while the back-bone was a foot and a half in thickness. (PLINY, *Natural History* 9, 4, 5)

8

Embalming

Embalming was uncommon in ancient Rome – much more of an Egyptian thing – but Nero and his wife Poppaea Sabina took embalming to new heights. In AD 58, Rome was threatened by a scandal, in the person of the empress (AD 30–65). Tacitus, no fan, tells us that she was the woman who had everything – everything, that is, apart from integrity. She inherited glory and good looks from her exceptionally beautiful mother; she was rich, eloquent and smart – *docta puella* (*sermo comis nec absurdum ingenium*) – and she preached modesty (*modestia*) but practised salaciousness (*lascivia*). She was something of a recluse, but when she did go out, she wore a veil – either to tantalize men or to accentuate the allure of her beauty – and her predilection for bathing in asses' milk started a craze.

Poppaea aimed high: her resolve was to persuade Nero to assassinate his mother, Agrippina, and then marry her. According to Dio, Seneca also urged Nero to commit matricide. In AD 62, Nero married Poppaea, but while she was awaiting the birth of her second child in the summer of 65, she argued violently with Nero over him spending too much time at the races. Outraged, Nero kicked her in the stomach and killed her. Tacitus (*Annals* 16, 6) writes that Poppaea was embalmed by having her body stuffed full of herbs and spices. Nero burned a year's worth of Arabia's very expensive incense production at her state funeral.

A mummy of a middle-aged woman in a lead coffin was discovered in 1962 during an excavation in Thessaloniki. Researchers from the Institute of Anatomy at the University of Zurich showed that a number of oils, spices and resins were used to embalm the body, which dates to AD 300, when Greece was under Rome's imperial rule. Not only did this method help preserve the skeleton, but some soft tissues were also partially preserved, including hair and blood cells, and a hand muscle, as well as a gold-embroidered silk cloth that covered the body.

9

Deformity and Disability

Generally speaking deformity and disability never really exercised the Romans. The Romans were decidedly casual, and by modern standards, insensitive, inhumane and just plain wrong. Most deformed infants were simply abandoned or murdered at birth. But you didn't need to have a disability to be dumped, literally, on the scrap heap. Girls, by their very nature of not being boys, were similarly exposed because they were a financial liability waiting to happen; they were going nowhere professionally or politically, they were not going to join the army, and they would only be married off on provision of an expensive dowry. It is right that we deplore this, but we should also remember that what most people would today call 'proper and empathetic inclusion of disabled people into wider society' is still a relatively new development in the West. The hugely popular Victorian freak shows only ended one hundred or so years ago. Our so-called caring society and inclusive attitudes relating to disability are developments of the very late twentieth century, mere footnotes in the great scheme of things.

Just being what others considered to be ugly could, incredibly, have fatal consequences in the ancient world. In the late sixth century BC, Hipponax, that poet famous for adumbrating the darker corners of Ionian society, himself notable for his own ugliness and deformity, wrote that at the festival of Thargelia on the day of the sacrifice, the two ugliest men that could be found were led along with strings of figs around their necks and whipped on the genitals with rods of figwood and onion bulbs. They were then stoned to death, their corpses burnt and the ashes scattered into the sea as a fertilizer. These scape-goated victims were called *pharmakoi*, their odious treatment supposedly having a purgatory effect on a purification of a city in peril; interestingly, the same word denotes a magician, poisoner or, in its feminine form, a witch – all groups that have suffered similar indignities, marginalization and prejudice down the ages (TZETZES, *Chileads* 5, 728).

To get an idea of the life Hipponax lived and the otherness of the people he described living their low lives on the edges of society we only need look at some of the fragments that survive which depict the liminal sort of existence the disabled and the deformed experienced: in fragment 12 Hipponax lambasts, 'Bupalus, the mother-fucker (μητροκοίτης) with Arete', the latter evidently being the mother of Bupalus, yet Arete is presented as performing fellatio on Hipponax in fragment 17, while, elsewhere, Hipponax moans, 'Why did you sleep with that scoundrel Bupalus?', again apparently referring to Arete whose name ironically is Greek for 'virtue'.

So-called ugly people and the disabled were scape-goated and victimized in Greece because they were considered freaks – beyond the realms of nature, sent to Earth, like women, as a punishment to mankind by the gods. It was their fault when anything bad befell the community. Deformity was, therefore, heaven sent. As early as Hesiod in the *Works and Days*, the euphemism for a 'normal' child was one who 'resembled his father'. Before the battle of Plataea in 479 BC, the horrible consequences of not 'resembling your father' were quite clear from the battlefield oath: 'If I remain faithful to the inscribed oath, may women give birth to children who resemble their parents. If not, may they give birth to monsters.' This must have been a boon for religious conformity and piety – not just among the soldiers that day but with their womenfolk, who must have been terrified.

We have noted how girls were casually abandoned and exposed if they were deemed surplus to the requirements of the family, a burden on the household (*oikos*). The Athenian comic poet Posidippus puts it succinctly: 'Everyone, even a poor man, raises a son. Everyone, even a rich man, exposes a daughter.' In eugenicist Sparta, it was simpler still: the abandonment of handicapped infants was manda-tory in law. Elsewhere in Greece, mothers may have been less cold

Terracotta figurine of a person who possibly has
acromegaly – a rare disease in which the pituitary
gland produces too much growth hormone, leading
to various symptoms, such as swelling of parts of
the body, including facial features and organs –
from Smyrna, 100 BC–AD 100.

and brutal, if Plato's remarks in the
Theaetetus are anything to go by.
Referring disparagingly to a
'lifeless phantom not worth
rearing', he then asks: 'Or
do you think your infant
must be reared anyway
and not exposed? Can
you bear to see it exam-
ined and not be upset if it is taken
away, even if it is your first-born?', suggesting that some Athenian mothers
did love their children, however differently abled, enough to raise them within
the family. Aristotle is with Plato when,
in the *Politics*, he advocates a law crimin-
alizing the rearing of deformed children.

Surviving statuary and wall paintings
project an idealized and airbrushed image
of fine men and women as today. However,
recent research reveals that, contrary to the pleasant and pleasing
images conveyed by many of the frescoes and mosaics discovered in
Pompeii and Herculaneum (among other sites), around 10 per cent
of the local women were obese and hirsute; furthermore, they suffered from chronic headaches and diabetes. Skeletal examinations
revealed a small bony growth on the inside of their skulls behind the
forehead, indicative of a hormonal disorder, hyperostosis frontalis
interna (HFI), which causes these symptoms. We don't see many
statues or paintings of slaves or women grafting away in the baths
and the bakeries do we?

War correspondence, too, can help to make the picture more real and credible. Julius Caesar reports that in one battle during the civil war, four out of the six centurions in one cohort were blinded by enemy action – probably not that uncommon, given the number of missiles that were flying about:

> So, there were six battles in that one day, three at Dyrrachium and three at the outworks; when we add them all up we found that about two thousand of the Pompeians had fallen ...of our men no more than twenty were lost in all six battles. But in the redoubt every one of the men who was wounded and four centurions out of one cohort lost their eyes. As proof of their industry and the danger they were in, they counted out to Caesar about thirty thousand arrows which had been discharged at the redoubt, and when the shield of the centurion Scaeva was brought to him, one hundred and twenty holes were found in it. (*Bellum Civile* 3, 53)

Deliberate blinding was also a popular form of torture inflicted on prisoners of war and as a punishment for insubordination.

VOCABULARY IS OFTEN a good signpost to a society's attitude and cultural values. There is no exact word in Greek or Latin for 'disabled', but the Greeks use *teras* and the Romans *monstrum* to convey their meaning; semantically, it is but a short step from 'a wonderful thing' to a 'monster'. Interestingly, the original meaning of *monstrum* was, according to Charlton Lewis and Charles Short's *Latin Dictionary* (1879), 'a divine omen indicating misfortune', but it can, more positively, also mean 'wonderful things'. Varro, in his work on linguistics, *Etymologia*, says that the gods use defective births to show what the future holds (11, 3, 8); indeed, the word 'monster' comes from *monstrare*, 'to show'. All congenital malformations had to be reported to the authorities to check if they were a sign from above.

The noun *monstrum*, however, is ominously related to the verb *monere*, meaning 'to give warning', and can, as in Tacitus, even mean 'to punish' (*Annals* 5, 9). Disability, then, was never good news for the able. *Teras* elided from being a wonder or a marvel into 'a huge, unearthly creature, a monster', as in Homer and Plato. Linguistically, this means that disabled people are classified the same as such mythological monstrosities as the Gorgon Medusa.

The Latin word *mutus* describes both something or somebody unable to speak, or a dumb animal or a brute. Linguistic inadequacy this may just be, but the inevitable result is an association of the disabled with the monstrous and ugly. Pliny the Elder tells us that the Greeks also call such people *ektrapeloi* (freaks), a word that changed from meaning 'strange' or 'devious' to a description of people as monstrous, as in enormous children; he adds that the Romans have no word for them.

Pliny is the last word on gigantism and dwarfism, although we would rightly argue today that these are not indicators of either disability or deformity:

> Our histories do not tell us the height of Nævius Pollio; but we learn from them that he nearly died in the rush [of people] to see him, and that he was looked upon as a prodigy. The tallest man that has been seen in our times, was called Gabbaras, brought from Arabia by the Emperor Claudius; his height was nine feet nine inches [3 m]. In the reign of Augustus, there were two people, Posio and Secundilla, who were half a foot taller than him; their bodies have been preserved as objects of curiosity in the museum of the Sallustian family.
>
> In the reign of the same emperor, there was a man famous for being very small indeed being only two feet and a palm in height [68 cm]; his name was Conopas, and he was a big pet of Julia's, the wayward daughter of Augustus. There was a woman too, the same size, called Andromeda, a freedwoman of Julia Augusta. We learn from Varro, that Manius Maximus and M. Tullius, members of our equestrian order, were only two cubits in height (3 foot [1 m]); and I have myself seen them, preserved in their coffins. It is well known

that children are occasionally born a foot and a half in height, and sometimes a little more; such children, however, have died by the time they are three years old. (*Natural History* 7, 16)

Phlegon of Tralles records, for example, a hermaphrodite from 125 BC who caused such a commotion that the august Sibylline Oracles no less were consulted, because no one knew what to do with him; a highly thought of slave woman who in AD 49 gave birth to an ape; a four-headed child that was presented to Nero with eight arms and eight legs; and a child born with its head protruding from its shoulder (*Marvels* 20, 23).

According to the revered *Twelve Tables* (4, 1), deformed babies of either sex should be disposed of as soon as possible after birth. Dionysius of Halicarnassus (2, 15) alleges that Romulus (in the so-called *Law of Romulus*) 'obliged the inhabitants to bring up all their male children and the first-born of the females, and forbade them to destroy any children under three years of age unless they were maimed or monstrous from their very birth'.

In the ancient world, it comes as no surprise to learn that superstition often accompanied and shrouded deformity. Livy tells in 207 BC of a 'monstrously' deformed child being cast adrift, alive in a box, to rid Rome of such a 'repulsive portent':

a new report came, this time from Frusino, saying that a child had been born there in size and features equal to one four years old . . . it was impossible to say whether it was male or female. The soothsayers . . . said that this was a terrible portent, and the thing must be banished from Roman soil, not permitted to touch the earth, and buried at sea. They enclosed it still living in a box, took it out to sea, and dropped it overboard. (27, 37)

So, deformity in a baby told a parent in no uncertain terms that the gods were less than pleased: a deformed baby was seen as a manifestation of divine punishment visited upon its parents. By extension, deformity in a newborn spelled doom for the state. The deformed baby presaged disaster, and so the association of disability with misfortune served to fuel further the general suspicion and anxiety surrounding disabled people.

SUETONIUS DESCRIBES A decree in 63 BC that all boys should be exposed:

> According to Julius Marathus, a few months before Augustus was born a portent was generally observed at Rome, which gave warning that nature was pregnant with a king for the Roman people; thereupon the senate in consternation decreed that no male child born that year should be reared; but those whose wives were with child saw to it that the decree was not filed in the treasury, since each one appropriated the prediction to his own family. (*Augustus* 94,3)

The absence of registration meant that it never became law; however, the main point is that a king (*rex*) was anticipated and kings were reviled in Rome since the fall of the monarchy.

Musonius Rufus in the first century AD deplored child murder (*Reliquae* 80); and Soranus, the gynaecologist, saw fit to provide a checklist for midwives to help them determine the newborn disorders that permitted exposure (*Gynaekia*). Unwanted babies might be abandoned at the Temple of Pietas or the Columna Lactaria; those with serious abnormalities would simply be drowned or suffocated.

Generally speaking, then, the deformed and disabled were regarded – as a worst case – decidedly odd, bad news and something to be rid of; in the best case, they were an object of fun and mockery, as when Pompey put them on the stage in his theatre exploiting their novelty value for personal kudos and the titillation of the gawping, scoffing and mocking masses; or indulged as a pet (*delicia*), as with Julia, daughter of Augustus – however, although this was often a sentence to an apparently privileged life, it was not one without its sexual obligations.

Quintus Pedius

Other examples exist in which we see kind and compassionate behaviour. Pliny the Elder tells how Quintus Pedius (not to be confused with his grandfather, the Roman general and great nephew of Julius Caesar)

> had a grandson [also Q. Pedius], who being dumb from his birth, the orator Messala, to whose family his grandmother belonged, recommended he should be brought up as a painter, a proposal which was also approved of by the late Emperor Augustus. He died, however, in his youth [about AD 13], after having made great progress in the art. (*Natural History* 35, 4)

Quintus has the distinction of being the first recorded person with hearing issues known by name; it is also the first instance we know of the education of a hearing-impaired child. Octavia, Augustus' sister, was extremely solicitous, and encouraged Quintus' development and progress.

Claudius and Cerebral Palsy

The first-century Roman emperor Claudius was the butt of everyone's jokes and mockery. Suetonius shows the embarrassment he caused Augustus and Livia, his empress, notably in a letter from the former to the latter in which the emperor agonizes over the extent to which he should allow Claudius to officiate at public events and be seen, indeed gawped at, in the imperial box with him. But Claudius was by no means the idiot everyone liked to think he was (and still do to some extent, no thanks to Robert Graves): 'Despite the disability – a limp, a stutter and some deafness – caused by his lifelong illness – probably cerebral palsy – Claudius was a writer of some distinction and a competent student of Greek culture; he was also something of a linguist and introduced three new letters into the Roman alphabet' (SUETONIUS, *Claudius* 41–2).

For whatever reason – frustration, disappointment, embarrassment – Claudius' mother, Antonia Minor, was, to modern sensitivities, vile to Claudius, calling him a monster (*portentum*) and a half-complete creation (*nec absolutum a natura*), and describing others she considered stupid (*socordiae*) to be even dafter (*stultiorem*) than Claudius. His sister Livilla, on hearing that one day he might become emperor, is reported as saying that the Roman people did not deserve such a cruel misfortune. According to Suetonius (*Claudius* 3), his mother Livia rarely spoke to him.

DWARFS AND HUNCHBACKS were seemingly as much in high demand as singers, dancers, musicians, jugglers and clowns. Freak shows would have been all the rage. In his *A Feast of Lapithae*, Lucian describes a buffoon (*morio*) called Satyrion as 'an ugly, shaven little fellow' who provides some of the mid-prandial dinner-party entertainment:

> Now came one of the usual short breaks in the procession of dishes; and Aristaenetus, to avoid the embarrassment of a pause, told his jester to come in and talk or perform, by way of putting the company even more at their ease. So in came an ugly fellow with a shaven head – just a few hairs standing upright on the crown. He danced with dislocations and contortions, which made him still more absurd, then improvised and delivered some anapaests in an Egyptian accent, and wound up with witticisms aimed at the guests. (18)

Cicero, however, advises restraint against mockery, because the ridicule can backfire:

> In deformity, also, and bodily defects, is found fair enough matter for ridicule; but we have to ask the same question here as is asked on other points, 'How far the ridicule may be carried?' In this respect it is not only directed that the orator should say nothing impertinently, but also that, even

if he can say anything very ridiculously, he should avoid both errors, lest his jokes become either buffoonery or mimicry. (*De oratore* 2, 239)

The show goes on . . . Suetonius tells how Augustus exhibited a man called Lycius who was under 60 centimetres (2 ft) tall, weighed only 8 kilograms (17 lb) and had a stentorian voice, this despite Augustus being reported by Suetonius as seriously averse to dwarfs and the like, believing them to be ill-omened (*Augustus* 83). According to Dio (67, 8, 4), as we know, dwarfs were recruited by Domitian to perform as gladiators against women as warm-up acts for the main event.

Pygmies (*pugmaios*) – simply small people – are described most famously at the opening of Homer's *Iliad* Book 3. Alarmingly, the exploitation of dwarfs continues apace today in 'dwarf-tossing' in Canada, the United States and France: a modern manifestation of people exploited as spectacle solely because of their untypical physical form, because they differ from the so-called norm. At the most repellent end of the spectrum, we have already baulked at how Commodus allegedly served up a pair of hunchbacks smeared with mustard on a silver platter (*Scriptores Augustae, Commodus* 11, 1).

Sadly, some societies appear not to have moved on from the sick and sadistic reign of Commodus 1,800 years ago: individuals with skeletal dysplasia such as dwarfism often have specific medical conditions and vulnerabilities that increase the risk of further health complications. Throwing or tossing individuals with a growth disorder can have serious consequences, especially in cases involving kyphosis and scoliosis. Various medical sources and organizations have warned about the dangers of dwarf tossing, and there are known cases where individuals have suffered severe injuries and even died as a result of it.

It is but a short step from this cheap, voyeuristic sort of exploitation to sexual exploitation of the disabled. Pliny the Elder reports sex with a hunchback slave (*Natural History* 34, 11–12), while Martial launches an excoriating attack on a woman, Marulla, who apparently cultivated a predilection for sex with the facially deformed.

Petronius, in the feast of Trimalchio from the novel *Satyricon* (39), refers to people with convergent strabismus, that is, people who are cross-eyed: 'Under Sagittarius are born cross-eyed people who look at the vegetables and take the bacon.'

On a slightly more inclusive, constructive and less exploitative note, Tiberius, Claudius, Nero and Domitian all were happy to admit disabled slaves into their entourages of advisors and confidants. Suetonius says that Tiberius's dwarf court jester was particularly influential and, when he asked during a banquet about a man who had been charged with treason, Tiberius reacted and expedited the man's trial (*Tiberius* 61); Claudius enjoyed the company of Julius Paelignus, 'despised alike for his stupid mind and contemptible body' (TACITUS, *Annals* 12, 49 1), appointing him as governor of Cappadocia. Domitian kept a dwarf by his side at gladiatorial displays for the kudos, and just to be different: 'a boy dressed in scarlet with an abnormally small head' – microcephaly, presumably. These people were later to become the 'pinheads' in early circus sideshows, and put on display as 'missing links', the link between humans and lower mammals (SUETONIUS, *Domitian* 4, 2).

The *Historia Augusta, Commodus* (10,9), gossips that Commodus 'also had in his company a man with a male member larger than that of most animals, whom he called Onos. This man he treated with great affection, and even made him rich and appointed him to the priesthood of the Rural Hercules.' Elagabalus (r. AD 218–22) kept so many human 'curiosities' that looking after them became a financial liability.

Some people with mobility issues could scratch a living as potters, teachers and metal workers; indeed, the lame Greek god Hephaistos was a blacksmith and something of a role model for the disabled, despite the attempts of his mother, Hera, to murder him at birth, and forever being the butt of the other gods' ridicule. More lucrative, and certainly more dangerous, was employment as a spy or informer: Tacitus describes Vatinius as

> ranked among the filthiest prodigies of that court; the
> product of a cobbler, blessed with a misshapen body and

a scurrilous wit, he had been taken on from the start as a target for buffoonery; then, by falsely accusing every decent man, he acquired a power which made him a leading villain, in influence, in wealth, and in the capacity to inflict harm. (*Annals* 15, 34)

In the reign of Domitian (AD 81–96), a blind man called Catullus Messalinus became a very successful informer, described by Juvenal as 'a great and renowned monster (*monstrum*), a blind flatterer' (4, 115–16); he must have relied solely on what he heard.

Pliny the Younger tells us about the sad story of Domitius Tullus, a paralysed man who was sufficiently wealthy to be able to afford carer slaves, whom he hired from their owners to assist him with daily living. Pliny the Younger (*Epistles* 8, 18) says that Domitius Tullus did not feel lucky but rather somewhat humiliated at being so dependent on his slaves and his dedicated wife for the most basic functions and tasks: 'A quadriplegic, he could only enjoy his huge wealth by gazing at it and could not even turn in bed without help. He even had to have someone clean his teeth for him, a pathetic thing.'

However, begging on the streets, petty crime, fetishistic prostitution, casual, seasonal work and reliance on family charity must have been the order of the day for most disabled people, who usually were consigned and confined to or beyond the margins of Roman society.

The gods often dealt a devastating double blow when a disabled person happened also to be a slave. There must have been many such unfortunates: if they weren't disabled when they started their labours as slaves, they often would be later owing either to slaves being worked within an ace of death or through injuries sustained in battle before being consigned as war booty to servitude as a defeated prisoner of war. It seems likely that when a slave became too weak or disabled to be of any further practical use to his master, he was simply murdered: Claudius' law ruling that disabled slaves should be abandoned rather than killed probably testifies to this. Manumitting a disabled slave was probably the cruellest act of all:

MIRACULA

in effect, that slave was being consigned to a life of penury and abuse on the streets; it did, however, save the master money.

Perhaps the most extraordinary, and untypical, story relating to a disabled person is left to us by Pliny the Elder when he describes what happened to the slave Clessipus, named by Pliny as 'an ugly hunchback' (*Natural History* 34, 11). A wealthy woman called Gegania went out shopping one day and decided to buy an expensive Corinthian chandelier for the prodigious sum of 50,000 sesterces; for good measure, the auctioneer threw in Clessipus as well, so she left the shop with a bronze candelabra and a deformed slave. Making the most of it, Gegania showed him off at parties and had him parade naked for the titillation of her guests. However, she also fell deeply in love with him, aroused possibly by his scoliosis, took him into her bed and even changed her will to make him a beneficiary. On her death, Gegania's huge fortune came to Clessipus, who presumably spent the rest of his days giving thanks to the candelabra. Whether Clessipus was just a very clever fortune-hunter we will never know; we can only hope that he genuinely deserved his good luck.

Not surprisingly, some hunchbacks were very self-conscious about their condition. Suetonius tells that Horace's notorious teacher, the 'flogger' Lucius Orbilius Pupillus, was typically rude to distinguished men; when he was unknown and was giving testimony in a crowded courtroom, when asked by Varro Murena, the lawyer on the other side, what he did and what his profession was, he replied: 'I take hunchbacks out of the sun and put them into the shade.' Murena was a hunchback.

We know that that some Romans maimed their slaves out of sheer sadism, either to satisfy sexual deviance or just to create the extraordinary in order to impress, a kind of perverted status symbol for the home that had everything. There was nothing like a dwarf, hunchback, manic depressive, blind, death, dumb or blind man or woman to impress the neighbours or dinner guests – all readily available from that hideous special section of the slave market.

Plutarch describes this odious place (τεράτων ἀγορὰν, 'teraton agora' or the 'monster market'):

Therefore, just as at Rome there are some who take no account of paintings or statues or even, by Heaven, of the beauty of the boys and women for sale, but haunt the monster-market, examining those who have no calves, or are weasel-armed, or have three eyes, or ostrich-heads, and go searching to see if there has been born some commingled shape and misformed prodigy; yet if one continually conducts them to such sights, they will soon feel they've had enough and feel sick; so let those who are curious about life's failures, the blots on the coat of arms, the delinquencies and errors in other people's homes, remind themselves that their former discoveries have brought them no favour or profit. (*De curiositate* 10/*Moralia*, 520c)

An enlightened Longinus is yet more critical of this inhumane behaviour:

And so, my friend adds, if what I hear is true, not only do the cages in which they confine the pygmies or dwarfs, as they are called, stunt the growth of their captives, but their bodies even shrink due to the close confinement, on the same principle that all slavery, however fair it may be, might be described as a cage for the human soul, a common prison. (*De sublimitate* 44, 5)

Children too were deliberately mutilated to ramp up the pity – and therefore the money – they would bring in while begging on the streets: Seneca the Elder (*c*. 54 BC–*c*. AD 39) tells the shocking story of a man on trial for snatching exposed children and mutilating them:

Here roam the blind, leaning on sticks, here others carry round stumps of arms. This child has had the joints of his feet torn, his ankles wrenched; this has had his legs crushed. Another's thighs he has smashed, though leaving feet and legs unharmed. Finding a different savagery for each, this bone-breaker cuts off the arms of one, slices the sinews of another's; one he twists, another he castrates. In yet another he stunts the shoulder-blades, beating them into an ugly hump, looking for a laugh from his cruelty. Come on, bring out your troup half-alive, shaking, feeble, blind, crippled, starving; show us your prisoners. I want to get to know that cave of yours, that stripping-place for children. (*Controversiae* 10, 4, trans. Michael Winterbottom)

Despite it all, the deformed slave was sometimes regarded as something of a talisman, a good luck charm, a living force against malicious curses and evil spells. He or she also served to satisfy a sense of *schadenfreude* in the owner, or, more charitably, a living, daily reminder that 'there but for the grace of the gods, go I'.

Seneca the Younger's wife owned a dwarf named Harpaste who irked the philosopher no end:

You know Harpaste, my wife's female clown; she has stayed in my house, a burden inherited from a legacy. I especially disapprove of these freaks; whenever I wish to enjoy the gags of a clown, I don't have to go very far; I can just laugh at myself. Now this clown suddenly went blind. Incredible as it sounds, I swear that it is true: she does not know that she is blind. She keeps asking her attendant to change her quarters, saying that her apartment is too dark. (SENECA, *Epistles* 50, 2)

Lucian reminds us that the disabled apparently brought their own ill omens: 'Especially in the morning we avoid people who limp with their right leg, and, if anyone sees a monkey or a eunuch just as he's leaving home, he goes back in, convinced that everything will turn out bad that day' (*Pseudologists* 17).

When in Messene a storage jar shattered during a downpour, a triple head of a human body emerged sporting two sets of teeth. The Messenians 'transplanted' the monstrosity in another jar and looked after it more carefully thereafter. The head belonged to no other than the Homeric hero Idas (PHLEGON OF TRALLES, *Marvels* 11).

While digging fortifications on an island off Athens, the diggers came upon a coffin that measured 100 cubits (46 m/150 ft) in length. Inside was a withered body, which filled it, and an inscription that revealed the deceased to be Makroseiris, who lived for 5,000 years (*Marvels* 17).

Pygmies

We have already touched on the pygmy in the classical world in this occasionally disturbing discussion. In many ways, the pygmy might be seen as indicative of the repellent (by our standards) way Romans often treated disability – preferring to treat the deformed and disabled as objects of derision, abuse and entertainment instead of showing compassion and concern. Of course, we see all of this from the perspective of our own modern eyes, which, for the most part, are anxious to preserve the dignity and humanity of the disabled; the

Attic red-figure *oenochoe* showing a Pygmy fighting a crane, *c.* 430–20 BC.

Romans – indeed, ancient civilizations in general – still had a long way to go . . . However, unlike people of particularly short stature (or with the genetic condition achondroplasia), the references to pygmies in the literature quoted here show no specific discrimination aimed at the race of Pygmies; rather they are seen as a positive wonder due to their diminutive stature.

The Pygmies were a mythical race of small creatures who, like many other things that were thought odd by the Romans, existed at the edge of the world – in Africa, India or even in *Ultima Thule* (an island to the north of Britain used metaphorically to denote 'beyond the known world'). We know them best from the Geranomachy, their endless battling with the cranes that habitually swooped down on Pygmy communities, bringing death and destruction. The myth can be found as early as the Homer's *Iliad* (3, 1–7) and reappeared in subsequent literature and art as late as Isidore of Seville (d. AD 636).

10

Female Genital Mutilation (FGM)

As a prelude to this disturbing chapter, let's look at the key facts supplied by the World Health Organization (WHO) as of 5 February 2024:

- More than 200 million girls and women alive today have undergone female genital mutilation (FGM) in thirty countries across Africa, the Middle East and Asia, where FGM is practised.
- FGM is mostly carried out on young girls between infancy and the age of fifteen.
- FGM is a violation of the human rights of girls and women.
- Treatment of the health complications of FGM is estimated to cost health systems U.S.$ 1.4 billion per year, a number expected to rise unless urgent action is taken towards its abandonment.

In the UK, the website for the National Health Service (NHS) states:

- Female genital mutilation (FGM) is a procedure where the female genitals are deliberately cut, injured or changed, but there's no medical reason for this to be done.
- It's illegal in the UK and is child abuse.
- It's very painful and can seriously harm the health of women and girls.
- It can also cause long-term problems with sex, childbirth and mental health.

Today, we rightly recoil at the routine practice of FGM inflicted on young girls in certain societies by their relatives and religious authorities. This dehumanizing torture is, of course, nothing new. Over time, a number of so-called civilizing cultures and civilizations have indulged in this odious act, including those who saw themselves as harbingers of civilization in a world they xenophobically viewed as being populated largely by so-called barbarians.

Clitoridectomy and FGM

Female genital mutilation was well known in the ancient world; it seems to have originated with the Egyptians. When the practice was adopted in Greece and Rome it would appear that male anxieties about women and sexual pleasure, and the obsession some males had surrounding the virginity of their brides and the fidelity of their wives, were the driving forces behind the mutilating procedure.

A papyrus dated 163 BC refers to the operation being performed on girls in Memphis, Egypt, to coincide with the time when they received their dowries, suggesting that FGM originated as a form of marital initiation of young women.

The Romans developed a procedure that involved slipping *fibulae* (brooches) through the *labia majora* of female slaves as a form of contraception. Galen references FGM: 'When [the clitoris] protrudes to a great extent in their young women, Egyptians consider it appropriate to cut it out' (*Introductio sive Medicus* 10, 14, 76, 12–15). As does the Greek physician Soranus (AD 98–138):

> Concerning an immensely great clitoris an uncouth size is present in certain clitorises and brings women into disorder by the deformity of the private parts. As most people say, these same women, affected by the lust (or erection) typical of men, take on a similar desire, and they approach sexual intercourse with men only under duress. If it comes to that [an operation], the women is to be placed lying on her back and with thighs closed, lest the viscera of the vagina become distended. Then the excess part is to be held in place with a

small forceps and cut back with a scalpel in proportion to its unnatural size. (*Gynaecologica* 4, 9)

Soranus also cautions against excising too much, since there is considerable blood loss.

Clitoridectomy is recorded by the Byzantine Greek physician Aëtius Amidenus (*fl.* mid-fifth century to mid-sixth century), citing the physician Philomenes. The procedure was performed in cases where the clitoris, or nymphê, grew large or triggered sexual desire when rubbing against clothing. Post-operative, the genital area was cleaned and sterilized with a sponge, frankincense and wine or cold water, and wrapped in linen bandages dipped in vinegar until the seventh day, when calamine, rose petals, date stones or a 'genital powder made from baked clay' might be applied.

There is evidence that another form of FGM, female infibulation, was practised on prepubescent girls, if Strabo and Philo are to be believed. This is where the the labia are removed and the girl's legs are bound to allow the formation of a skin over the vagina as the wound heals; a small hole is made to allow for urination and menstruation. Its purpose then, as now, in some societies, was to reassure a husband that he is marrying a virgin.

LANGUAGE

II

The Greek Alphabet Derived from the Phoenician Alphabet

Before about 1950 BC, what we now call ancient Greek would have been unheard in what we now call ancient Greece. The Greek alphabet was developed around the early eighth century from the earlier Phoenician alphabet and was the first alphabetic script to offer distinct letters for vowels as well as consonants. It is the ancestor of the Latin and Cyrillic scripts.

Here is Herodotus' account (*Histories* 5, 58; adapted from A. de Sélincourt's translation of 1954), written in the 450s BC:

> The Phoenicians who came with Cadmus . . . introduced to Greece, after settling in the country, a number of accomplishments, of which the most important was writing, an art, I believe, unknown to the Greeks before that time. At first they used the same characters as all the other Phoenicians, but as time went by, and their language developed, they also changed the shape of their letters. Then, most of the Greeks in the neighbourhood were Ionians; they were taught these letters by the Phoenicians and adopted them, with a few alterations, for their own use, continuing to refer to them as the Phoenician characters . . . In the temple of Ismenian Apollo at Theba in Boeotia I have myself seen cauldrons with inscriptions etched them in Cadmean characters – most of them not so very different from the Ionian.

Hyginus, writing in the early Roman Empire, gives an account of the development of ancient Greek which owes little to history or philology: 'The three Fates created the first five vowels of the alphabet and the letters B and T' (*Fabulae*, 277ff).

The Latin language

If you want to know more about the Latin language from a contemporary then Varro (116–27 BC) is your man, a polymath with expertise in history, science, agriculture and linguistics. He was a prolific writer, being the author of over one hundred books: his *De lingua Latina* alone comprised 25 books – an introductory volume followed by six books on etymology, six on morphology and twelve on syntax. Sadly, though we do have in almost complete form books five through ten, the rest are lost.

The oldest example of Latin that has survived, perhaps from the seventh century BC, consists of a four-word inscription of Greek characters on a cloak pin. Today, the *Oxford Latin Dictionary* (OLD) is the standard English lexicon of Classical Latin for which the compilation of the more than 1 million quotations on which the work was based began in 1933. The dictionary was originally published in eight fascicles at two-year intervals from 1968 until 1982. The complete dictionary contains around 40,000 entries.

12

The Written Word and Bad Books

The Greeks and the Romans were pioneers of the written word: the book was as 'invented' in classical Rome, and the information contained therein went on to inform and shape civilizations after Rome, their religions, politics, philosophy, literature, morals, medicine, science and engineering. What has survived of the great literatures and scientific writings of Greece and Rome was able to embrace cultures and civilizations in the Middle Ages, the Renaissance, the Enlightenment and up to the modern period.

Here we expose the first science-fiction novel ever written, the thorny question of hair, Homer as an imposter poet and glue-sniffing with books as well as the act of stealing books from the library. And finally we have a contrite Odysseus' letter to sexy Calypso after he had dumped her for his Penelope, his ever-patient wife – some would say over-patient.

IT WAS NOT always a simple case of writing in straight lines from left to right:

> Homer's teacher, Pronapides of Athens according to Diodorus Siculus (*The Library* 3, 67), developed writing in lines, just as we still do today. Before that, people either wrote in coils, or in rectangles or in columns, or in *boustrophedon* (as when oxen turn when ploughing), that is, right to left and left to right alternately. (SCHOLION TO DIONYSIUS THRAX, *Art of Grammar* 183)

At the Library of Pantainos, Athens, a famous inscription has provided the template for library rules ever since: 'It shall not be permitted to anyone to take the books off the premises because we have taken an oath. The library is to be open first hour until the sixth.' The Bodleian in Oxford and the American School of Classical Studies library in Athens still require users to take an oath, to be read aloud upon seeking admission to the collections. (These oaths are also inscribed on collectibles, which can be bought from the institution's gift shops.)

Roman 'texts' had an unusual currency in the eighteenth century: Ferdinand I, Bourbon king of the Two Sicilies, swapped eighteen of the priceless Herculaneum papyri found in 1785 for eighteen kangaroos to populate his mistress's theme park.

Trivia

The Danish scholar Niels Iversen Schow was offered fifty rolls of Greek texts by a group of Egyptian peasants; he bought one and the peasants burnt the rest to enjoy the smell they gave off. Papyrus sheets, you see, are held together by a gum or glue in the plant (PLINY, *Natural History* 13, 82).

The smallest surviving book from Antiquity, the Cologne Mani-Codex (*Codex Manichaicus Coloniensis*), is a tiny parchment codex, dated to the fifth century AD, that was found near Asyut (the ancient Lycopolis), Egypt; it contains a Greek text describing the life of Mani, the founder of the religion Manichaeism. The 192 pages measure 3.5 by 4.5 centimetres each with 23 fine lines of Greek.

The smallest biggest book? According to Pliny (*Natural History* 7, 85) Cicero mentions a copy of the *Iliad* written on parchment and secreted in a nutshell. Just for the record, the seventeenth-century French bishop Pierre-Daniel Huet transcribed eighty verses of the *Iliad* onto a single line of a sheet of paper. From this we can extrapolate that he could have fitted 19,000 verses on the page – 3,000 more than the *Iliad* actually contains.

Ever wondered what the number of syllables is that can be produced by combining the letters of the alphabet? Well, Xenocrates has the answer (frg. 89): 1,002,000,000,000.

The longest word recorded in classical Latin is the 24-letter third declension *subductisupercilicarptor*, meaning a person who criticizes while drawing his eyebrows from below – as in Aulus Gellius' *Attic Nights*. Mary Poppins would have been impressed. This is positively brief, though, when compared to the longest word in compound-friendly ancient Greek:

Lopadotemachoselachogaleokranioleipsanodrimhypotrimmatosilphioparaomelitokatakechymenokichlepikossyphophattoperisteralektryonoptekephalliokigklopeleiolagoiosiraiobaphetraganopterygon.

This almost incomprehensibly long phrase is the name of a sixteen-ingredient dish mentioned in Aristophanes' *Eccleziazusae* (1169–75). It is a transliteration of the word:

λοπαδο-τεμαχο-σελαχο-γαλεο-κρανιο-λειψανο-δριμυπο-
τριμματο-σιλφιο-καραβο-μελιτο-κατακεχυ-μενοκιχλ-επι-
κοσσυφο-φαττο-περιστερ-αλεκτρυον-οπτο-κεφαλλιο-
κιγκλο-πελειο-λαγῳο-σιραιο-βαφη-τραγανο-πτερύγων.

Henry George Liddell and Robert Scott, in their *A Greek–English Lexicon* (1843), translate, with commendable economy, this as 'name of a dish compounded of all kinds of dainties, fish, flesh, fowl and sauces'. The Greek word has 172 letters and 78 syllables; the transliteration has 182 Latin characters. It is one of the longest words ever to appear in literature according to the 2024 *Guinness World Records*. (The longest (compound) word is 195 Sanskrit characters (transliterating to 428 letters in the Roman alphabet) describing the region near Kanci, Tamil Nadu, India, which appears in a sixteenth-century work by Tirumalāmbā, Queen of Vijayangara.)

Antiphanes would have agreed with the twentieth-century poet T. S. Eliot when he said, 'For last year's words belong to

last year's language/ And next year's words await another voice'
(*Four Quartets*):

> Antiphanes said as a joke that in a certain city words froze
> with the cold the moment they were spoken, and later, as
> they thawed out, people heard in the summer what they
> had said to one another in the winter; it was the same way,
> he asserted, with what was said by Plato to men still in their
> youth; not until long afterwards, if ever, did most of them
> come to get the meaning, when they had become old men.
> (PLUTARCH, *How to Assess One's Progress in Virtue* 70a)

Homer as Imposter

Homer is nothing more than a myth according to Photius (*Library*,
151b): in fact, a woman from Memphis (aptly) called Phantasia composed the *Iliad* and the *Odyssey* long before Homer is supposed to
have. Homer plagiarized her when he took the books from their
deposit in Memphis. And if it wasn't Phantasia, then it was Helen:

> Helen appeared to Homer by night and commanded him to
> compose a poem about those who went on the expedition
> to Troy, since she wished to make their death more envied
> than the life of the rest of mankind; and they say that, while
> it is partly because of Homer's skill, the *Iliad* has become
> so universally famous chiefly through her. (ISOCRATES, *In
> Praise of Helen* 65)

When Alcibiades asked his teacher for a copy of the *Iliad*, the
teacher replied that he had no Homer. Alcibiades punched him
(PLUTARCH, *Sayings of Kings and Commanders* 186d).

Odysseus as Sycophantic Bullshitter

An unconvincingly contrite Odysseus's letter to Calypso after he had dumped her for his wife:

Dear Calypso

This is just a note to tell you that, after I left you in the ship I had hastily knocked together, I was shipwrecked, and just about escaped with the help of Leucothea into the country of the Phseacks, who sent me home to Ithaca, where I found lots of men going after my wife, and having a riot in my house at my expense. Anyway, I killed them all, but was afterwards killed myself by my son Telegonus – by Circe, apparently – and am now in the Island of the Blessed. Every day I deeply regret not staying with you and not taking up your offer of immortality. If I can find a convenient time, I'll give them all the slip and come and see you.

Yours, Odysseus

(LUCIAN, *A True Story* 101)

The First Science-Fiction Book

Lucian's second-century AD *A True Story* is the earliest known work of fiction to include interplanetary travel in outer space, alien life-forms, interplanetary warfare, colonization of planets, artificial atmospheres, liquid air, a reflecting telescope, creatures as products of human technology (robots) and worlds operating a set of alternate 'physical' laws. As such, it is recognized as the first known text that could be called science fiction.

Despite the title, Lucian prefaces the work with the admission that the story is a pack of lies. Nevertheless, the novel opens with Lucian and his crew sailing past the Pillars of Heracles and blown off course by a storm. They reach an island with a river of wine filled with fish and bears, indicating that Heracles and Dionysus had been there before them; the trees looked like women, suggesting that maybe something more mind altering than wine was involved. Soon after leaving the island, a whirlwind blows them up to the Moon, where they are implicated in a full-scale war between the king of the Moon, Endymion, and Phaethon, the king of the Sun, over colonization of the Morning Star. Both armies deploy strange hybrid lifeforms to fight their enemy. The armies of the Sun are victorious when they shroud the Moon in cloud, blocking out the Sun's light. Both parties then conclude a peace agreement. After the war, Lucian describes life on the Moon and how it differs from life on Earth.

On returning to Earth, the adventurers are swallowed up by a 320-kilometre-long (200 mi.) whale, in whose stomach they discover a variety of fish people, against whom they wage war and vanquish. They kill the whale by starting a bonfire and escape by propping its mouth open. Next, they come up against a sea of milk, an island of cheese and the Island of the Blessed, where Lucian meets the heroes of the Trojan War, other mythical men and animals, as well as Homer and Pythagoras. They see notorious sinners being punished, the worst of whom are the ones who had written books laced with lies and fantasies, including Herodotus and Ctesias. On leaving the Island of the Blessed, they deliver a letter to Calypso given to them by the deceased Odysseus explaining that he wished he had stayed with her, kicking himself that he did not take up her offer of immortality. They then discover a trench in the ocean, but eventually sail around it; they find a far-off continent and decide to take a look. The book ends abruptly with Lucian stating that their future adventures will be described in the forthcoming sequels – 'the biggest lie of all'.

Towards the end of this fantastic voyage, Lucian and his crew have an encounter with the donkey-hoofed Ass-shanks, who have a predilection for passing men. On landing at a small island, they find it inhabited by what they take to be women, who speak Greek. They come and greet the explorers with kisses, dressed like courtesans, all young and pretty, and with long robes sweeping the ground. Cabbalusa was the name of the island, and Hydramardia the city. These women paired off with the men and led them away to their separate homes. Lucian delays a little, feeling a bit uneasy, especially when he peers a bit closer and sees a pile of human bones and skulls lying around. Not wanting to raise the alarm by gathering his men and resorting to arms, he instead draws out his mallow plant, and prays intently to it for an escape. Shortly after, when being served by a hostess, Lucian sees that instead of human feet she has donkey's hooves; he draws his sword, and seizes, binds and interrogates her. Reluctantly she confesses that the strange women are sea-women called Ass-shanks, who feed on passing travellers. 'When we have made them drunk,' she says, 'and slept with them, we murder them while they sleep.' After this confession Lucian shouts out for his comrades. When they appear, he tells them all, showing them the bones of former victims, and brings them to see the prisoner, who immediately vanishes, turning to water. On thrusting the sword into the puddle, the water turns to blood.

Men's Hair . . . or Not?

Moving on from science fiction we come to a disquisition on the vexed subject of men's hair, or the lack of it: Dio Chrysostom (*c.* AD 40–*c.* 115), a Greek orator, writer, philosopher and historian of the Roman Empire, is survived by eighty of his *Discourses*, as well as a few letters and the humorous essay 'In Praise of Hair'. Here is how the essay begins:

> Dio of the golden tongue has composed a discourse entitled *An Encomium on Hair*, which is a work of such brilliance that the inevitable result of the speech is to make a bald man feel ashamed. For the speech joins forces with nature; and by nature we all desire to be beautiful, an ambition whose realization is greatly assisted by the hair to which from boyhood nature has accustomed us. In my own case, for example, even when the dreadful plague was just beginning and a hair fell off, I was smitten to my inmost heart, and when the attack was pressed with greater vigour, hair after hair dropping out, and ultimately even two or three together, and the war was being waged with fury, my head becoming utterly ravaged, then indeed I thought myself to be the victim of more grievous injury than the Athenians suffered at the hands of

Archidamus when he cut down the trees of the Acharnians, and presently, without my so intending, I was turned into a Euboean, one of the tribe which the poet marshalled against Troy 'with flowing locks behind.'

Aeschylus died when an eagle dropped a tortoise onto his bald head. The eagle was only doing what comes natural to a raptor: it was using the tragedian as a stone on which to smash open the tortoise shell and get at the prey's flesh (VALERIUS MAXIMUS, *Memorable Deeds and Sayings* 9, 12). (Sophocles was not much luckier whichever way you look at it: he met his final act when he choked on a grape, or when he died of joy on hearing that his last play was the winner, or he literally ran out of breath when reading a long section of *Antigone* that had no pauses or punctuation (*Life of Sophocles*).)

A Review to Die for

Theocritus of Chios heard a recital by a mediocre poet who then asked him which bits he thought were good. Theocritus replied, 'the bits you left out' (*Gnomologium Vaticanum* 338). And the premiere of Terence's second-century BC *Hecyra* was a flop because the audience left the theatre to go to watch a tightrope walking display nearby instead.

Nero perfected the concept of the captive audience, with performances to die for:

> While he was singing no one was allowed to leave the theatre even for the most urgent reasons. And so it is said that some women gave birth to children there, while many who were worn out with listening and applauding, secretly leaped from the walls, since the gates at the entrance were closed, or feigned death and were carried out as if for burial. (SUETONIUS, *Nero* 23)

Even the cruellest of men can be moved to tears:

Epaminondas had learned how savage Pelopidas was, and how little regard he had for right and justice, in that sometimes he buried men alive, and sometimes dressed them in the skins of wild boars or bears, and then, as a game, set his hunting dogs on them and either tore them to pieces or shot them down; and at Meliboea and Scotussa, allied and friendly cities, when the people were in full assembly, he surrounded them with his body-guards and slaughtered them from the youth up ... Once when he was watching a tragedian act the 'Trojan Women' of Euripides, he suddenly left the theatre, and sent a message to the actor bidding him be of good courage and not make any less effort because of his departure, for it was not out of contempt for his acting that he had gone away, but because he was ashamed to have the citizens see him, who had never taken pity on any man that he had murdered [in real life], weeping over the sorrows of Hecuba and Andromache. (PLUTARCH, *Life of Pelopidas* 29)

The Life of Aeschylus (1. 9) reveals that when Aeschylus brought the chorus of the Eumenides onto the stage, one at a time, it was so disturbing that children fainted and pregnant women miscarried.

Unfortunate Words and Names

Nothing reveals better the innate xenophobia of the Greeks than the Greek language itself. Many verbs with foreign associations are freighted with negative connotations and are stereotypes:

Kretizein – to act like a Cretan, to tell lies.
Lesbiazein – to act like a person from Lesbos, that is, to suck off, because fellatio was believed to have been developed by the people of Lesbos.
Siphniazein – to act like a person from Siphnos, that is, to perform elaborate musical compositions but then to touch someone on the buttocks with one's finger.
Sybarizein – to be like a person from Sybaris – to live decadently.

Bum Town and Fart Moon

Pygela, a town in Ionia, got its embarrassing name, Bum Town, after Harpocration wrote that, according to Theopompos (frg. 59), some of Agamemnon's men stopped off there embarrassed by 'an ailment of the buttocks' – *pygae*. Pygela was changed to Phygela when Pliny rewrote history, and the etymology, recording and pretending that the city was founded by *phygades* (fugitives; *Natural History* 5, 114).

Similarly, Strabo advocated changing Pardosolene (*Geography* 13, 2) to Paroslen because Pardoselene meant 'fart moon'.

Wordsearch

The Sator Square (or Rotas Square), found at Herculaneum in Campania, Italy, is a word square containing a five-word Latin palindrome. It consists of a sentence written in Latin: SATOR AREPO TENET OPERA ROTAS.

S A T O R

A R E P O

T E N E T

O P E R A

R O T A S

In particular, this is a square 2D palindrome, which is when a square text has four symmetries: identity, two diagonal reflections and 180-degree rotation. The text can be read top to bottom, bottom to top, left to right or right to left, and even if rotated 180 degrees, it can still be read in all those ways. It is the earliest 2D palindrome that we can date, and its translation has been the subject of speculation and argument.

13

The Pontius Pilate Stone, Tiberius Julius Abdes Pantera and Jesus of Nazareth

A damaged block of carved limestone with a fragmentary inscription attributed to, and referring to, Pontius Pilate, the famous prefect of the Roman province of Judaea from AD 26 to 36, was discovered at the site of Caesarea Maritima in 1961. It represents the earliest surviving record and evidence for the existence of the hand-washing Pilate: 'To the Divine Augusti [this] Tiberieum ... Pontius Pilate ... prefect of Judea ... has dedicated [this]'.

This probably referred to a temple. The stone was later recycled in the fourth century as a building block for a set of stairs in a building behind the stage house of the Herodian theatre, discovered there still attached to the ancient staircase.

There is nothing particularly remarkable about the tombstone inscription of Tiberius Julius Abdes Pantera (*c.* 22 BC–AD 40) found in Bingerbrück, Germany, in 1859: 'Tiberius Julius Abdes Pantera from Sidon, aged 62 years served 40 years, former standard bearer(?) of the first cohort of archers lies here' (*CIL* 13, 7514).

What is remarkable, though, is the claim that Pantera is the father of Jesus of Nazareth, based on the belief of the philosopher Celsus, who, according to the Christian writer Origen in his *Contra Celsum*, was the author of an anti-Christian work titled *The True Word*. Celsus' work is lost, but, if Origen is to be believed, Jesus was born of an affair between his mother Mary and a Roman soldier. He said she was 'convicted of adultery and had a child by a certain soldier named Panthera'. Tiberius Pantera could easily have been serving in the region at the time: both the Talmud and medieval Jewish writings support this, referring to Jesus as 'Yeshu ben Pantera' (Jesus, son of Pantera). If it is indeed true, Pantera's adultery may go some way to explaining the vexed question of the immaculate conception for Joseph.

Did Jesus of Nazareth exist?

The question regarding the historicity of Jesus is never far away from any work dealing with the politics of early empire Judaea and its Roman occupation. It seems that it is broadly accepted that Jesus was a real person and that he did come into contact with John the Baptist and the Roman prefect Pontius Pilate. The former, a preacher and baptizer at the Jordan River, is a key figure in Christianity and Islam: 'the forerunner, herald and baptizer of Jesus of Nazareth'. He is mentioned by Josephus in his *Antiquities of the Jews* (18, 5, 2) and is a major religious figure in Christianity, Islam, the Bahá'í faith and the Druze faith.

While describing the Great Fire in Rome of AD 64, Tacitus refers, in *Annals* 15, 44, to the origins of Christianity and the execution of Christ as given in the gospels.

14

The Spoken Word: Rough-Speaking Romans

A facility for Latin was one of the hallmarks of *Romanitas* – Roman-ness. Many Romans in the senatorial and equestrian classes had a supremacist outlook on the world, believing themselves to be better than all who were not Roman – that is, anyone who lived beyond the frontiers of the Roman Empire. In fact, these people were labelled *barbaroi* because they were thought to speak in a kind of ovine gibberish. The Roman concept of *urbanitas* (sophistication) required you to not only speak, read and understand Latin, but be able to speak it proper(ly), so rural and provincial Romans as well as foreigners were lambasted. Evidence comes from Edwin Ramage in his article 'Cicero on Extra-Roman Speech' (1961):

> Thus it is that Plautus makes fun of the Praenestines for using Latin vocabulary and pronunciation that were rustic and so unacceptable to the refined city dweller. Lucilius' jibe at Caecilius' country pronunciation and Cato's attempt to identify the *homo urbanus*, or city wit, are also early manifestations of this attitude.

According to Plutarch (*Cato* 12, 4–5), in 191 BC, a precious Cato defiantly addressed a Greek audience in Athens in Latin to make his point about Roman superiority.

Cicero too was a stout advocate of *Romanitas*. The Latin language, or rather the ability to speak it, and the practice of Roman law were equally potent emblems of Roman-ness. Here is Cicero championing and advocating the use of Latin by traders beyond Rome's borders:

Ordinary men, born in obscurity, go to sea and they go to places which they have never seen before; places where they can neither be known to the men among whom they have arrived, nor where they can always find a lawyer. However, due to this singular faith in their Roman citizenship, they think that they will be safe, not only among our own magistrates, who are constrained by fear of the law and of public opinion, but also with our fellow citizens who are joined with them, among many other things, by a common language and laws; but wherever they come they think that this will protect them. (*In Verrem* 2, 5, 167)

In *Brutus* (37, 140), he is even more explicit, declaring that it is a matter of shame not to know Latin; a facility for Latin was for Cicero a mark of the good Roman citizen. Suetonius (*Tiberius* 71) tells us that the emperor Tiberius believed it important that soldiers in the Roman army be able to speak Latin from an incident when he refused a Greek soldier permission to reply in Greek when summonsed to give evidence.

We rarely hear the foreigner's – or non-Roman – side of the story, so it is refreshing, not to say amusing, when an outlander is recorded giving his view of the Roman, his urbanity and his *Romanitas*. The comeuppance in question was in the second century AD, when 'a Cheran king named Netunceral attacked and seized Roman ships'. The *Patirruppattu* describes how the king 'captured the uncivilised *Yavanas* [Romans] of harsh speech, poured oil on their heads and tied their hands to their backs and took their precious and beautiful vessels and diamonds'. They were either enslaved or a ransom was required for their release. How funny to see the Romans for a change being criticized for their diction, by these 'bar-bar'-speaking 'barbarians' from India.

15

Graffiti

Considering that in the first century AD only 20–30 per cent of men, and less than 10 per cent of women, were what we would call literate, there's a lot of graffiti scrawled on the walls of Pompeii, the population of which was about 20,000 in AD 79. Altogether archaeologists have uncovered more than 11,000 examples since the nineteenth century.

Graffiti in Pompeii proclaims that the local women were 'up for it' while for the ladies 'Glyco does cunnilingus for two asses.' Martimus, though, is not such a good deal: he charges four but will accommodate virgins for free. All this suggests a lively trade for the bored Pompeii housewife. One resident of the town found that his beautiful whore was still full of the semen deposited by a previous client and was sufficiently annoyed by this to record the fact on a wall. Likewise, this disappointed customer from an early second-century AD house in southern Spain: 'I nearly froze to death in her cunt' (*CIL* 4, 1516).

Here are more:

Tavern of Verecundus: Restitutus says: 'Restituta, take off your tunic, please, and show us your hairy privates.'
Bar/Brothel of Innulus and Papilio: Weep, you girls. My penis has given you up. Now it penetrates men's behinds. Goodbye, wondrous femininity!
House of the Citharist, below a drawing of a man with a large nose: Amplicatus, I know that Icarus is buggering you. Salvius wrote this.

Street wall: Theophilus, don't perform oral sex on girls against the city wall like a dog.

Barracks of the Julian-Claudian gladiators: Celadus the Thracian makes the girls moan!

House of Orpheus: I have buggered men.

Atrium of the House of Pinarius: If anyone does not believe in Venus, they should gaze at my girlfriend.

Vicolo del Panattiere, House of the Vibii Merchants: Atimetus got me pregnant.

Eumachia Building, via della Abbondanza: Secundus likes to screw boys.

The Lupinare: I screwed a lot of girls here.

The Lupinare: On 15 June, Hermeros screwed here with Phileterus and Caphisus

Street of the Theatres: A copper pot went missing from my shop. Anyone who returns it to me will be given 65 bronze coins [sestertii]. Twenty more will be given for information leading to the capture of the thief.

Above a bench outside the Marine Gate: If anyone sits here, let him read this first of all: if anyone wants a screw, he should look for Attice; she costs 4 sestertii.

The following were scratched in the basilica: I could caress Venus's ribs with a stick, and whip her buttocks; she pierced my heart, and I would gladly break her head with a cudgel!

Chie, I hope your haemorrhoids rub together so much that they hurt worse than when they ever have before!

Grab your servant girl whenever you want to; it's your right.

He who buggers a fire burns his penis.

O walls, you have held up so much tedious graffiti that I am amazed you have not already collapsed in ruin.

Banal as most of it is, it does show that little changes in the world, even across 2,000 years.

16

Aphorisms: True or Not So True?

Whether there is any truth in the following truisms or not is debatable:

- Only humans can count. (ARISTOTLE, *Topics* 142b)
- Bathing, wine and sex ruin our bodies; but bathing, wine and sex are what life is all about. (*CIL* 6, 15258)
- Only humans can be tickled because they have delicate skin and they are the only animals that laugh [Don't tell the hyenas . . .]. (ARISTOTLE, *On the Parts of Animals* 673a)
- Other animals' sexual urges are restricted to specific times of year but human beings have them continually until old age. (XENOPHON, *Memoirs of Socrates* 1, 4)
- The people of Miletus are not stupid; they just do the sort of things stupid people do. (ARISTOTLE, *Nicomachean Ethics* 1151a)
- Weasels give birth through their ears, though some say through their mouths. (TIMOTHEUS OF GAZA, *On Animals* 39)
- You can remove tattoos by smearing on them a mixture of very sharp vinegar and the stuff that sticks to the insides of a chamber pot. (PAUL OF AEGINA, *Medical Compendium* 4.7)
- Men ejaculate when they die. (CASSIUS IATROSOPHISTA, *Problems* 47)

SEX
AND
SEXUALITY

17

Fetishes and Voyeurism

Fetishistic food sex – eating, drinking, defecating and fornicating, often at roughly the same time – occurs in Hipponax's (late sixth century BC) fragment 92, in which the poet describes a sexual encounter in a stinking toilet where a Lydian-speaking woman performs some mysterious and obscene rites on the poet, which include whacking his genitals with a fig branch and inserting a foreign body up his anus, provoking incontinence and an attack by dung beetles. It's a repugnant and bizarre scene that inspired the 'Oenothea' episode in Petronius' *Satyricon*.

Another early example of sexual fetishes is a red-figure cup by the Brygos Painter, depicting an orgy scene from about 480 BC in which a woman is beaten with a slipper. Some centuries later, Suetonius (b. AD 69), in the *Life of Vitellius* 2, tells the strange story of Vitellius' shoe fetish: he would beg Messalina, third wife of the Roman emperor Claudius, to allow him to remove her shoes, whereupon he would secrete one of them in his clothing, removing it from time to time afterwards to kiss it. This was not Vitellius' only paraphilia; he was also in the habit of mixing the saliva of a freedwoman mistress with honey and using it as a lotion for his neck and throat.

When it comes to voyeurism, perhaps the most unusual, and worrying, example concerns a plant called the Gorgon. We know of it from Michael Psellus, a Byzantine Greek monk from the eleventh century AD, who in his *Opusculum* (32) cites the work of Sextus Julius Africanus (AD *c.* 160–*c.* 240), a Christian traveller who compiled the *Kestoi* – an encyclopaedia that contains much that was strange and miraculous. The entry describes the voyeuristic activities of this Gorgon, which usually grows underground; if a girl has sex near to it, it shoots up and watches proceedings intently. Africanus, it might be added, had the useful, if unusual, ability to restore a woman's virginity even if she had engaged in sex multiple times.

The Secret Cabinet in the National Archaeological Museum in Naples

The Gabinetto Segreto and its fascinating contents have been open to the public since 2000. Before the millennium, it was closed off, bricked up in 1849, re-opened and closed again in a silly attempt to shield the curious public from some of the finest erotic art ever to be produced – in wall paintings, mosaics, frescoes, inscriptions and myriad objects such as oil lamps, door chimes and amphorae. The irony is that the cabinet was actually accessible to 'people of mature age and respected morals', which meant only educated men. Quite unsuitable for the eyes of women! At nearby Pompeii, locked metal cabinets blocked out erotic frescoes, but these could be shown, for an additional fee, to gentlemen – again, not to ladies. This charade, this censorship, was still in place at Pompeii in the 1960s.

18

Pederasty: The Sexual Pursuit of Boys by Men

Paiderastia is the Greek word for the sexual pursuit of boys by men. This was a relationship between an older male and a boy, a boy being a 'boy' until he sported a full beard, at which point he became a man. Pederasty then usually extended from about twelve years of age to around seventeen. The older man was the *erastes*, and his role was to educate, protect, love, provide moral improvement and be a role model for his *eromenos*.

The myth of Ganymede's abduction by Zeus was invoked as a precedent – a justification even – for the pederastic relationship, as Theognis (*fl.* sixth century BC) says to Simonides:

> Alas, I am in love with a soft-skinned boy who shows me off to all my friends in spite of my unwillingness. I'll put up with the exposure – there are many things that one is forced to do against one's will – for it's by no unworthy boy that I was shown to be captivated. And there is some pleasure in loving a boy, since once in fact even the son of Cronus, king of the immortals, fell in love with Ganymede, seized him, carried him off to Olympus, and made him divine, keeping the lovely bloom of boyhood. So, don't be astonished, Simonides, that I too have been revealed as captivated by love for a handsome boy. (*Fragment* 1, 1341–50)

It all seems to have started in ancient Crete. Strabo gives us the history. Cretan pederasty was an early form of paedophilia dating from the Minoan period, around 1650–1500 BC, that involved the ritual kidnapping (*harpagmos*) of a boy from an elite background by an aristocratic adult male, with the consent of the boy's father. This male was known as *philetor*, befriender; the boy was *kleinos*, glorious. The man took the boy out into the wilderness, where they spent two months hunting and feasting with friends. If the boy was pleased with how this went he changed his status from *kleinos* to *parastates*, or comrade, signifying that he had metaphorically fought in battle alongside his *philetor* and went back and lived with him. The *philetor* showers the boy with expensive gifts, including an army uniform, an ox for sacrifice to Zeus and a drinking goblet – a symbol of spiritual accomplishment. At the same time, according to Strabo, the boy must choose between continuing with or putting an end to the relationship with his abductor, and whether to denounce the man if he has misbehaved in any way.

Strabo gives us more detail (*Geographia* 10, 4, 21):

[The Cretans] have a strange custom regarding love affairs, for they win the objects of their love, not by persuasion, but by abduction; the lover tells the friends of the boy three or four days beforehand that he is going to make the abduction; if the friends hide the boy, or restrain him, it is indeed a most disgraceful thing, a confession, as it were, that the boy is unworthy to obtain such a lover; and when they meet, if the abductor is the boy's equal or superior in rank or other respects, the friends pursue him and lay hold of him, though only in a very gentle way, thus satisfying the custom; and after that they cheerfully turn the boy over to him to lead away; if, however, the abductor is unworthy, they take the boy away from him.

Failure to attract a *philetor* was stigmatic for a good-looking or noble boy; on the other hand, *parastates* are honoured and are given privileged positions in dances. Once they have grown into manhood, they wear a special dress which shows them to have been a distinguished *kleinos*.

The Roman historian Cornelius Nepos in *Praefatio* (3–5) claims that Cretan youths had more than one lover. Apart from teaching

Graeco-Roman cameo depicting sexual intercourse between a man and a boy.

the boy essential adult skills, pederasty allegedly also demonstrated who the best men were. We learn from Aristotle that it was originally instituted as a form of population control (*Politics*, 2, 10): '[They] segregated the women and set up sexual relations among the males so that women would not have children.'

19

Sex: From Buttocks Partialism to Zoophilia

Ask an ancient Greek why his bed was so important to him and, likes as not, he will, in all seriousness, respond that it was where he discharged his statuory duty as a citizen to keep up his *oikos*, his house(hold) and his family line, and thereby replenish and increase the citizenry of his *polis* (city-state) by having lots of children, ideally boys. On a less official level, his bed was also where he might enjoy a fling on the side with impunity, and where he might extend some overtime to his female slaves, or else entertain prostitutes or concubines when his wife was indisposed by virtue of being heavily pregnant (again) or had recently given birth, or if she was unadventurous or plain uninterested, possibly because she felt slighted because of his serial adultery. Alternatively, he might invite his boy lovers there in his role as a pederast, or he might consort there with an effeminate adult male or two.

For a woman, it was a more functional location and was the place where she had sex with her husband in order to mother as many children as possible – again, ideally boys – and so fulfil her responsibility as a provider of citizens to populate the army and the state machinery. However, it was all somewhat academic since (male) doctors, poets, historians and philosophers had all decreed that sex, and by extension, bed, was neither a thing nor a place of pleasure for women.

SEXUAL HYPOCRISY: DID the writers quoted here have any idea of what they were talking about?

Sexual intercourse has never done anyone any good, and we should be thankful if it does us no harm. (EPICURUS, frg. 62)

It is quite clear that reasonable people do not have sex for pleasure, but rather to relieve a troublesome urge. (GALEN, *The Affected Places* 8, 419k)

To get a sleeping woman to confess the name of her lover, put a bird's tongue under her lips or on her heart and ask the question. She will say the man's name three times. (*Greek Magical Papyri* 63, 8)

People have died of too much pleasure before now. (GALEN, *Semen* 4, 588k)

Democritus was never keen on sex: to him, 'Sexual intercourse is a brief attack of apoplexy' (frg. 32).

Rabbi Eliezer, writing in Palestine in AD 80 and quoting from the Torah, prescribes the following class-based programme of routine sexual activity by occupation:

- for students and the unemployed, every day
- workers, twice a week
- donkey drivers, once a week
- camel drivers, once a month
- sailors, once every six months

As arbitrary as it is, no Roman (man) would argue with that, except perhaps the odd sailor becalmed at sea and a camel driver or two. Two hundred years later, Rabbi Abba Bar Ayvo, founder of the Rabbinnic Academy in Sura, Persia, would seem to endorse this when he euphemistically says of someone he 'knows' that 'she eats with him every Friday night' (RABBI ELIEZER, *m. Ketubot* 5, 6. Rav at *yketubot* 5, 8, 30a–b).

Forget about chickens and eggs, who gets the greater pleasure out of sex – man or woman? Dicaearchus of Messana was an obscure

Greek philosopher, cartographer, geographer, mathematician and writer, and a student of Aristotle's in the Lyceum. Despite his obscurity, however, we are all eternally grateful to him for solving that age-old conundrum (frg. 37). Here is the answer we've all been waiting for:

> When Tiresias, the blind seer, came across a pair of snakes copulating, he killed the female with his staff. An angry Hera turned him into a woman as a result. Obviously 'she', Tiresias, learned a lot of interesting things about women in this time, but when, eight years later, 'she' happened on another pair of mating snakes, 'she' – in a historical case of shape-shifting reciprocity – trampled on the male and promptly turned back into a man. An avidly curious Zeus and Hera asked him which of the two sexes enjoyed sexual intercourse more: the man, as Hera claimed; or, as Zeus said, the woman. Tiresias, with the unique wisdom of having experienced both, divulged that sex was more enjoyable when he was a woman: 'Of ten parts a man enjoys one only'. This was not what Hera wanted to hear so she punished him

Anal and oral sex on the rim of a red-figure *kylix*, Athens, *c.* 510 BC, attributed to the Pedieus Painter. Both acts were deplored by the Romans – real men always did the penetrating, be it to a man or a woman.

for heresy with blindness; Zeus, however, inclined to the opposite and invested in Tiresias the power of prophecy and the gift of longevity lasting for seven generations. (PHLEGON OF TRALLES, *Marvels* 4)

Which just goes to show that for the Greeks there's a silver lining to every blinding.

Gallic Incest and Wife-Sharing

The Stoic Musonius Rufus (AD *c.* 25–95) would not have agreed with Tiresias, as we have just seen. Sex was not for pleasure, and he was certainly not alone in thinking that: 'Those who are not decadent or immoral should see sexual intercourse as justified only if it takes place within marriage and for the procreation of children, as the law says. Sex in pursuit of pleasure alone is unjustified and illegal, even within marriage' (*Discourse* 12).

British women must have seemed very loose to even the most licentious Roman invader in 44 BC; Caesar observed that up to ten or twelve men shared one wife, with brothers and fathers even partaking in what was an incestuous act when they had sex with their brothers' or son's wife. Any offspring was officially fathered by the man who took the woman's virginity (*Gallic Wars* 5, 14). Imagine the arguments that must have started!

Dio adds to this controversy when he describes an encounter between Julia Domna (AD 170–217), empress of Septimius Severus, and the wife of a Caledonian chieftain. Julia Domna primly remarks on how somewhat free the tribal women are with their sexual favours; the 'barbarian' lady replies tartly, 'We satisfy our desires in a better way than you Roman women do. We have sex openly with the best men while you are seduced in secret by the worst' (77, 16, 5).

Buggery and the Catamite

A catamite (*catamītus*) was a pubescent boy who was the intimate companion of an older male, usually in a pederastic relationship.

The absolute cardinal thing for the Roman in sexual matters was the dichotomy between the active and dominant sexual partner and the passive and receptive. The male was – or should have been, if he knew what was good for him – active while the female, or a man of lower social standing such as a slave or a *cinaedus*, was passive. *Cinaedus* is a pejorative word denoting a male who was gender-deviant; his choice of sex acts, or preference in sexual partner, were overshadowed socially by his perceived deficiencies as a 'man' (*vir*).

When a man graduated to being a *paterfamilias*, it was not just the power of life and death over his wife, his children and his slaves that he assumed. He also was legally permitted to sodomize his male slaves, but only as an active participant: passivity, or being sodomized, was anathema to the Roman, a sign of depravity and feebleness, something foreigners or barbarians did. It was crucial that the Roman man remained at all times a sexually impenetrable penetrator, and that he thereby maintained his sexual integrity.

Seneca neatly sums the situation up: 'Sexual passivity in a free man is a crime, for a slave a necessity, for a freed slave a duty.' Seneca, however, is quick to point out the humorous side of this when he tells us that *officium* (duty) soon became a witty euphemism for being buggered (*Controversiae* 4, Prologue 10).

Virtus was the important word in the sexual lexicon relating to the masculinity of the Roman synonymous as it was with good, powerful descriptors like 'virtue', 'manliness', 'military prowess' and 'bravery'. *Virtus* too was imbued with nostalgia – it is what all the Romans' ancestors exhibited in the good old days, how they conducted themselves before, apparently, being overcome by the effeminate feebleness that insinuated itself in Roman life swept in from Greece and all points east. These notions of ancient behaviour (some no doubt the product of selective memory) were collectively called the *mos maiorum*, the way our ancestors did things – larded with honour, self-control imbued with *virtus*.

Virtus was also synonymous with Roman-ness; it was the word that the true Roman yearned to see on his role of honour up there with all his other achievements in life, his *res gestae*. The word soon took on connotations of probity and shrewd discrimination:

knowing the difference between right and wrong, according to the satirist Gaius Lucilius (*c.* 160–103 BC). Sexual passivity, or being on the receiving end, was most definitely one of the bad things in life, as emphasized by Lucilius in another fragment in which he insults freeborn men who made their *scultima* (anus) available for penetration as a *scultimidonus*, or 'arsehole offerer'.

The moral rectitude police were never far away. The *lex Scantinia* of 216 BC had criminalized *stuprum* (illicit sex) against a freeborn male minor and penalized adult male citizens who took a passive role in sex with other men. Allowing one's body to be used for pleasure by others in sodomy and oral sex was now punishable in law but how it was effectively policed when perpetrated in private is anyone's guess.

There is, nevertheless, evidence for male prostitutes selling penetrating services: a voyeuristic Hostius Quadra watched himself being penetrated in his mirrors; it gained a grubby kind of royal assent with emperors Nero and Elagabalus notoriously scouring the streets for well-endowed men; Plautus refers to it in his *Curculio* (482–4) as does the writer of mimes Pomponius Bononiensis (frgs 148–9; 151–2R), and Martial (2, 51; 3, 71; 6, 50). The pseudo-Virgilian *Catalepton* (13, 23–6) tells us about sailors down by the Tiber offering the same senior service. Doryphorus – a freedman gladiator of Nero's – assumed the role of groom and would penetrate Nero, his bride, to the accompaniment of wailing virgins being raped (TACITUS, *Annals* 15; SUETONIUS, *Nero* 29).

We have defined the *cinaedus* above as the man on the receiving end, so to speak. He enjoyed a reputation as being available for a spot of adultery and was often, as a dancer, recognizable by his exaggerated and provocative bum-wiggling and his effeminate hair coiffure. Aulus Gellius describes one such man as given to him by the general Scipio Africanus Aemianus (185–129 BC): 'the sort of perfumed man who peacocks every day in front of the mirror, trims his eyebrows and prances about with well-groomed beard and depilated thighs' (*Attic Nights* 6, 12).

Nevertheless, the market open for the androgynous *cinaedus* extended beyond the *virtus* deficient male: they also attracted the

attentions of some women who were drawn to the more effeminate man. However, to name but one detractor, Justinian I, emperor
(r. AD 527–65), codifier and legislator, the 'man-woman', or effeminate male, was disgusting: they 'do unspeakable things' and 'practice
this sort of degradation' (*Apology* 1, 27, 2).

As an indicator of just how common the word *cinaedus* was, and
its place in common parlance as an insult or in defamation, we know
of thirty instances of it in Pompeii graffiti along with 126 references
to oral sex, 83 references to anal or vaginal penetration and two
mentions of *pathicus*, a synonym of *cinaedus*. *Cunnilingus* was the
licker not the act, as revealed by the discovery of a third-century AD
brick in modern Bulgaria describing Euphiletos as a 'cunt-licker'
(*kusthekleikhon*).

Physiognomy and other physical properties had their place
in the demonization of the *cinaedus*. Ask Favorinus of Arelate
(*c.* AD 80–*c.* 160), a top rhetor, whose womanish looks triggered not
only the vitriol of Polemon, his rival, but one of ancient history's
most savage (and successful) character assassinations (*Anonymus
Latinus* 40; Philostratus, vs 489). As if being born without testicles was not bad enough in his alpha-male world, Favorinus was
described as 'greedy and immoral beyond all measure', had many
feminine features (such as soft cheeks and limbs, abundant hair
and a woman's voice, neck and walk), was a 'deceitful magician'
and 'a leader in evil and a teacher of it'. Philostratus called him a
hermaphrodite.

The Persian eunuch Bogoas was mocked just as savagely; lover
of Darius III and Alexander the Great no less, Bogoas suffered badly
at the hands of Roman senator and historian Q. Curtius Rufus,
whose tirades involved calling him effeminate, sluttish and dissolute,
and through the Persian governor Orsines, he is a whore, a pervert
and lower in station than a woman.

Buttocks Partialism (Pygophilia)

In the male and sometimes the female gaze, female buttocks have
always been an erogenous zone and a symbol of fertility and beauty.

Statues created as early as 24,000 BC, such as the Venus or Woman of Willendorf, found in Austria, have exhibited exaggerated buttocks, hips and thighs. Pygophilia is sexual arousal brought on by someone else's buttocks.

Athenaeus tells the engaging story of the well-read *hetaira* (courtesan, high-class escort) Mania, mistress of Philip II, quoting Sophocles:

> Mania once was asked by King Demetrius, for a good look at her fine buttocks; and she, in return, demanded that he should grant her a favour. When he agreed, she turned her back, and said, – 'O son of Agamemnon, now the Gods grant you to see what you so long have wished for.' (*Philosophers at Dinner* 13, 42)

There is more buttock-revealing, or at least a request for it, and an exquisite put-down from another *hetaira*, Gnathaena, whose impressive client list reveals that she flourished in the fourth century BC: 'They say that one fine day a youth from Pontus was sleeping with Gnathaena, and in the morning he asked her to show her buttocks to him. But she replied, "You have no time for that now, it's time for you to feed the pigs".'

Buttocks apart (sorry!), Gnathaena was a truly exceptional woman in traditionally repressive Greek society: as a *hetaira*, Gnathaena both attended and hosted symposiums, using her popularity to attract upper-class men to dine and to match wits with her. In defiance of established Athenian social norms she was never beholden to a man in the way that most Athenian women were. Gnathaena's treatise, *Rules for Dining in Company*, listed her rules stating which men were allowed access to her and her daughters' house to participate in the symposia they hosted, as well as how the men should conduct themselves once in there.

Demophoon, a friend of Sophocles', was also partial to his *hetaira*'s buttocks: 'And it is said this woman had nice buttocks, And when Demophoon tried to hold them, "A pretty thing," said she, "that what you get from me, you may present to Sophocles."'

In the endless ancient Greek pursuit of the acme of physical beauty, the buttocks were very important, as indeed they were in social intercourse. The ideal was portrayed on a Greek bronze, now lost, but a fine first-century BC Roman copy in marble called the Kallipygean Venus can be seen in the Naples Archaeological Museum. How did the bronze come to be? Athenaeus tells how a Syracusan farmer had two daughters who could not agree on which had the better buttocks, so they enlisted the opinion of a young boy passing by. He preferred the buttocks of the older sister and fell in love with her. His inquisitive younger brother fell likewise for the younger sister; the two married their Kallipygian girls, who commissioned a temple to the Kallipygean Aphrodite and erected a cult statue within. The Christian Clement of Alexandria was not at all impressed and later described the masterpiece as 'shamefully erotic examples of pagan religious art'.

Talking of buttocks, the box tree (*pyxos*) is sacred to Aphrodite, or, more specifically, to her buttocks (*pygae*). Cornutus described Aphrodite as *callipygos*, 'with a lovely bum' (*On the Nature of the Gods* 46).

Agalmatophilia

Agalmatophilia, from the Greek *agalma* (statue) and -philia (φιλία, love), is a paraphilia involving sexual attraction to a statue, louvre or mannequin. This may embrace a desire for sexual contact with the object, viewing such encounters or sexual pleasure from thoughts of being transformed or transforming another into the preferred object. Athenaeus describes an instance of an unfulfilling heart of stone:

> Cleisophus of Selymbria . . . fell in love with a statue of Parian marble that then was at Samos, and shut himself up in the temple to gratify his affection; but when he found that he could make no impression on the coldness and unimpressibility of the stone, then he discarded his passion. (*Philosophers at Dinner* 605f)

Another man got away lightly, perhaps, for his 'deviation':

> At Delphi, in the museum of the pictures, there are two boys
> wrought in marble; with one of which, the Delphians say,
> a visitor fell in love so strongly, that he made love to it, and
> shut himself up with it, and presented it with a crown; but
> when he was discovered, the god ordered the Delphians,
> who consulted his oracle about it, to let him off.

Agalmatophilia first became a subject of clinical study with the publication of Richard von Krafft-Ebing's *Psychopathia sexualis* (1886), in which he recorded the case of a gardener in 1877 falling in love with a statue of the Venus de Milo and being discovered attempting to have sex with it.

Oral Sex: What Goes in the Mouth Stays in the Mouth

Orogenital sex was by no means uncommon in certain circles in Rome. *Os impurum* (filthy mouth) was an excoriating term of abuse reserved for those who provided oral sex and was used as such with relish by the poets Catullus, Horace and Martial. Cunnilingus, like fellatio, suggested questionable oral hygiene, anathema to many Romans, who held the purity of the mouth in high esteem. The reason being that it was the mouth that was the vehicle for oratory and declamation, roads to political and social success; moreover, it was the custom among Romans to kiss on meeting, so bad breath, also a symbol of moral turpitude through its connection to oral sex, was extremely embarrassing. Insults did not come any more acerbic than accusing a man of fellatio with another man. It was indicative of the sexual passivity and receptiveness that was so reviled by the Romans; moreover, it was something older men did when they were unable to summon up an erection. The Campanians had a predilection for oral sex, resulting in a high incidence locally of *campanus morbus*, oral lesions caused by human papillomavirus.

Fellatio is privileged with two precise nouns in Latin: *irrumatio* is the action of the penis; *fellatio*, the action of the mouth, and obviously a popular alternative to coitus for some clientele of prostitutes. It may also have had a contraceptive role, in a bid to avoid pregnancy, not just in extramarital relationships but within marriage, as an attempt to break the relentless serial childbearing. In Martial, we hear of Vetustina's warm mouth and how Thais sucks. In his poem about Galla and Aeschylus, he advises that if you are going to do it, then you should keep your mouth shut about it, as it were; he accuses Aeschylus of paying over the odds to ensure that the knowledge of his fellatio goes no further than sucker and sucked, mindful no doubt of the disgust that attended this sexual proclivity. Suetonius deplores Quintus Remmius Palaemon's predilection for cunnilingus. Galen, the celebrated medical scientist and doctor, believed that orogenital sex was unnatural.

That Martial refers to oral sex in twelve of his epigrams might suggest that the poet was obsessed with the act. He excoriates Nanneius, an inveterate cunnilinguist suffering from lingual dysfunction after contracting a disease of the tongue. So prolific was he that whores preferred to perform fellatio on him rather than kiss him on the mouth because his penis was much cleaner. Catullus associated fellation with the urinary function of the penis: he refers to 'the repellent spit of a pissed-over prostitute' and lambasts a Celtiberian for brushing his teeth with urine. Martial says that a nicely scented perfume turns to fish sauce (*garum*) when sniffed by a man whose breath was rank from oral sex. You can tell a *fellator* because when he breathes on a hot cake to cool it down, it turns to excrement. Ausonius in the fourth century AD echoes Martial in a blistering and disgusting attack on Eunus, whom he accuses of licking his pregnant wife's putrid genitals, anxious to tongue the buttocks of his unborn sons: fellatio, antenatal sexual child abuse and incest all in one fetid breath (*Epigrams* 86).

Catullus asserts that any woman who has sex with the odious Aemilius (*Carmen* 97) might as well lick the anus of a hangman with diarrhoea. Cicero delivers the most excoriating of insults on Sextus Cloelius when he accuses him of performing cunnilingus on a menstruating woman.

Perhaps the most celebrated description of oral and anal rape is in Catullus' *Carmen* 61:

Fuck you, boys, up the butt and in the mouth, you queer Aurelius and you fag Furius! You size me up, on the basis of my poems, because they're a little sexy, as not really decent. A poet has to live clean – but not his poems. *They* only have spice and charm, if somewhat erotic and really not for children – if, in fact, they cause body talk (I'm not talking teenagers, but hairy old men who can barely move their stiff bums). But you, because you happen to read about 'many thousands of kisses,' you think *I'm* not a man? Fuck you, boys, up the butt and in the mouth!

In art, cunnilingus is usually portrayed as one half of 'soixante-neuf'. Some women hired male prostitutes for the specific purpose of receiving cunnilingus; one political graffito invites the electorate to 'Vote Isidore for aedile; he's the best at licking cunt!' Nevertheless, graffiti tells us that the adept *fellatrix* was much in demand. Wall paintings in the Suburban Baths in Pompeii depict cunnilingus; here the beautiful, naked prostitute adopts a dominant role while her fawning, fully clothed male client is something of a comedic figure, indicating the scorn oral sex attracted and the opportunity it gave for parody and humiliation.

Anal Sex

Martial moans about his woman's reluctance to indulge in anal sex, scandalously claiming the traditionally virtuous Cornelia, Pompey's wife Julia and Brutus' wife Porcia all to have been willing participants in the act. Sodomy was not unknown on the wedding night for some brides. In homosexual sex, some men 'took it like a woman' when penetrated (*muliebria pati*); but when a man sodomized a woman, she played the boy role. Martial (12, 75 and 96) prefers anal sex with boys, even though his wife reluctantly allows him anal sex to keep him happy.

In the first century AD, Strato, in the *Greek Anthology*, expresses a preference for boys because girls get little enjoyment from anal sex and are frigid when sodomized. Martial says as much when he rebukes his wife for describing her *culus* as a sphincter when, according to him, she really has two vaginas (*cunni*).

Reproduction

Aristotle, or one of his followers, spent a lot of time researching generation of species and reproduction; here are some of his startling findings:

- Crows indulge 'but rarely' in sexual intercourse.
- The human penis protrudes and recedes 'in the opposite way' to that of a cat.
- A man becomes bald only once he has become sexually active.
- The more powerful a person's sexual activity is, the quicker they will shed eyelashes.
- The female cat is 'naturally lecherous', and 'wheedles' the male on to sexual commerce, caterwauling throughout.
- The penis of the male seal is 'exceptionally large'.
- Octopuses have sex through an 'interlacing of their tentacles', coming together at the mouth.
- Pigeons kiss one another just when the male is on the point of mounting the female, 'and without this preliminary the male would decline to perform his function'.
- Hedgehogs copulate erect, 'belly to belly'.

(PSEUDO-ARISTOTLE, *Problems* 878b)

Bestiality

Bestial practices it seems are as old as mankind: one of the earliest depictions is a cave painting from Val Camonica in Brescia, Italy, circa 8000 BC, which clearly shows a man pleasuring a donkey. A common Egyptian curse went 'May a donkey fuck your wife and children!' We have heard about a woman having sex with a goat in Herodotus' descriptions of some bizarre Egyptian habits; there is also the example of the highly sacred Egyptian Apis bull with its strong association with fertility: when a new bull was born to replace the deceased one, only women were allowed to look after it for the first forty days of its life. To encourage fertility throughout its life, women would lift their cloaks and display their vulvas. Theocritus describes shepherds and goats in 'hideous coupling' at Thyout while, in what could be described as early pornography, a petroglyph found at Naquane, north Italy, shows a man happily buggering a quadruped while gaily waving at the viewer. In the various books on dream interpretation from ancient Greece, we hear of women fantasizing about sex with mice, horses, donkeys, rams, wolves, lions, crocodile, snakes, baboons, ibis and falcons.

The Greeks had a long tradition of bestiality going back to King Minos and his receptive bull who, in punishing Athens for her deception, required every nine years Athens to send seven boys and seven girls to Crete to be sacrificed to the Minotaur (the offspring from the zoophilic encounter of Minos' wife Pasiphaë with the Cretan Bull). Also on Crete, the gods, as usual, did not set the best example, with Zeus furtively having sex with Leda, as a swan, and unashamedly seducing Europa, Minos' mother, in the guise of a white bull.

We cannot know exactly how far this divine bestiality extended into real Greek life. Herodotus narrates that within his lifetime, a billy-goat had intercourse with a woman in Egypt – moreover, it was in plain sight and he describes the incident in a masterful understatement as 'a most surprising incident' (2, 46). Pliny records that Semiramis, a ninth-century BC Assyrian queen, copulated with a horse (*Natural History* 8, 64); he also tells us about the actor Bathyllus and the erotic dance in which he dresses up as Leda to have sex with a swan – no doubt in an enactment of Zeus' encounter with Leda and much to the apparent excitement and arousal of the women watching. Dio has the story of a prostitute masquerading as a leopard to gratify a senator. Examples are thin on the ground, no doubt because having sex with an animal is probably something most people would want to keep between themselves and the animal.

Images of Leda and the swan are particularly common on oil lamps: one lamp from mid-third-century AD Athens made by the lamp maker Preimos shows a woman on a bed entertaining a pony; in another, from the first century, a naked – and courageous – woman on top of a crocodile, possibly a humorous swipe at Cleopatra VII. Others show women performing with donkeys and dogs. Such images go back a long way: there is a red-figure cup by Epitketos from the end of the sixth century BC that depicts a maenad being taken by a donkey. Other early examples include a satyr penetrating a buck on a black-figure cup from about 520 BC. Representations of bestiality almost always involve women receiving excited quadrupeds – only one example of a man penetrating a mammal, a donkey, survives.

Pan having his way with a goat, marble found in Herculaneum. Pan also gets the credit for teaching young shepherds how to masturbate.

Martial in his *De spectaculis* (On the Spectacles) suggests that bestiality was reenacted on stage at the inaugural games of the Flavian Amphitheatre in AD 80. The punishment that was death by bestiality was the most terrible of fates. Martial also commends the realism of a re-enactment of the Bull of Pasiphaë myth in the arena; presumably body fluids from a cow on heat were used to arouse and attract the bull to the woman. Juvenal, bitter and misogynist, says that women are so sexed up at the festival of Bona Dea that if men are not available these 'drunken Maenads, they will fornicate with an adulterer, by the *adulter's* son, or by slaves, or the water carrier; as a last resort, a donkey will take them in the arse: *inposito clunem sumittat asello* (6, 314–34). Apuleius, in the *Metamorphoses* (16; 17), describes how Lucius, when a donkey, has vigorous (and consensual) intercourse with an insatiable woman who pays Thiasus, his master, for the pleasure. Thiasus sees an opportunity here, and Lucius is booked for a celebrity engagement in front of an ecstatic amphitheatre audience, caged up with a woman condemned to be fed to wild animals; before the bestial spectacle can begin, however, he makes good his escape.

When we think of bestiality, or zoophilia (which is presumably not very often for most people), we tend to assume that it is the man or the woman who is the instigator rather than the animal. Not so Athenaeus: he can offer a catalogue of instances where the animal has been the driving force in zoophilic relationships, although we have no way of knowing if there was ever an actual sexual element involved:

> And even brute beasts have fallen in love with men: for there was a cock who took a fancy to a man of the name of Secundus ... and the cock was nicknamed the Centaur ... And, at Aegium, a goose took a fancy to a boy; as Clearchus relates in the first book of his Amatory Anecdotes ... And Hermeias says that a goose also took a fancy to Lacydes the philosopher. And in Leucadia a peacock fell so in love with a maiden there, that when she died, the bird died too ... at Iasus, a boy whose name was Dionysius who, when leaving the palaestra with the rest of the boys, went down to the sea

to bathe to be met by a dolphin which came forward out of the deep water to meet him, and taking him on his back, swam away with him a considerable distance into the open sea, and then brought him back again to land . . . Coeranus was saved by a dolphin. And when, at last, he died of old age in his native country, as it so happened that his funeral procession passed along the sea-shore close to Miletus, a great shoal of dolphins appeared on that day in the harbour, close to those who were attending the funeral, as if they also were joining in the procession and sharing in the grief. (*Wise Men at Dinner* 13, 73)

We learn too from Athenaeus of an affectionate, maternal elephant called Nicaea that crosses the species boundary: the wife of the king of India on her deathbed entrusted her one-month-old child to the elephant, who demonstrated extraordinary affection for the child. It could not bear the child to be out of its sight, and whenever it did not see him, it became dejected:

And so, whenever the nurse fed the infant with milk, she placed it in its cradle between the feet of the beast; and if she failed to do so, the elephant would not eat . . . while the child was sleeping, it would beat away the flies . . . And whenever the child cried, it would rock the cradle with its trunk, and lull it to sleep. And very often the male elephant did the same.

If zoophilia is repellent then necrophilia can only be equally, if not more, repulsive.

Necrophilia

In a rare divergence from societal norm, from the sixteenth century BC to the thirteenth century BC Hittite law explicitly permitted sexual relations with the dead. Egypt, according to Herodotus, had a problem with necrophilia among its embalmers:

The wives of [Egyptian] men of rank when they die are not handed over immediately to be embalmed, the same applies to very beautiful women; it is only on the third or fourth day after their death (and not before) that they are delivered to the embalmers. This is so that the embalmers may not abuse the women, for they say that one of them was caught doing just that to the corpse of a woman recently deceased, and his colleagues blew the whistle on him.

Herodotus alludes to Periander, the tyrant (*c.* 627–587 BC) – an effective ruler who exploited to the full the economic and cultural potential of Corinth, his city. Some remembered him as one of the Seven Wise Men of Greece; however his extreme measures and despotic gestures make him more suited to a list of famous tyrants than of wise men. Periander was the author of a collection of didactic maxims in 2,000 verses. The most famous episode Herodotus regales us with is how Periander was 'baking his bread' in Melissa's 'cold oven', that famous euphemism:

[Periander] stripped all the women of Corinth naked, because of his own wife Melissa [whom he had killed]. He had sent messengers to the Oracle of the Dead on the river Acheron in Thesprotia to enquire about a deposit that a friend had left, but Melissa, appearing as a ghost, said that she would tell him nothing, nor reveal the location of the deposit. Why? Because she was cold and naked. The clothes, she said, which Periander had buried her in had not been cremated, and were consequently of no use to her. Then, to prove to her husband that she was telling the truth, she added that Periander had put his loaves into a cold oven. When this message was brought back to Periander he knew that it was true because he had actually had intercourse with Melissa's corpse. Immediately, he proclaimed that all the Corinthian women should come out into the temple of Hera which they did, as if attending a festival, wearing their finest clothes; Periander posted his guards there and stripped every one of them, ladies and slaves alike, and heaped all their clothes in a pit, in which, as he prayed to Melissa, he set fire to them. When he had done this and sent a second message, the ghost of Melissa told him where the friend's deposit was. (5, 92)

The Babylonian Talmud relates that King Herod of Judea (73–4 BC) was besotted by a virgin girl who was so distressed by his persistence that she killed herself to avoid marrying him; he preserved her body in honey for seven years in order to have regular sex with her corpse.

Xenophon of Ephesus (*An Ephesian Tale* 5, 1) leaves us with the odd and unedifying story of another deviant, the poor Spartan Aigialeus and his common-law wife Thelxinoe, who had died; Aigialeus kept her body at home, embalmed Egyptian-style. 'I speak to her as though she is still alive,' he says, and 'I lie down next to her and have my meals with her' (another euphemism?). This can't fail to evoke Euripides' play *Alcestis* (348–53), where Admetus promises to keep a likeness of his dying wife in his bedroom.

Diodorus Siculus reminds us that poorer Egyptians would keep mummies at home rather than placing them in tombs because they believed that the dead could still enjoy earthly pleasures such as food and drink. Aigialeus says of Thelxinoe's corpse, 'I'm forever kissing her and passing the time with her,' with the strong suggestion of necrophilia (1, 92,6).

Hipponax (*fl.* 540 BC) gives us an unhealthy fusion of both incest and fellatio in his iambic fragments, adumbrating the seamier depths of Ionian life; he calls the sculptor Bupalus a mother-fucker (μητροκοίτης), with Arete (the name means 'virtue'); elsewhere Hipponax tells us that Arete performed fellatio on him. The vitriol apparently stemmed from the fact that Hipponax had hopes of marrying Bupalus' daughter, but he was rejected on account of his being ugly and deformed and was cruelly represented as such by sculptors' work. Hipponax's response was so devastating that Bupalus hanged himself (frgs 12, 15, 17). Hipponax was no lover of women generally, if the famous line 'There are two days when a woman is a joy: the day someone marries her and the day when someone carries out her dead body' is indeed by him.

Sexual Positions

Top of the range *hetairae* could name their prices according to the sexual positions they were proficient in. One who had mastered twelve positions charged the most for one position called *keles* – 'racehorse' – in which the woman was on top.

For the lower rent *khamaitypês* (χαμαιτυπής), the service and the client experience were much less comfortable or dignified; they had to perform 'in the dirt', as they had no beds or rooms. We see them on vases as either performing rear entry 'doggy-style' or on all fours on the ground, also taking it from the rear. Epicurean Lucretius in the first century BC was to describe this as *more ferarum* – 'the way that animals do it'.

A vase shows us a sex worker standing in improvised doggy-style holding on to a tree trunk to steady herself. Her legs are spread apart and the man enters her from behind, his hands on the sides of her buttocks; she is helping in the thrusting. The artist has painted a smile on the woman's face, suggesting that she was enjoying it – or more probably, pretending to while contemplating her fee. Another vase demonstrates the *cyon*, or the 'dog', from which the term doggy-style presumably comes, and which has the woman on all fours and the man entering from the rear. In a famous vase in the British Museum, we can see a *hetaera* sitting on her client's lap facing him, assisted by two slave girls in rising and falling up and down on her man's penis. The 'leapfrog' – an act of sodomy where the woman is 'folded in two' with her hands flat on the ground – appears on another vase.

Petronius and Apuleius, two early empire Roman novelists, describe the lubricious movements of the dominant woman. Horace compares the whore (*meretricula*) with a horse rider. The *mulier equitans* appears to have been popular with the woman 'riding' on top; it was also called the 'Hector horse', as mythical Hector and Andromache allegedly enjoyed sex that way.

There are numerous visual representations of the sexually dominant woman, many from the ceramics found in the Rhone Valley dating from AD 70 to 250: some show the woman to be the soldier in a reversal of the *miles amoris* (soldier of love) trope: *orte scutus est* – 'look out, that's a shield you've got there!'; the man is flaccid. A medallion shows the woman on top with the text *vides quam bene chalas*: 'see how well you open me up'. The famous *Navigium Veneris* – 'navigation of Venus' or, more loosely, 'cock steering' – medallion is still attached to its original jug and shows a very dexterous man steering his penis into his partner's ample rear, in much the same way as he would manipulate a boat's rudder, hence the nautical metaphor. Ceramic evidence shows that before this, Greek man and woman were up to the same antics.

It may be that the *figura veneris* where the woman crouches and lifts her buttocks, the 'lioness', was primarily for anal intercourse; prostitutes who specialized in this were praised as 'good anal' (*culibonia*), although it was probably adopted more as a way of avoiding pregnancy than for client satisfaction.

Masturbation

Man and woman have been masturbating since the dawn of time: a clay figurine of the fourth millennium BC from Malta shows a woman masturbating. In ancient Sumer (*fl.* between the fourth and second millennium BC) masturbation, either solitary or with a partner, was thought to enhance sexual potency. In ancient Egypt, male masturbation when performed by a god was considered an existential or magical act: Atum created the universe by masturbating, and the ebb and flow of the Nile was attributed to the frequency of his ejaculations. Egyptian pharaohs were required to masturbate ceremonially into the Nile.

To the ancient Greeks, masturbation was a normal and healthy substitute for other sexual pleasures – a handy safety valve against destructive sexual frustration. The few references to it in the literature may be explained away by the fact that it was such common practice that something so routine did not warrant much attention.

Anyway, it's not the sort of thing you want to broadcast or share with anyone but your closest friends.

Nevertheless, it may well have been deemed, publicly at least, to be the preserve of slaves, lunatics and other liminal peoples. Elite opinion would have regarded the act literally as a waste of time and semen, since it was one of the prime cultural responsibilities of the Greek male to further the family line and extend the household.

One Greek word for masturbation is *anaphlao*, a verb that Aristophanes disparagingly uses to describe the Spartans pleasuring themselves in the *Lysistrata* (1099). *Anaphlasmos* is the word for masturbation used in *Autolycus* (21) by the playwright Eupolis (446–411 BC). Satyrs were inveterate masturbators, and there are sixth-century BC *kraters* that survive showing them in the act with their prominent erections.

Diogenes the Cynic (412–323 BC) relates a myth in which Pan learned how to masturbate from his father, Hermes, and then taught the habit to lonely, sequestered shepherds (DIO CHRYSOSTOM, *Discourses* 6, 20). The decidedly odd Diogenes routinely masturbated in public, defending his actions by saying, 'If only it were as easy to banish hunger by rubbing my belly' (APULEIUS, *Florida* 2, 49). Interestingly, Diogenes attracted censure not just for masturbating in the open air, but for eating in the *agora*, indicating perhaps that masturbating in a public place was regarded as no more serious a crime than eating in one.

Masturbation to the more earnest of Romans was utterly pointless, as it was to the Greeks, because it could not result in conception. The word is generally derived from *manu stuprare* – to defile with the hand. Women used phallic objects, such as dildos and cucumbers, solely to prepare themselves for penetration by their husbands, not, seemingly, for any pleasure; one of the less foundational cornerstones of medical science teaches that women suffer less frequently with bladder stones because they do not masturbate. We have a graffito inscription from Pompeii to thank for an example of masturbating a woman – *cunnum tibi fricabo* – as opposed to a woman masturbating. For worldly Martial, masturbation is low-grade sex – something slaves do, although he does admit to masturbating when he cannot afford a beautiful slave boy: 'my hand relieved me as a substitute for Ganymede.' Lucilius (307, 959) mocks a personified penis whose girlfriend Laeva (Left-hander) wipes away his 'tears'. The left hand was the preferred hand for masturbating, as it was for bum-wiping, as confirmed by this graffito from Pompeii: 'when my worries oppress my body, with my left hand I release my pent-up fluids' (*CIL* 2066).

Martial, fantasizing in a poem where he whinges about a wife's coolness towards his sexual advances, alludes to a long tradition of female masturbators, beginning with ever-patient Penelope, and Hector's steadfast wife, Andromache. *Veneri servit amica manus* – 'Your hand serves as the mistress of your pleasure,' writes Martial (*Epigram* 33), famously.

Much later, the libertine Pacificus Maximus (*fl.* AD 1500), writing in Latin, asks, 'Is there no boy nor girl to hear my prayers? No one comes? Then my right hand must perform the accustomed office.' Another wonderful pun. And in bitter Catullus: 'O Caelius, our Lesbia, Lesbia, that Lesbia whom Catullus more than himself and all his kin did love, now in the public streets and in alleys wanks off the magnanimous descendants of Remus' (*Carmen* 58).

Honoré Gabriel Riqueti (1749–1791), comte de Mirabeau, tells us that Mercury taught the art to his son Pan, who was distracted by the loss of his mistress, Echo, and that Pan afterwards taught the skill to lonely shepherds. Mirabeau also mentions a curious practice that he declares to be prevalent among the Grecian women of modern times: that of using their feet to bring on orgasm for their lovers. The pedicure to end all pedicures.

Wet Dreams (Nocturnal Emissions) and Artemidorus, the Father of Erotic Dreams

The gold standard and go-to reference on dream interpretation in antiquity is the *Oneirocritica*, extensively researched and compiled by Artemidorus of Ephesus in the second century AD and based on his own work and that of sixteen predecessors, now unfortunately all lost. Ask Freud: 'In later antiquity Artemidorus of Daldis was regarded as the greatest authority on dream-interpretation' (*The Interpretation of Dreams* (1900)). To give an idea of its exhaustiveness the 82 sections in Book One interpret the appearance in dreams of subjects as diverse as head size, eating and sexuality.

According to Artemidorus, penis dreams are related to one's parents because of the reproductive process that made the dreamer the child of those parents; they also are indicative of children, because the penis helps in the production of children. Penis dreams can likewise signify a wife or a mistress, as the penis is the vehicle for sexual intercourse. Additionally it implicates brothers and other close relatives since the *oikos* (household) is reliant on the penis to populate the household. It is a token of both strength and vigour, which explains why some call the penis 'one's manhood'. More obscurely the penis is also a sign of wealth and possessions because, like them, it too expands and contracts and is productive (*Oneirocritica* 1, 45).

Dreaming about legal, consensual intercourse with a wife bodes well, while coercive sex has the opposite impact. Accounting for prostitutes in your dreams is complicated, but dreaming about bought sex with prostitutes working in brothels, not surprisingly, signifies a bit of a scandal in the offing and a small financial outlay in the future. Going into a brothel and getting out is good. Artemidorus describes 'an acquaintance' who dreamt that he went into a brothel and could not get out; more of a nightmare than just a dream, he died in real life a few days later – the logical outcome of his dream, because 'a brothel, like a cemetery, is a place "common to all" and the destruction of many human seeds takes place there'. Prostitutes sitting in their stalls, selling their services, receiving their fee or visibly copulating add up to a good sign, but streetwalkers in a dream are even better.

Familiarity is everything: if a man dreams he is having intercourse with a woman he does not know, if she is attractive and elegant, is decked out in fine, expensive clothes and gold necklaces and gives herself willingly, this augurs very well for the dreamer and indicates forthcoming success. However, not surprisingly, 'if she is an ugly, shapeless, shabbily dressed old woman dragging out a life of pain, and she does not consent to sex, it signifies the opposite.'

The interpretations, or prophecies, get a little contrived and self-fulfilling and, it seems, provide some sex education: going back to sex with the woman the dreamer knows and is consensual, the man will benefit from such a woman because a woman who gives her body freely would very likely also give him 'her life savings. Often a dream of this kind has helped the dreamer when coping with the mystery of woman, since the woman in such a dream also allows him to touch her secret parts' (ARTEMIDORUS, *Oneirocritica* 1, 78).

Artemidorus is right to introduce a degree of caution: it is a bad thing to dream of having sex with a legally married woman, because that dream delivers the same punishments as the law – a man caught in adultery in real life is sentenced to death.

Artemidorus continues in the same section to advise that dreams relating to female homoeroticism were all about secrets. Everything will be revealed to the partner when a woman dreams that she is pleasuring another woman. The same happens when a woman dreams that she is the object of pleasure, with the disadvantage, though, that she will either be separated from her husband or she will be widowed.

To Artemidorus, oral sex was one of those aspects of sexuality he considered to be outside the law. Anyone dreaming that he has had fellatio performed on him by a friend, relative or a child will grow to hate the perpetrator; if the child is an infant, then that infant will die because he can no longer kiss him or her. If fellatio is performed by someone he does not know, then he will pay a penalty for 'the useless emission of semen'. If, however, the man performs fellatio on some-one he knows – man or woman – then he will come to hate that person, again because they can no longer kiss each other. But if he does not know the person on whom he performs fellatio, then harm will come to all – except those who make a living by using their mouths, such as flute players, trumpeters, orators and philosophers.

The interpretation of incestuous dreams about having sex with one's mother is dealt with in 1, 79 and things are, unsurprisingly, not so straightforward: 'the case of one's mother is both complex and manifold and admits of many different interpretations . . . the manner of the embraces and the various positions of the bodies indicate different outcomes.'

This is how Artemidorus interpreted dreaming of having sex with your mother:

First, then, we will discuss face-to-face intercourse between a dreamer and his living mother, since a mother who is alive does not have the same meaning as a mother who is dead. Therefore, if anyone takes his mother through face-to-face intercourse, which some also call the 'natural' method, if she is still alive and his father is in good health, it means that he and his father will become enemies because of the jealousy that generally arises between rivals [which would be greater in their case]. But if his father is sick, he will die, since the dreamer will take care of his mother both as a son and as a husband . . . And if the dreamer is estranged from his mother, they will become friends again because of the sex . . .

It is not good to have a mother who is looking away from you. For then either the mother herself will look away from the dreamer, or his native land, his trade, or any present undertaking. It is also unlucky to have intercourse with one's mother while she is standing. For men use this position only when they have neither bed nor mattress. Therefore it signifies constraint and oppression. It is also bad to have intercourse with your mother while she is kneeling (and still more unseemly, while she is prostrate). For it signifies great poverty because of the mother's immobility . . .

Woe betide the son who allows his mother to be on top: 'Taking one's mother from underneath while she is in the "rider" position is interpreted by some as signifying death to the dreamer.'

Artemidorus helpfully teaches that

it is not lucky to use many different positions on one's mother. For it is not right to insult one's mother . . . the worst dream by far is one in which the dreamer practices fellatio with his mother. For this signifies to the dreamer the death of children, the loss of property, and serious illness. I know of a man who, after this dream, lost his penis. For it was understandable that he was punished in the part of the body with which he had sinned.

Things only get worse, with necrophilia now in the mix: if, though, his mother is dead in the dream, the dreamer will himself die very soon afterwards.

The two oddest dreams ever:

A man dreamt that he had three penises. He was a slave at the time and was set free. He then had three names instead of one, since he acquired an additional two names from the man who had set him free. (ARTEMIDORUS, *Interpretation of Dreams* 5, 91)

A man dreamt that he had a mouth in his rectum complete with big, beautiful teeth and through it he ate, spoke – all the usual oral functions. Later he was exiled for making tactless statements' [or, talking out of his arse?] (*Interpretation of Dreams* 5, 68)

Cross-Dressing

The Greeks and Romans were quite comfortable with males dressing up as women, and women getting up as men although instances of the latter were, as far as we know, considerably fewer than the former. The practice was helped by the fact that in the theatre female roles were assumed by men (see Plautus' *Casina* for example), and by the precedents set by members of the Greek pantheon, which, to some degree, led to it being tolerated, even supported, as an element of religious devotion. Despite this relaxed attitude, we have evidence of hostility in Greek and Roman sources because cross-dressing by men is also linked to effeminacy and homosexuality. Julius Caesar, for one, never lived down his flirtation with the practice in Bithynia (a scene discussed later in this book).

Indeed, Abbey Kayleen Elder cautions in her article 'Cross-Dressing in Greek Drama', 'the modern idea of the "transgender" individual should not be applied to an ancient Greek, as no such construct of identity existed in that time period, so far as the evidence available suggests.' The emperor Elagabalus (r. AD 218–22) is remembered for numerous eccentricities, not least his predilection for cross-dressing. His daily ritual often involved dressing up in women's clothing, and wearing make-up and wigs, all of which were viewed as outrageous and highly scandalous and inappropriate for a Roman emperor. A team of beauty assistants fussed around him, pandering to his whims and fancies. But it goes much further back than the third century AD. Tiberius, Caligula and Nero in the first century AD all were partial to a spot of cross-dressing.

One heroic mortal woman who deserves mention is Epipole, for her exploits in the Trojan war. Although not mentioned by Homer, Epipole was a daughter of Trachion of Carystus in Euboea. She so much wanted to fight with the Greeks against Troy that she bravely dressed up as a man and inveigled her way into the massed armies – a very early case of classical cross-dressing. Unfortunately, when the Euboean prince Palamedes discovered her sex, she was stoned to death by the somewhat intolerant Greek army.

Hard man Heracles too had a humiliating role-reversal episode in which he donned women's clothing. It took place in Omphale's court, where he was overpowered, stripped of his trademark hide of the Nemean lion and relieved of his club only for the women of the court to deck him out in their (or possibly Omphale's) clothes, and give him a distaff so that he can help them with their spinning. Omphale rubs it in when she asserts her authority by donning the lionskin, and wielding the club. Omphale was queen of Lydia who exerted on Heracles the sentence of one year's servitude for his accidental murder of Iphitus. Both Lucian (*Dialogues of the Gods* 15) and Tertullian (*De Pallio* 4,3) tell the story.

We can add the following:

- Achilles was dressed up in women's clothing by his mother Thetis at the court of Lycomedes, to hide him from Odysseus who wanted him to conscript him to join the Trojan War.

- Athena often went to the aid of people dressed as men in the *Odyssey*.
- Tiresias was turned into a woman after angering the goddess Hera by killing a female snake that was copulating.
- In the cult of Aphrodite, worshippers routinely cross-dressed, men wore women's clothing and women dressed in men's clothing, with false beards.

Allegations of cross-dressing were held against another military alpha male. Ephippus of Olynthus, the pamphleteer and historian, in a surviving fragment (5) describing the court of Alexander the Great in 324–323 BC alleges that Alexander liked to cross-dress as the Greek goddess Artemis. It seems that Alexander often appeared in public as Artemis dressed up like a Persian complete with a bow and spear. However the passage may be a libel aimed at slurring Alexander, whose father Philip had layed waste Ephippus' home city of Olynthus in 348 BC.

Publius Clodius dressed up as a woman to gain access to the Bona Dea rites held at the home of Julius Caesar in his pursuit of Caesar's wife, Pompeia, with whom he was allegedly having an affair. Caesar then had to divorce Pompeia so as not to sully his reputation and remain above suspicion. Cicero led the prosecution of Clodius for *incestum* (sacrilege), and was merciless in his scathing attack.

20

Satyrs and Satyriasis

Satyrs are woodland creatures; with their obnoxious, bestial equine or goat-like features, 'animal-like men with the tail of a horse, donkey ears, upturned pug noses, reclining hair-lines, and erect penises', they have a reputation for being inveterate masturbators with a penchant for rape, sodomy and necrophilia – all of which goes some way to account for their binary bestial form. A satyr is a true party animal with a Dionysian insatiable passion for dancing, women and wine. The trouble is that their's was not the sort of party most women would want to be invited to. Nonnus (*fl. c.* fifth century AD) vividly describes one such shindig:

> Many of the horned [horny?] Satyroi joined furiously in
> the festive dancing with nimble steps. One felt within him
> a new hot madness, a sign of passion, and threw a hairy arm
> round a Bacchanal girl's waist. One shaken by the madness
> of mind-crazing drink laid hold of the girdle of a modest
> unwedded virgin, and as she was not up for sex pulled her
> back by the dress and fondled her rosy thighs from behind.
> Another dragged back a resisting mystic maiden while kind-
> ling the torch for the god's nightly dances, laid tentative
> fingers upon her bosom and pressed the swelling circle of
> her firm breast. (*Dionysiaca* 12, 330ff)

The vase painters had an interesting time depicting the Satyrs; the sileni (as they were also known) were accomplished on the *aulis*, a phallic-shaped double reed instrument; some vase paintings show Satyrs ejaculating while playing, and one even shows a bee deftly

avoiding the discharge in mid-flight. Another vase illustrates a hirsute satyr masturbating while shoving a dildo of sorts into his anus.

Apart from inspiring some astonishing depictions on ceramics, satyrs have left us the word 'satyriasis': male hypersexuality, as
classified today in ICD–10 (the *International Classification of Diseases*,
10th Revision, of the World Health Organisation); nymphomania
being the term used for women. In 1951 it was still listed as a 'sexual
deviation'.

Aretaeus denies its existence in women, just like the American
Psychiatric Association today, saying that others believe that it
manifests, as in men, as a desire for sex; Soranus, that other famous
doctor, adds that the 'itching' felt in the genitals that makes women
'touch themselves' increases their sexual urge and causes 'mental
derangement', and an immodest desire for a man. Soranus' treatment involved bleeding the patient, a liquid diet, refreshing poultices
applied to the genitals and avoiding anything that caused flatulence
or sexual desire. Galen called it 'uterine fury' (*furor uterinus*). In
the fourth century, Theodorus Priscianus termed it *metromania*. The
therapy recommended by Rufus of Ephesus in the late first century included bloodletting, taking honeysuckle seed and the root
of the waterlily, hot baths and the avoidance of all things erotic.
Rufus compares the treatment of female satyriasis with the therapy
for spermatorrhea – an involuntary ejaculation of sperm that was
thought to occur in both men and women.

The Satyroi Nesioi were a tribe of wild Satyrs native to the
islands known as the Satyrides – somewhere off the coast of north
Africa you would be advised to avoid. According to Pausanias, when
some sailors were unluckily forced to land on the island, the Satyroi
captured and, true to type, savagely violated one of their female
passengers:

> As soon as they caught sight of their visitors, they [the
> Satyrs] ran down to the ship without uttering a cry and
> assaulted the women in the ship. At last the terrified sail-
> ors sent a foreign woman on to the island [as a sacrificial
> decoy]. The Satyroi violated her not only in the usual way,

but also in a most shocking manner as well. (*Description of Greece* I, 23, 6)

Not much of a TripAdvisor recommendation there then.

Satyros Argios was a Satyr who frequented the Lernaean Springs of Argos and who attempted to rape King Danaus' daughter, Amymone, when she came to fetch water. (Amymone had thrown a spear at a deer and hit a sleeping Satyr by mistake.) Poseidon, however, appeared on the scene and chased the Satyr away. Once the Satyr had fled, Poseidon, not wanting to miss an opportunity, made love to Amymone.

Satyrs were no strangers to Greek literature, and they don't disappoint, not least in Satyr plays, the only complete extant one being Euripides' *Cyclops* (a burlesque of a scene from the eighth-century BC epic the Odyssey). In Sophocles' satyr play *Ichneutae* (Tracking Satyrs), the chorus of satyrs is described as 'lying on the ground like hedgehogs in a bush, or like a monkey bending over to fart at someone.' The character Cyllene rebukes them: 'All you [satyrs] do you do for the sake of fun! ... Stop expanding your smooth phallus.' In Dionysius I of Syracuse's fragmentary satyr play *Limos* (Starvation), Silenus attempts to give the hero Heracles an enema.

21

Priapus and Priapism

Priapus, the phallus with a face, was a rustic fertility god who looked after livestock, fruit plants, gardens and male genitalia. He is characterized by his oversized, permanent erection, which gives us the medical term 'priapism' and is the subject of an obscene collection of verse called the *Priapeia*. Diodorus Siculus, *Bibliotheca Historica*, 4.6.1; Pausanias, *Description of Greece* 9.31.2 and Tibullus, 1.4.7 all try to untangle his ancestry. He was unfortunate enough to be on the wrong end of Hera's anger: she cursed him with impotence, ugliness and a filthy mind; this was in revenge for Paris judging Aphrodite more beautiful than Hera. Ovid (*Fasti* 6, 398) tells how he attempted to rape the goddess Hestia but was thwarted by an ass, whose braying caused him to lose his erection at the critical moment and woke Hestia. Not surprisingly the incident left him with a lasting hatred of asses and a willingness to see them all slaughtered. The other gods evicted him from Olympus, abandoning him on a hillside to be eventually found by shepherds and raised by them. Body image and self-esteem must have been at an all-time low for Priapus.

We have to go to Egypt for the earliest evidence of the cult of the phallus. Isis, after Osiris had been dismembered, couldn't find his penis; the goddess then fashioned an erect phallus for mankind to worship. This cult of the phallus spread to Greece as the *falloforia* and thence to Italy. Plutarch (*De cupiditate divitiarum* 8, 527d) describes the *falloforia* – processions in honour of Priapus and Dionysus – staged by Ptolemy of Alexandria, which featured a procession with celebrants carrying a 50-metre-long (165 ft) phallus covered in gold. Athenaeus (5, 52) ascribes it to Antiochus, king of

Syria, in a festival in Alexandria in 275 BC that was the last word in extravagance, exoticism and sumptuousness:

> In other carts, also, were carried a Bacchic wand of gold, one hundred and thirty-five feet [41 m] long, and a silver spear ninety feet [27 m] long; in another was a gold phallus one hundred and eighty feet [55 m] long, painted in various colours and bound with fillets of gold; it had at the extremity a gold star, the perimeter of which was nine feet [2.5 m].

In Greece, the phallus was thought to have a mind of its own, animal-like, outside the control of man.

In Rome, the phallus goes back to the days of Romulus: Plutarch, in his *Life of Romulus*, tells the story of Tarchetius, the cruel king of Alba Longa. An enormous phallus emerged from his hearth and started flying around the house; oracular consultation revealed this to be the god Mars displaying his anger, as he was impatient for Tarchetius to produce a successor to the throne. Mars demanded a virgin to sate the phallus because the child born of this coupling would excel in virtue, fortune and strength. Attempts by Tarchetius to persuade his daughter to have sex with the phallus failed; instead she ordered a slave girl to stand in for her. The result? Romulus and Remus were duly born: Tarchetius abandoned the twins only for them to be adopted by the she-wolf, *lupa*, and nurtured. They, of course, went on to found Rome in 753 BC.

One of Priapus' roles was as a useful piece of garden furniture, either as a statue, to ward off thieves, or in fields, vineyards and gardens as a bird scarer, or on chariots, acting as a modern go-faster sticker. Priapus was everywhere – indicative of how strongly Romans of both sexes felt about male power, virility, procreation and sex. He turns up over doors, outside businesses, in paving stones, on amulets and on windows.

The phallic god Priapus was integral to Roman society; in one poem, Priapus threatens anal rape against any would-be thief. Upsetting Priapus might result in impotence, or perpetual sexual arousal from which there was no relief or release. Priapus once laid a curse on a thief that ensured he had no recourse to women or boys to relieve his erection; the thief eventually burst.

The Priapeia comprises 95 poems about Priapus and is found on various statues of the god in the shape of large phalluses. It is a fertile source of Latin profanities:

> O young woman, no fairer-skinned than the Moor, but limper than any catamite, shorter than the Pygmies fearful of the crane, harsher in aspect and shaggier than a she-bear, roomier [in your vulva] than the trousers of the Medes and Indians, you can wait here or leave as you wish. For, though I may seem fully equipped, it would be the work of ten handfuls of herbs to scrub through the ditches between your thighs, and kill the worms swarming in your cunt! (46)

And:

> Priapus! perish, I am not ashamed to use words obscene and wicked:
> But when you, a god
> display your bollocks,
> With Cunt the Cock I must baldly name.

Or:

> We have each distinguishing features in the formation of our bodies: in Phoebus 'tis luxuriant locks, in Hercules muscular power; and the effeminate Bacchus has the figure of a girl. Minerva's eye is light in colour, Venus's prettily blinking ... Aesculapius always wears a never shaven beard. No man is more broad-chested than the warlike Mars; but if 'mid this array there remain any place for me, than Priapus no Deity hath a larger or better-hung cock!

22

Candaules, 'Dog Throttler', Father of Candaulism (and Voyeurism)

Candaules, also known as Myrsilos, was a king of Lydia from 735 to 718 BC. Herodotus says his name meant 'dog throttler' (1, 7, 2–13). In telling this story he delivers a disturbing tale of caution in which a vengeful woman takes centre stage: Candaules was murdered by his wife, Nyssia, tired as she was of his arrogance. For Herodotus, she was responsible for allowing the Lydian throne to slip out of the hands of the Heraclid dynasty – after 505 years and 22 generations – to the Mermnad dynasty in the guise of Gyges. How? Candaules habitually boasted about his wife's prodigious beauty to his bodyguard, Gyges; she took exception to such inappropriate and disrespectful behaviour when he made her nudity a public spectacle. This is what Candaules said to Gyges: 'If you don't believe me when I tell you how lovely my wife is, a man always believes his eyes more than his ears; so do as I tell you – get an eyeful of her taking her clothes off.'

At first Gyges was outraged and refused, only too aware of the taboos surrounding nudity in Persian society and concerned how unpredictably Candaules might actually react if and when the seedy deed was done and he had sight of a naked Nyssia (1, 8, 2; 1, 10, 3).

Candaules did eventually persuade him, asserting that Nyssia knew no shame when her clothes were off. He revealed a plan in which Gyges would lurk behind a door in the royal bedroom to watch Nyssia undressing; Gyges would then steal away unnoticed while the queen's back was turned with no one any the wiser:

Near the door there's a chair on which she will put her clothes as she takes them off, one by one. You will be able to

William Etty, *Candaules, King of Lydia, Shews His Wife by Stealth to Gyges, One of His Ministers, as She Goes to Bed*, 1830, oil on canvas.

watch her with perfect ease. Then, while she's walking away from the chair towards the bed with her back to you, slip away through the door – and watch she doesn't catch you.

So, that night, Gyges took up his position and leered as planned, but the queen caught a glimpse of him and realized in an instant that she had been betrayed, shamed and humiliated by her own husband. Nyssia swore revenge and formulated her own plan. The next day, she summoned Gyges and confronted him: 'One of you must die. Either my husband, or you, who have violated convention by seeing me naked.' Eventually, Gyges, quite understandably, chose to betray the king and save his own skin. Nyssia's vengeful scheme involved an element of *déjà vu*, literally: Gyges hid behind the door of the bedroom again, this time armed with a knife provided by the queen, and slew Candaules in his sleep. Gyges married the queen and became king.

Candaules did not pay just with his life. He has the dubious privilege of lending his name to candaulism, a deviant sexual practice in which a man exposes his (usually) female partner, or images of her, to other people for their voyeuristic pleasure. The term is also applied to the practice of undressing or exposing a female partner's body to others or forcing her into having sex with a third person, or into prostitution or pornography. Today, all this is worryingly familiar: the term is increasingly applied to the posting of revealing images of a female partner on the Internet, often via smartphones, or forcing her to wear sexually suggestive clothes for depraved and prurient public consumption. There is clearly nothing new in the world.

Nyssia was obviously a dignified and shrewd woman, a fact which, for the average Greek, makes Herodotus' story all the more disturbing – and persuades that average Greek to be all the more careful to keep his women under wraps and shielded from the prying eyes of depraved strangers. Nyssia defends the conventions that her husband spurned and proved him wrong when he insinuated that women lose their shame when naked. She punishes the violation and restores normality: in the end, only her husband had still ever seen her naked, even if that necessitated a radical change of spouses.

Herodotus also exposes the exhibitionism displayed by the Egyptians en route to the festival of Artemis: many Egyptians came on barges, and the men would play flutes and the women sing, clap and clack castanets. When they passed by a town, they would bring their barge close into the shore and the women would 'shout abuse at the women of the place, or start dancing, or hitch up their skirts' (*Histories* 2.60).

23
Lesbianism and Sappho

For Roman men, the shame implicit in penetration by another male may go some way to explain the disgust commonly felt towards lesbians who might perform penetrative sex. We can clearly see from Sappho's poems that female homoerotic relations were an integral part of a girl's education in *thiasoi* (girls' schools) in Mytilene (capital of Lesbos), possibly as a precursor to homosexual marriage. Sappho (*c.* 630–570 BC) may have run such a *thiasos* – a place with a dual focus: to deliver a basic education and, at the same time, expose the girls to homosexual love, sometimes for and from their teachers. Sappho herself writes of her affection for various students – and sometimes their love for each other. As the *polis* evolved as a viable political and social entity, however, heterosexual marriage became the social norm, effectively closing down the *thiasoi*, and with them that early flowering of sexual freedom and independence, neither of which could find a home in the new world of heterosexual love and marriage.

The linguistic link of lesbianism and the island of Lesbos had yet to be made: Aristophanes (446 BC–386 BC) only uses the verb *lesbiazein* to refer to fellatio, because the inhabitants of Lesbos apparently had a predilection for oral sex (*Frogs* 1308; *Wasps* 1346; and *Ecclesiazusae* 290). It was not until the second century AD that the island started to be associated with female homoeroticism, probably due to the Sappho factor.

Before the end of the nineteenth century, the adjective 'lesbian' could refer to anything related to the island of Lesbos, including a type of wine. Lesbianism, to denote erotic relationships between women, is only recorded from 1870. In 1890 'lesbian' had an entry in a medical dictionary to define tribadism – as 'lesbian love'; by 1925, the word became a noun in English for the female equivalent of a sodomite.

For the Greeks and Romans, medically speaking, the consensus was that love between women was 'not quite right', if the Greek physician Asclepiades (*c.* 124–40 BC) is representative of contemporary medical opinion. Despite critical acclaim from Plato who saw Sappho as the tenth muse and said so in a couplet – high praise indeed (*Palatine Anthology* 9, 506) – this chimed with male derision and contempt directed at Sappho both as a female poet (poets were routinely men) and as a tribade, thus initiating centuries of male sexism and misogyny born of male insecurity which only relented in the twentieth century. The stereotypes came thick and fast with Sappho depicted in the literature as a stout and plain woman who turned to women only because she could not attract a man. Others slandered her, because female homoerotic acts were tantamount to prostitution.

Despite the near universal derision, Plato was not alone in his admiration. For example, Solon, the famous statesman and contemporary of Sappho, reputedly wanted to learn a Sapphic poem so that it could be his swansong:

> Solon the Athenian, the son of Eksêkestides, when his nephew sang some song of Sappho at a drinking party, took pleasure in it and asked the young man to teach it to him. When someone asked why he was eager to learn it, he responded: 'So, once I learn it, I may die.' (AELIAN, Fr. 187/190 (from STOBAEUS 3.29.58))

Maximus of Tyrus asserted that Sappho should be regarded as the 'mother' of Socrates' speech in the *Symposium*:

> What else could one call the art of love of the Lesbian woman other than the Socratic art of love? For they seem to me to have practised love after their own fashion, she the love of women, he of men. For they said they loved many, and were captivated by all things beautiful. (*Dissertations* 18.9)

In the first century BC Catullus, the great Roman love poet, paid homage when he adapted one of her fragmentary songs (31) – about sexual frustration – into Latin (*Carmen* 51) in the Sapphic metre.

Aristotle, though, is genuinely surprised that the 'people of Mytilene honour Sappho'. Why surprised? Because 'she is a woman' (*Rhetoric* 1398b). Over the centuries, the issues regarding Sappho have spawned endless (largely speculative) debate and passionate arguments over her character, public life and sexual orientation. Even though there is no direct reference to either homosexual or heterosexual sex in her work, hypocritical religious leaders down the ages, including Pope Gregory VIII, who called her a lewd nymphomaniac in 1073, ordered her books be burned. He was probably influenced by the early Christian father Tatian (AD 120–*c*. 180), who described Sappho as a 'sex mad little whore'. Tatian, in turn, was influenced by the homophobic apostle Paul: 'This Sappho is a sex mad little whore, and sings of her own promiscuity; but all our [Christian] women are chaste, and the young girls at their distaffs sing of divine things more nobly than that woman of yours. So be ashamed' (*Address to the Greeks* 33). (It is worth pointing out that this Tatian is the same Christian man who described the 'invention' of marriage as being the work of the Devil.)

When Plato's Aristophanes attempts to describe women who desire other women words fail him because there is no such word in the Greek lexicon; he uses the term *hetairistria* with its obvious connotations.

Caelius calls lesbians *tribades* – women who are 'more eager to lie with women than men and in fact pursue women with almost masculine jealousy . . . they rejoice in the abuse of their sexual powers'. This may reflect a general male homophobia, an antipathy to lesbianism. Caelius is unable to help – to him, the condition is quite incurable; these 'disgraceful vices' are an affliction of the mind that must be controlled. The situation was hopeless: he believed that homosexuality intensified with age, resulting in 'a hideous and ever increasing lust'.

Reference to Lewis and Short's *Latin Dictionary* will show that *tribas* is derived from the Greek *tribo* (I rub), a pejorative term which was first used in the first century AD; it is defined as 'a woman who practises unnatural vice with herself or with other women', and in Latin, 'a woman who practices lewdness with women'. Latin was quite versatile here and so we get other words for lesbian: *fricatrix* (she who rubs) and *virago*. Many Romans found the idea of *tribades* repellent; this presumably stems from the generalization that tribadism always necessitated penetration – by a dildo, for example, or a large clitoris. Men were being somewhat proprietary here – and most probably disingenuous and hypocritical – since we have already seen that penetration was regarded as the exclusive preserve of men.

You would expect someone with the amatory knowledge and experience of Ovid to be au fait with all of this but Ovid is as mystified as the next man: he finds it 'a desire known to no one, freakish, novel … among all animals no female is seized by desire for female'. With justification Martial calls Philaenis a *tribas* in his obscene diatribe in which she buggers the boys as vigorously as any man and performs cunnilingus on the girls. As far as insults go, this was extreme and double-edged: not only was Philaenis penetrating just like a man, she was licking, too – cunnilingus, be it homo- or heterosexual, was to Roman men utterly repellent and degrading. Bassa is a similar case; on first sight she appears as chaste as a Lucretia, because she reputedly has never been involved with a man, but really, she is a penetrating *fututor*, a 'fucker', bringing together two *cunni* and pretending to be a man. To Artemidorus, that expert interpreter of dreams, lesbian sex was as perverted as the notion of having sex with the gods, with animals and with the dead. A woman dreaming of having sex with another woman had its pitfalls, and not just for her: pleasuring another woman meant that she will have to share all her secrets with that woman; if she is herself pleasured by another woman she will lose her husband or be widowed, the only compensation being that she gets to learn the other woman's secrets.

Stoic Seneca the Younger writes that women in general 'satisfy the strangest of sexual tastes, acting as men among men', when they deploy dildos for penetration. To him homosexuality was simply unnatural, *contra naturam*. His father Seneca the Elder cites a case in which a man murders his wife and her lover *in flagrante delicto* which in law he his permitted to do; however, before the blood bath he prudently checks to confirm beyond any doubt that the lover was 'natural' (a man) or 'artificial' – a woman wearing a dildo. We know not which. What we do gather from this is that the Romans had no law of adultery when it was committed between women.

Despite all of this ballyhoo, lesbians there were in Rome and in the wider empire; literary evidence includes a Pompeii graffito (*CIL* 4, 5296) that has a woman addressing her lover, another woman, as 'my darling' (*pupula*). Lucian in his *Erotes* (28), and we've been here before, creates a rhetorical exercise the purpose of which is to establish whether love for a man (homosexuality) is better than love for a woman (heterosexuality), or vice versa. The conclusion is inconclusive, but along the way the accompanying images are truly graphic including its dildos, those 'strange and monstrous tools of lechery without semen'.

In Carthage, all Tertullian (AD 160–240) saw around him was so-called *matronae* dressed like prostitutes or *frictrices*. Indeed, he has some warnings relating to hygiene when he advises against drinking from the same cup as a *frictrix*, a castrated priest of Cybele (assumed to be a homosexual), a gladiator or an executioner. Homosexuals were tarred with the same Christian brush as killers. *The Apocalypse of Peter* (17) has it on good authority that effeminate men and *tribades* spend their time in Hell continually jumping off a very high cliff.

Two of Lucian's *hetairae*, Clonarion and Leaena, discuss the pros and cons of lesbian sex, and so prove that such services were readily available on the streets and in the brothels (LUCIAN, *Dialogues of the Courtesans* 5). The girls tell of Megilla, a rich woman who had the hots for Leaena as much as any man would; both courtesans agree that this was unnatural, commenting that in Sparta they have tribadists just like Megilla who actually look like men.

To the fable writer Phaedrus, *tribades* with their strap-on dildos, and soft (*molles*) men, enjoy a deformed pleasure (4, 12; 1–2, 12–14).

24

Hermaphrodites and Other Wondrous Beings

Pliny says that the Greeks call hermaphrodites *ektrapeloi* (freaks), but that there is no Latin equivalent for the Romans. Hermaphrodites (*androgyni*) enjoyed a reputation as prodigies, until Pompey took away their dignity by downgrading them to objects of ridicule and by putting them on the stage in his theatre (*Natural History* 7, 34).

They shared the limelight with such miraculous people, or celebrities, as Eutyches, who was led to her funeral pyre by twenty children, to celebrate the thirty individual babies she had given birth to; Alcippe, the proud mother of an elephant (PLINY, *Natural History* 7, 3, 1); and the slave girl who was delivered of a snake when Apollo killed the huge snake Python at Delphi. A temple dedicated to him was set up at the site, which replaced Gaea's earlier sanctuary and appropriated her oracle. For the next 1,000 years people consulted the prophecies of Apollo here while Pythia was a priestess at the temple, imbued with the spirit of the god.

There is a connection to the Bible: in Acts 16:16–24, the apostle Paul meets a slave girl at Philippi with a 'spirit of python', who can tell the future. Paul meets the slave girl and exorcizes the 'spirit of python' from her. This action also had the effect of depriving her of her prophesying skills, angers her owners and lands Paul and his companion Silas in prison after a severe flogging.

Beings that were half-man, half-horse were not uncommon, it seems: Pliny (*Natural History* 7, 35) and Phlegon (*Marvels* 34) describe one such creature that was spotted smeared in honey. A somewhat discerning baby was born in Saguntum, soon after the city was sacked by Hannibal (219 BC): the baby took one look around, was not impressed by what it saw and went straight back to the safety of its mother's womb.

The fourth-century CE writer Julius Obsequens, author of *Prodigiorum liber* (Book of Prodigies), describes hermaphrodites, monstrous children and the like taken from Livy. Here is a random sample:

- A two-headed lamb, and a boy with three hands and as many feet were born [at Atellae] ...
- At Vulsinium ... a two-headed, four-footed, four-handed girl with twin sets of female genitalia was born dead ...
- At Faesulae roaring was heard from the earth. A boy was born of a slave-girl without an aperture in his genitals through which urine might pass.
- A woman was found with two sets of genitalia. A torch was seen in the sky.
- A bull spoke.
- At Volaterrae a river flowed with blood. At Rome it rained milk.
- At Arretium two hermaphrodites were found. A farm-yard chicken was born with four-feet. (50, 51, 53)

Diodorus in the late first century BC described hermaphrodites as marvellous creatures (*terata*) who announce the future, for good and bad. Phlegon of Tralles tells the story of Kainis, who, in the land of the Lapiths, was raped by Poseidon. As compensation, the god promised her anything she wished for; she desired to be changed into a man so as never to endure rape again, and so, Kainis became Kaineus (*Marvels* 5).

The wedding day of a thirteen-year-old virgin in Antioch from a well-to-do family and sought after by many suitors was not everything it should have been. Just as she was leaving her home she was afflicted by an eye-watering pain; this continued for three days with no relief, and no diagnosis, until on the fourth day it intensified, and male genitals burst from her; the virgin became a man. Claudius built a temple for Jupiter the Avenger in her honour (*Marvels* 6).

The very same thing happened to a virgin called Philotis (*Marvels* 7) in Mevania and to Sympherousa in Epidauros. Phlegon (*Marvels* 8) adds the revealing postscript that Sympheron spent the rest of his life as a gardener.

In around AD 500, Isidore of Seville described hermaphrodites as having the right breast of a man and the left of a woman, and after sex can both sire and bear children. In Roman law, a hermaphrodite was, confusingly, classified 'as either male *or* female'. After Pompey made celebrities out of them, they had, by Pliny's time, become objects of delight and fascination (*deliciae*) highly sought after in the slave markets.

Hypospadias (or Male Pseudo-Hermaphroditism)

Diodorus Siculus (32, 10) leaves us with an intriguing story about a man from Macedonia called Diophantus who lived in Abae, Arabia; he married an Arabian woman and had a son, who died young, and a daughter, Heraïs, whom he married off to a man named Samiades. After a year, Samiades embarked on a long journey, leaving Heraïs, who fell ill 'of a strange and altogether incredible infirmity' – an aggressive tumour presented at the base of her abdomen that became more and more swollen, accompanied by fevers; her physicians diagnosed an ulcer at the mouth of the uterus. On the seventh day without cure, the tumour burst to reveal a penis projecting from her groin with testicles. When this happened, only her mother and two slaves were present; they looked after Heraïs to the best of their ability and said nothing of what had happened to anyone. Heraïs recovered and tried to get on with her life, still wearing women's clothes, looking after her house and remaining true to her absent husband. It was assumed by the few people in the know that she was a hermaphrodite, and that since conventional sexual intercourse was not an option, she would have to have sex with her husband anally.

Samiades eventually returned but Heraïs, out of shame, could not bear to be near him. He was angry and quarrelled with Diophantus, and resorted to legal action; the jurors debated whether the husband should have jurisdiction over his wife or the father over his daughter. When the court found in favour of Samiades, she undid her robe and exposed her penis – much to the astonishment of all present. Heraïs swapped her women's clothes for a man's. The doctors concluded that her penis had been concealed in an egg-shaped part of her vagina, encased by a membrane; an opening had formed through which urine and menses were discharged. Heraïs underwent surgery. In consequence they found it necessary to scarify the perforated area – that is, make shallow incisions in the skin – and induce cicatrization (the contraction of fibrous tissue formed at a wound site by fibroblasts, reducing the size of the wound while distorting tissue): the aim was to bring the penis into a viable shape. She changed her name to Diophantus, joined the cavalry and fought in the king's army, as you do.

Diodorus described a similar case in Epidaurus some thirty years later involving a patient called Callo who was an orphan and priestess of Demeter. Callo was only able to urinate through a kind of penis (*pecten*). Nevertheless, she married, but she was unable to have natural sexual intercourse and 'was obliged to submit to unnatural embraces' – sodomy. She eventually developed a painful tumour on her genitals; none of the doctors she attended would treat her, other than an apothecary who cut into her groin only to reveal testicles and an imperforate penis. 'Cutting into the glans he made a passage into the urethra, and inserting a silver catheter drew off the urine. Then, by scarifying the perforated area, he brought the parts together.'

The venal apothecary then demanded double his fee, justifying that it was because he had received a female patient and made her into a healthy young man. Callo, meanwhile, 'laid aside her loom-shuttles and all other instruments of woman's work, and taking in their stead the garb and status of a man changed her name ... to Callon' (DIODORUS SICULUS 32, 11). Unfortunately for Callo, because she had been a priestess and had witnessed things to which men should not be privy, she was tried for impiety.

Urologists have identified this as a clear case of hypospadias (or male pseudo-hermaphroditism), where the hole through which urine passes (*meatus*) is not at the tip of the penis. Instead, the hole may be anywhere along the underside of the penis, or even within the scrotum; the foreskin is all at the back of the penis, leaving none at the front, and the penis may be bent when erect: around 15–50 per cent of cases are in such a condition, called 'chordee'. Corrective surgery aims to straighten the penis, relocate the meatus to the tip of the penis and to carry out a circumcision by removing the excess foreskin. According to the Urology Care Foundation of the American Urological Association, 'Hypospadias is fairly common, being found in about 1 in every 200 boys.'

As noted, as an indicator of the casual way the Romans treated 'intersex babies', they are often recorded alongside unusual animal births, such as 'a lamb with a pig's head' (Livy 31.12.6–8), which illustrates how such children were considered, in the Roman mind, to be of a kind with the non-human. Indeed, the expiation ceremonies – rituals to appease the gods – to rid the state of what were considered ill-omened prodigies usually coincided with times of political tension, evidenced by a ritual carried out in 207 BC during the Second Punic War. Intersex infants were used as scapegoats in troubled times, just as Vestal Virgins were.

25

Gender Reassignment, Miraculous Births and Sexual Ecstasy

Pliny (*Natural History* 7, 34) is insistent on the phenomenon of instantaneous transgender transgression or gender reassignment: *ex feminis mutari in maris non est fabulosum non est speculum* ('it is no dream').

In 171 BC a girl from Casinum instantaneously changed into a boy before her parents' eyes: the augurs were not impressed and banished her to an island. Licinius Mucianus records the case of Arescon, a man from Argos who married a man as Arescusa; she then developed a beard and other male features and got married to a woman. There was a similar sighting in Smyrna. Pliny himself saw a bride turn into a man on their wedding day.

The mother of a boxer, Nicaeus of Byzantium, was born from her mother's adulterous affair with an Aethiopian: the mother was born white but Nicaeus, one generation later, was born black.

Pliny goes on to assert that certain Indian tribeswomen bear children from age seven and are old by the time they reach forty, while others conceive aged five and die three years later; the children of others go grey immediately after birth. Women who want a black-eyed baby must eat a shrew during their pregnancy.

There are no reported cases of women dying from overexertion during sex, but Pliny (*Natural History* 7,53,1) reports that both Cornelius Gallus, the well known first-century BC poet, and the otherwise obscure equestrian Titus Hetereius died in the throes of sexual ecstasy – with women, he primly adds.

26

Aphrodisiacs and Anti-Aphrodisiacs

Galen believed that any food that produced flatulence also had aphrodisiacal qualities – a not altogether magical combination. This was still believed until the eighteenth century. Pliny the Elder recommends 'a man's urine in which a lizard has been drowned' as an aphrodisiac. If there is no lizard to hand, 'the right section of a vulture's lung worn as an amulet in a crane's skin' did just as well. If all else failed, a disappointing member might be activated by recourse to the dark arts: for an on-demand erection, simply smear 'your thing' with crushed pepper in honey (*Greek Magical Papyri* 12, 36).

Theophrastus (*Enquiry into Plants* 9, 18) tells us about a big Indian man who had an inedible plant that when rubbed on his penis gave him sufficient hardness to service as many women as he liked. Some users boasted they had managed twelve times, but the big Indian claimed he once had seventy women one after another. Admittedly, by the end, his semen was ejaculated in drops and was bloody, but seventy times all the same . . . Women too became 'unusually eager for intercourse' when applying this drug. Sadly for drug manufacturers, Theophrastus omits to name the plant.

The *Kyranides* (1, 18), a compendium of dubious magico-medical works in Greek compiled in the first century AD, includes an aphrodisiac to be worn as an amulet: it comprises lapis lazuli engraved with an ostrich holding a fish in its mouth. An orchid seed and a sliver of the gizzard goes into the ostrich's stomach; wearing it ensures good digestion and an erection, and 'fosters an interest in sex; specially good for old men and those who want sex often; it also makes the wearer seductive'. Another from the same source (2, 7) requires a weasel's right testicle to be reduced to ashes and mixed with myrrh to form a paste on a ball of wool and inserted into the woman's vagina before intercourse; the result is immediate conception. The left testicle has the opposite effect as a contraceptive. The author invites sceptical readers to try it for themselves on a bird that is laying eggs.

Anti-aphrodisiacs included nymphaea, a herb guaranteed to 'relax' the phallus for a few days. One writer even boasted that it would 'take away desire and even erotic dreams for forty days!' Pliny reveals that there was much confidence in animal body parts, especially those of the hippopotamus. Hippo parts generally were effective as antidotes for snakebite: all a victim had to do was swallow a coin-sized piece of hippo testicle with water. Hippos, though, were the beast of choice for temporarily inhibiting sexual desire: simply take the hide from the left side of a hippo's forehead, then attach it firmly to the groin – the woman's groin, that is. If this was not repellent enough to stifle any residual passion, it certainly made for an excellent barrier contraceptive. Pliny adds another:

A most powerful medicament is obtained by reducing to ashes the nails of a lynx, together with the hide . . . these ashes, taken in drink, have the effect of checking abominable desires in men . . . and if they are sprinkled upon women, all libidinous thoughts will be restrained. (*Natural History* 28, 32)

Perhaps the most effective anti-aphrodisiacs, however, were the radish and mullet. If a husband caught his wife and an adulterer in the act, he was at liberty to do more or less whatever he liked to them. One of the punishments for adultery with a married woman was to have a radish shoved into your anus – 'radish reaming' or 'radish rape' – a symbol of the erect male penis (and cuckold) delighting in revenge. The verb is ῥαφανιδόω (*rhaphanidoo*). The bad news was that if a radish was not found, then a mullet would be substituted; the even worse news was that mullets have spikes . . .

Another humiliating punishment guaranteed to lower the libido was singeing off the adulterer's pubic hair with hot ashes in the marketplace to make the adulterer look effeminate (SCHOLION TO ARISTOPHANES, *Wealth* 168).

Pliny (*Natural History* 28, 256) prescribes a potion that makes sex repugnant to women: it involves smearing the genitalia of the woman with blood from a tick that resides on a wild black bull. If she then drinks goat's urine, she will find love repellent too. Smearing blood had a strange effect on Faustina, the wife of emperor Marcus Aurelius: she was smitten by a gladiator and finally confessed her passion to her husband. On advice from the Chaldeans, the gladiator in question was executed and Faustina was made to bathe in his blood and then have sex with her husband, still covered in the blood. Any erotic thoughts of the gladiator apparently vanished (Historia Augusta, *Marcus Aurelius*).

The *Paignia* of Democritus (7, 167–86) tells us how erectile dysfunction can be overcome by coating the penis with a mixture of honey and pepper to produce an erection, or by boiling a donkey's genitals in oil and using it as an ointment (PLINY 28, 262, crediting Salpe, a female obstetrician).

27

The Roman *Joy of Sex*

O vid's Roman equivalent to Alex Comfort's 1976 bestselling *Joy of Sex*, his *Amores*, taps into a rich tradition of classical sex writing. Ovid himself refers to a number of sex manuals, all now lost, some of which may have been regarded as what we now call pornographic; many were Greek.

An otiose Lucius Cornelius Sisenna translated Aristides into Latin under the title *Milesiae fabulae* around 78 BC; Ovid calls it an anthology of misdeeds (*crimina*), full of smutty jokes. The Milesian tale (Μιλησιακά in Greek, in Latin *fabula milesiaca*, or *Milesiae fabula*) had a long history, even by Ovid's day. It is usually defined as a short, erotic story featuring love and adventure. In his dialogue on the kinds of love, *Erotes*, Lucian praised Aristides as 'that enchanting spinner of bawdy yarns'. After the Battle of Carrhae (53 BC), the victorious Parthians were shocked to find the *Milesiaca* in the baggage of Crassus's officers:

> Surena . . . laid before them certain wanton books, of the writings of Aristides, his *Milisiaka*; neither, indeed, was this any forgery, for they had been found among the baggage of Rustius, and were good ammunition with which to supply Surena with insulting remarks about the Romans, who were not able even during war to forget such writings and practices. (PLUTARCH, *Crassus* 32)

The *milesiaca* influenced the racier parts of Petronius' *Satyricon* and Apuleius' *Golden Ass*, as well as *Cupid and Psyche*. Some of the medieval *fabliaux* were influenced by Aristides, including Chaucer's *The*

Miller's Tale, part of Boccaccio's *Decameron* and the *Heptameron* of Margaret of Angoulême.

Technical and scientific manuals were big business in the classical publishing world: it was not just men who taught the *artes amatoriae*; women contributed to the sex manual publishing programmes. Martial alludes to books by Elephantis in his review of the work of Sabellus: she was the author of a famous book on sexual positions, a Roman *Kama Sutra* or another *Joy of Sex*. Suetonius tells us that Tiberius packed a copy for reference when he left for his retreat on Capri. Martial recommends the books written by Sulpicia to women and men alike, if they want guidance on how to achieve the perfect marriage – on both sides of the bedroom door. Elsewhere, women lend a helping hand when he recommends that Istantius Rufus has his girl masturbate him as he reads the salacious books (*pathicissimi libelli*) of Musaeus.

The erotic – pornographic, if you will – was all around. Ubiquitous erotic wall decoration in public buildings and expensive private homes and the effect it was having on impressionable young girls was a cause for concern for Propertius. The Cynthia-obsessed love poet deplores the *obscaenae* and the corrupting effect they have on the innocent eyes of young women. He has an agenda, though: what he is really worried about is that the pictures will engender in female viewers a promiscuity that will not always be to his personal advantage. Ovid writes to Augustus from exile in Tomis, describing quite casually the *tabella* he has seen there that depict *concubitus varii* (different ways of having sex) and *figurae veneris* (sexual positions). In the Pompeiian wall paintings, women are frequently shown playing an equal or dominant role in the sex act; women were not only willing and equal partners here, they would have been just as likely to enjoy the paintings and sexual graffiti as men, or indeed to assume a matter-of-fact attitude to them. The reception of erotic wall paintings by the Roman man and woman was surely very different to the reception of the Victorians and later societies, for example, who hid the paintings away from us, locked up away out of sight many years.

So, erotic images, symbols and literature were visible to all, women and men alike, and presumably enjoyed by both sexes:

sex for the Roman was more of a pleasure than a sin, or anything to feel ashamed or embarrassed about. Sex was a public affair for Roman men and women, indicative of pleasure. In Rome, when a sexual act is displayed on a house wall, on a lamp or on a wine jug, it becomes part of the domestic wallpaper, accepted as normal by everyday people. Mundane objects such as mirrors and jugs, for example Arretine ware, were often embellished with the erotic, ranging from routine 'courting' to explicit penetration by the erect penis into the vagina.

Laddish graffiti proclaims that all the wives of Pompeii were 'up for it'. For the ladies, 'Glyco does cunnilingus for two asses.' Martimus, however, is not such a good deal: he does it for four but will entertain virgins for free – all suggesting a lively trade in male prostitution for the bored housewives of Pompeii. Horace gives us an example of voyeurism as the pimping husband watches as his wife enjoys sex with all manner of men, with the candles burning brightly for all to see.

Group sex (*koine cupris*) was an occupational hazard, or maybe a business opportunity, for prostitutes: Gallus describes three men penetrating Lyde; Nicarchus, in the first century AD, describes another foursome where the three men draw lots for which orifice they get. One of the scenes at the Suburban Baths in Pompeii shows one man taking a woman from behind while he receives a man standing behind him. Catullus, in *Carmen* 56, re-enacts it, considering it hilarious. Another scene shows a foursome in which a man sodomizes another man on whom a woman gives fellatio; another woman performs cunnilingus on her.

According to Suetonius, Horace himself preferred sex at home to visiting brothels, inviting escorts back to his place where the mirrors in his bedroom literally reflected his sexual activity: coitus from every angle (HORACE, *Odes* 3, 6. *Greek Anthology* 5, 49; 11, 328). Martial knows exactly what he wants from a prostitute: a low price and a willingness to take three clients at a time; the older the whore, the less he pays (9, 32; 10, 75).

Juvenal and Strabo describe temple prostitution: sex that was rife in temples such as Eryx in Sicily and at Corinth. Prostitutes also provided a lucrative sideline for low-rent hotels (*tabernae cauponiae*), bars and inns, offering their services as *noctilucae*, night-lights, in the tiny cubicles out the back with their stone beds and straw mattresses. One amusing inscription from Aesernia describes a client paying his hotel bill; the extras included the services of a girl, costing eight asses, and hay for the mule, costing two: the guest protests that it is the mule that is the likely cause of his financial ruin.

Incidentally, Cicero in his *Brutus* (154) explains why the phrase 'with us' in Latin is written *nobiscum* rather than the expected *cum nobis*; conflate two words and you get something that sounds like *cunno bis*, 'a pair of cunts'. French has the same problem with *qu'on*, which sounds like *con* (cunt) and swerves round it by adding *l'* to form the less ambivalent *que l'on*. Helen's 'cunt' is described by Horace by synecdoche as the cause of the Trojan war (*Satires* 1, 2 and 1, 3).

28

Dildos

Miletus was the centre of excellence, the global manufacturing and exporting centre of the *olisbos* from ὀλισθεῖν (*olisthein*, to slip, glide) and known to us as the dildo, a type of sex toy. We learn from Jonathan Amos's BBC report 'Ancient Phallus Unearthed in Cave' of 25 July 2005 that the world's oldest known dildo is a 20-centimetre (9 in.) phallus from the Upper Palaeolithic period some 30,000 years ago, found in Hohle Fels cave near Ulm in Germany. Nick Belardes, in his *Random Obsessions: Trivia You Can't Live Without* (2009), adds that

> What can only be described as dildo-like breadsticks, *olisbo-kollikes* (singular *olisbokollix*), were known in ancient Greece before the fifth century BC. More often, dildos were made of either wood or pressed leather and, obviously, were liberally smeared with olive oil before use, if only for lubrication and taste.

A third-century BC mime by Herodas, *A Quiet Chat* (*Mime* 6), features a conversation between two young women, Metro and Coritto: Metro wants to borrow Coritto's dildo, but Coritto says that Nossis has it, and she got it from Euboula. Coritto then explains that she bought it from Kerdon, the maker of the dildo, who conceals his black-market trade by masquerading as a cobbler who 'works at home and sells secretly'. Metro then vividly describes Kerdon's expertise. She then leaves to seek him out. In *Mime* 7, Metro takes some friends to Kerdon's shoe shop, and the sexual innuendo continues with footwear, a metaphor for sex toys.

The *olisbos* is also mentioned in Aristophanes' *Lysistrata* (107ff). We see dildos too on Greek vases: one famous example from the sixth century BC depicts an erotic scene in which a woman bends over to perform oral sex on a man, while another man is about to thrust a dildo into her anus. Another is the red-figure amphora attributed to the Flying-Angel Painter, circa 490 BC, now in the City of Paris Museum of Fine Arts.

The Vindolanda Phallus

In February 2023 Mark Brown reported in *The Guardian* on a 2,000-year-old object found at Vindolanda in 1992. This object had been reassessed by archaeologists, their results outlined in the journal *Antiquity*:

> Archaeologists believe they may have found the only known lifesize Roman dildo, discovered in a ditch along with dozens of shoes and dress accessories as well as craft waste products such as leather off-cuts and worked antler . . . If it was not used as a sexual implement then the object may have been an erect penis-shaped pestle, or it could have been a feature from a statue that people touched for good luck . . . What it definitely is not is what it was catalogued as in 1992: a darning tool . . . The Vindolanda phallus is 16cm long . . . The analysis has revealed it to be, at the very least, the first known example of a disembodied phallus made of wood recovered anywhere in the Roman world.

SOCIAL SCIENCES

29

Bad Parenting, Good Parenting?

What is good parenting and what is bad? Here are some tips from the ancient world on caring for children. First off, honey, the ultimate pacifier – not good for the teeth though:

> People used to take a pot full of honey with a sponge blocking the opening and put it into children's mouths to keep them quiet and to stop them from crying to be fed. (SCHOLION TO ARISTOPHANES, *Acharnians* 463)

How about corporal punishment and psychological abuse?

> Without flogging, no one can be educated. (PSEUDO-MENANDER, *Sayings* 73)

> The Mitylenæans, having taken control of the sea, imposed as a punishment on the allies who had revolted from them that they should not teach their children to read, nor allow them to be educated. The Mitylenæans believed that to be bred ignorantly and illiterately was the harshest of all punishments. (AELIAN, *Miscellaneous History* 7, 15)

For hyperactive children, Pliny recommends putting goat's dung in children's nappies to soothe them, especially girls (*Natural History* 28, 259). And Seneca lays down rules to stop tantrums:

> We must not allow outbursts of anger in them, or blunt their individuality . . . a boy's boisterousness increases with too

much freedom while it is depressed with repression. Praise lifts the spirits and engenders confidence; too much praise, though, causes arrogance and anger. We must steer him through a middle course, then, deploying carrot and stick. Don't treat him like a slave or degrade him; don't let him beg for anything and don't give him anything for begging. Anything he gets must be as a reward for good behaviour or the promise of good behaviour. In competition with his peers don't let him sulk or lose his temper . . . he can have leisure time but don't make him lazy or slothful . . . the boy who always gets his own way, whose anxious mother is forever drying his tears, who always gets one over his teacher, that boy will never cope with the real world. (*On Anger* 2, 21, 1–6)

But if these don't work, then there's always . . .

The example of Hera, queen of the gods and the goddess of women, marriage and family, the disputatious wife and sister of Zeus, who threw her son off Mount Olympus because he was ugly. Despite her unimpeachable honorifics, Hera was never going to be the ideal mother: having given birth to the blacksmith god Hephaestus without any physical involvement by Zeus in an immaculate conception of sorts, she was so disgusted by Hephaestus' looks that she cast him off the mountain; result: his characteristic hobble and limp and, no doubt, some lifelong issues, not least PTSD. Hera went on to produce Hebe after being impregnated by a head of lettuce.

If Hera despised Hephaestus, Hera loathed Heracles, her stepson. When Heracles was still a baby, Hera sent two serpents to kill him as he dozed in his cot; Heracles, however, showing signs of things to come, was unphased by this and simply throttled them both. The Milky Way was formed when Zeus tricked Hera into nursing Heracles: when she realized who the baby was, she tore him from her breast, and a spurt of her milk projected and created the starry smear across the sky that we now know as the Milky Way.

If Penelope was the role model for the good and virtuous Greek wife, then Clytemnestra was the polar opposite. No waiting

Sarcophagus relief, Rome, marble, *c*. AD 150. Orestes appears three times on the front of this sarcophagus, always wielding a short sword. In the centre he stands over the body of his mother Clytemnestra, and at centre left over the body of her lover Aegisthus.

faithfully and patiently working the wool for her: Agamemnon bitterly and graphically describes to Odysseus during the necromancy in *Odyssey* 11 how the unexpected high point of his eventual return from Troy was him being butchered by his wife:

> Aegisthus and my wicked wife were the death of me between them. He asked me to his house, feasted me, and then butchered me most miserably as though I were a fat beast in a slaughter house, while all around me my comrades were slain like sheep or pigs for the wedding breakfast, or picnic, or gorgeous banquet of some great nobleman.

Indeed, as far as Agamemnon is concerned, Clytemnestra, like Pandora before her, has unwittingly added to the script for the male reception of women forever. All women are blemished from now on; that eternal hostility, fear and suspicion begins here. In fact, so bitter is Agamemnon that, ironically, he warns Odysseus to beware Penelope when he arrives home, fearing a similar bloody and

deceitful reception from her. From a distance, we can understand from the example of Penelope that by no means were all women bad: a stereotyping and bitter Agamemnon naturally sees it very differently, and mud sticks.

If Clytemnestra is bad, then Medea is worse still and must rank as one of literature's most repugnant and reprehensible mothers. She unequivocally declares her hatred for her children early on in the play that bears her name: 'You accursed sons of a mother who know nothing but hate, damn you, your father and your whole house' (EURIPIDES, *Medea* 112). Medea is the gold-standard witch, the one to equal, to emulate and to echo. Others run her close – Homer's Circe and Lucan's Erichtho, for example – but Medea comes out top of the funeral pyre. Her meticulous instructions on how to rejuvenate through jugulation – throat-cutting made simple – are beyond compare.

Rejuvenation and reanimation were important skills in the witch's armamentarium. Medea was an expert in making the young old – with devastating consequences. Lucan's Erichtho, as we shall see, performs what is probably one of history's most ghastly acts of reanimation, raising the black art to gruesome new heights, or rather plunging them to new depths. She was also a dab hand at ad hoc blood transfusion.

Euripides opens his *Medea* with the nurse telling us that Medea is 'unhinged in her love for Jason'; up to this point she is the perfect Greek type of wife who did everything her husband asked, making great sacrifices for him. In return, he cruelly betrayed her love, with shocking consequences for their children. For Medea, love was for life: in the *Argonautica* (3, 126–8) by Apollonius of Rhodes, she swears, 'in our lawful marriage-chamber you shall share my bed, and nothing will separate us in our love until the appointed death enshrouds us.' Not so in the case of Jason. Her rejection by Jason has sown an unnatural hatred in her heart that results ultimately in the infanticide of her children. According to Diodorus Siculus (*Library of History* 4, 50, 6), she was connected to that satanic family, the unholy trinity, which boasted Hecate as Circe's mother and Circe as her sister:

> [Medea] said [to the Argonauts] that she had brought with her many drugs of marvellous potency which had been discovered by her mother Hecate and by her sister Circe; and though before this time she had never used them to destroy human beings, on this occasion she would, and by means of them easily wreak vengeance upon men who were deserving of punishment.

30
Sexism and Misogyny

Greek and Roman literature is littered with sexist expression and misogyny, starting way back in the seventh century BC with Hesiod, who set the tone and template for the next 1,100 years of the classical period and then the Middle Ages, the Renaissance and so on into the modern period. Here is some of the cream of the classical crop. The vitriol is tangible; the antipathy towards women incessant and unrelenting. No wonder then that prejudice against women is still with us to some extent: it was always going to last over 1,500 years when endorsed by some of the supposedly best-educated and most intelligent men in antiquity whose influence down the centuries has been huge and remains unabated.

Greece

It did not take long before Greek women attracted a very bad press among the writing classes: women were trouble, even in mythology. According to Hesiod, Greece's first woman, Pandora, was the embodiment of everything to loathe in a human being because man had made the fatal mistake of learning from Prometheus the secret of producing fire. Pandora was man's eternal punishment; she was fashioned out of the earth by Hephaestus, by command of Zeus; other gods and goddesses supplied all the other unhealthy physical attributes and characteristics of women traditionally hated and feared by men: seduction, dishonesty and manipulation. What you could see before your eyes was beautiful, making her irresistible to men; on the other hand, it was the invisible features donated by the Olympian gods that constituted her true personality: these would bring endless grief, injury, harm and much trouble to man:

> Prometheus, surpassing all in cunning, you are glad that you have outwitted me and stolen fire – a great plague on you and to all future men. But for the payback for fire I will give men an evil thing in which they may all be happy while they embrace their own destruction. (*Works and Days* 55ff)

When Pandora unscrewed the lid of the fateful jar given by Zeus, she was also screwing man:

> the tribes of men lived on earth remote and free from ills and hard toil and heavy sicknesses which bring the Fates to men; for in misery men grow old quickly. But the woman took off the great lid of the jar with her hands and scattered, all these and her thought caused sorrow and mischief to men. Only Hope remained there in an unbreakable home under the rim of the great jar ... But the rest, countless plagues, spread amongst men; for earth is [now] full of evils, and the sea is full too. Diseases come upon men continually by day and by night, bringing stealthy mischief to mortals.

With an air of weary resignation, Hesiod spoke for generations of Greek men when he concluded that 'men could not live with [women] and could not live without them'. Hesiod, apart from echoing the sentiments of his contemporary menfolk, influenced successive generations of men against women, injecting prejudice, discrimination, misogyny, fear and distrust into one half of the population against the other. By opening that fateful jar, Pandora had taken the lid off the bad things in life; she had ended the Golden Age, brought a close to the good old days and ushered in a world that from now on was going to be much harder work. And who's fault was it? It was women's fault. But the 'grim cares of mankind' were now out in the open in plain sight: all men could do now was hope against hope.

And so, lumbered with this poisoned chalice, man had to make the most of it; here is Hesiod's prescription for choosing a good wife:

> Marry a virgin, so that you can teach her careful ways, in particular, marry one who lives near you, but have a good look around and ensure that your marriage will not be the laughingstock of the neighbourhood. For a man wins nothing better than a good wife, and nothing worse than a bad one, a greedy soul who roasts her man without fire, as strong as he might be, and brings him an early old age. (*Works and Days* 699ff)

Hesiod reiterates the doom-laden message in *Theogony* when he asserts that bachelorhood is no escape from misery: a wretched old age awaits the single man, as there will be no one around to provide all that vital home care. Incidentally, in so doing, the poet inadvertently admits to one of the benefits a good woman can provide: care for a husband in his dotage:

> For from Pandora comes women and female kind: of her is the deadly race and tribe of women who live amongst mortal men to their great trouble, no help meets in hateful poverty, but only in wealth ... Zeus ... made women to be an evil to mortal men, with a nature to do evil ... whoever avoids marriage and the sorrows that women cause, and will not wed, reaches deadly old age without anyone to tend his years. (590ff)

Women enjoyed precious few freedoms in Athenian society, and Solon (638–558 BC) did his best to restrict these yet further:

> He also subjected the public appearances of the women, their mourning and their festivals, to a law which abolished disorder and licence. When they went out, they were not to wear more than three garments, they were not to carry

more than an obol's worth of food or drink, nor a pannier more than a cubit high, and they were not to travel about by night unless they rode in a wagon with a lamp to light their way. He banned self-harm by mourners, and lamentations, and the bewailing of any one at the funeral ceremonies of another. The sacrifice of an ox at the grave was not permitted, nor the burial with the dead of more than three changes of clothes, nor the visiting of other tombs than those of their own family, except at the time of burial ... offenders shall be punished by the board of censors for women, because they indulge in unmanly and effeminate extravagances of sorrow when they mourn. (PLUTARCH, *Life of Solon* 20, 4; PLUTARCH, *Plutarch's Lives*, trans. Bernadotte Perrin (Cambridge, 1914))

A woman couldn't even grieve or mourn. Look at this litany of misogyny from the privileged but influential few that has echoed down the ages constantly promulgated by each period's literati:

Man is naturally superior to women and so the man should rule and the woman should be ruled. (ARISTOTLE, *Politics* 4 (1254b 13–14))

We keep *hetaerae* for pleasure, female slaves to look after us and wives to give us legitimate children and to take care of our households. (DEMOSTHENES, *Apollodorus Against Neaera* 3, 122)

A man who teaches a woman how to write should know that he is giving poison to an asp. (A school exercise attributed to the Athenian fourth-century BC playwright Menander; *Synkrisis* 1, 209–10)

I am only a woman, a thing which the world hates. (Phaedra in Euripides' *Hippolytus*)

> It's a strange thing that whereas there are antidotes, revealed
> to men by some god, against the venom of fierce serpents,
> nobody has yet discovered a remedy for a plague worse than
> fire or any viper – the plague of Woman. Such a curse our sex
> is to mankind. (Andromache in Euripides' *Andromache*, 108)

Euripides, it seems, armed his women characters with self-deprecating
and misogynistic poisoned arrows. Iphigenia, in *Iphigenia in Aulis*,
urges her father to sacrifice her to Artemis, claiming it is better for
one man to live than 10,000 women (1394).

Aristophanes chimed in with Lysistrata declaring her disappointment with her sisters: 'Calonice, it's more than I can take,
I'm boiling over with embarrassment for our sex. Men say we're slip-
pery rogues'; and Calonice, on the subject of staging a female coup
in Athens, asks: 'How could we pull off such a great and clever deed?
We women who live quietly adorning ourselves in a back-room
with gowns of lucid gold and gawdy toilets of stately silk and dainty
little slippers.' Exaggerated as it may be, the men in Aristophanes'
audience would have warmed to this condescending portrayal of the
little woman fussing over her toilette (*Lysistrata* 8–11; 42–5).

We have already noted the profound statement by Hipponax
when he declared relief first for father and then husband: 'There are
two days on which a woman pleases most: the day when someone
marries her [and he carries her into his house], and the day when her
husband carries out her dead body' (HIPPONAX, frg. 68).

Hyperides asserted: 'A woman who goes outside her house
should be old enough for people to ask whose mother she is, not
whose wife she is' (frg. 204).

But there is much worse: Semonides' seventh-century BC misogynistic satire on women is comparatively little known (even
though it competes with Hesiod in vitriol), and what attention it
has received from classicists is scant and not very complimentary.
Lines 1–94 describe ten types of women: seven are animals, two
are elements and the final woman is a bee. Of the ten, nine are
destructive: the pig, fox, dog, earth, sea, donkey, ferret, mare and
monkey. Only the woman who originates from the bee is considered

to make a good wife, and she is, by comparison, miraculous. These other apparently execrable types include:

- *the pig woman*: squatting in a dung heap, growing obese, her clothes and house filthy; no personal hygiene;
- *the yapping bitch of a dog*: the ultimate busybody; you couldn't shut her up by knocking her teeth out with a rock to the face, or with kindly persuasion;
- *donkey woman*: only threats and a cudgel will cure this stubborn woman who when it comes to love will take anyone;
- *horse woman*: the ultimate lazy mare, avoiding housework, bedecked as she is in finery and over-perfumed, bathing her grimy body two to three times a day;
- *monkey woman*: the greatest disaster Zeus ever inflicted on man – ugly, a laughing spectacle, long legs and no bum, mobility issues, the ultimate trouble.

The second part of the poem comprises a moan about the evils of women in general.

Such unhealthy leitmotifs emanated from ingrained stereotypes from the past (not least from Hesiod) and, in the future, went on to paint themselves indelibly onto the male Greek way of thinking about women. It remains one of the earliest and most vituperative texts attesting to the misogyny in ancient Greek thought.

Rome

Obviously, Greece was not alone. Other cultures and civilizations in the region and beyond were fiercely patriarchal, and their societies were run on lines that showed very clearly women's place and role within said societies and political administrations.

As Rome developed and extended its hegemony within and without the Italian peninsula through incessant warfare, expansionism and trade, so it took with it its policy and attitudes relating to women – social, political, economic and religious. Looking back over the best part of two centuries, Livy puts it well, and beyond dispute, in the debate on the repeal of the Oppian Law in 195 BC: 'Women cannot hold magistracies, priesthoods, celebrate triumphs, wear badges of office, enjoy gifts, or booty; [on the other hand,] elegance, finery, and beautiful clothes are women's emblems, this is what they love and are proud of, this is what our ancestors called women's decoration' (34, 7). What he is saying, in effect, is just let women go shopping and they'll be happy.

Around the same time, the conservative Cato the Elder, or someone with similar views, assured his contemporaries that

> Woman is a violent and uncontrolled animal, and it is pointless letting go the reins and then expect her not to be 'difficult'. You must keep her on a tight rein ... Women want total freedom or rather – as they would call it – complete licence. If you allow them to achieve complete equality with men, do you think they will be easier to live with? No way. Once they have achieved equality, they will be your masters.

This is commonly misappropriated: it is actually made up of a paraphrased speech of Cato's quoted at Livy 34 2–4. The Oppian Laws were hugely restrictive of women's behaviour and dress, and of the women who were protesting to get it repealed. They succeeded.

Looking back on Greeks, Romans and Christians, John Chrysostom, the fourth-century AD Archbishop of Constantinople, said it all in his *The Type of Women Who Ought to be Taken as Wives*: essentially he argues that a woman's role exclusively is to care for children, for her husband and for her home. God assigned a role to each of the sexes: women look after the home, men take care of public affairs, business and military matters – in other words, everything outside the home. He was echoing the words of Livy some three hundred years earlier.

Indeed, the Romans neatly precised the mantra in their pithy *domum servavit, lanam fecit* ('she cleaned the house and did the sewing'), four Latin words of wisdom that turned up on many a middle-class tombstone as the go-to epithet for the dutiful wife, summarizing her life.

On the scientific side, Pliny the Elder warns us that menstrual blood was highly toxic and had a pronounced dulling effect on all things shiny; both he and Columella expatiate at length on the supposed ill effects of the menses (PLINY, *Natural History* 7, 63–5, with 19, 176–7 and 28, 77–80; and COLUMELLA, *On Agriculture* 11, 3, 51). To Pliny (28, 77), this discharge contained limitless and outstanding powers (*post haec nullus est modus*). Natural catastrophes such as hailstorms, whirlwinds and lightning could be averted by a menstruating woman. Menstrual blood could also sour crops, wither fruits and vegetables, kill bees, drive dogs mad, dull the shine of mirrors, blunt razors, turn linens black, and rust iron and bronze. Columella (11, 3, 50) assures us that a menstruating woman could kill a seedling just by looking at it (*visu quoque suo novellos fetus necabit*). Menses had the power to destroy plants such as rue and ivy, described as having 'the highest curative power', which led a number of scholars down the years to believe a bleeding woman represented 'a latent threat to humanity'.

Plutarch dismisses the notion that women might have emotions – 'A wife should have no feelings of her own, but share her husband's seriousness and sport, his anxiety and his laughter' – and even advocated that women should not be allowed their own friends, but were to share instead their husband's mates:

> A wife shouldn't make friends of her own, but should enjoy her husband's friends with him. The gods are the first and most important friends and so it is right for a wife to worship and to know only the gods that her husband believes in, and to shut the front door tight upon all strange rituals and outlandish superstitions. No god likes stealthy and secret rites performed by a woman. (*Moralia: Advice to Bride and Groom* 19)

Success in the marriage bed comes with a nice juicy quince: 'Solon ordered that the bride should nibble a quince before getting into bed, intimating, presumably, that the delight from lips and speech should be harmonious and pleasant at the outset' (*Moralia* 1).

Indeed, much of Plutarch's marriage guidance centres around the Greek custom of keeping their women socially ostracized and confined to the domestic setting, where, even there, they might be housed in separate quarters for much of the time; he found a precedent in Egyptian society: 'The women of Egypt, by custom, were not allowed to wear shoes, so that they would stay at home all day; and most women, if you take from them gold-embroidered shoes, bracelets, anklets, purple, and pearls, do stay indoors' (*Moralia* 30).

Theano, when putting her cloak on, exposed her arm. Somebody exclaimed, 'What a lovely arm.' 'But not for the public,' she responded. Not only the arm of the virtuous woman, but her speech as well, ought to be not for the public, and she ought to be modest and guarded about saying anything in the earshot of outsiders, since it is an exposure of herself; for in her talk can be seen her feelings, character, and disposition. (*Moralia* 31)

There is a lesson to be learned from the animal world when we often dress cautiously when in the presence of elephants due to their aversion to vivid colours; we don't bang drums near tigers because they go mad at the noise; women should do the same if certain things annoy their husbands:

Those who have to go near elephants do not put on bright clothes, nor do those who go near bulls wear red because they are furious by these colours; and tigers, they say, when surrounded by the noise of banging drums go completely mad and tear themselves to pieces. Since, then, the same applies to men where some are unable to tolerate scarlet and purple clothes, while others are irritated by cymbals and drums, how hard can it be for women to refrain from such things, and not upset or irritate their husbands, but live with them in constant kindness? (*Moralia* 45)

31

Domestic and Sexual Abuse

Whenever a Roman father exercised his right to expose his unwanted infant daughters, he invoked the traditional power invested in the *pater familias* – the head of the family – the Law of Life and Death: *ius vitae necisque*. Exposure allowed a hard-up family to rid itself of an extra mouth to feed and to eliminate the dowry liability that daughters brought to the family on marriage. Infant disability also opened the door to exposure, while the *Twelve Tables* took things a stage further when one of the laws decreed that a father should raise all his sons, but only one daughter. A man could kill or thrash his wife for having a drink or for walking outdoors with her face uncovered, and a cuckolded husband was entitled to kill his unfaithful wife and her lover if found *in flagrante*.

Exposure assumed a degree of domestic violence – physically against the child and psychologically against the mother. Nevertheless, Roman law later criminalized domestic abuse by a husband towards his wife. Cato the Elder said that the man who struck his wife or child laid violent hands on the holiest of holy things. He also thought it a better thing to be a good husband than a good senator (PLUTARCH, *Cato the Elder* 20, 2). Wife-beating thus became grounds for divorce or other legal action against the husband.

Counselling for alcohol abuse or wife-battering was doubtless unavailable but marriage guidance and anger management, there was. The temple of Juno Viriplaca, or 'husband appeaser', on the Palatine Hill offered reconciliation between squabbling couples; a Roman relationship counselling service, or Relate.

A marriage contract of 13 BC survives from Egypt and, although it probably owes as much to Egyptian legislation as it does to

Woodcut illustration of Poppaea Sabina and Nero, from a German translation
of Boccaccio's *De mulieribus claris* (On Famous Women) (*c.* 1474).

Roman, it is, nevertheless, interesting because domestic violence features as one of the seemingly routine things that the husband will promise not to commit.

> To Protarchus from Thermion daughter of Apion, with her guardian Apollonius son of Chaereas, and from Apollonius son of Ptolemaeus. Thermion and Apollonius son of Ptolemaeus agree that they have come together to share a common life, and the said Apollonius son of Ptolemaeus acknowledges that he has received from Thermion by hand from the house a dowry of a pair of gold earrings weighing 3 quarters and silver drachmas; and from now Apollonius son of Ptolemaeus shall furnish to Thennion as his wedded wife all necessaries and clothing in proportion to his means and shall not ill-treat her nor cast her out nor insult her nor bring in another wife, or he shall straightway forfeit the dowry increased by half, with right of execution upon

both the person of Apollonius son of Ptolemaeus and all
his property as if by legal decision, and Thermion shall fulfil
her duties towards her husband and their common life and
shall not absent herself from the house for a night or a day
without the consent of Apollonius son of Ptolemaeus nor
dishonour nor injure their common home nor consort with
another man, or she again if guilty of any of these actions
shall, after trial, be deprived of the dowry, and in addition
the transgressing party shall be liable to the prescribed fine.
The 17th year of Caesar, Pharmouthi 20 [the eighth month
of the ancient Egyptian and Coptic calendars].

The Bona Dea (The Good Goddess) rites have their mythical
roots in domestic violence, provoked ominously by a woman taking
a drink. Although Bona Dea was celebrated by men and women
alike, in the domestic rite, which took place on 3 December, all
males were banished, even male animals and pictures or statues of
males. Only Roman matrons (*matronae*) and the Vestal Virgins were
present; the Vestals brought in Bona Dea's image from her temple
and a meal of sow's entrails was eaten – sacrificed to her on behalf
of the Roman people – alongside sacrificial wine. The fun (*ludere*)
lasted all night, with female musicians, games and wine, euphemistically called 'milk', from a 'honey jar'. This was not a weak attempt
to conceal clandestine drinking; rather, it came about when Faunus,
married to the Good Goddess, caught her drinking surreptitiously
and beat her to death with a myrtle branch. Myrtle was also associated with both Aphrodite and sex, and so myrtle was alien to the
rites and banned. The *matronae* refrained from sexual relations in the
run-up to the festival. According to Cicero, any man caught observing the rites could be punished by blinding (*De haruspicum responsis*
17, 37; 18, 38). So, a bit of a girl's night, but there was a very serious
side to it – from both a religious and a political view.

Bona Dea was jealously protected by its followers, so when the
high-profile rites of 62 BC were infiltrated by an equally high-profile
man, the ensuing scandal was immense, not least because Caesar's
mother, Aurelia Cotta (a paragon of feminine virtue), Pompeia (his

wife), his sister, Julia, and the Vestals were all present. According to Juvenal, any sexual propriety that remained in Rome evaporated that night: Publius Clodius Pulcher sacreligiously gatecrashed the rites that were being held *chez* Caesar, that year's *pontifex maximus* (high priest). The scandal led to Caesar divorcing Pompeia: she was implicated by her very presence, and Caesar's wife cannot be under suspicion.

The quintessentials of Roman womanhood can be found in the concept of *matrona*: the Roman wife and woman of the household. The qualities and virtues of the matrona include *pudicitia* (sexual propriety, modesty, virtuousness, loyalty, strength of character and fortitude), *pietas* (pious devotion) towards the family, a

Ancient Greek *pelike*,
4th century BC, depicting a
woman acrobat shooting an arrow
with her feet.

one-man-woman (*univira*) and unquestioned devotion to her children. A girl took on these responsibilities the minute she arrived at her husband's house during her wedding.

We have another casual reference to domestic violence: causes of miscarriage can be found in the Hippocratic Corpus and include domestic violence: carrying too heavy a weight, being beaten up, jumping up into the air (an occupational hazard for professional acrobats and dancers), lack of food and fainting, fear, loud shouting, flatulence and too much drink were all triggers for miscarriage.

When it comes to domestic abuse, Nero is probably the worst of the emperors. He was alleged to have arranged for his first wife (and stepsister) Claudia Octavia to be murdered, after he had subjected her to torture and incarceration (TACITUS, *Annals* 16, 6). Nero then kicked Poppaea Sabina, his second wife, to death when she was heavily pregnant:

> [Nero] loved Poppaea dearly; he married her twelve days after his divorce from Octavia, yet he killed her too by kicking her when she was pregnant and ill. She had rebuked him for coming home late from the races. He had a daughter by her, Claudia Augusta, but lost her when she was still a baby.
> (SUETONIUS, *Nero* 35, 3)

Poppaea's death (murder?) served only to exacerbate Nero's simmering psychotic and unbalanced behaviour. He yearned for Poppaea so much that he kidnapped and debauched a woman who was unfortunate enough to resemble her; later he had a boy called Sporus castrated (since he, too, looked like Poppaea) and proceeded to use him like a wife. In time, though already 'married' to the freedman Pythagoras, he bigamistically 'married' Sporus in Greece; Tigellinus gave the eunuch away; Nero contributed a dowry and organized a lavish wedding ceremony. The wedding to Pythagoras in AD 64 had also been celebrated in full regalia with Nero wearing bridal veil, with dowry, marriage bed and torches all on public view. According to Tacitus (*Annals* 14, 60–64). Nero now shared the marriage bed with two men: Pythagoras played the role of husband, and

Sporus that of wife. The latter was called 'lady', 'queen' and 'mistress'. If Commodus had read his Suetonius he would have found the perfect role model in Nero.

COMMODUS KILLED HIS cousin and his sister. To give some idea of his unspeakable sadism and his whimsical megalomania, here is what the *Historia Augusta* says of him:

Even as a child he was gluttonous and lewd. While a young- ster, he disgraced every class of men in his company and was shamed in turn by them. If anyone ridiculed him he threw them to the wild beasts. One man, who had merely read the book by Tranquillus on the life of Caligula, he com- manded to be cast to the wild animals, because Caligula and he shared the same birthday. He performed a laparotomy on one corpulent man causing his intestines to gush out. Other men he dubbed one-eyed or one-footed, after he himself had gauged out one of their eyes or cut off one of their feet. Among his people were men he named after the genitalia of both sexes, whom he liked to kiss. He frequently mixed human excrement with the most expensive foods, and would taste it . . . he displayed two misshapen hunchbacks on a silver platter after smearing them with mustard. He would enter the temples of the gods defiled with adulteries and human blood. He even aped a surgeon, going so far as to bleed men to death with scalpels.

And so in the light of this it comes as no surprise that he went on to have his sister, Lucilla, the eldest of four, slain while exiled on Capri. Lucilla had made the mistake of conspiring in her broth- er's assassination with the help of two men alleged to have been her lovers, Marcus Ummidius Quadratus Annianus (the consul of 167, also her first cousin) and Appius Claudius Quintianus. They botched the job and were seized by the emperor's bodyguard and subsequently executed.

His mistress, Marcia, encouraged Commodus to murder a number of potential enemies including his cousin Annia Fundania Faustina, who met her end in AD 192. Marcia, like everyone else, was getting tired of all this and so it was with utter horror that when she discovered a list of people Commodus intended to execute she saw her own name on it. Dio (73, 22) tells us that with two co-conspirators Marcia 'plotted to assassinate the emperor. On 31 December, Marcia poisoned Commodus' food, but he vomited up the poison, so the conspirators sent his wrestling partner Narcissus to strangle him in his bath.'

Social breathalysing, automatic and harsh punishment and financial penalties and death awaited some women who had had a drink. Egnatius Mecenius clubbed his wife to death for drinking:

> At Rome [in the early days of the monarchy after 753 BC] it was illegal for women to drink wine ... the wife of Egnatius Mecenius was killed by her husband with a club, because she had drunk some wine. He was declared innocent of the murder by Romulus [founder of Rome]. Historian Fabius Pictor [254 BC–190], in his *Annals*, has stated that a woman was starved to death by her family for opening a purse in which the keys of the wine-cellar were kept; and Cato the Elder tells us that it was customary for male relatives to kiss the females of the family in order to establish if they smelt of *temetum*, wine, hence our word *temulentia*, meaning inebriation. Judge Cn. Domitius once ruled that a woman appeared to him to have drunk more wine than was good for her, and without her husband knowing, so he relieved her of her dowry. (VALERIUS MAXIMUS, *Memorable Words and Deeds* 6, 3, 9)

Aspasia Annia Regilla was a rich, aristocratic and powerful woman who was distantly related to several Roman emperors and empresses. She was the wife of the prominent Greek Herodes Atticus. Regilla was kicked to death by one of Atticus' freedmen called Alcimedon, who struck her repeatedly in the stomach.

According to Philostratus, Appius Annius Atilius Bradua brought charges in Rome against his brother-in-law, alleging that Herodes Atticus was the murderer.

The frequency with which physical violence features in Roman love poetry might suggest that it was not uncommon; in the late Republic Catullus hates and at the same time loves his woman (*Carmen* 85) – *odi et amo*.

At the dawn of empire Propertius outlines the serious consequences of his mistress's infidelity: 'But you will not get away: you should really die with me; the blood of both of us will drip from the same sword, the murder may well disgrace me but however much a disgrace it is, you are going to die anyway' (2, 8). Here he ambivalently rejects physical violence as being beneath him, but in doing so gives us what sounds like a characteristic repertoire of physical abuse:

> Is it true Cynthia that throughout all Rome you have a reputation for living a life of shame? Do I deserve this? You faithless woman, I will punish you ... I won't tear the clothes from your duplicitous limbs, nor will my anger break down the doors you barricade against me; I would not dare in my anger to tear your plaited hair, nor bruise you with a cruel punch. Let some boor look for fights as demeaning as this. (2, 5, 21–6)

Near contemporary Tibullus describes a scene of marital discord and domestic violence between a farmer and his wife:

> The countryman drives home from the wood half-drunk half-sober, with wife and children in his cart, but then they evoke love's war, and the woman regrets her torn hair and the broken-down doors. The battered woman weeps for her tender cheeks, but the victor weeps too that his hands were so strong in his mad rage ... enough to have torn the thin clothes from her body, enough to have dishevelled her hair, enough to have made her cry. (1, 10, 51–8)

Ovid echoes this, although there is a hint that he derives some perverse pleasure from the violence:

> Come on, if you're really friends, tie up these hands which, with unholy anger have wounded a mistress . . . I have broken the most religious ties, both to my parents and the gods: I tore (o god) her finely braided hair, how charming she looked in her disarray . . . with streaming cheeks, and with dishevelled hair. Such lips were formed for kinder words than these, wounds made by lovers' furious ecstasies. Though like a torrent I was hurried on, a slave to passion which I could not shun, I might have only pierced her tender ear with threatening language, such as virgins fear. Fear having chilled the current of her blood, she pale as Parian marble statue stood.
>
> Tears, which suspense did for a while restrain, gushed forth, and down her cheeks the deluge ran . . . and three times did she fight back against me the criminal. (*Amores* 1, 7)

We find evidence for physical abuse in a woman's funerary inscription for Margarita, her dog – here the statement that she had never been assaulted may indicate that domestic violence was a routine part of life for others: '[I was] never accustomed to being held in heavy chains or to suffer savage beatings to my snow-white body' (*CIL* 6, 29896).

This papyrus describing an indictment by a Christian wife against her husband for various offences reveals some disturbing details:

> For seven whole days he shut up his own slaves and mine with my foster-daughters and his agent and son in his cellars, having abused his slaves and my slave Zoe and beat them half to death, and he set fire to my foster-daughters, having stripped them naked, which is against the law. (*Oxyrhynchus Papyri* 6, 903)

Episodes of physical violence are sometimes evident in skeletal remains. In 2002, in excavations in the Collatina necropolis in Rome, the skull of a fifty-plus-year-old woman exhibited a number of traumatic injuries suggestive of physical abuse throughout her life.

Of course, violence against women was not confined to the home. When the Romans sacked a city, the booty became the property of the victorious army; that booty included the women and girls of the town, so we frequently find that they were raped or sold into slavery.

The ferocious sack of Cremona by Antonius Primus in AD 69 was notorious for the systematic rape and butchering of women, men and the elderly on a prodigious scale:

> Forty thousand soldiers burst into Cremona with even more army suppliers and camp followers who were further corrupted by lust and savagery. Age and dignity provided no protection as they interchanged rape with slaughter and slaughter with rape. Old men and aging women – useless as booty – were dragged into the 'fun'; any grown-up girl or fine-looking man who came along was torn apart at the violent hands of the rapists. (TACITUS, *Histories* 3, 32–4)

In the 1930s, Eric Birley found two skeletons under the floor of a building during his excavations of Housesteads Roman Fort, on Hadrian's Wall. This is possibly one of the earliest instances recorded of domestic violence and murder in Britain. One skeleton was a man with the tip of a knife in his ribs, and the other was probably a woman. They had been buried in the clay floor beneath a rear room of what was likely an inn or brothel, and then concealed under a clean layer of clay.

More mystery surrounds the excavations in the armoury of the Pompeii gladiatorial barracks, which unearthed eighteen skeletons in two rooms, presumably the skeletons of gladiators; but they were not alone. The bones of a woman wearing gold and an emerald studded necklace were also found; she clearly was not there just to serve the rations . . .

32

On Being a Left-Hander, and Toilet Etiquette

For those of us who have had to endure a life burdened with the stigma of being a cuddy wifter and the dyspraxia that left-handedness can bring, this chapter will be of special interest. But how did such an affliction begin?

We have looked at aspects of superstition earlier, but this particular one deserves special attention. The Roman superstition that the left-hand side of things was not good, indeed that it signified evil, while the right-hand side represented good, can be demonstrated by our word 'sinister', which derives from the Latin word meaning 'on the left side'. On the other hand, the corresponding word for 'right' is *dexter*, which obviously suggests dexterity – a good thing. The French word for left is *gauche*, which has connotations when used in English of gaucheness or clumsiness.

It all goes back to the Indo-Europeans, who between about 9,000 and 6,000 years ago spread into Europe from Asia. According to Anatoly Liberman, author of *Word Origins . . . And How We Know Them* and *An Analytic Dictionary of English Etymology: An Introduction*, the Indo-Europeans believed

> prayers should be addressed to the sun as it rose in the east thus placing the left hand at the north while making a prayer; and the direction north represented evil because it was thought to be the location of the Indo-European underworld, or 'kingdom of the dead.' Over time the left-hand side came to be seen as evil, rather than the direction north.

The Romans shared this left-leaning superstition with other descendants of the Indo-Europeans, including the ancient Greeks, Germans and Celts. It led to all sorts of irrational beliefs and practices:

- The Latin word *sinister* was used in Roman augury, where an unfavourable omen was likely if birds flew to the left.
- Left-handed people were considered undependable.
- Noble Romans hired 'footmen' to enter a house before them using their right foot.

Which brings us on to toilet hygiene. Philippe Charlier and others, in their 2012 article 'Toilet Hygiene in the Classical Era' in the *British Medical Journal*, tell that 'The Romans had two primary ways to clean themselves post-bathroom break. Option one? A tool called a *tersorium*, which was used to clean the buttocks after defecation.' We are invited to

Imagine a loofah, but made of fresh sea sponge, attached to a wooden rod – similar to back-washers sold in drugstores today. After using the stick to aim and the sponge to wipe, the person would [hopefully] dunk the sponge in a bucket full of water or vinegar to clean it off for the next user. While water wouldn't do much in terms of sterilization by modern standards, vinegar would prove much more – if not totally – effective.

Tersoria were quite common in Roman cities throughout the Roman Empire. For example, in 1972 soiled public-use sponges were found in a Roman sewer in Eboracum (present-day York). Waste water from the nearby baths and latrines would have been washed away down there. It extended for 44 metres (144 ft) and was built high enough to accommodate slaves crawling inside to clean it out. Also found were side gullies, sluices and manhole covers. When sewage found there was analysed it showed the residents of York to have been riddled with worms and bowel parasites. The discovery of spicules from these marine sponges confirms what we already knew from literary evidence: that bathers in the numerous bath houses used sponges provided for general and not individual, personal use.

But, as with modern-day toilet paper, there were times when the trusty *tersorium* was simply not available, or they were simply too expensive. In that case, you had no option but to depend on one of the most readily available – and free – commodities in the world: discarded pottery. Most common vessels, from amphorae holding wine or oil to small lamps, were made of clay; thus, Greco-Roman dumps, as we have seen, were full of pottery shards – or *pessoi* (Greek for "pebbles").'

Considerable care was needed in your choice of shard: you didn't just pick up any fragment and start wiping. In the Athenian agora, archaeologists found *pessoi* that had been 're-cut from old broken ceramics to give smooth angles that would minimize anal trauma', according to Charlier et al. They discuss a stunning wine cup, or *kylix*, that shows 'a man, semi-squatting with his clothing raised'. On this sixth-century BC vessel, a man balances himself with a cane in his right hand while 'wiping his buttocks using a pessos with his left hand'.

Our sinister flirtation with shards does not end there; it was common practice among the Greeks when they exiled their political opponents to scratch the names of the soon to be exiles on shards, or *ostraca* – hence our word 'ostracize'.

33
Men and Boys

We might be intrigued to know more about the ancient world's opinions on hair, and the lack thereof. To start, dying your hair got you nowhere in alpha-male Sparta:

> A Cean, an old man, conceited and ashamed of his age came to Sparta; this is why he tried to conceal the grayness of his hair by dying it. Coming before the Lacedemonians he declared his business. But Archidamus, King of the Lacedemonians stood up and declared, 'What truth, said he, can this man speak, who does not only lie in his heart, but in his hair?' So he rejected him. (AELIAN, *Miscellaneous History* 7, 20)

The headline act? Smashing your skull and covering it with boiling tar:

> There are men at the theatre who offer a frequent and diverting spectacle to the public: namely, of the artificially, not of the naturally bald, for he goes to his barber many times a day, and appears before the public for the very purpose of showing the strength of his head, to which no fearful thing is fearful, for he exposes it to boiling tar, and to head-butts from a trained ram ... and to the Megarian vases which shatter on his noble cranium. His skull is duly lacerated, and not one of these displays fails to make the audience shudder. (SYNESIUS, *A Eulogy on Baldness* 13)

An exhibition of sword-swallowing was no less riveting:

At Athens, recently, in front of the Painted Porch, I saw a juggler swallow a sharp-edged cavalry sword complete with its lethal blade, and later I saw the same bloke, spurred on by a small donation, ingest a spear, sharp end downwards, right into his stomach. Suddenly a beautiful boy clambered up the wooden bit of the inverted weapon and danced a dance, twisting and turning, as if he'd no muscle or spine, astounding everyone there. (APULEIUS, *Metamorphoses* 1, 4)

Pelops

Pelops got off to a bad start in life when his father, Tantalus, chopped him up and made a stew for the gods from the body parts; only a distracted Demeter, grieving over Persephone, had the misfortune to have a taste – his shoulder. Things picked up, though, when the Fates restored the boy, replacing the missing shoulder with a newly constructed prosthesis in ivory. Poseidon fell in love with him and taught him to drive the divine winged chariot. Later, however, Pelops only had eyes for Hippodamia and wished for her hand in marriage; but that was a problem: her father, King Oenomaus, was understandably worried about a prophecy that predicted he would be killed by his son-in-law. As a consequence, the king had already killed eighteen suitors after beating each of them in a chariot race; he stuck their heads on the wooden columns around his palace as trophies. Pelops was naturally quite concerned when he saw this, so he called up Poseidon, reminding him of their love – 'Aphrodite's sweet gifts'. Poseidon helped by magicking up a chariot drawn by untamed winged horses (PINDAR, *First Olympian Ode* 71; CICERO, *Tusculanae Disputationes* 2,27, 67).

Things got complicated, and decidedly messy, when a less-than-confident Pelops, on the eve of the race, convinced Oenomaus' charioteer, Myrtilus, to help him win. The prize for the deception was half of Oenomaus' kingdom and the first night of marriage in bed with Hippodamia. Myrtilus replaced the bronze linchpins attaching the wheels to the axle with ones made of bees-wax, and just when Oenomaus was catching up to Pelops and getting ready to kill him, the wheels flew off; Myrtilus nevertheless survived, but Oenomaus was dragged to death by his horses. Pelops murdered Myrtilus by throwing him off a cliff into the sea after he had attempted to rape Hippodamia.

In his youth, King Laius of Thebes abducted and violated Chrysippus, the son of friend and host Pelops, king of Pisa in the Peloponnesus, and took him back to Thebes; this is the subject of one of the lost tragedies of Euripides, *Chrysippus*. Laius, who was Chrysippus' tutor, never recovered from this violation of the laws of hospitality; he was advised by the oracle never to have a son but, one night while drunk, he had sex with his wife, Jocasta, who (regrettably for all) later gave birth to Oedipus – the rest is ancient history . . .

Laddism

Posh Boys' Antics, Pre-dating the Oxford University Bullingdon Club

I hear, gentlemen of the jury, that a certain Bacchius, who was executed by your court, and Aristocrates, the man with the bad eyes, and others of this sort, and Conon, the man here, were friends as young men and had the nickname 'Triballoi'. These men would regularly gather offerings to Hecate and also pigs' testicles, the ones used for purification when there is going to be a public meeting, and dine on them every time they got together, and they swore oaths and perjured themselves as casually as can be. (DEMOSTHENES, *Against Conon* 14, 39)

Living in a Tub

Diogenes the Cynic won fame by living in terra cotta tub, but he was not alone: 'Because of a housing shortage, the people who swarmed into Athens from the countryside during the Peloponnesian war lived in jars and caves' (SCHOLION TO ARISTOPHANES, *Knights* 792).

Jean-Léon Gérôme, *Diogenes*, 1860, oil on canvas. The Greek philosopher Diogenes
(404–323 BC) is pictured here sitting in his 'home', the earthenware tub, in the
Metroon, Athens, lighting the lamp in daylight by which he was fruitlessly
searching for an honest man. His companions were dogs that also served as
emblems of his 'Cynic' (Greek: *kynikos*, dog-like) philosophy, which promoted an
austere existence.

The Benefits of a Big Belly or a Fat Arse

'It is best for a boxer to have a small belly as this permits him
to move quickly and breathe easily. However, a big belly has
the advantage of impeding your opponent when he is trying
to punch you.' (PHILOSTRATUS, *The Gymnast* 34)

Or take, Katomochanos, 'with an arse so flabby you could sling it
over your shoulder' (HIPPONAX, frg. 28).

Pisspaste

A dazzling smile can be a piece of piss: before the days of safe-to-use
tooth whitener, Catullus, the love poet, put a rival's dazzling smile
down to the Spanish custom of tooth brushing with urine from the
latrinae publicae – a product usually reserved for laundry (39).

Disrespecting the King's Wife's Vagina, and a Farting Philenus

Sotades of Maroneia, author of a lost version of the *Iliad* in a metre of his own invention, died due to his lack of tact towards royalty and was dumped in the sea in a leaden urn for his trouble. Famously, he had criticized Ptolemy Philadelphus for marrying Arsinoe, his own sister, saying 'he is pushing his prick into an unearthly hole' (frg. 1). Just as tactless was his description of a farting Philenus, who was the father of Theodorus the flute-player: 'And he, opening the door which leads from his arse, sent forth vain thunder from a leafy cave, Such as a mighty ploughing ox might emit' (ATHENAEUS, *Philosophers at Dinner* 621a).

Biting the Snake that Bites You

'A venomous snake was no match for Pythagoras. When one bit him he bit it back and killed it.' (ARISTOTLE, frg. 191)

Betting on the Chariots Was Certainly No Fun for Cats

Drown the cat, and stick three metal sheets, one in its anus, and one in its throat; and write the formula [of the magic curse] on a clean sheet of papyrus, with cinnabar [ink], and then the names of the chariots and charioteers and the horses. Wind this around the body of the cat and bury it. (*Greek Magical Papyri* 3, 15).

The Best Sort of Hair Cut

'A loquacious barber asked King Archelaus of Sparta how he'd like his hair cut. He replied "in silence".' (PLUTARCH, *Sayings of Kings and Commanders* 177a)

The Modern Man in Inaction

Iberia, it seems, was not the ideal place for a woman to go into labour: Strabo the geographer reports that when a Spanish woman is in labour, her husband lies in bed and *she* looks after *him* (*Geography* 3, 4, 17).

Diodorus Siculus says much the same thing of Corsica, where the mother and baby experience leaves a lot to be desired: mother and baby are more or less ignored and all attention focuses on the father. He falls down in agony and goes into a phantom labour for a number of agonizingly painful days (*The Library* 5, 14).

Sling for Your Supper in the Balearics

Recruits are to be taught the art of throwing stones both with the hand and sling. The inhabitants of the Balearic Islands are said to have been the inventors of slings, and to have managed them with surprising dexterity, owing to how they bring up their children. The children were not allowed to have their food by their mothers till they had first struck it with their sling. (VEGETIUS, *Military Affairs* 1, 16)

A Wine-Wasting Tree Hugger and a Ban on Trousers

Gaius Sallustius Crispus Passienus, great grandnephew of Sallust the historian and stepfather to Nero, was a wine-wasting tree hugger: 'He loved a very ancient tree in the grove of Diana in Tusculum. He would often kiss and hug it, would sleep under it and pour wine around it' (PLINY, *Natural History* 16, 242).

Vulgar trousers: the emperor Honorius forbade the wearing of trousers in Rome in AD 397; trousers were considered barbaric.

Gay Julius Caesar?

We usually associate Julius Caesar with assassination, new calendars, the scourge of the Gauls and incursions into obscure, cold, wet and windy islands on the northwest of the Roman 'empire'. He is usually thought of as the archetypal alpha male – but he may well not have been. There were many more strings to the man's bow, as these extracts demonstrate.

Homosexuality among the political and military elite was nothing new and has one of its more celebrated exponents in Julius Caesar. Caesar was emulated by Tiberius, Caligula, Nero and Galba, among others. According to Suetonius (*Caesar*, 49), while staying at the Bithynian court of Nicomedes IV, 'he submitted to the king's pleasure'. It was time well spent, however, as Nicomedes later bequeathed his entire kingdom to Rome.

Nevertheless, the episode continued to haunt Caesar with repeated innuendo and political slur: to Licinius Calvus Bithynia was 'Caesar's buggerer'; to Curio Caesar was the 'queen's concubine' and refers to the 'whorehouse of Nicomedes' and the 'Bithynian brothel'; to Marcus Brutus, Caesar was queen to Pompey's king. Gaius Memmius describes him as cupbearer to Nicomedes along with other catamites. Cicero reminded Caesar in court – while he was defending Nysa, Nicomedes' daughter – that 'it is well known what he gave you and what you gave him.' Even his soldiers had a good laugh over the rumours, giving vent to a ribald marching song during the Gallic campaign: 'Caesar had his way with Gaul; Nicomedes had his way with Caesar; behold now Caesar, conqueror of Gaul, in triumph, Not so Nicomedes, conqueror of Caesar.' When he was granted the provinces of Gaul and Illyria by the senate, he responded that he would be 'mounting on their heads', that is, committing oral rape on the enemy, and had to suffer the quip that that would be rather difficult for a woman to perform. Caesar quicky responded that Semiramis and the Amazons were examples of women combatants successful in war.

Innuendo apart, apparently, he was a great dictator (no pun) and could keep seven scribes busy at any one time; he could even dictate letters to two or more scribes at the same time while on horseback (PLUTARCH, *Life of Julius Caesar* 17; PLINY, *Natural History* 71).

When Cato the Younger invited Caesar to divulge the contents of a letter he was surreptitiously reading in the senate (thinking it would incriminate him in the Catilinarian conspiracy) it turned out to be a spicy love letter sent to him by Cato's half-sister (PLUTARCH, *Life of Brutus* 5; *Life of Cato the Younger* 24). Own goal?

Don't Look Back

Caesar could give as good as he got: when Pompey was showing off a facial wound he had received when fighting for Caesar, the latter retorted, 'You should never look back when you're running away' (QUINTILIAN, *Education of the Orator* 6, 3, 75).

The Hubristic Publius Claudius Pulcher and the Chickens

In 249 the Romans led by the consuls Publius Claudius Pulcher and Lucius Junius Pullus laid siege to Lilybaeum ... but to no avail. Hannibal broke the siege by day and replenished the garrison by night. Claudius attacked Drepana and ordered his fleet to leave the harbour for the open sea: the result was a Roman naval calamity of massive proportions with multiple collisions and total confusion. Pullus committed suicide rather than return to Rome in disgrace. Cicero tells us in his *De natura deorum* (2, 7) that the defeat was due to Claudius' disrespect for the pre-battle auspices. The sacred chickens refused to eat the grain – a terrible omen that indicated the gods clearly were not in favour of a battle. In a foolish bid to calm his frightened crew, Claudius unceremoniously threw the chickens overboard, pronouncing, 'Let them drink, since they won't eat' (*bibant, quoniam esse nolunt*). The arrogant and hubristic Claudius survived the battle but not the aftermath: he returned to Rome in disgrace and was charged with treason – not for naval ineptitude, but for sacrilege. For killing the chickens, he was exiled.

HISTORY
AND
ETHNOGRAPHY

34

Aethiopians and Black People

South of the grain-rich province of Roman Egypt was what was to become known by the Romans as Aethiopia, where lived the Aethiopians outside the southern border (*limes*) of the Roman Empire in what approximates to modern Sudan. In the ancient world, they were among the tallest of all the races known to Rome; they were slender and athletic, as indeed some Ethiopians still are to this day. The Romans clearly respected the Aethiopians and their military prowess, since they were often deployed as special forces – archers wielding 2-metre (6 ft) bows, spears and clubs. When their quivers were spent of arrows, they resorted to clubbing their foes to death. Added terror came with their predilection for wearing the skins of wild animals such as lions and leopards, and the lurid war paint smeared on their faces and bodies. Diodorus (3, 8) adds to the characteristic black skin and wooly hair that they arm their women and allow them to fight and 'most observe the custom of wearing a bronze ring in their lip'. The word 'Aethiopian' came to mean to the Romans any person with black skin.

However, racism reared its ugly head when the author of *Physiognomonics*, once thought to be by Aristotle, wrote that 'Those who are too black are cowards, like for the instance, the Egyptians and Ethiopians.' Marcus Manilius, the Syrian poet and astrologer, was no less racist when in AD 35 he said in his five-volume *Astronomicon*: 'The Ethiopians stain the world and depict a race of men steeped in darkness.'

Jan van Bijlert, *Caspar*, *c.* 1640–50, oil on panel.

Physiognomics

By Aristotle's time, physiognomics had developed as an art in its own right with its particular expert practitioners, for example Zopyrus. Antigonus the paradoxographer adds for us:

> 114(a) He derives character from some features as follows: those who have a large forehead are sluggish, while those with a small one are agile – adding that it is for the most part in each case; those who have broad foreheads are excitable. (b) Level eyebrows are indicative of a gentle nature; those bent towards the nose, a harsh; towards the temples, a mocking and ironic. (c) If the corner of the eye is fleshy, it indicates a dishonest nature; middling ears are indicative of the finest character, but those which are large and protruding, of foolish talk and prattling.

Extant works post-Aristotle include Polemo of Laodicea, *de Physiognomonia* (second century AD), in Greek; Adamantius the Sophist, *Physiognomonica* (fourth century), in Greek, and the anonymous Latin *de Physiognomonia* (*c.* fourth century). Pythagoras – who some believe to be the father of physiognomics – is believed to have turned down Cylon as a prospective follower because the philosopher thought he didn't look quite right.

Physiognomics had connections to not only medicine but magic and divination. Caspar was one of the Three Wise Men, along with Melchior and Balthazar, mentioned in Matthew 2:1–9. A portrait of Caspar by Jan van Bijlert was painted around 1640. Caspar is important to us not just because he and his compatriots brought incense along the Spice Road, an expensive and lucrative commodity that was much in demand in Rome and the west, but, as a man of colour, he is representative of the many people of colour with whom the Romans came into contact. The Romans, for the most part, were unconcerned about anything like our modern notions of race or ethnicity: skin colour or physical appearance were of little consequence. People who looked different from the typical

Mediterranean were not excluded from any profession or discriminated against, and there are no records of stigmas or biases against 'mixed race' relationships.

Frank Snowden in his *Blacks in Antiquity: Ethiopians in the Greco-Roman Experience* summarizes it well:

> The ancients did not fall into the error of biological racism; black skin color was not a sign of inferiority. Greeks and Romans did not establish color as an obstacle to integration in society. An ancient society was one that for all its faults and failures never made color the basis for judging a man.

'Washing the Ethiopian White' is one of Aesop's Fables and speaks to the impossibility of changing character. Lucian makes an early allusion to the fable, using a phrase proverbially in his epigram 'Against an Ignoramus': 'You wash the Ethiopian in vain; why not give up the task? You will never manage to turn black night into day.'

35

Sparta and the Spartan Stasi

From about 900 BC, the city-state of Sparta was a thorn in the side of the rest of Greece. It was a fiercely independent and powerful military opponent of Athens, not least during the Peloponnesian War (431–404 BC).

Critias records how the Spartans did not trust their slaves and confiscated the shield handles of all the slaves when they were at home on leave (frg. 37). Special heavy-duty locks were produced for their doors to forestall any revolt. Plutarch in the *Life of Lycurgus* adds that the helots (Spartan slaves) were used as guinea pigs when they were brought into the mess halls of Spartan soldiers to demonstrate what it was like to be drunk (28). They were humiliated and ridiculed by being forced to dance and sing in a silly manner. Moreover, they were prey to the Spartan secret police (*krypteia*), the state's death squads. Plutarch goes on:

> This secret service worked like this. The magistrates from time to time sent out into the country at large the most discreet of the young warriors, equipped only with daggers and essential supplies. In the day time they scattered into obscure and remote places, where they hid themselves and lay quiet; but in the night they came down into the highways and killed every Helot whom they caught. Often, too, they actually crossed over the fields where Helots were working and slew the strongest and best of them. So, too, Thucydides [4, 80] tells us that the Spartans put wreaths on the heads of those Helots who had been judged by them to be the bravest as part of their emancipation, and led them round

the temples of the gods in procession. Soon after they all disappeared, more than two thousand of them.

But it wasn't just the helots who suffered terribly at the hands of these special forces. Spartan boys, according to Plutarch in the *Ancient Customs of the Spartans,*

> were lashed with whips during the entire day at the altar of Artemis Orthia, frequently to the point of death, and they bravely endured this, cheerful and proud, challenging one another as to which one of them could endure being beaten the longest and take the most blows. And the one who was victorious was held in special regard. This competition is called 'The Flagellation', and it takes place each year. (239d)

What is said in the *syssitia* stays in the *syssitia*: 'To each one of those who comes in to the public meals the eldest man says, as he points to the doors, "Through these no word goes out"' (PLUTARCH, *Ancient Customs of the Spartans* 236f). The *syssitia* was communal eating in messes, analogous to the symposium system. The word 'xenophobe' could have been coined for the Spartans:

> It was not allowed them [Spartans] to go abroad, so that they should have nothing to do with foreign behaviour and rowdy ways of living. Lycurgus also introduced the practice of banning all foreigners from the country, so that these should not insinuate themselves [in Spartan society and] teach the citizens bad things. (*Ancient Customs of the Spartans, Moralia* 238f)

Unlike in the rest of Greece, women played an active and vital role in keeping the renowned war machine at Sparta well oiled and efficient. Since Spartan men were preoccupied with military training, bonding with comrades in mess life and constantly doing battle, it fell to women to run the farms and households back home and keep the *polis* going in their absence. Working the wool was never as important in a Spartan woman's life as it was in the rest of Greece: she had many more important things with which to fill her day. If we are to believe the hostile press the Spartans get from their Greek neighbours, Spartan women showed, by our standards, an astonishing lack of maternal affinity or unconditional love towards their sons. The following encounter occurred when a mother was told of the death of her five sons in battle; she retorted to the messenger: 'don't tell me about that you fool; tell me whether Sparta has won!' And when he declared that Sparta was victorious, 'Then,' she said, 'I accept gladly also the death of my sons' (PLUTARCH, *Sayings of the Spartans* 6, 7). Just as sensitive was the wife and mother who told her son departing for yet another war to come home carrying his shield, or, if not, carried on it (*Sayings of the Spartans* 6, 16). The bereaved mothers of the fallen at the Battle of Leuctra in 371 BC are said to have had beaming smiles on their faces out of sheer pride.

By the same token, producing a son who turned out to be a coward was a cause for great shame and sorrow. One traitor, Pausanias, met a terrible end when he took refuge in a sanctuary to Athena: his mother, Theano, instead of pleading for his life, picked up a brick and placed it in the doorway: very soon, others followed her lead and completely bricked up the temple door. Pausanias died a slow death, suffocating and starving inside.

This probably sums it up; Pheidippides at Marathon was not the only ill-fated messenger: 'One woman, seeing her son coming towards her, asked, "how is our country?" And when he said, "everyone's dead", she picked up a tile and, hurling it at him, killed him, saying, "And so they sent you to bring the bad news to us!"' (*Sayings of the Spartans* 6, 5).

Xenophon spells out how the coward quickly became a social pariah:

> In other states when a man proves to be a coward, the only consequence is that he is called a coward. He goes to the same market as the brave man, sits beside him, attends the same gymnasium, if he chooses to. But in Sparta everyone

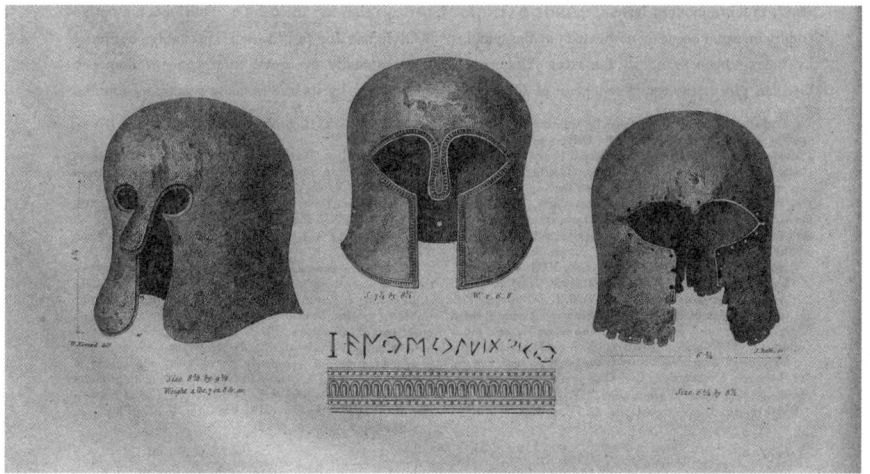

Ancient bronze helmets in Corinthian style, from Patras.

would be ashamed to have a coward with him in the mess or to be partnered with him in a wrestling bout.

Often when choosing sides for a ball game the coward is the odd man left out: in the chorus he is banished to the worst position; in the streets he has to give way; when he takes a seat he must give it up, even to a junior; he must support his unmarried sisters at home and must explain to them why no one will marry them: he must make the best of a fireside without a wife, and yet pay the fine for not marrying: he will be beaten up by his neighbours if he goes about with a smile on his face or behaves as though he were innocent. (*On the Constitution of the Spartans* 2–4)

Indeed, the ritual humiliation by no means ends there: the coward must go around looking scruffy with a patched-up cloak and with one side of his beard shaved off (PLUTARCH, *Life of Agesilaus* 30).

Brad Kallet, writing on the 2024 Spartan Trifecta World Championship – a gruelling combination of events that participants need to complete in a calendar year – said, in his blog for race organizers Spartan, that

Twenty-five hundred years ago, 300 ancient Spartans put everything on the line in the fight for good against evil. Grossly outnumbered, they lost their lives in the Battle of Thermopylae. Their bodies perished, but the memory of their fight, their persistence, and their bravery lives on all these centuries later.

But despite that, there is no statue or monument honoring those 300 legendary warriors. (To be fair, there is a monument of Leonidas in Sparta, but there isn't one specifically dedicated to the 300) . . . Now, on the 2,500-year anniversary of the Battle of Thermopylae, Sparta is building a monument in the city of Sparta to honor the 300. It will be a 35-foot-tall metal statue of an ancient Spartan helmet, and the plan is for it to be completed in time for the 2024 Spartan Trifecta World Championship in Sparta.

36

The Death of Pyrrhus: History's Best-Aimed Tile

A mother sends military assistance for her soldier son in his combat with the Greek king: Plutarch reports on the unusual, almost comic, death of Pyrrhus in 272 BC after he was wounded by an Argive – not a hero of any kind, simply the son of a poor old woman who was viewing the action in a teichoscopy:

> His mother, like the rest of the women, was at this moment watching the battle from the roof, and when she saw that her son was fighting with Pyrrhus she was distressed by the danger he was in, so, picking up a tile with both hands she hurled it at Pyrrhus. It hit his head just below his helmet and crushed the vertebrae at the base of his neck, making his sight blurred and his hands drop the reins. Then he sank down from his horse. (*Pyrrhus* 34, 1)

Plutarch continues to describe how the old mother's well-aimed tile was followed by a very messy decapitation of the dazed and injured Pyrrhus. Her missile has been called the most historically significant roof tile.

37

Mithridates: Professional Poisoner

In the early first century BC, Mithridates, king of Pontus and enemy of the Roman Republic,

> captured Manius Aquilius, one of the ambassadors and the one who was most to blame for this war. Mithridates led him around, bound on an ass, and compelled him to introduce himself to the public as 'maniac'. Finally, at Pergamon, Mithridates poured molten gold down his throat, thus rebuking the Romans for their bribe-taking. (APPIAN, *Mithridatic Wars* 18)

In 88 BC, Mithridates opened hostilities with the Battle of the River Amnias in Paphlagonia against Nicomedes IV of Bithynia; Mithridates was victorious, thus depriving the Romans of the province of Asia for some years. The Pontic general Archelaus made excellent use of his scythed chariots: according to Appian in *The Mithridatic Wars*,

> the chariots caused such horrific wounds ... cutting some of them in two, and ripping others to shreds. So horrified was the Bythinian army at the sight of men sliced in half while still breathing, or their mangled body parts hanging off the scythes, that they were overcome rather by the sheer horror of the spectacle than by the loss of the battle. (XII.3.18)

Epicurean philosopher Lucretius (99 BC–55) provides a scientific, if lurid, explanation for scythed chariot trauma:

They say that in the heat and indiscriminate carnage of battle limbs are often lopped off by scythe-armed chariots so suddenly that the fallen member hewn from the body is seen to writhe on the ground. Yet the mind and consciousness of the man cannot yet feel the pain: so abrupt is the hurt, and so intent the mind upon the business of battle. With what is left of his body he presses on with battle and bloodshed unaware, it may be, that his left arm together with its shield has been lost, whirled away among the chargers by the chariot wheels with their predatory blades. (*On the Nature of Things* III.642ff)

Mithridates trusted no one: he concocted a complex 'universal antidote' against poisoning; Celsus describes a version of it in his *On Medicine* (5, 23, 3), the *Antidotum mithridaticum.* Our word 'mithridate' is derived from it – a remedy with as many as 65 constituents, used as an antidote for poisoning. It was much in demand in the Middle Ages by imbibers hoping to fight off the plague and for centuries during the Renaissance in Italy and France. A revised recipe, theriac (*Theriacum andromachi*), was prevalent in the nineteenth century. The Italian and Romanian words for administrating a poison are still *mitridatizare* and *mitridatiza*, respectively.

Pliny the Elder's version described 54 ingredients to be matured for at least two months. Paranoid and hyperchondriac all at once, Mithridates' anti-poison regimes were overseen by the *Agari*, the Scythian shamans who never left his side. A horse, a bull and a stag, which would neigh and bellow whenever anyone approached the royal bed, stood sentinel at his bedside when he was asleep (Aelian, *On Animals* 7, 46). Apparently, the recipe for the antidote was found written in his own hand and was taken to Rome by Pompey, who had it translated into Latin by Pompey's freedman Lenaeus. Later, attempts to make it yet more efficacious were made by Nero's physician Andromachus, and by Galen, physician to Marcus Aurelius.

A. E. Housman describes Mithridates' antidote in the final stanza of his poem 'Terence, This Is Stupid Stuff' in *A Shropshire Lad* (1896):

There was a king reigned in the East:
There, when kings will sit to feast,
They get their fill before they think
With poisoned meat and poisoned drink.
He gathered all that springs to birth
From the many-venomed earth;
First a little, thence to more,
He sampled all her killing store;
And easy, smiling, seasoned sound,
Sate the king when healths went round.
They put arsenic in his meat
And stared aghast to watch him eat;
They poured strychnine in his cup
And shook to see him drink it up:
They shook, they stared as white's their shirt:
Them it was their poison hurt.
– I tell the tale that I heard told.
Mithridates, he died old.

Alongside his proficiency in toxicology, Mithridates was a formidable linguist. Pliny records that 'It is well known that Mithridates is the only person who has ever been able to speak 22 languages. Throughout his reign of 56 years, he never once spoke through an interpreter to his subjects' (*Natural History* 25, 6).

38

Socrates: He Danced Alone

Even saturnine Socrates enjoyed a good dance, if Xenophon is to be believed from the *Symposium* written in the late 360s BC . . .

> For instance, what could be more enchanting than a Socrates who solo-dances for joy and exercise, so unlike the Socrates we know from Plato? In Xenophon's *Symposium*, Socrates asks the Phoenician dance-master to show him some dance moves. Everyone laughs: what will you do with dance moves, Socrates? He replies: 'I'll dance, by God!' A friend of Socrates then tells the group that he had stopped by his house early in the morning, and found him dancing alone. When questioned about it, Socrates happily confessed to solo-dancing on a regular basis. It's great exercise, it moves the body in symmetry, it can be done indoors or outdoors with no equipment, and it freshens the appetite.

The perfect advert for social prescribing. Here is more fascinating detail showing how the philosopher enjoyed a good party:

> Now the tables were pushed back, the libation poured, and the hymn sung. Adding to the revelry, a Syracusan came in with a trio of assistants: the first, a flute-girl, expert in her art; and next, a dancing-girl, skilled to perform all kinds of wonders; lastly, in the bloom of beauty, a boy, who played the harp and danced with infinite grace . . . After the girl had played her flute, the boy his harp, and both performers had filled the hearts of every one with joy, Socrates turned

Socrates 'dad-dancing': Honoré Daumier, 'Socrates at Aspasia's House', 1842, lithograph.

to Callias: 'My word, what a feast, you prince of entertainers! Was it not enough to set before your guests a perfect dinner, but you must then feast our eyes and ears on the most delicious sights and sounds.' (XENOPHON, *The Symposium* 2)

Agility, both physical and musical, are much in evidence as the performance takes an acrobatic turn:

Immediately Ariadne came in, dressed up as a bride, and sat down in the chair . . . Then a hoop was introduced with swords fixed all around it, pointing upwards, and placed in the middle of the hall, the dancing-girl immediately leaped head first into it through the middle and then out again with wonderful agility . . . I see the dancing-girl entering at the other end of the hall, and she has brought her cymbals along with her . . . At the same time the other girl took up her flute; the one played and the other danced to much admiration; the dancing-girl throwing up and catching again her cymbals, so as to answer exactly the rhythmic pattern of the music, and that with amazing dexterity.

Centuries later, another philosopher, Friedrich Nietzsche (1844–1900), followed Socrates when he pronounced in *Thus Spoke Zarathustra*, 'I would believe only in a god who could dance. And when I saw my devil I found him serious, thorough, profound, and solemn: it was the spirit of gravity – through him all things fall.' Near contemporary Charles Baudelaire (1821–1867) too was a fan: 'Dancing can reveal all the mystery that music conceals.'

Dirty Dancing

Or, as a Roman would say, *saltatrices*. Like Socrates, the Romans loved a good dance, and the activity's popularity extended to men and women of all classes, free and enslaved, rich and poor. The classical dancer rubbed shoulders with those other *probrosae*: actors, adulterers, prostitutes and workers in the baths. Moralists discouraged lasciviousness. Most of the action took place in the private villas of the rich and powerful accompanying themselves with a form of castanet, delighting their audiences with performances which could, and did, elide into strip shows and prostitution; privately, they could extend their passion and satisfy demand as private dancers. According to www.sacred-texts.com,

The costume of female acrobats was of the scantiest. In some designs the lower limbs of the figures are shown enveloped in thin drawers. From vase paintings we see that female

acrobatic costume sometimes consisted solely of a deco-
rated band swathed round the abdomen and upper part of
the thighs, thus resembling in appearance the middle band
adopted by modern acrobats. Juvenal speaks of the 'barbarian harlots with embroidered turbans', and the girls standing
for hire at the Circus; and in Satire xi he says, 'You may perhaps expect that a Gaditanian singer will begin to tickle you
with her musical choir, and the girls encouraged by applause
sink to the ground with tremulous buttocks.' This amatory
dancing with undulations of the loins and buttocks was
called *cordax*; Plautus and Horace term a similar dance *Iconici
motus*. [Friedrich Karl Forberg], commenting on Juvenal,
says, 'Do not miss, reader, the motive of this dance; with
their buttocks wriggling the girls finally sank to the ground,
reclining on their backs, ready for the amorous contest.

Wall painting of male and female dancers, *c*. 480–70 BC, Tomb of the Triclinium,
near Tarquinia. The Etruscans taught the Romans many things, how to dance being
one of them.

Different from this was the Lacedaemonian [Spartan] dance *bíbasis*, when the girls in their leaps touched their buttocks with their heels. Aristophanes in *Lysistrata* writes – 'Naked I dance, and beat with my heels the buttocks.' And Pollux, 'As to the *bíbasis*, that was a Laconian dance. There were prizes competed for, not only amongst the young men, but also amongst the young girls; the essence of these dances was to jump and touch the buttocks with the heels. The jumps were counted and credited to the dancers. They rose to a thousand in the *bíbasis*.' Still worse was the kind of dance which was called `*eklaktisma*, in which the feet had to touch the shoulders.

Julius Caesar Scaliger (1484–1558) said, 'One of the infamous dances was the *díknpma* or *díknoûothai*, meaning wriggling the haunches and thighs, the *crissare* of the Romans. In Spain this abominable practice is still performed in public.' Martial also stated that these dances were sometimes accompanied by the cymbal and he spoke of dancers from Cadiz who were skilled in the art of 'licentiously undulating their loins; and of Telethusa's lascivious gestures and agile posturing in the Gaditanian fashion to the sound of the castanets', according to an 1890 translation of the *Priapeia* – a selection of short, chiefly witty and occasionally pornographic Latin poems associated with worship of the Greek fertility god Priapus – by Leonard C. Smithers and Richard F. Burton. Moreover, Vergil also alludes to this kind of dancing with castanets in the *Thesaurus Eroticus*, where he describes them as naked dancing-girls who through their salacious movements provoked the lust of their spectators, while the *tractatrices* 'were softly kneading and pressing the limbs of their masters and soliciting an erection with their apt touches'.

39

The Celts

To Aelian, the Celts are utterly fearless:

> The Celts court dangers more than any other people.
> Anyone who dies gallantly in battle is celebrated in song.
> They fight wearing crowns, and glory in their actions, and
> leave monuments to their valour in the Greek manner. To
> them it is dishonourable to flee; they will not leave their
> houses even when they are falling down or burning, though
> they see themselves surrounded with fire. Many defy the
> waves of the sea and some even take up arms and attack the
> powerful waves with naked swords and brandished lances,
> as if they are able to terrify or wound them. (*Miscellaneous
> History* 12, 23)

The Gauls too are formidable. Steer clear of their women:

> Almost all the Gauls are of tall stature, fair and ruddy, ter-
> rible for the fierceness of their eyes, fond of quarrelling, and
> of overbearing insolence. In fact, a whole band of foreign-
> ers will be unable to cope with one of them in a fight, if he
> calls in his wife, stronger than he by far and with flashing
> eyes; least of all when she swells her neck and gnashes her
> teeth, and poising her huge white arms, proceeds to rain
> punches mingled with kicks, like shots discharged by the
> twisted cords of a catapult. The voices of most of them are
> formidable and threatening, just the same when they are
> good-natured or angry.

But all of them with equal care keep themselves clean and neat, and in those districts, particularly in Aquitania, no man or woman can be seen, be she never so poor, in soiled and ragged clothing, as elsewhere. All ages are fit for military service, and the old man marches out on a campaign with a courage equal to that of the man in the prime of life; since his limbs are toughened by cold and constant toil, and he will make light of many formidable dangers. Nor does anyone of them, for dread of the service of Mars, cut off his thumb [to make them unfit for military service], as in Italy: there they call such men 'murci', or cowards. (AMMIANUS MARCELLINUS 15, 2, 1)

The Irish more so – sensationally depicted as champions of cannibalism and incest:

There are also other small islands around Britain; but one that is big, Ierna, lying parallel to it towards the north, long, or rather, wide; concerning which we have nothing certain to say, other than that its inhabitants are more savage than the Britons, feeding on human flesh, are very big eaters, and consider it a good thing to devour their dead fathers, as well as openly to have sex not only with other women, but also with their own mothers and sisters. (STRABO, *Geography* 4, 5, 5)

The early Byzantines, however, couldn't care less, for

they live in taverns, abandoning their own houses, and letting them to visiting strangers, and not just to them but to their wives too for use as brothels. Thus they by this one act are guilty of two crimes, drunkenness and prostitution. Moreover, flowing in wine and drunkenness, they love to hear the pipe, and make piping their main business. But they cannot endure to hear any sound of a trumpet; clearly the Byzantines are wholly averse to arms and war. And so

Leonides their general, in a desperate siege, seeing that when the enemy was assaulting the walls the Byzantines left the battlements and got on with their usual entertainments, commanded that taverns should be set up for them on the walls. (AELIAN, *Miscellaneous History* 3, 14)

But it wasn't just so-called barbarians who were incestuous. When the wife of Nausimenes the Athenian caught her son and daughter having sex, she was so horrified that she was literally struck dumb. According to Valerius Maximus in his *Memorable Words and Deeds* (1, 8, 26), the siblings committed suicide. This work, of about AD 30, offers the following on miracula: 'because it is hard to understand them, or why they happen, they are deservedly called miracles'. Examples of these unexplained phenomena include a child 'born with an elephant's head'; stones raining from the sky in Picenum; in Gaul, a wolf running amok with a sword taken from a sentinel's scabbard; shields in Sicily that sweat blood; bloodied ears of corn harvested in the fields near Antium, and – to continue this bloody theme – the waters of Caere running red with blood. And during the Second Punic War, an ox belonging to a man was heard to say, 'Beware, O Rome.'

40

Dinner with Attila the Hun, AD 450

Attila the Hun was, to say the very least, a very powerful man, possibly the most powerful in the world at a time when Rome was beset by barbarian incursions and the fall of the Roman Empire was a few years away. He was the ruler of the Huns from AD 434 until his death, in early 453. He was the leader of an empire comprising Huns, Ostrogoths, Alans and Bulgars, among others, in Central and Eastern Europe. Dinner dates don't come more edgy than this.

Priscus of Panium was a fifth-century Roman diplomat and Greek historian and rhetorician. We join him on a diplomatic mission to the court of Attila the Hun with Maximinus, the head of the Byzantine embassy, representing Emperor Theodosius the Younger (r. AD 408–50). It's hard to believe that Priscus could have had much of an appetite, but there again, he could hardly insult Attila by not eating his food.

> The next day I entered Attila's palace, bearing gifts to his wife, whose name was Kreka ... I found her reclining on a soft couch ... Having approached, saluted, and presented the gifts, I walked to another house, where Attila was, and waited for Onegesius, who, as I knew, was with Attila ... Attila sat in the middle on a couch; a second couch was set behind him, and from it steps led up to his bed, which was covered with linen sheets and wrought coverlets for ornament, such as Greeks and Romans use to deck bridal beds. The places on the right of Attila were held highest in honour, those on the left, where we sat, were only second ...

When evening fell torches were lit, and two barbarians sang songs they had composed, celebrating Attila's victories and deeds of valour in war. And of the guests some were pleased with the verses, others reminded of wars were excited, while others, whose bodies were feeble with age shed tears. After the songs a Scythian, whose mind was deranged, appeared, and by uttering outlandish and senseless words forced the company to laugh. After him Zerkon, the Moorish dwarf, entered and threw all except Attila into fits of unquenchable laughter by his appearance, his dress, his voice, and his words, which were a confused jumble of Latin, Hunnic, and Gothic.

Attila, however, remained immovable and expressionless; nor by word or act did he betray anything approaching a smile of merriment except at the entry of Ernas, his youngest son, whom he pulled by the cheek, and gazed on with a calm look of satisfaction. I was surprised that he made so much of this son, and neglected his other children but a barbarian who sat beside me and knew Latin, bidding me not reveal what he told, gave me to understand that prophets had forewarned Attila that his race would fall, but would be restored by this boy. When the night had advanced we retired from the banquet, not wishing to drink any more. (frg. 8, in *Fragmenta historicorum Graecorum*, adapted from translation by J. B. Bury)

GREEK
AND
ROMAN SOCIETY

41

Children and Schooling

'The breeding of children is a self-inflicted grief.'
(PSEUDO-MENANDER, Sayings 70)

'A mother's love is always stronger than a father's; for she knows the children are hers; he only thinks they are his.'
(EURIPIDES, frg. 105)

Plutarch's *De liberis educandis* (On the Training of Children) is the earliest extant essay on home education. When it came to nursing children, Plutarch was an advocate of the mother feeding her own children. Here he explains why women have breast milk and why they have two breasts:

> In my opinion on the nursing of children the mothers should do it themselves, giving their own breast to those they have given birth; it will certainly be performed with more tenderness and care by natural mothers who love their children intimately. On the other hand, hired wet and dry nurses are only in it for the money . . . Yes, even Nature seems to have assigned the suckling and nursing of the babies to those that bear them and to that end she has given every living creature that brings forth young the milk with which to nourish them. God has wisely ordered that women should have two breasts so that if any of them should happen to bear twins, they might have two springs of nourishment ready for them. (5)

Indeed, Plutarch seems to have been somewhat enlightened generally; here he is on education:

> Children should be won over to pursue their studies by encouragement and reason and on no account to be forced to learn by whipping or any other humiliating punishments . . . even slaves, when treated badly, are dulled and discouraged from their work, partly by the pain of their lashes and partly because of the disgrace thereby inflicted. (12)

We only have to go to Horace to confirm that corporal punishment was a part of the daily routine for some teachers, in this case the flogger (*plagosus*) that was Lucius Orbilius Pupillus (*Epistles* 2). He is recalled by Horace for the beatings meted out during lessons on Livius Andronicus' translation of the *Odyssey*, although he was honoured at Beneventum with a statue on the town's *capitolium*. An early example of the psychological suffering inherited from childhood trauma with which we are so acutely aware of today, and which often presents as PTSD many years after the event.

Suetonius gives us some fascinating detail about Orbilius in the first century BC:

> Lucius Orbilius Pupillus from Beneventum was made an orphan because of the death of his parents who were both murdered on the same day. After he retired from the military, he returned to his studies which he had not touched much since he was a boy . . . He also wrote a book, entitled *On Unreasoning*, which is full of complaints about insults which teachers receive either because of the negligence or arrogance of parents. He was, moreover, of a bitter nature not only in respect to his fellow scholars, whom he attacked at every chance, but also towards his students, which is what Horace means when he calls him 'the abuser' and Domitius Martius writes about: 'The people Orbilius murdered with a stick or a leather whip.' He did not avoid laying in to men of the highest classes. (*Lives of the Grammarians* 9)

Children playing ball games, marble, mid-2nd century AD. The girl
on the far right is tossing a ball in the air.

Plutarch offers more common-sense advice on good parenting and on child care, advice which sadly we still have to remind
ourselves of some 2,000 years later:

> Nursery education must not be left to chance. Even the
> myths our children hear should be carefully selected.
>
> Still more care is required in choosing a teacher. Above
> all, choose [as] teachers men whose lives are unblemished,
> whose characters are beyond reproach, and whose attain-
> ments are the highest, and when you have got your teacher
> don't leave him to himself. Test your children's progress every
> few days yourself.
>
> Philosophy [moral and religious education] is the
> main thing. Philosophy teaches us what is honourable or
> dishonourable, just or unjust, to revere the Gods, honour
> parents, respect the old, obey the laws, be subject to rulers,
> love our friends, be chaste to women, kind to children, and
> refrain from insolence to slaves. Above all, it teaches us
> the *mens aequa* [moderation] in everything.
>
> Fathers must set an example as to what is right by encour-
> agement, and not by violence, which will only stiffen and
> harden the child's character. They must use praise and blame
> judiciously; they must not love 'too well', as some parents
> do, and, therefore, in their desire for their children to excel,
> impose on them long and wearisome tasks, 'over-press' them,

in fact. They must be patient with faults, and if they must show temper, better be passionate than sullen. Above all, by abstaining from ill and doing all that is right, fathers must make their lives a pattern to their children, that, looking into their life, as into a mirror, they may abstain from evil in word and deed. (*On the Training of Children* 7)

Valerius Maximus spells out for us the love one father has for his son (*Memorable Deeds and Sayings* 7, 3):

But perhaps Octavius Balbus was more strongly and ardently affectionate towards his son. For when he was proscribed by the triumvirs, he got away through the back door of his house, and had already started on his escape; but upon hearing a false report that his son had been killed at home, he returned to the doom which he had avoided, and delivered himself up to be murdered by the soldiers. The moment wherein he saw his son safe, was of more value to him than his own preservation. Oh unfortunate eyes of that young man, with which he could not avoid beholding a most loving father dying for his sake!

No such love from Cassius (Valerius 8, 2):

Cassius, whose son was a tribune of the plebs, and was the first that promulgated an agrarian law, and by many other popular acts had won the hearts of the people; when he had laid down his office, by advice of his family and friends, Cassius condemned his son in his own house for seeking to be king: and after he had been whipped, commanded him to be put to death; and consecrated his property to Ceres.

42

The Games

When it came down to it, the two things that kept Romans happy and stopped them rioting, especially in the late Republic and early years of the empire, were the games and the bread dole – a sentiment immortalized in Juvenal's famous *panem et circenses* (AD 55–128) in *Satire* 10: 'For that sovereign people that once gave away military command, consulships, legions, and everything, now confines its desires, and is concerned only with two things – bread, and the games of the circus!'

Juvenal was telling his audience that the Roman people no longer cared for political involvement as they had in the early Republic and were kept down and quiet with a constant supply of cheap food and entertainment provided by politicians.

Honorius (r. AD 393–423) eventually abolished the public games after a monk who tried to stop a fight was stoned to death by angry spectators. But in the good old days, there was nothing more certain than death in the arena: someone always went round dressed as Mercury (the god who escorted you to hell) with a red-hot poker and prodded the casualties, just to make sure. To make doubly sure, a man dressed as Dis – god of the Underworld – followed him round with a sledgehammer (TERTULLIAN, *Apology* 15).

Caligula (r. AD 37–41), despite his many flaws and malevolent eccentricities, was always keen to save money: 'When meat was only available at a high price for feeding his wild beasts at the spectacles, he ordered that criminals should be fed to them, not bothering even to examine their charge sheets, ordering them to be dragged away.' This barbarity chimed with his casual mistreatment of anyone who crossed his path:

Another man, who had vowed to give his life but shrank from the sacrifice, Caligula gave him up, adorned as a victim with garlands and fillets, to youths who drove him through the streets, urging him to fulfil his vow, until they threw him headlong from the ramparts. After disfiguring many men of high rank by branding them full in the face with red-hot irons, Caligula condemned them to the mines, to work in repairing the roads, or to fight with wild beasts. Or he would tie them by the neck and heels, just like beasts carried to slaughter, and shut them up in cages or saw them in half. But these atrocities were not inflicted for serious crimes, but just for making remarks about his public games, or for not having sworn by the Genius of the emperor. He forced parents to watch the execution of their sons.

No one was safe:

He ordered the superintendent of the spectacles and wild beasts to be flogged in chains for several days in a row in his own presence and did not put him to death until he was sick of the stench of his putrefied brain. He also burned alive, in the centre of the arena of the amphitheatre, the writer of a farce for some witty verse with a *double entendre*. A Roman knight was thrown to the wild beasts crying out that he was innocent; Caligula called him back, and, having had his tongue cut out, threw him back into the arena. (All quotes: SUETONIUS, *Caligula* 27)

Pliny the Elder has the answer for anyone unfortunate enough to be concerned about animals in the arena that bite: simply sprinkle a copper concoction into the mouths of bears and lions and they won't be able to bite anymore (*Natural History* 34, 127). It is doubtful if anyone ever lived to benefit from this experiment, even if they had copper handy.

In Carthage, the largest town in Roman Africa, the townsfolk were one day, in AD 439, so absorbed in the games that the Vandal hordes of Gaiseric, king of the Vandals and Alans from 428 to 477, stormed the place and took it virtually unopposed.

Blood, sweat, mud, dirt and oil scraped off the bodies of gladiators was much in demand as an unguent, sold to the gullible public by officials on the make (Pliny, *Natural History* 15, 19; 28, 50).

Suetonius gives us vivid descriptions of lavish spectacles at *Caesar* 10 and *Nero* 11–12, the latter apparently featuring even bestiality and suicidal flying:

Nero also put on a naval battle in a saltwater lake with sea monsters swimming about in it, as well as pyrrhic dances by some Greek youths, to whom he handed certificates of Roman citizenship at the end of their performance. The pyrrhic dances represented various scenes: in one a bull mounted a woman nicknamed Pasiphae, who was concealed in a wooden image of a heifer – or at least many of the spectators thought so. Icarus at his very first attempt [to fly] fell close by the imperial couch and spattered the emperor with his blood.

The Circus Maximus was the top venue for chariot racing with its circa 600-metre (1,970 ft) track and 250,000 capacity, and for Ovid, this was *the* place to pick up a woman (*Ars amatoria* 312). For a thrilling commentary on a chariot race go no further than Sidonius Apollinaris, writing in the fifth century AD:

Brightly gleam the colours, white and blue, green and red. Servants hold mouth and reins and with knotted cords force the twisted manes, and all the while they incite the steeds, eagerly cheering them with encouraging pats and instilling a rapturous frenzy. There behind the barriers they rub, pressing against the fastenings, while a vapoury blast comes from the wooden bars and even before the race the field is filled with their panting breath.

They push, they bustle, they drag, they struggle, they rage, they jump, they fear and are feared; their feet are never still, but restlessly they lash the hardened timber. At last the herald with loud trumpet blast calls forth the impatient teams and launches the fleet chariots into the field . . . The ground gives way under the wheels and the air is choked with the dust that rises as they run. The drivers hold the reins and apply the lash; now they stretch forward over the chariots with stooping breasts, and so they sweep along, striking the horses' shoulders . . . everywhere the sweat of drivers and flying steeds falls in drops on to the field . . . Thus they go once round, then a second time; then goes the third lap, then the fourth . . . Now the return half of the sixth course was completed and the crowd is already clamouring for the prizes . . . Then the enemy in reckless haste overtakes you and, thinking that the first man had already gone ahead, shamelessly makes for your wheel with a sidelong dash. His horses are brought down, a multitude of intruding legs entangled in the wheels, and the twelve spokes were crowded, until a crack came from those crammed spaces and the revolving rim shattered the mangled feet; then he, a fifth victim, flung from his chariot, which fell on him, caused a mountain of manifold havoc, and blood disfigured his flat on the ground brow. (23, 323–424)

Jean-Léon Gérôme, *The Christian Martyrs' Last Prayer*, 1863–83, oil on canvas. Depicted are the Barbary lion and tiger (*Panthera tigris virgata*).

273

Here is Statius' celebration of the fantastic spectacle given by Domitian (AD 51–96) for the Saturnalia, a veritable *tour de force*; he certainly knew how to party for the people:

The Kalends of December

Father Phoebus, over-serious Pallas and holiday-time muses – get lost! We will call you back on January 1st. But Saturn, slip your shackles and come here, and December, well sloshed and joking Jester and shameless Wit – all of you come here while I tell of good old Caesar's happy holiday and the drunken feast that ensued.

It was barely dawn when fruit and nuts rained down from the ropes – the prevailing south easterly was spreading the dew: noble fruit from Pontic nut groves or dates from the fertile fields of Idume, or the plums which pious Damascus grows on its branches, figs which bibulous Caunus ripens, all fall freely like great big booty. Biscuits and soft pastries; apples and pears from Ameria – masses of them, their ripeness just right, and laurel cake and bursting nut-shaped dates – all fell down from palm trees you couldn't see. The downpours with which stormy Hyades rushes over the earth and soaking Pleiades – neither were as severe as this 'winter weather' hailing down on the Latin people from a storm free sky. Jupiter can lead his storm clouds over the world and threaten the wide-open fields with floods all he wants while our own Jupiter brings on these showers.

Look, more people are coming through the benches – a marvellous sight – they're all very well turned out and are as many as the people already sitting down in there. Some carry bread baskets and white napkins and even more sumptuous fare; others lavish languishing wine, you'd think they were as many as the servants of Ida! You are feeding, blessed Emperor, so many people; the circle of the great and good and, at the same time, the people who wear the toga – so let proud Annona not know about this day. Come now Ancient of Days and compare our age more with the Golden Age of antique Jove: the wine didn't flow as freely then and the harvest didn't last the lazy year. One table feeds every rank: little ones, women, the common people, knights, senators: liberty has relaxed the usual reverence. Indeed, even you Emperor (what god could have so much time or promise as much as you?), even you come and share our banquet with us. Now Everyman, needy and fortunate alike, glories in the fact that he is the guest of the Emperor.

Amid such clamour and unaccustomed luxuries the pleasure of the spectacle flew by. Women who have no inexperience in and who knew nothing about sword-craft got up and without embarrassment took on men's battles. You'd think that this was Thermodon's troops seething at Tanais or savage Phasis. A brave company of dwarfs comes on: Nature finished off creating them too soon and left them short and all bound up in a knotty lump. They take and dish out wounds in close combat and threaten to kill – what hands they have! Father Mars and bloody Bravery have a laugh at this and cranes waiting to fall on scattered booty are amazed by such ferocious fighters.

While Martial marvels at the sight of a rhinoceros:

The trainers were aggravating a rhinoceros and they were worried because it was taking so long for the mighty beast to get angry; they all despaired for the battle and the war that had been on the programme. But in the end the fury they had seen before returned. The rhino tossed a heavy bear with his twin horns just as a bull throws stuffed dummies into the air, just like young Carpophorus lets loose the Noric hunting spears with sure aim from his strong right hand. The rhino, its neck swivelling, hurls a pair of cows, overcomes a fierce oxen and a bison, a lion flees from him and runs straight onto the spears. Go now you mob and heckle any long delays! (*On the Spectacles* 22)

Seneca reminds us of two incidents when the participants in some games or other are so determined to escape the dreadful fate that awaits them that they take their own lives in the most horrible of ways. There is little glory, rejoicing or adulation here:

> Not long ago in a training-school for wild-beast gladiators a German, who was getting ready for the morning display withdrew in order to relieve himself, – the only thing which he was allowed to do in private and without the presence of a guard. While so engaged, he grapped a stick of wood with a sponge fixed on the end, which was used for cleaning excrement, and stuffed it, just as it was, down his throat thus blocking his windpipe, and choked to death ... a gladiator who had been sent out to the morning exhibition was being carried in a cart along with the other prisoners. He was nodding as if he were fast asleep and then he let his head fall over the side far enough so that it was caught in the spokes of the cartwheel; he kept his body there long enough to break his neck as the wheel went round. (*Epistles* 70, 19–21, 23)

According to Herodian (*Roman History* 1, 15, 7) the odious antics of Commodus (AD 161–192) in the arena repelled many Romans, prompting rumours that he was actually the son not of Marcus Aurelius, but of a gladiator whom his mother, Faustina, had taken as a lover at the seaside town of Caieta (*Historia Augusta, Life of Marcus Aurelius* 19). Of course, Commodus always won his battles in the arena. Privately, he used to slaughter his practice opponents. Every time he showed up, he charged the city of Rome an appearance fee of 1 million sesterces, putting massive strain on the Roman treasury (DIO, *Roman History* 73, 10, 3). Often, so as not to provide anything remotely competitive, wounded soldiers and amputees would be sent into the arena for Commodus to slay with his sword in the style of Hercules; or they would be tethered together for Commodus, pretending they were giants, to club to death (DIO 73.20.3). According to Dio in his *Roman History: Epitome of Book LXXIII* Commodus was obsessed with Hercules; Dio also records how he commissioned numerous statues to be made depicting him got up as Hercules with the trademark lion's hide and a club. Indeed, he had it in his head that he was the reincarnation of Hercules, as demonstrated by his frequent appearances in the arena emulating the legendary hero's famous feats and labours.

Commodus usually played out the role of a *secutor*: a gladiator who typically carried a short sword, a *gladius* or a dagger. The secutor was trained to fight a *retiarius*, a lightly armoured gladiator armed with a trident and net.

In the arena, exotic animals were no safer. Dio and the (tabloid) authors of the *Historia Augusta* agree that Commodus once killed one hundred lions in one day, and a giraffe. Later, he decapitated an ostrich running at full pelt with a specially designed dart and afterwards carried his sword and the bleeding head of the dead bird over to the section where the Senators sat and motioned as though to indicate they were next. According to Edward Gibbon's *History of the Decline and Fall of the Roman Empire*, on another occasion, Commodus killed three elephants single-handedly. He was a skilled archer, who could shoot the heads off ostriches who were running at full pelt, and kill a panther as it attacked a victim in the arena.

Dead Gladiators

What happened to the corpses of all those gladiators who were mauled to death or hacked to pieces by their opponents? Most amphitheatres had an area in front of the entrance to the arena called the *spoliarium*. Here the corpses were stripped of their weapons and armour, which were then left for the gladiator's slave owner or else donated to the local armoury (*armamentarium*). Presumably the bodies were thrown to wild animals or buried in mass graves outside the city. Celebrity gladiators, however, could expect to be exalted with a high-profile burial.

Female Gladiators

This popular form of live entertainment probably all started when female sword fighters performed at funerals in the very early days of Rome. When we think of gladiators now, we tend to think of men, thanks largely to the dominance of male actors in Hollywood films about gladiators. However, women were not uncommon competitors in the amphitheatres around the Roman world, playing out the phoney fights and grappling in close combat, much to the delight and titillation of the audiences; the nearest the modern world has come to it is probably female wrestling. These women, the *gladiatrix*, were usually warm-up acts, providing light relief in between the top-of-the-bill, crowd-pleasingly gruesome and gory acts.

Women gladiators might share their particular stage, for example, with an elephant walking a tightrope – as at games arranged by Nero in honour of his mother, Agrippina the Younger, whom he had recently murdered. There was, however, opposition: Tacitus was outraged at any form of female participation: 'Many ladies of distinction, however, and senators, disgraced themselves by appearing in the amphitheatre.' The fact that these were rich women who had no need of the extra money suggests that they did it for the high. Cassius Dio tells of another spectacle when Nero, entertaining King Tiridates 1 of Armenia, gave a gladiatorial show featuring Aethiopian men, women and children (*Roman History* LXIII.3.1). He adds:

> There was another exhibition that was at once most disgraceful and most shocking, when men and women not only of the equestrian but even of the senatorial order appeared as performers in the orchestra, in the Circus, and in the hunting-theatre [Colosseum], like those who are held in lowest esteem. Some of them played the flute and danced in pantomimes or acted in tragedies and comedies or sang to the lyre; they drove horses, killed wild beasts and fought as gladiators, some willingly and some very much against their will. (*Roman History* LXI.17.3)

Petronius describes a woman who challenges from a chariot, booked for a gladiatorial show at a festival in the manner of *essedarii* (*Satyricon*, XLV), a type of gladiator who fought from a chariot.

Women gladiators, of course, were just one of many variations on a bloodthirsty theme unleashed into the arena to keep the baying crowds entertained. In the hundred-day games staged by Titus (AD 79–81) to mark the opening of the Colosseum, they competed in a battle between cranes and one bout between four elephants – just a handful of the 9,000 beasts slaughtered in a single day, and, also according to Petronius, 'women took part in despatching them.' They must surely have participated in Trajan's (AD 98–117) games in AD 108, which lasted 123 days and in which 'eleven thousand or so animals both wild and tame were killed and ten thousand gladiators fought'. Martial, in his *On the Spectacles*, describes women battling in the arena. One is dressed as Venus, another as a *venatrix* (animal hunter) who subdues a lion: 'Caesar, we now have seen such things done by women's courage,' he marvels. An incredulous Statius (AD 45–96) describes in his *Silvae*, 'the sex untrained in weapons recklessly dares men's fights! You would think a band of Amazons was battling by the River Tanais.'

If some men were astonished at the thought and sight of women fighting in the arena, then they seem to have had no such qualms about dogs: in one of his epigrams, Martial tells the sad story of the hunting dog (*venatrix*) Lydia, who was brought up amid the trainers at the amphitheatres (*amphitheatrales*); she loved her job and was loyal to Dexter, her trainer. Age did not wither her; rather she was killed by a lightning-quick goring from a huge, slavering wild boar. Lydia had no complaints; she could not have asked for a nobler death.

Domitian put on 'hunts of wild beasts, gladiatorial shows at night by the light of torches, and not only combats between men but between women as well,' and Dio adds, 'sometimes he would pit dwarfs and women against each other.' Statius sums it all up: 'Women untrained to the *rudis* take their stand, daring, how recklessly, virile battles!' The *rudis* was the wooden sword given to a gladiator when he was freed after a series of conspicuous victories. Martial praises Titus for showing women fighting like Hercules.

Juvenal sardonically described 'Mevia' hunting wild boars in the arena, 'holding her spear, breasts exposed' (*Satires* 1, 19).

Elsewhere he was even more scathing:

> How shameful is a woman wearing a helmet, who shuns femininity and loves brute force . . . If a sale is held of your wife's effects, how proud you will be of her belt and arm-pads and plumes, and her half-length left-leg shin-guard! Or, if instead, she prefers a different form of combat, how pleased you'll be when the girl you love sells off her shin pads! . . . Hear her grunt while she practises thrusts from the trainer, wilting under the weight of the helmet. (*Satires* 6, 252ff)

In September 2000, the Museum of London announced that a grave had been discovered in Southwark of a female gladiator from the first century AD – the first ever to be found – although it is hotly disputed that this is actually a woman gladiator. A shard of pottery has been discovered with the inscription *VERECVNDA LVDIA LVCIUS GLADIATOR*, 'Verecunda the woman gladiator, Lucius the gladiator', but this may just be the paraphernalia typical of a woman who was married to or a mistress of a gladiator.

The woman was buried outside the main cemetery, along with pottery lamps of Anubis – whose role it was to guide the dead into the afterlife – a lamp depicting a dying gladiator and the burnt remnants of pine cones. The fragrant smoke of these last items was used as a purifier and cleanser. Elsewhere, remains of a massive, muscular human found during an archaeological dig in the English village of Credenhill in Herefordshire have also been speculated as those of a female gladiator.

The British Museum has a first- or second-century AD marble relief commemorating the release (*missio*) from service of two female gladiators with the 'stage names' Amazon and Achillia. It was found in Halicarnassus, modern-day Bodrum, Turkey. The women are depicted as armed with swords and shields and are advancing towards each other to attack. The *gladiatrix* on the right has lost her head – damaged, not decapitated. They are standing on a platform, and below on each side a spectator can be seen. It is inscribed above and on the platform in Greek with the two names and the word *apeluthesan*, which tells us their fight ended in a draw. The pair have the same equipment as male gladiators, except for helmets, and are heavily armed with a greave (shin armour), loin cloths and a belt; they each carry a mid-sized rectangular shield as well as a dagger in their right hands. They sport arm protection (*manica*); the armlets (*galege*) of both women are at their backs on the floor; their hair is cropped in the style of a slave and their breasts are bare. Such a spectacle must have been prestigious for it to be commemorated in this way.

43

The Law

Roman law, as with the legal systems of any jurisdiction, old or new, had its idiosyncrasies and its oddities. Pliny (*Natural History* 7, 40) tells how a woman claimed to have given birth after a thirteen-month pregnancy; the claim was allowed because there was no statute determining the length of a pregnancy. Justinian I (AD 483–565) was Eastern Roman Emperor from 527 until his death and gave us the penalty for parricide, the murder of a father. Spare a thought for the innocent dog, cock, viper and ape:

> The penalty for parricide, as prescribed by our ancestors, is that the culprit shall be beaten with rods stained with his blood, and then shall be sewed up in a sack with a dog, a cock, a viper, and an ape, and the bag thrown into the sea, if the sea is near at hand; otherwise, it shall be thrown to wild beasts, according to the Constitution of the Divine Hadrian.
> (JUSTINIAN, *Digest* 48, 9, 9)

Other horrendous punishments included *damnatio ad metallum*, meaning 'condemned to the mines'. This was a punishment typically reserved for enslaved people, prisoners of war and serious criminals. Conditions were unspeakably hellish: people were shackled to prevent escape and were forced to work endless hours in dangerous and unhealthy conditions. Chest diseases did for many a miner as did trauma from accidents and falling rocks; they battled against inky darkness, the poorest nutrition, dusty ventilation and the ever present risk of cave-ins. In the end many miners were simply worked to death.

44

Public Services

To run an empire the size of Rome's it was imperative that public services functioned properly. Aqueducts sprang up around all major towns to ensure a clean water supply, and many still remain today. Here are some other essential services:

Roads

We are told that Roman roads are straight, and often they are – but not always. For example, the distance between Lincoln (Lindum) and York (Eboracum) is, as the *corvus* flies, 88 kilometres (55 mi.); the Roman road is 116 kilometres (72 mi.) as it encounters swampy land en route and the river Humber.

Baths

At the end of the Republic, Rome had 170 public baths (PLINY, *Natural History* 36, 121); by the late empire, this had risen to over 1,000. Romans washed their arms and legs every day but bathed only on market days, every eighth day (SENECA, *Epistles* 86).

Latrines

Around the same time, the *Notitia regionum* informs us that there were 144 public *latrinae* in Rome. Civil engineers attest that the standard of engineering in these *latrinae* was not achieved again in Europe until the nineteenth century.

Roman public latrine found in the excavations of Ostia Antica. Unlike cultures today the Romans never had a problem with privacy or modesty.

Some *latrinae* had as many as 25 seats; some accommodated eighty people at the same time. Vespasian's Domus Flavia had a sixty-seater especially for the palace slaves. Vespasian's name would be given to public latrines in Paris in the nineteenth century after the man who introduced these sanitary measures to stop *al fresco* urination. Claude-Philibert Barthelot, comte de Rambuteau, was horrified to learn that people had named these new *pissoirs* after him. To rescue the dignity of his aristocratic name, he made haste to retro-rebrand them *colonnes vespasiennes* in honour of the emperor instead.

Chamber Pots

Despite this high standard of public provision, chamber pots were not only a necessity but sometimes a hazard and a weapon. One of the *Lille Papyri* (2, 24) tells how a plaintiff to King Ptolemy complained of an assault on him during a business trip by a woman called Psenobastis from Pysa. She drenched him when emptying a chamber pot out of an upper storey window into the street below.

When he protested she grabbed his cloak, exposing his chest, and spat in his face. Witnesses available.

Elsewhere, an elegantly turned plangent elegiac couplet explains, 'I have wet the bed, I admit I have done wrong, innkeeper. If you ask me why? There was no chamber pot' (*CIL* 4, 4957).

Only men could use the capacious urinals set up in the street; the contents were sold to launderers as a cleaning agent. A lead pipe lead directly to a laundry from the Baths of Mithras at Ostia.

The Miracles of Saint Thekla

On the subject of incontinence, the Miracles of Saint Thekla are a collection of miracle stories ascribed to Thekla, a follower of the Apostle Paul. In Miracle 7:

> Dexianos, bishop of Seleucia ad Calycadnum, was once attacked by a demon who was envious of his universally good reputation. One night, the demon appeared to Dexianos, while he was sitting on the toilet, looking wild, panting, leering and making insane noises, so the bishop was stupefied and completely overwhelmed with dread. Out of great fear, his head was dislocated and shook.

The martyr recognized the demon who had done this to Dexianos and delivered the bishop from his suffering so that his great affliction ceased immediately and disappeared.

45
Food and Feasting

Conviviality was a characteristic of Greek and Roman social life, particularly for those who could afford to entertain and be entertained, and who could prepare the best meals using the most exotic of ingredients.

Healthy Eating

Galen wrote extensively on the relationship between food and medicine; his works include 'On the Humours', 'On Black Bile', 'On Uneven Bad Temperament', 'On the Causes of Disease', 'On Barley Soup' and three books titled 'On the Power of Foods'. Not everything is what you might expect from a famous and prolific author-physician; he records some decidedly exotic foods (castrated puppy apart):

> Some people serve bear, and also lion and leopard, though these are much worse than bear. Many people also eat panther meat – indeed, some doctors recommend it. Plump young puppies, especially if they have been castrated, are popular food in many countries. Hunters serve fox meat in the autumn, when the foxes have grown fat on grapes. (*On the Power of Foods* 6, 664)

Who'd have thought it, but cress, that inconspicuous, unobtrusive edible herb, is brimming with virtues and benefits. The anonymous Byzantine *Farm Work* gives us some of them (although we can maybe ignore the bit about sex):

A family meal involving three or so generations, Pompeii, 1st century AD, mural.

- Drunk with wine and mint it expels roundworm and tapeworm.
- It drives away snakes when used as a fumigant.
- Those who eat cress have high intelligence.
- It inhibits the sex drive.
- It inhibits hair loss.
- It cures dandruff when mixed with goose fat.
- Cress juice when poured in through the ears cures toothache.

Unusual Delicacies and Staples

One of the *Orphic Fragments* (291) usefully tells us how to eat something approaching our parents' heads: 'If you put a bean into a new pot and cover it with manure for forty days, you will see that it is transformed, and looks like a flesh-covered human being.' That is why the poet says 'eating beans is the same as eating our parents' heads.'

No vegetarian, Plautus's vampire owl from hell will eat you from the inside:

> I don't cook a dinner too, like other cooks, who bring me up seasoned meadows of grass upon their dishes; who turn the guests into oxen, and supply the grass. This herbage, too, they further season with other herbs: put in coriander, fennel, garlic, orage; they add, too, sorrel, cabbage, beet, and spinach. In this they dissolve a pound weight of asafœtida. The roguish mustard is pounded, which makes the eyes of those that pound it drop tears before they have pounded it. These fellows, when they cook dinners, when they season them, not with seasonings, but with vampyre owls which eat out the bowels of the guests while still alive. This is why that people here live such short lives, because they heap up these herbs in their stomachs, dreadful to be mentioned, never mind eaten. Herbage the cattle don't eat, just men. (*Pseudolus* III.2).

Fish sauce made from the blood and intestines of fish (*garum* or *liquamen*) was a popular staple that was enjoyed by not just Romans in Rome and Italy but provincial officials, export businessmen and soldiers all over the empire. It is possible that Lea & Perrins' Worcestershire Sauce has its origins in *garum*: it was exported to India by the Romans and was still enjoyed there as Worcestershire Sauce in the nineteenth-century British Raj. Anchovies are one of the ingredients. *Garum* factories proliferated in towns near to the sea and have been excavated at Barcino, Barcelona and Pompeii. A recipe can be found in the *Geoponica* (20, 46, 1–5).

Fast Food

We tend to think of fast food as a modern convenience. Not so. Apicius had just the thing for the peckish in-a-hurry Roman, be they private citizen or legionnaire. His take on the classical burger-type snack was known as *isicia amulata* (meatballs) and consisted of meat (beef or pork) or fish (a kind of fishcake); and then there was *lucanica*, a smoked sausage, the word for which has survived to this day in Italian. The ever-creative Apicius – the *Apicius* is the go-to Roman recipe book; compiled in the late fourth or early fifth century AD, it is often referred to as *De re coquinaria* – recommends peacock, pheasant, rabbit, chicken and pork as possible fillings.

Here is how to make it:

pound minced lean meat with crustless bread soaked in wine. Pound with pepper, *garum* (optional, fish sauce), and myrtle berry after having removed the seeds. Shape little

Thermopolium in Ostia Antica, south of Rome, 3rd century AD. Thermopolium, which literally means 'a place where something hot is sold', was a commercial establishment where it was possible to purchase ready-to-eat street food. The items served are sometimes compared to modern fast food and street food.

meatballs, placing inside pine nuts and pepper. Wrap in caul fat and cook with *caroenum*. (*De re coquinaria* 2, 1, 7)

For the omnivore and the carnivore there is always cannibalism when the cress runs out.

Cannibalism

Eating one's fellow man (or woman) provided an answer to wasted food: Zeno of Citium, the founder of Stoicism (frg. 253), had an answer for food shortages when he said that the dead ought to be given to the living as food, rather than be thrown on a funeral pyre. Galen noted that when people unwittingly ate human flesh, served up to them by unscrupulous restaurant owners, they remarked how similar it was to pork (*On the Power of Foods* 2).

Aretaeus says that eating the brains of a vulture, the uncooked heart of a seagull, or a domestic ferret work against seizures. He then goes on to add that he once witnessed epileptics drinking the warm blood of a recently killed man. He also knows of a person's liver being eaten (*On the Treatment of Chronic Diseases* 1, 4).

Epileptics do swear by drinking the blood of gladiators. According to Pliny, you shouldn't do this to wild animals, never mind human beings. He also mentions epileptics eating the leg marrow and brains of infants (*Natural History* 28, 4). He adds that human blood is very effective in the treatment of tonsillitis and confirms that if smeared on the mouth of someone suffering convulsions, they will get up straightaway.

Don't fall ill if you're a Padaei! They have a cure-all for any form of illness: they combine murder and cannibalism with a form of euthanasia.

> Other Indians, to the east of these, are nomads and eat raw flesh; they are called Padaei. It is said to be their custom that when anyone of their fellows, whether man or woman, is sick, a man's closest friends kill him, saying that if wasted by disease he will be lost to them as meat; though he denies

that he is sick, they will not believe him, but kill and eat him anyway. When a woman is sick, she is put to death like the men by the women who are her best friends. As for any one that has reached old age, they sacrifice him and feast on his flesh; but not many get this far as before that everyone who falls ill they kill. (HERODOTUS 3, 99)

Such was the ruthlessness of many a Roman siege that the besieged inhabitants were sometimes forced to cannibalism. For example, Sulla and the siege of Athens:

A great and pitiless slaughter ensued in Athens, the inhabitants, for want of nourishment, being too weak to escape. Sulla ordered an indiscriminate massacre, not sparing women or children. He was angry that they had so suddenly joined the barbarians without cause, and had displayed such violent animosity towards him. Most of the Athenians, when they heard the order given, rushed upon the swords of the slayers voluntarily. Sulla forbade the burning of the city, but allowed the soldiers to plunder it. In many houses they found human flesh prepared for food. The next day Sulla sold the slaves at auction. (APPIAN, *Mithridatic Wars* 21)

When the Persian king Cambyses II (the second King of Kings of the Achaemenid Empire, who ruled from 530 to 522 BC) conquered Egypt, his thirst for more conquest led him to send spies south to investigate and invade Meroe. The signs were good, so he led his huge army into Nubia; but Cambyses badly underestimated the operation and soon the soldiers started eating the pack animals. Once these had all been consumed, grass and herbs were all that was left to sustain them. When the army went into the desert they resorted to cannibalism. A shocked Cambyses turned back to Egypt, but not before he had lost a significant number of his men.

The siege of Jerusalem by Roman forces in AD 70 led by future emperor Titus is one of history's most shocking military atrocities. Titus slyly ramped up the pressure on the food and water supplies when he permitted pilgrims to enter the city for Passover, and then refused to allow them to go back out again. Josephus' description of the most harrowing aspects of the predicted famine is truly Lucanesque in its horror: these are the lengths to which the Romans were prepared to go to avenge Beth Horun when 6,000 men and the legion's *aquila* were lost with the remainder wounded or fleeing in confusion.

Children pulled the morsels that their fathers were eating out of their very mouths, and what was still more to be pitied, so did the mothers from their infants; and when those that were most dear were dying under their hands, they were not ashamed to take from them the very last drops that might preserve their lives: and while they ate like this the rabble every where came upon them immediately, and snatched away from them what they had got from others; for when they saw any house shut up, this was to them a signal that the people within had some food; whereupon they broke open the doors, and ran in, and took pieces of what they were eating almost up out of their very throats, and this by force: the old men, who held their food fast, were beaten; and if the women hid what they had within their hands, their hair was torn for so doing; nor was there any commiseration shown either to the aged or to the infants, but they lifted up children from the ground as they hung upon the morsels they had got, and shook them down upon the floor. But still they were more barbarously cruel to those that had prevented their entry, and had actually swallowed down what they were going to seize upon, as if they had been unjustly defrauded of their right.

They also invented terrible methods of torments to discover where any food was including bunging up their anuses, in which case they would drive sharp stakes up their arses; and a man was forced to bear what it is terrible even to hear, in order to make him confess that he had but one loaf of bread, or that he might discover a handful of barley-meal that was hidden; and this was done even when these aggressors were not themselves hungry . . . but it was done so as to make provisions for themselves for the following days. (JOSEPHUS, *Jewish War* 5, 10, 3)

Incredible as it may be, this description is eclipsed by Josephus when he gives an illustration of a woman called Mary who is forced by starvation into cannibalism. She roasts her breastfeeding baby and devours half the body:

> she killed her son, and then roasted him, and ate one half of him, and kept the other half by her hidden. When the rebels entered and smelled the horrid scent of this food, they threatened that they would cut her throat immediately if she did not show them what food she had prepared. She replied that she had saved a portion of it for them, and uncovered what was left of her son. They were seized with horror and astonishment, and stood frightened . . . and left the rest of that meat to the mother. (*Jewish War* 6, 201–13)

The city eventually fell to the Romans on 7 September and was systematically destroyed. Josephus records that 1.1 million people were butchered after the siege, most of whom were Jewish; 97,000 were captured and sold into slavery. He sums up the carnage as follows: 'The slaughter inside was even more awful than the spectacle seen from outside. Men and women, old and young, insurgents and priests, combatants and those who wanted mercy, were mowed down in indiscriminate carnage. The legionaries had to clamber over heaps of dead to proceed with their extermination' (*Jewish War* 6, 9, 3).

Food Nightmares

Be very careful what you dream: 'Dreaming about cakes made without cheese is a good omen, but cheesecakes signify deceit and trickery' (ARTEMIDORUS, *Interpretation of Dreams* 1, 72).

It's a Dog's Life

According to Hippocrates, 'The lightest meats for the body to digest are well-boiled dog, poultry and hare' (*Affections* 52). Not only that, but 'Dog meat warms and dries the body, and builds you up,' however, 'it is not easy to excrete. Puppy flesh moistens the body, and is easy to excrete' (*Diet* 2.46).

Doom Cafés

Death cafés have got nothing on this. Come dine with me *chez* Domitian:

> On another occasion he [Domitian] entertained the senior men among the senators and knights in the following fashion. He prepared a room that was pitch black on every side, ceiling, walls and floor, and had made ready bare couches of the same colour resting on the uncovered floor; then he invited in his guests alone at night without their attendants. And first he set beside each of them a slab shaped like a gravestone, bearing the guest's name and also a small lamp, such as hang in tombs. Next comely naked boys, likewise painted black, entered like phantoms, and after encircling the guests in an awe-inspiring dance took up their stations at their feet. After this all the things that are commonly offered at the sacrifices to departed spirits were likewise set before the guests, all of them black and in dishes of a similar colour. Consequently, every single one of the guests feared and trembled and was kept in constant expectation of having his throat cut the next moment, the more so as on the part of everybody but Domitian there was dead silence, as if they were already in the realms of the dead, and the emperor himself conversed only upon topics relating to death and slaughter.
>
> Finally he dismissed them; but he had first removed their slaves, who had stood in the vestibule, and now gave his

guests in charge of other slaves, whom they did not know, to be conveyed either in carriages or litters, and by this procedure he filled them with far greater fear. And scarcely had each guest reached his home and was beginning to get his breath back, as one might say, when word was brought him that a messenger from the Augustus [Domitian] had come. While they were expecting to perish this time in any case, one person brought in the slab, which was of silver, and then others in turn brought in various articles, including the dishes that had been set before them at the dinner, which were constructed of very expensive material; and last of all came that particular boy who had been each guest's familiar spirit, now washed and adorned. Thus, after having passed the entire night in terror, they received the gifts. (DIO, *Roman History* 67, 9)

Phew ...

Gluttonous Gastronomy

Untrammelled gluttony was alive and well:

Milon of Croton ... ate twenty pounds of meat, and an equal quantity of bread, and drank two gallons of wine. And once at Olympia he took a four-year-old bull on his shoulders, and carried it all round the course, and after that he killed it and cut it up, and ate it all up by himself in one day ...

Astyanax of Miletus, when he was victorious at Olympia three times in the *pancratium*, was invited to supper by Ariobarzanes the Persian, and offered to eat everything that had been prepared for the whole party, and he did! ... And when he died, and when his body was burnt, his bones filled two urns ... they say that the dinner which he ate by himself at Ariobarzanes' table had been prepared for nine guests. (ATHENAEUS, *Philosophers at Dinner* 413e)

The emperor Vitellius was a notorious glutton during his eight-month reign in AD 69:

> He divided his feasts into three, sometimes into four a day, breakfast, lunch, dinner, and a drinking session; and he was easily able to do justice to all of them through his habit of taking emetics ... Most notorious of all was the dinner given by his brother to celebrate the emperor's arrival in Rome, at which two thousand of the choicest fishes and seven thousand birds are said to have been served. He himself eclipsed even this at the dedication of a platter, which on account of its enormous size he called the 'Shield of Minerva, Defender of the City.' In this he mingled the livers of pike, the brains of pheasants and peacocks, the tongues of flamingos and the milt of lampreys, brought by his captains and triremes from the whole empire, from Parthia to the Spanish strait ... he could never refrain, even when sacrificing or making a journey, from snatching bits of meat and cakes amid the altars, almost from the very fire, and devouring them on the spot; and in the cookshops along the road, viands smoking hot or even those left over from the day before and half eaten. (SUETONIUS, *Life of Vitellius* 13)

But the glutton Clodius Albinus (r. AD 196–7) may have out-eaten even Vitellius: he is said to have consumed at one sitting 500 dried figs, 100 peaches, 10 melons, 9 kilograms (20 lb) of grapes, 100 small birds and 400 oysters (*Historia Augusta, Clodius Albinus* 11). No constipation there then.

Recipes

Brain pudding (Isicia de Cerebellis)

Put in the mortar pepper, lovage and origano, moisten with broth and rub; add cooked brains and mix carefully to get rid of any lumps. Add five eggs and continue mixing well to have a good mixture that you can thin with broth. Spread this out in a metal pan, cook, and when cooked, unmould it onto a clean table. Cut into handy sizes. Now prepare a sauce. Put in the pepper, lovage and oregano, crush, mix with broth. Put into a saucepan, boil, thicken and strain. Heat the pieces of brain pudding in this sauce thoroughly, dish them up, sprinkled with pepper, in a mushroom dish (*Apicius* 1, 2, 45).

For Flamingo and parrot (In phoenicoptero)

Scald the flamingo, wash and dress it, put it in a pot, add water, salt, dill, and a little vinegar, to be parboiled. Finish cooking with a bunch of leeks and coriander, and add some reduced must to give it colour. In the mortar crush pepper, cumin, coriander, laser root, mint, rue, moisten with vinegar, add dates, and the fond of the braised bird, thicken, strain, cover the bird with the sauce and serve. Parrot is prepared in the same way (*Apicius* 5, 6).

46

Drink and Drinking

'Drunkenness is nothing but voluntary madness.'

(SENECA, *Letters* 83, 18)

Some sound advice from Mnesitheus (prophylactic vomiting and dilution apart it still holds good today):

> Three things to bear in mind when you're drinking a lot: do not drink cheap wine; do not drink undiluted wine; do not eat snacks during a drinking session. When you've had enough to drink, do not go to bed without vomiting as much as you can. When you have vomited enough, have a quick bath and rest. [That's five]. (frg. 40)

In one of Cleopatra's party tricks when at a feast with Mark Antony, she would invite her guests to drink their garlands by putting them into their wine. When Mark Antony was about to drink his, she put her hand over his cup and summoned a condemned prisoner, who drank the wine and dropped down dead (PLINY, *Natural History* 21, 12).

Seneca advocates a modicum of partying, going wild and getting a bit drunk:

> But, as in freedom, so in wine there is a wholesome moderation. It is believed that [austere] Solon and Arcesilaus were fond of wine, and Cato has been reproached for drunkenness; but whoever reproaches that man will more

easily make reproach honourable than [strait-laced] Cato immoral. Yet we ought not to do this often, for fear that the mind may contract an evil habit, nevertheless there are times when it must be drawn into rejoicing and freedom, and gloomy sobriety must be banished for a while. For whether we believe with the Greek poet that 'sometimes it is a pleasure also to rave,' or with Plato that 'the sane mind knocks in vain at the door of poetry,' or with Aristotle that 'no great genius has ever existed without some touch of madness' – be that as it may, the lofty utterance that rises above the attempts of others is impossible unless the mind is excited. (*On the Tranquillity of the Mind* 17, 4)

Or, in a word: only drunk men dance.

The wonders of wine, according to Pliny the Elder:

There are some miraculous properties, too, in certain wines. It is said that in Arcadia there is a wine grown which makes women fertile and men mad (at the same time?); while in Achaia, and more specifically in the vicinity of Carynia, there is a wine which causes abortion; an effect which is also produced if a pregnant woman happens only to eat a grape of the vine from which it is grown, although it tastes no different from ordinary grapes: again, it is confidently asserted that those who drink the wine of Trœzen never bear children. Thasos, it is said, produces two varieties of wine with quite opposite properties. By one kind, sleep is induced, by the other it is prevented. There is also in the same island a vine known as the 'theriaca,' the wine and grapes of which are a cure for the bites of serpents. The Libanian vine also produces a wine with the smell of frankincense, with which they make libations to the gods, while, on the other hand, the produce of that known as 'aspendios,' is banished from all the altars: it is said, too, that this last vine is never touched by any bird. (*Natural History* 22, 180)

We can rely on the *Geoponica* to advise how to make a drunk person sober: 'Vinegar copiously drunk, and radishes eaten, and pastry made with honey, and sweet cakes, make drunk persons, and so do disquisitions on ancient history, and chaplets of various flowers set on the person's head.' Or, to prevent inebriation in the first place:

> Having roasted the lungs of a goat, eat them, or, when fasting, eat five or seven bitter almonds or eat raw cabbage and you will not be inebriated. A person that drinks likewise will not get drunk if, in drinking the first cup, he repeats this verse of Homer: 'Thrice thunder'd Jupiter from Ida's height.' (*Geoponica* 7, 33)

Diodorus reports a right royal hangover:

> So as to ward off the headaches which every man gets from drinking too much wine [Dionysus] bound round his head, they report, a band (*mitra*), which was why he was called Mitrephorus and it was this head-band, they say, that in later times led to the introduction of the crown for use by kings. (*Library* 4, 4)

Plutarch questions why women seem to rarely get drunk; he references Aristotle, who

> affirms that those that drink fast, and take a large swig without taking a breather, are seldom overtaken by drink, because the wine does not stay long in their bodies, but having acquired an impetus by this greedy drinking, suddenly runs through; and women are generally observed to drink like that. Besides, it is probable that their bodies, by reason of the continual defluction [urination] of the moisture in order to their usual purgations [periods], are very porous, and divided as it were into many little pipes and conduits; the wine falls into these and is quickly carried away, and does not lie in and

fret the principal parts, from whose disturbance drunkenness proceeds. (*Table Talk* 650a)

Interesting as this is, the answer is more likely to lie in the fact that women in Greece and Rome were strongly discouraged from drinking alcohol.

A hilarious fragment of Timaeus' (149) reveals that there was a house in Acragas called the 'Trireme'. It got its name from the young men who drank there and imagined they were sailing in a trireme that was beset by a storm. They were so inebriated that they threw all the furniture and bedding out of the house, as if they were jettisoning cargo in the storm.

Stay off the eels: St Isidore says that 'People who drink wine in which eels have drowned lose their appetite for drinking wine' (*Etymologies* 12, 6, 41).

It's not just liver disease that can be life-shortening; some drinking games can be fatal too:

Some Thracians make hanging into a game at their drinking-bouts; they attach a noose at a certain height, directly under which they place a stone which may be easily rolled by any who step on it. They then draw lots, and the one who receives the lot stands on the stone, holding a pruning-knife, and places his neck in the noose; another comes along and pushes the stone away. While the stone is rolling from under him, the man hanging there dies if he does not quickly cut himself loose with the knife in time. The others laugh, taking the poor devil's death as a great joke. (ATHENAEUS, *Philosophers at Dinner* 155e)

Plutarch describes (*Table Talk* 621e) party games at *symposia* that know no bounds for the lads: stutterers are commanded to sing; bald men to comb their hair; the lame to dance on a greasy oilskin. To make fun of Agapestor, who had a withered leg, all the drinkers were required to drain their cups of wine while standing on one leg – or else pay a fine. However, this was tame compared with the goings-on in the court of the Seleucid king Antiochus VIII Grypus (Hook-Nose):

> Antiochus the king, who was surnamed Grypus, when he was celebrating the games at Daphne, gave a magnificent banquet; at which, first of all, a distribution of entire joints [of meat?] took place, and after that another distribution of geese, and hares, and antelopes all alive. 'There were also,' says he, 'distributed golden crowns to the feasters, and a great quantity of silver plate, and of servants, and horses, and camels. And every one was expected to mount a camel [in the get-on-its-back sense], and drink his wine; and after that he was presented with the camel, and with all the gear that was on the camel, *and* the boy who looked after it.' (POSIDONIUS, frg. 72a)

If you've ever wondered if there is a difference between being drunk with wine and being drunk with beer, then Aristotle has the answer (frg. 106): 'Those who get drunk on wine fall flat on their faces while those who have drunk beer lie flat on their backs. Wine causes headaches, whereas beer stupefies.'

Alcohol, of course, also takes its toll on virility, but Aristotle has the answer to this as well:

> Why is it that those who are drunk are incapable of having sexual intercourse? Is it because to do so a certain part of the body [the penis] must be in a state of greater heat than the rest, and this is impossible in the drunk owing to the large quantity of heat present in the whole body ... Furthermore the semen is derived from food and all food is concocted, and those who are full with food are more inclined for sexual intercourse. This is why some people say that with a view to having sex one should take a midday meal but only a light supper, so that there may be less un-concocted than concocted matter in the body. (*Problems Book III: Problems Connected with the Drinking of Wine and Drunkenness*)

Democritus has the last word: 'Life without celebration is a long road without an inn' (frg. 230).

47

Slaves and Revolting Slaves

'A slave is a possession that is alive.'

(ARISTOTLE, *Politics* 1253b)

'Poor people have no slaves and have to use their wives and children as their servants.'

(ARISTOTLE, *Politics* 1323a)

Galen concedes that he has never punched his slaves – his father had explained how his friends suffered bruised tendons after hitting their slaves in the teeth and how they deserved to suffer spasms and death from the inflammation when they could quite easily have beaten them with a stick or a strap (*On the Diagnosis and Cure of the Afflictions of the Mind* 4). Seneca the Younger claimed that 'Slaves are allowed to run and take sanctuary at the statue of a god; *though the laws allow a slave to be ill-treated to any extent,* there are nevertheless some things which the common laws of life forbid us to do to a human being' (*De Clementia* (On Clemency) Book 1, Chapter 18).

Slaves were a crucial and ubiquitous facet of Greek and Roman life; the more Rome expanded with conquest and trade the more slaves were absorbed into Roman society (as with other cultures of the time and before slavery was considered normal, if not essential). They were employed in every aspect of subservience, their worst experience being in the mineral mines around the Roman world. They were generally treated badly, but not always. From the days of empire, freedmen (slaves given their freedom) rose to significant hieghts in some of the imperial courts and public service.

When we think of slave revolts, we tend to think of Spartacus and, indeed, his rebellion has gone down, thanks largely to Hollywood, as the greatest servile insurrection of them all in the classical era. There is, however, a long tradition of servile rebellion in Greece and Rome, before and after Spartacus. It seems wherever a large number of slaves are gathered together, there will be a dash for freedom.

The first major incident was the First Servile War (135–132 BC) which ignited on a large farm (*latifundium*) owned by a Greek from Henna called Damophilius. In 136 BC, Eunus (d. 132 BC), a slave from Apamea in Syria (his followers were called the 'Syrians'), occupied the town of Henna (Enna) in central Sicily with four hundred other runaways. Eunus soon gathered a large following, bolstered by his boast that he was related to the Syrian mother goddess Atargatis, the equivalent to the Greek goddess Demeter, who had a shrine at Henna. According to Florus, a poet and author of the *Epitome of Roman History*, one of his party tricks during his oracular trances was fire-eating, which he brought off by secreting in his mouth a nut filled with sulphur and exhaling a flame every time he spoke. This 'miracle' was given as proof of his supernatural powers and brought in 2,000 recruits. A tip proffered at the performance guaranteed the donor protection come the revolution.

The revolt spread; Eunus' army – now up to 200,000 men strong, if Diodorus is to be believed, 70,000 if Livy and Orosius – defeated the army led by the praetor of Sicily. Eunus and another leader called Cleon then moved south to capture Agrigentum, and Tauromenium and Catana in the east. Eunus was declared king of Sicily and renamed himself Antiochus, a common regal name in Seleucid Syria and other states in the region. Interestingly, with Orwellian irony, the dynastic implications of the name are diametrically opposed to the personal liberty Eunus was trying to achieve for his fellow slaves.

IN ROME, IF a slave murdered his master, then all the slaves shared collective responsibility and collective punishment; Tacitus gives an

Fyodor Bronnikov, *Cursed Field. The Place for Execution in Ancient Rome. Crucified Slave*, 1878, oil on canvas. Crassus took the long road back to Rome along the Appian Way, a putrefying exhibition of warning against any future slave revolts after the failed attempt by Spartacus; 6,000 prisoners were crucified along the road.

example from AD 61 that went ahead despite public protest. All four hundred 'implicated' slaves died that day.

> Soon afterwards one of his own slaves murdered the city-prefect, Pedanius Secundus, either because he had been refused his freedom, for which he had struck a deal, or in sexual rivalry. Ancient custom required that all the slaves living under the same roof should be dragged off to execution, when a sudden gathering of the people, which was for saving so many innocent lives [including patently innocent women and children], started a riot. Even in the Senate there was a strong feeling on the part of those who shrank from the harshness, though the majority were opposed to any bending of the law. (*Annals* 14, 40)

As noted, hard labour in a silver mine was particularly brutal:

The slaves who work in [the silver mines] produce for their taskmasters revenues beyond belief, but in doing so they exhaust their bodies day and night in their excavations, dying in droves due to the exceptionally bad treatment they endure. There is no respite or break from their work, but they are driven on under the blows of the overseers to endure the most severe of plights, exhausting their lives in this wretched way ... indeed to them death is preferable to life, such is the enormity of the hardships they must endure. (DIODORUS SICULUS 5, 38, 1)

Mill work was no better; here the lives of the slaves were as unspeakably atrocious as those who entered the mines. We might compare the life of a mill worker to that of the donkey into which Lucius had been transformed in Apuleius' second-century novel *Metamorphoses*:

Dying of hunger as I was I was nevertheless curious and anxious and fascinated to see the routine of that terrible baker's mill . . . good God, what pathetic slaves they were! Some had skin black and blue all over from the beatings, some had their backs striped with lashes just covered rather than clothed with torn rags, some had their groins only concealed by a loin cloth; so ragged were they that they might as well have been naked; some were branded on the forehead; some had their hair shaven; some had shackles on their ankles; their skin was an ugly sallow; some could barely see, their eyes and faces were so black with smoke, their eye-lids all glued up with the gloom of that fetid place, half blind and sprinkled black and white with dirty flour like boxers. (9, 12)

Pliny the Elder tells us how the sadistic Vedius Pollio liked to throw slaves into a pool of *muraenae* (Roman eels) to see them being torn to pieces:

Vedius Pollio, a Roman equestrian and a friend of the late Emperor Augustus, found a way of practising his cruelty by means of the muraena; he had any slave condemned by him thrown into pools filled with muraenae. Not that any land animal would have done the job: he would not then see a man so comprehensively and instantly torn to shreds by any other kind of animal. (*Natural History* 9, 39, 77)

Here is Dio's version of events:

[Pollio] kept huge lampreys in his ponds, huge lampreys that had been trained to eat men, and he was accustomed to throw to them such of his slaves as he desired to put to death. Once, when he was entertaining Augustus, his cup-bearer broke a crystal goblet, and without regard for his guest, Pollio ordered the fellow to be thrown to the lam-preys. Hereupon the slave fell on his knees before Augustus and begged him for mercy, and Augustus at first tried to persuade Pollio not to commit so monstrous a deed. Then, when Pollio ignored him, the emperor said, 'Bring all the other drinking vessels which are like that one, or any others of value that you have, in order that I may use them,' and when they were brought, he ordered them to be broken. When Pollio saw this, he was annoyed, of course. (*Roman History* 54, 23)

The famous incident was also used in a didactic context, for which see Seneca the Younger, *De ira* (On Anger), 3, 40, and *On Clemency*, and as education (PLINY THE ELDER, *Natural History* Book 9, 39 or TERTULLIAN, *De Pallio*), which all goes to show how over a long period of time this was probably seen as a disgusting and barbaric form of sadism against a slave.

48

The Public Baths, Sex
and Hair-Pulling

'Baths, wine, and sex corrupt our bodies; but the baths, wine, and sex are what we live for.'

Going to the baths – much like the games, drinking in bars and worshipping in the temple – was a routine facet of Roman social life. All sorts of things went on at the baths; they were the archetypal community centre, combining the ancient equivalents of the modern pub, parish hall, Women's Institute, post office and church congregations. So you could go there for a good gossip, some light education, a massage and other beauty treatments such as dermabrasion – sanding down the skin with strigil and oil – exercise, people watching, a quick sauna, a bit of sly sex (and not-so-sly sex) and many similar sociable, mildly energetic things that are good for you and not so mildly energetic such as boxing, discus throwing, weight lifting, and wrestling activities on the palaestra or in the gymnasium.

One such activity you could book as man or woman was a hair-pulling session (depilation) by a professional hair-puller. *Psilothrum* or *psilotrum* (ψίλωθρον) and *dropax* (δρῶπαξ) were depilatories in ancient Greece and Rome. The head, eyebrows, eyelashes, arms and legs, face, abdomen, back, buttocks, anus, areola, chest, nostrils and ears all fell under their sway – all subject to invasion.

Not quite 'Romans, lend me your shears' but the hair-puller, he or she, would oblige by yanking out your underarm hair and unwanted pubic hair, or any superfluous hair for that matter; the aim of which was to reduce body odour and improve body image, especially as nudity was a feature of bath life and clean, smooth skin was 'a good thing' and sexually attractive. Vanity was also a powerful factor. The tool of the trade was tweezers made of red-hot bronze and fashioned into the shape of a sickle – more an instrument of torture than an implement in a relaxing beauty session.

As English Heritage reminds us, body-hair removal was one of the great civilizing things that the Romans brought with them to Britain, along with clean, piped water and underfloor heating: 'From painful waxes to irritating shaves, we can trace the modern obsession with hair removal back to the Romans.' Tweezers are also big news in archaeology; English Heritage claims: 'We do have an amazing number, English Heritage has 50 Roman sites, 10 of which have produced tweezers. We have a total number of 94, 60% of those came from Wroxeter. So yes, we've cornered the market in tweezers.'

Tweezers, though, were nothing compared with other tools for dermabrasion, which included using flint, seashells, beeswax, various other depilatory utensils and exfoliator substances, such as tar and resins, some of which were obviously highly caustic, toxic and painful. One example is white lead, known to have caused sterility, as well as affecting the brain cells. White lead was used as a foundation until the 1800s. Apparently, the dead skin scraped up from the floor after gladiators had taken their post-performance baths was used in face creams and as an aphrodisiac. Julius Caesar and Augustus led the way for alpha males by scorching their legs with red-hot shells of walnuts to achieve softer skin.

Not everyone, however, warmed to the community atmosphere and conviviality of the local baths, Seneca for one:

Just imagine all those voices, which make you begin to hate your own ears. When those body-builders work out by swinging around lead weights in their hands and exert themselves (or pretend to), you can hear them groaning. Whenever they exhale the air they have been holding in, you can hear it escape with a wheezing, squealing sound. Whenever you see a chilled-out type who is happy with a low rent massage, you can hear from the sound of the masseur's hand slapping the shoulder if the hand was flat or cupped. A ball player running in to announce the score is the straw that breaks the camel's back.

Then picture a yob or a pickpocket being arrested and the man who likes to hear himself sing in the bath, and to that you can add those who belly flop into the water with a loud splash. As well as these people, whose noise is at least natural, you have to imagine the shaver who is always shouting in his piercing voice in order to grab the attention of passers-by. He never shuts his mouth, except when he is yanking out armpit hairs and lets someone else shriek in his place. Then there are the booze sellers with their multifarious cries, the sausage sellers, the pastry bakers and the barmen, each one extolling his services in every possible way. (*Letters* 56, 1,2)

On hygiene generally, Plutarch advises men against bathing with women: apart from being indecent, he assures us that some effluvia and excretions from women's bodies are harmful to men. Pliny deplores the vogue for effeminate ointments among wrestlers,

The *tepidarium* (warm room) and the *caldarium* (hot room) of the Roman public baths in Kourion, Cyprus.

hot baths and depilation by women, especially in the pubic area. A graffiti writer from Pompeii shares Pliny's distaste, coming down on the side of depilation deprivation because 'it [the unshaven vulva] stays warm and excites the [male] organ.'

Celsus was a pioneer of social prescribing in the first century AD when he reeled off a whole medical lexicon of ailments that would benefit from a day out at the baths. Alarmingly, no mention of cross-infection here, though: 'dysentery, typhus and malaria, tuberculosis (in particular *tabes dorsalis*), paralysis, liver tumours, cholera, bowel disorders, diarrhoea, worms and maggots, gonorrhoea, rabies, boils, psoriasis, coeliac disease, diseases of the eye and lice that have attached themselves to the eyelashes'.

We have noted how the girls (*probrosae*) who worked in the baths were thought to be on a par with dancers, actors, adulterers and prostitutes. Martial describes the *tractatrix* – the masseuse who spreads her practised (*manus docta*) hand over every limb and joint – the *unctores* (perfumers), *fricatores* (rubbers) and *fractatrices* (masseuses), *alipilarii* (depilators) and the *picatrices*, the young girls who trimmed what was left of your pubic hair into a neat symmetrical arrangement. And then there were the unfortunate *paratiltriae*, children hired for the cleansing of all the orifices of the body, the ears, anus, vulva and so on. Not quite so sensual (or disgusting) were the *dropacistae*, who attended to your corns.

In Pompeii, the Suburban Baths have a series of paintings depicting a range of erotic scenes, which is probably an advertisement for the services offered by the slave girls working there.

49

The Hell that Is Urban Living

A pragmatic solution to all the fiddling, greed and excess associated with Roman society and politics was to pack it all in and move out to the country, or to the seaside. And that's what those who could afford it often did – failing that, they enjoyed the luxury of a nearby holiday home somewhere more salubrious than Rome or similar urban hell holes. In *Satires* 2, 6 Horace's sheer delight at being out of the city and at his place in the country is quite tangible. The huge difference between waking up on his Sabine farm and his noisy, busy, pressured day-to-day life in Rome is remarkable to him.

Martial echoes this to some extent, and while appreciative of attempts to improve local services, is clearly exasperated by his life in the city, with its perils and its turgid monotony. Like Horace, he is clearly attracted to a more otiose lifestyle outside Rome. Elsewhere in 3, 58 he gives us the real benefits of his Baian villa, although country living can have its drawbacks too (7, 36). In 12, 57 Martial deplores the noisiness of Rome – he can only get a good night's sleep at his country villa. His annoyance at the inadequacies of his water supply should not be underestimated in a city that depended for its water supply almost entirely on the sophisticated and enduring system of aqueducts. For the last word on this, see Frontinus (*On the Aqueducts of the City of Rome* 2, 98–129) and Vitruvius (*Architecture* 8, 6).

If we want Pliny the Younger's take on the matter, he describes the perfect day in Tuscany: a bit of work, some gentle exercise, a power nap, a bath, a quiet meal and some good conversation – the perfect way to recharge the batteries before returning to enjoy the more civilized pursuits of the city. He describes in some detail – and

Delivery time in a choked-up Rome with cart and pack animals, detail from Trajan's Column (original, Roman, AD 13).

to our ears, somewhat smugly – his country retreat and the pleasure it brings.

Such rational thinking is quite alien to Juvenal's rant. His vituperative attack illustrates just how awful life in Rome could be. One-sided and somewhat exaggerated it may well be, but it is quite likely that Horace, Martial and Pliny would have agreed with him to a large extent. To Juvenal, Rome has nothing at all to commend it, and he ends his tirade as he begins it with a calm, reflective bucolic-tinged coda recommending a life in the country. But the diatribe in between is an excoriating attack on all things Roman, or rather non-Roman. Moral bankruptcy and social turpitude are everywhere.

The ubiquity of *delatores* – paid informers – receives special attention and reminds us unsettlingly of what Tacitus said about the corrupt nature of the state (*Annals* 1,74, 1–2; 4,30, 3–5; 3,3, 26; see also Seneca (*De beneficiis* 3, 26)). Jews and especially Greeks feel the lash of Juvenal's tongue in an attack that would not be out of place today in an argument over immigrants and immigration. Juvenal's urban world is a world turned upside down by these foreigners, by their institutionalized sycophancy, effeminacy, corruption, gluttony and arrogance.

Although upset by the departure of my old friend, I nevertheless applaud his decision to set up home in quiet Cumae and to give the Sibyl her one and only citizen. It is the gateway to Baiae, a pleasing seaside and a pleasant retreat. I prefer even Prochyta to the Subura: a place so wretched and desolate but better than living in fear of fires, buildings falling down all the time and a thousand other dangers in this savage Rome – and bloody poets reciting all through August . . .

Who in cool Praeneste fears or has ever feared that his house would fall down? The same goes for Vosinii situated on the wooded slopes, or rural Gabii, or the citadel of Tivoli on the slope. We live in a Rome shored up to a great extent on lightweight props. That's how the bailiff stops his building from falling down, papering over the ancient cracks, and telling the tenants to sleep soundly while collapse is imminent. I need to live in a place where there are no fires, nothing to fear in the night. Ucalegon demands water now, now he's moving out his bits and pieces and there's already smoke coming from your place on the third floor – and you knew nothing about it! If the alarm is raised at ground level the last man to burn will be the one who is protected from the rain only by the roof tiles where the delicate doves lay their eggs . . . (*Satires* 3)

Athenaeus adds in the *Deipnosophistae* (12, 518 c–d):

And the Sybarites were the first people to forbid those who practice noisy arts from dwelling in their city; such as blacksmiths, and carpenters, and men of similar trades; providing that their slumbers should always be undisturbed. And it used to be unlawful to rear a cockerel in their city.

50

Parking Restrictions and Potholes

We tend to think of parking restrictions and unloading times to be things that have afflicted us since the motorcar and white van became ubiquitous. Not really: Harold Whetstone Johnston in his *The Private Life of the Romans* (1903, revd 1932) tells us that

> The streets of Rome were so narrow that wagons and carriages were not allowed in them at hours when they were likely to be thronged with people. Through many years of the Republic, and for at least two centuries afterwards, the streets were closed to all vehicles during the first ten hours of the day, with the exception of four classes only: market wagons, which brought produce into the city by night and were allowed to leave empty the next morning, transfer wagons (*plaustra*) conveying material for public buildings, the carriages used by the Vestals, *flamines*, and *rex sacrorum* in their priestly functions, and the chariots driven in the *pompa circensis* and in triumphal processions. Similar regulations were in force in almost all Italian towns.

All of this is very familiar today, particularly in surviving Roman towns and cities like York, for instance.

And then there were potholes: the Roman road in Ipplepen, Devon, reveals ruts were caused by horse-drawn carts and holes in the road. But generally the Romans spent a lot of time and money keeping the roads in good condition. Roman roads were built to last.

51
All Creatures Great and Small

S ome important questions and facts:

Why do all animals have an even number of feet? (PSEUDO-
ARISTOTLE, *Problems* 893b)

There is also a type of mullet called the grayfish which
feeds on its own slime; and the octopus sits through the
winter devouring himself. (PLUTARCH, *On the Cleverness of
Animals* 965a)

Anyone who is stung by a scorpion should sit on a donkey,
facing backwards towards the tail. For this transfers the pain
to the donkey and makes it fart. (ANON., *Geoponica* 13, 9)

When autumn comes, the hedgehog creeps under the vines
and with its paws shakes down grapes from the bunches
and, having rolled about in them, gets up again with them
stuck to its quills. Once when I was a child I saw one and
it looked just like a creeping or walking bunch of grapes!
Then it goes down into its hole and delivers its load to its
young for them to enjoy and feed from. (PLUTARCH, *On the
Cleverness of Animals* 972a)

As authors go, Aelian (*c.* AD 175–*c.* AD 235) was the king of the
animal world. As we have seen, his encyclopaedic *On the Nature
of Animals* is a compilation in seventeen books of short passages
concerning natural history. Some have a moral dimension; others are

simply outrageous and astonishing. His expatiation on the beaver is typical:

> The Beaver is an amphibious creature: by day it lives hidden in rivers, but at night it roams the land, feeding itself with anything that it can find. It knows full well why hunters come after it with such eagerness and urgency, and so it lowers its head and with its teeth severs its testicles and throws them into their path, just like a prudent man who, up against robbers, sacrifices all that he is carrying, to save his life, and gives up his possessions by way of ransom paid. If, however, the beaver has already [in an earlier incident] saved its life by self-castration and is hunted down again, then it stands up and reveals that it offers no reason for their eager pursuit, and saves the hunters the bother because they consider its flesh now to be of less value. Often, however, Beavers with testicles intact, after getting as far away as possible, have drawn in the scrotum, and with great skill and ingenuity tricked their pursuers, pretending that they no longer possessed what they were hiding [and what they were hunting]. (17, 6, 34)

Aelian's anecdotes on animals rarely depend on direct observation: they are almost entirely taken from existing sources, not only Pliny the Elder, Theopompus and Lycus of Rhegium, but other authors and works now lost, making his work a valuable resource.

The obscure second-century AD writer Nepualius delivers some indisputable animal facts in his *On Antipathy and Sympathy*:

- Storks put a tortoise bone and the leaves of a plane tree in their nests to deter bats.
- Owls put a bat's heart in their nests to stop ants stealing their eggs or hatchlings.
- Warm goat's blood dissolves diamonds.
- A horse goes numb if it steps on the tracks of a wolf.
- Lions are scared of hens – especially white ones.

- If you smear yourself with elephant fat no wild animal will come near you.
- Smearing yourself with hen fat stops a lion from charging at you.

Nepualius clearly had some veterinary knowledge and shows how sick animals are very resourceful when it comes to healing themselves:

- Sick dogs eat green dog's-tooth grass and vomit bile.
- A sick deer eats a crab.
- A sick lion eats a monkey.
- A sick hyena eats a dog puppy.
- A sick panther drinks dog's blood.
- A sick tiger eats human faeces.
- A sick camel eats green oak leaves and vomits black bile.
- A sick monkey drinks its own urine.
- A sick eagle eats a turtle.
- A sick swan eats frogs.
- A sick leopard drinks blood of a wild goat.
- A sick cat eats flies.
- A sick bear eats ants.

Additionally, fire does not burn a salamander, and hot blood of a goat dissolves a diamond.

The victory at Marathon (490 BC) followed a vow made by Athens before the conflict to sacrifice to Artemis a number of goats equal to the number of Persians slain. So great was this number (6,400) and the toll on the goat population that the decision had to be modified to offer five hundred goats a year until the number was fulfilled. Xenophon records that in his day, some ninety years after the battle, goats were still being slaughtered in sacrifice (XENOPHON, *Anabasis* 3, 2, 11).

Tailgating

Arabia has two marvellous and unique kinds of sheep. One of these has tails no less than nine feet long. Were the sheep to trail these behind them they would suffer from chafing their tails on the ground; but every shepherd there knows enough about carpentry to make little carts which they fix under the tails, binding the tail of each sheep onto its own cart. The other kind of sheep has a tail three feet broad. (HERODOTUS 3, 113)

They say that male camels in Arabia do not mate with the females and will not do so even if force is used. A story is told that once when no stallion was available the man in charge surreptitiously introduced a colt. The colt completed the mating but soon after bit the camel driver to death. (PSEUDO-ARISTOTLE, *On Marvellous Things Heard* 2)

They say that there are no wolves, bears or snakes in Crete, because Zeus was born there. (*On Marvellous Things Heard* 83)

In the first century BC, Varro, in his *Country Affairs* (2, 1), noted that ewes under three years old are unsuitable for breeding and so are fitted with chastity belts: little baskets made of reeds or similar, fitted over their reproductive organs. He also sagely points out that it is easier to take care of them if they are pastured separately from the rams.

If you've ever wanted to catch a long-tailed monkey, here's how:

There are two ways to catch a monkey. Monkeys are imitative animals so when they take refuge up among the trees the hunters place a bowl of water that the monkeys and they, the hunters, splash their eyes with. Next they replace this with a basin of bird-lime, go away, and lie in wait some distance away. The monkey leaps down, and smears itself with the bird-lime: when it blinks, the eyelids are stuck together and the hunters come and capture it.

The other method is as follows: the hunters dress themselves in baggy trousers, and go away, leaving behind them other trousers which are downy and smeared over with bird-lime. The monkeys put them on, and are easily captured. (STRABO, *Geography* 15, 29–30)

Delayed Death Syndrome

Galen taught that some animals, when on the slab to be sacrificed, continued to breathe and bellow even though their hearts had been removed – and that some even got up and ran away, eventually dying of blood loss (*On the Doctrines of Hippocrates and Plato* 2, 4, 45).

Net-Shredding Fishing Wolves

Wolves can be very assertive: around the Sea of Azov, they work with the fishermen in catching fish, but, if a fisherman does not reward them with what they consider to be an appropriate share of the catch, they rip their nets to shreds (ARISTOTLE, *History of Animals* 620b).

SuperCroc and Oral Hygiene

Gadoufaoua (Touareg for 'the place where camels fear to tread') is a site in the Tenere desert of Niger – where Rome extended her trade tendrils – famous for its huge fossil graveyard, where remains of *Sarcosuchus imperator*, popularly known as SuperCroc, have been found. *Sarcosuchus* is a distant relative of living crocodilians, with fully grown individuals reaching up to 9.5 metres (31 ft) in length and 4.3 metric tons in weight.

When the crocodile yawns, the trochilus (willow warbler) flies into his mouth and cleans his teeth. The trochilus gets his food in this way, and the crocodile can relax and take comfort in the knowledge that his dental hygiene has been taken care of; it makes no attempt to injure its little friend, but, when it wants it to go, it shakes its neck in warning, lest it should accidentally bite the bird. (ARISTOTLE, *History of Animals* 6, 6)

- A win-win for crocodiles and warblers. But not when the mongooses are out and about: 'Egyptian mongooses lie in wait for the crocodiles, when the latter are basking in the sun with their mouths open; they then drop into their jaws, and eating through their intestines and belly, emerge from the dead body' (STRABO *Geography* 17, 39). Pliny corroborates this when he describes the mongoose as 'hurtling itself like a spear through the crocodile's jaws' (*Natural History* 8, 89).
- Even Alexander the Great was bothered by wild animals. His camp in India was assailed by white lions, bigger than bulls; gigantic pigs of all colours; bats as big as doves with teeth the size of humans; an *Odontotyrannus* bigger than an elephant and with three horns; and poisonous shrews, bigger than foxes (Alexander's *Letter to Aristotle about India* 7).
- The pigs that were stolen by pirates off the coast of Tuscany certainly brought home the bacon. The owners watched the kidnap and when the pigs were far out to sea they called the pigs back with their usual cry. The pigs heard this and clamoured onto one side of the boat, capsizing it. The pirates drowned, but the pigs swam back to shore (AELIAN, *On Animals* 8, 19).
- On the day that Alexander died in 323 BC, a Babylonian oracle tells us of a horrible omen: the birth of a lamb with three heads and three buttocks; it also usefully informs us that it was cloudy that day in Babylonia.
- Pliny says that frogs, like centipedes, explode when you spit on them (28, 38) and that the liver of a chameleon, when smeared with a frog's liver, makes an excellent depilatory (28, 117). Moreover, the ashes of a frog mixed with stale grease is good for gout and arthritis (32, 110), and poorly

pigs are cured if they drink water in which a frog has been thoroughly boiled (32, 141).

• We get our saying 'lick into shape' from bears who give birth to shapeless and limbless baby bears; the mother licks them into the shape we know so well (PLUTARCH, *On Natural Affection Towards One's Offspring* 2).

Antigonus of Carystus (*fl. c.* 240 BC), paradoxographer and worker in bronze, provides a positive treasure trove of fascinating facts about, above all, animals, birds and insects; here are just a few extracts from his *Compilation of Marvellous Accounts* (Ἱστοριῶν παραδόξων συναγωγή):

[20, 1] the gecko which whenever it sheds its skin, having turned it around, swallows it: for it is, they say, as Aristotle writes, a cure for epilepsy. Likewise, the seal is said to vomit out its whey – this indeed is useful for the same disease [20,2]. Mares [20,3] eat off the excrescence on their embryos called 'hippomanes': this occurs on the forehead and is sought for many purposes. The doe buries her right horn in the earth: this, too, is useful in many ways. [20,4]

[21] The embryos of dog-fish on being born, are dispensed from the stomach but crawl back into the mouth. The lioness does not conceive twice: for, as Herodotus says, she ejects the womb with the new-born. Nor does the viper, for the embryos eat its stomach.

[22] The bat alone of birds has teeth and breasts and produces milk. Aristotle says that the seal too, and the whale give milk ... he says that in Lemnos milk was expressed from a he-goat, enough to make cheese.

[29] Doe deers give birth by the roadside, to avoid predatory animals, for wolves are least likely to attack them there; they lead their offspring to their lair, so as to get them used to that from which they must flee – this is a precipitous rock with only one exit ... Deer are captured by whistling and singing so that they lie down, overcome with pleasure.

[34] The tortoise whenever it eats a snake, then eats oregano; and once, when someone had stripped off the leaves, it died since it did not have oregano to eat.

[47] The fish called the 'fishing frog' hunts little fish with protrusions from its eyes, like hair, but with an attachment at the tip like round bait: so it hides and sticks this out.

[53] They say that the bison has no upper teeth, like the ox or any other two-horned beast, and in other respects is similar to the bull. When it is pursued, it projects its excrement some considerable distance; whenever it does this in fright, its dung burns in such a way that the pursuing hounds' hair falls out, but if it does it free from fear, nothing suffers or is injured.

[54a] If a bull elephant mates with a female and makes it pregnant, it never touches that female again.

[54b] They say that the King of Scythia had a fine mare; he led one of its foals to her so that it might mate, but [the foal] was not interested. Then they covered the mare's head: the foal mounted her, but when she had been unveiled and the foal saw her face, he fled and threw himself off the cliffs.

[61] All the land animals which have lungs breathe but wasps and bees do not breathe.

[67] The genitals of the weasel are bony.

[69] The heart of the horse is bony, as is that of some cattle.

[72a] Snakes have thirty ribs. [b] And if one pricks their eyes out, they grow back again, just like those of the swallow.

[75] In Phrygia there are cattle which can move their horns.

[79] Aristotle says that ants, when sprinkled with oregano and sulphur, abandon their anthill.

[80] The eel is neither male nor female.

[81] With partridges, if the female stands downwind of the male, it becomes fertilized.

[84b] The salamander extinguishes fire.

[89] Snakes have an unhealthy relationship with human corpses: when the spinal cord of certain corpses rots, small snakes are generated from the spine, if the person breathed in the odour of a dead snake before death.

[95] Every creature bitten by a rabid dog becomes rabid, except man.

[98] The young of the swallow regain their sight if anyone should blind them.

[103a] Goats and sheep give birth, for the most part, to male offspring if they copulate while there is a north wind, but to female in the case of a south wind. [b] The offspring are white if there are white veins under the tongue of the ram, but black if the veins are black. The same principle holds for red offspring. [c] [Those] that drink salted water are the first to be mounted.

[104] Laconian dogs copulate better when tired out.

[105a] The procreation of mice is amazing because of its speed: a pregnant female once got trapped in a jar and after a short time one hundred and twenty mice came to light. [b] In some places in Persia, when the female mouse is dissected the embryos are discovered to be already pregnant.

And then we have: 'When a lion is ill, the only thing that will cure him is eating an ape' (AELIAN, *Various History* I, 9).

Elephants at War and Peace (WMDS)

The elephant was the first 'weapon of mass destruction' and a major actor in ancient battlefield 'blue on blue'.

The Pyrrhic War (280–275 BC) was notable for the first deployments of elephants, elephantries, by the Greeks against the Roman army. According to P. C. Chakravarti, in *The Art of War in Ancient India* (1941), the Indians pioneered the use of elephants as an instrument of war: they feature in the Sanskrit epics, later stories of the Mahabharata and the Ramayana in the fourth century BC. An army without elephants was as unthinkable and unacceptable as a forest without a lion, a kingdom without a king or valour unaided by weapons. Their deployment spread westwards, reaching the Persians in their wars with Alexander the Great with the first confrontation coming at the Battle of Gaugamela in 331 BC, when the Persians used fifteen elephants. Such was their impact that Alexander felt the need to sacrifice to the God of Fear on the eve of the battle. Alexander won the battle and was so impressed by this new killing machine that he enlisted the captured fifteen into his own army, gradually adding to the complement as he overran the rest of Persia.

The elephantries continued to increase when, facing King Porus, in the modern-day Punjabi region of Pakistan, Alexander's army found itself confronting up to a hundred war elephants at the battle of the Hydaspes River (326 BC). Small fry compared to what the kings of the Nanda Empire (Maghada) and Gangaridai (present-day Bangladesh and the Indian state of West Bengal) could throw against him: between 3,000 and 6,000 war elephants had the crucial effect of effectively halting Alexander's invasion of India. Returning home, he set up a unit of elephants to guard his palace at Babylon and established the office of *elephantarch* to take command of his elephants.

H. H. Scullard, in his *The Elephant in the Greek and Roman World* (1974), tells that war elephants made their European debut in 318 BC when Polyperchon, one of Alexander's generals, besieged Megalopolis with the help of sixty elephants. Pyrrhus is due credit for the introduction of the combat elephant to Italy, at the battle of Heraclea. Here the elephants were of the Indian variety and were given the sobriquet 'Lucanian oxen' by the awe-struck Roman soldiers. The Lucanians were an Italic tribe living in Lucania, in southern Italy.

The Battle of Raphia (or the Battle of Gaza) was fought in 217 BC near modern Rafah between Ptolemy IV Philopator, king and pharaoh of Egypt, and Antiochus III the Great of the Seleucid Empire during the Syrian Wars. It was one of the largest battles fought by the Hellenistic kingdoms and was one of the biggest battles of the ancient world. Polybius records that Ptolemy had 70,000 infantry, 5,000 cavalry and 73 war elephants, and Antiochus 62,000 infantry, 6,000 cavalry and 102 elephants. This is the only battle we know of in which African and Asian elephants were used against each other. Ptolemy's elephants were the now-extinct North African Forest elephants from present-day Eritrea; those of Antiochus were the larger Asian elephants, brought from India. According to Polybius, the African elephants could not bear the smell, sound and sight of their Indian counterparts, as well as their greater size and strength, and would flee.

'Friendly fire' would have been a common occurrence in the head-on, close-combat fighting of the tightly knit Greek and Roman combat units. The absence of distinctive uniforms, the similar languages between enemies and allies and the general turmoil and panic would have heightened the chances of fighting, or raining missiles down on, friends and allies. Thucydides had vividly described the mayhem of the Athenian defeat at the night-time battle of Epipolae in 413 BC – a blueprint for battlefield confusion. He asks how anyone can really know what is going on in the dark: 'many parts of the enemy ended by falling upon each other, friend against friend, citizen against citizen.' This nightmare scenario must have been repeated endlessly down the years. Despite attempts to control and to deter, the elephant only added to the opportunities for 'friendly fire'. Regardless of its benefits as a potent psychological and physical instrument of war, the cumbersome beast was prone to panic, difficult to control and indiscriminately deadly when on the rampage. Time and time again, when a startled, frightened elephant turned and fled, it trampled its army's own soldiers in its blind rush to flee the field of battle.

We noted earlier that Aelian (*On Animals* 11, 14) tells how a female elephant called Nicaea took over as nurse to a baby when his keeper's wife died, rocking the cradle with its trunk when the infant cried. Nicaea was one of the elephants that belonged to the king of Macedon Antigonus Gonatas; the herd was panicked during the siege of Megara when pigs were hurled over the city wall after they had been doused in oil and ignited (*On Animals* 16, 36).

Roman mosaic showing the procession of Dionysus, who is shown riding a lion, while Silenus is riding a camel behind, from the ancient city of Thysdrus (El Djem), Tunisia, 2nd century AD.

Camels in Roman London

Were there camels in Roman Britain? Archaeological evidence indicates that camels were used across the empire well into the early medieval period. As historian and archaeologist Caitlin Green, who authored 'Were There Camels in Roman Britain?' for *Forbes Magazine* in November 2017, suggests, their reach included the province of Britannia. 'Camel teeth found at Greenwich Park, near . . . Londinium likely come from a temple complex that sat along a busy Roman road,' Green states, concluding that the finds from Greenwich would seem to fit into the general pattern of Roman-era finds of camel remains across Europe, and provide evidence of the presence and use of Roman camels, probably primarily as pack animals/beasts of burden. She points out that if the Romans were willing to transport elephants across the Channel, as they may well have done, then there seems little reason to think that they wouldn't have done the same with camels, particularly given that camels were apparently being fairly widely employed elsewhere in northwestern Europe at that point.

An Aviary of Birds

It was thought that when vultures got a whiff of myrrh – 'if anyone smears it on them or gives them anything steeped in myrrh to eat' – they perished. 'In the same way beetles are said to die from the scent of roses' (PSEUDO-ARISTOTLE, *On Marvellous Things Heard* 147). Vultures themselves were considered curious creatures:

> From a pair of mating eagles every second one of their off-spring is a sea-eagle. From sea-eagles are born the osprey and from these hawks and vultures; these vultures produce great vultures which have no young. This is proved by the fact that no one has ever seen a nest of great vultures. (*On Marvellous Things Heard* 835a)

Hawks were popular, as was care of the hawk – although this remedy seems a little unpalatable: 'If your hawk snores and is in pain and cannot eat, it has contracted an inflammation of the throat. Feed it meat sprinkled with iron filings and it will be cured' (Demetrius of Constantinople, *Hawk Wisdom* 151).

Ever wondered why cranes stand on one leg?

> When they light upon some water-spring and rest for the night and sleep, three or four of the cranes mount guard for all the others; and in order to avoid falling asleep during their watch they stand on one leg, but in the other that is tucked up they clutch a stone firmly and securely in their claws. Their purpose is that, if they should inadvertently drop off to sleep, the stone will fall and wake them with its noise. (AELIAN, *On Animals* 3, 13)

The story of Apsethus the Libyan teaches us never to trust a parrot:

Apsethus the Libyan really longed to become a god; but when, after repeated intrigues, he failed totally to accomplish his desire, he nevertheless wished to *appear* to have become a god; and he did at all events appear, as time wore on, to have in reality become a god. For the gullible Libyans were accustomed to sacrifice to him as to some divine power, supposing that they were giving credence to a voice that came down from above, from heaven.

For, collecting into one and the same cage lots of birds, – parrots, – he shut them up ... This man, having for a time fed the birds, was in the habit of teaching them to say, 'Apsethus is a god.' After, however, the birds had practised this for a long period, and were accustomed to the utterance of that which he thought, when said, would make it believed that Apsethus was a god, then, opening the cage, he released the parrots, each flew in a different direction ... the Libyans, being astonished at the voice of the birds, and not spotting the knavery perpetrated by Apsethus, held Apsethus to be a god. One, however, of the Greeks, by accurate examination, perceiving the trick of the supposed god ... by confining many of the parrots, taught them anew to say, 'Apsethus, having caged us, forced us to say, Apsethus is a god.' But having heard the recantation of the parrots, the Libyans, coming together, all unanimously decided to burn Apsethus at the stake. (HIPPOLYTUS, *Refutation of all Heresies* 6, 3)

Photius, however, reminds us just how clever parrots are when he describes how they learn to talk (*The Library* 223.215b): 'You should speak to it from behind a mirror. The parrot is tricked into thinking it is listening to another parrot and quickly repeats what it hears.'

According to Aristotle, 'Short-necked birds with crooked talons and flat tongues tend to be mimics. The Indian bird, the parrot, is like this. And it gets particularly bolshie when it drinks wine' (*History of Animals* 597b).

Weasels Give Birth through their Ears or Mouths

If Galen is to be believed, the etymology of *strouthokamelos* (στρουθοκάμηλος, the word for a camel), would suggest that our humped friend is a cross between a sparrow and a camel (*Properties of Foodstuffs* 6, 702).

'Mice are said to nibble iron and silver. That is why gold miners cut them open and extract the gold' (PHOTIUS, *The Library* 278, 528).

'If a mouse cannot reach the oil in a lamp with its tongue, it inserts its tail and then licks the oil off it' (TIMOTHEUS OF GAZA, *On Animals* 38). Timotheus has another priceless fact for us: 'Weasels give birth through their ears, though some say through their mouths' (*On Animals* 39). Talking about weasels ... 'Weasels are to be found on one side of the road that runs across the island of Pordoselene, but not on the other' (ARISTOTLE, *History of Animals* 605b).

In other news, 'The blood of the chameleon, and likewise that of green frogs, is thought to remove the hairs on your eyelids' (DIOSCORIDES, *Medical Material* 2, 79). And 'Indian dogs are said to be a cross between tigers and bitches ... they take the bitches out to a lonely spot. Many get eaten if the tiger is not in the mood for mating' (ARISTOTLE, *History of Animals* 607a).

Pigs might fly: 'I hear that there once was a flying pig near the city of Clazomenae, and that it devastated the whole countryside. That is why there is a famous place there called "The Place of the Winged Sow"' (AELIAN, *On Animals* 12, 38).

And other mythical beasts may wander: 'Hippocentaurs were not uncommon. One was captured in Saune in Arabia and taken to Rome via Egypt where it was embalmed. Its face was fiercer than a human face, its arms and fingers were hairy and its ribs joined onto its front legs and its stomach' (PHLEGON OF TRALLES, *Marvels* 34).

Some ancients believed (for example, Virgil in *Georgics* 4) that you get bees from the putrefying corpse of an ox that had been beaten to death. Varro and Pliny both tell us that goats breathe through their ears (*On Farming* 2, 3; *Natural History* 8, 202). Oppian, in the *Cynegetica*, says that these goats breathe through a channel between their horns, and that they can be suffocated by pouring wax around said horns (2, 338–42). What the ancients didn't know was that some turtles breathe through their rectums. Snakes, meanwhile, are partial to wine (PLINY, *Natural History* 10, 198).

Bad Animals

Aelian gives us a classic whodunnit and an eight-armed robber. A Spanish fish merchant in Pozzuoli could not work out how their stocks of pickled fish were seriously depleted every morning, even though the doors, walls and roof were always undamaged. It turned out that an octopus was coming up through the sewers every night and taking its fill (*On Animals* 13, 6).

Herodotus describes man-eating, gold-digging ants:

In this sandy desert are ants, not as big as dogs but bigger than foxes; the Persian king has some of these, which have been caught there. These ants live underground, digging out the sand in the same way as the ants in Greece, to which they are very similar in shape, but the sand which they carry from the holes is full of gold. It is to get this sand that the Indians set off into the desert. They ride three camels each. (3, 102–4)

The baby-snatching strix, or screech owl, is particularly odious:

Big is their head, goggle their eyes, their beaks are made for rapine, their feathers blotched with grey, their claws fitted with hooks. They fly by night and attack nurseless children, and defile their bodies, snatched from their cradles. They tear at the flesh of these babies with their beaks, their throats are full of the blood which they have drunk. Screech-owl is their name: the reason of the name is that they are wont to screech horribly by night ... In the chambers Proca, a child five days old, was a fresh prey for the birds. They sucked the infant with their greedy tongues, and the poor child squalled and craved help. Alarmed by the cry of her fosterling, the nurse ran to him and found his cheeks scored by their rigid claws. What was she to do? The colour of the child's face was like the common hue of late leaves nipped by an early frost. (OVID, *Fasti* 6, 131)

The exact nature of a fabulous beast called the manticore exercised the ancients. Pausanias was sceptical:

The beast described by Ctesias in his Indian history, which he says is called martichoras by the Indians and 'man-eater' [androphagos] by the Greeks, I am inclined to think is the tiger. But that it has three rows of teeth along each jaw and spikes at the tip of its tail with which it defends itself at

Miniature of a manticore from the Rochester Bestiary, *c.* 1230–40. Pausanius in particular was sceptical about the existence of such a beast.

close quarters, while it hurls them like an archer's arrows at
more distant enemies; all this is, I think, a false story that the
Indians pass on from one to another owing to their excessive
dread of the beast. (*Description of Greece* 9.21.4)

Pliny, less so:

> Ctesias informs us that among these same Æthiopians, there
> is an animal found, which he calls the mantichora; it has a
> triple row of teeth, which fit into each other like those of a
> comb, the face and ears of a man, and azure eyes, is of the
> colour of blood, has the body of the lion, and a tail ending
> in a sting, like that of the scorpion. Its voice resembles the
> harmony of the flute and the trumpet; it is of excessive
> swiftness, and is particularly fond of human flesh. (*Natural
> History* 8, 30)

Flavius Philostratus (*c.* AD 170–247) reserved judgement:

> 'There are,' replied Apollonius, 'tall stories current which
> I cannot believe; for they say that the creature has four feet,
> and that his head resembles that of a man, but that in size it
> is comparable to a lion; while the tail of this animal puts out
> hairs a cubit long and sharp as thorns, which it shoots like
> arrows at those who hunt it.' (*Life of Apollonius of Tyana* 1,
> Book III, Chapter 45)

Pliny's description of the basilisk is no less terrifying:

> It is produced in the province of Cyrene, being not more
> than twelve fingers in length ... When it hisses, all the other
> serpents fly from it ... It destroys all shrubs, not only by its
> contact, but those even that it has breathed upon; it burns
> up all the grass too, and breaks the stones, so tremendous is
> its noxious influence. It was formerly a general belief that if
> a man on horseback killed one of these animals with a spear,

the poison would run up the weapon and kill, not only the rider, but the horse as well. To this dreadful monster the effluvium of the weasel is fatal, a thing that has been tried with success, for kings have often desired to see its body when killed: the animal is thrown into the hole of the basilisk. The weasel destroys the basilisk by its odour, but dies itself in this struggle of nature against its own self. (*Natural History* 8, 33)

But it is the catoblepas (the Antelope Gnu?) that holds the greatest threat to the human race – total devastation no less:

Near this fountain [of Nigris], there is found a wild beast, which is called the catoblepas; an animal of moderate size, and in other respects sluggish in the movement of the rest of its limbs; its head is remarkably heavy, and it only carries it with the greatest difficulty, being always bent down towards the earth. Were it not for this circumstance, it would prove the destruction of the human race; for all who behold its eyes, drop dead on the spot. (PLINY, *Natural History* 8, 32)

Aelian notes its grim countenance, its bloodshot eyes, its 'down-looking', described thus on account of its weighty head, its toxic cough and fetid breath that, if inhaled, causes convulsions in the victim (*On the Nature of Animals* 7, 5). The amphisbaena, an ant-eating snake, is particularly difficult to deal with because it has a head at both ends (9, 23). Aelian waxes lyrical about the Indian parrot (Book 15, 2): ' I am told that there are three kinds, and all learn like children; and become talkative in the same way and speak like human beings.' And monkeys (15, 10):

there is a race of monkeys with human intelligence; in appearance they are as large as Hyrcanian hounds . . . The beard that grows beneath their chin is like that of a satyr; while the tail is as long as a lion's. The whole of their body is white except for the head and the tip of the tail, which are

red. They are sober and naturally tame. They visit the sub-
urbs of Latage [a city in India] in great numbers and feed
on the boiled rice which the king has served out to them.

And then there are

in the Indian Ocean sea-monsters five times the size of the
largest elephant (15, 12) and pangolins: an animal somewhat
like the land-crocodile. It is the size of a Melitean lapdog.
The scales that cover it are so rough and of such close texture,
that when flayed they perform the functions of a file. They
will even cut through bronze and eat their way through iron.
They call the creature Phattagē (15, 6).

52

Pets

'Cows are like dogs: they recognize their herdsmen's voice when he calls their name, and they do what he tells them to do.'

(According to the *Geoponica* (17, 2))

One of the great paradoxes in Roman society and one which defies explanation is how the Romans showed inestimable affection and devotion towards their family pets yet clamoured to enjoy watching other animals be mutilated by gladiators or ripping one another to shreds in the arena. It seems that on one day Romans could mourn and bury their deceased pets with fondness, and the very next would go to the games and watch scores of lions, giraffes, antelope and rhinos, and other such magnificent beasts, massacred before their eyes, all the while baying for their blood.

Cats

Like the weasel, ferret and snake, the cat performed a role in eradicating mice and rats from the home. They may also have doubled up as pets, as they often do today. Domestic cats, however, were a rare pet; weasels were the hunter of choice in the war against rodents. Seneca asks why mice fear cats but not dogs. Juvenal, Hyginus (*c.* 64 BC–AD 17) and Aulus Gellius all refer to the house cat as *aelurus*. Palladius (*fl.* AD 350) is the first to use the word *cattus* in his *Opus Agriculturae* (20, 8), when he bizarrely recommends them for catching moles in artichoke beds. On a larger scale, Evagrius (*c.* AD 593) tells us that, as a boy, St Simeon Stylites walked his tame pet panther around on a lead (*Historia Ecclesiastica* 6, 23). In two of his epigrams, Agathias (AD 527–565) records that his house-born cat ate his tame partridge when it should have been pursuing mice (*Anthologia Palatina* 7, 204; 7, 205). When we look at medicine we see how Aetius recommended inserting the liver of a cat inside a tube fitted to the woman's left foot as a contraceptive device.

Diodorus Siculus tells us how a Roman soldier serving in Egypt in the reign of Ptolemy XI Alexander II (r. 80 BC) was attacked by an angry mob when he had the misfortune to accidentally kill a cat (1, 71). Cats, of course, were treated as kings and gods in Egypt; Herodotus famously wrote (2, 66) that if a cat died in the house, the occupants shaved off their eyebrows. The Egyptian word for a cat was 'maou' – the last word in onomatopoeia.

Katharine Rogers, author of *Cat* (2006), tells us that Aristotle in his *History of Animals* believed that 'female cats are naturally lecherous.' Plutarch associated cats with cleanliness, noting that perfumes could send them mad. Interestingly this comes in his 'Advice to Bride and Groom' in his *Moralia*: 'They say that the cat is excited to frenzy by the odour of perfumes. Now if it happened that women were similarly made furious and frantic by perfumes, it would be a dreadful thing for their husbands not to abstain from perfume.'

Pliny (*Natural History* 10, 83) associated them with lust, and Aesop with deviousness and cunning as in his fable 'The Cat and the Fox'. We learn from Donald Engels in his *Classical Cats* (1999) that in Ovid's *Metamorphoses*, when the gods flee to Egypt and take on animal forms, the goddess Diana (the Roman equivalent of Artemis) turns into a cat. In *Letters* 121, 18 Seneca ponders 'Why should baby chickens fear a cat and not a dog?'

We get some fascinating depictions of domesticated cats in Roman sculpture, as for example one on a sarcophagus from the first half of the first century AD inscribed with the occupant's name, Calpurnia Felicla – 'pussy' (*CIL* 6, 14223). In the Capitoline Museums in Rome, we can see a cat being trained to dance by a woman to the strains of a lyre with a tempting brace of birds suspended above it. The Musée d'Aquitaine in Bordeaux has on display a delightful relief showing a girl holding a kitten while a cockerel pecks at its tail. In the Muséum d'Histoire Naturelle d'Auxerre, a fragmentary statuette has a cat wearing a collar.

Dogs

The guard dog on the *cave canem* ('beware of the dog') mosaic from Pompeii has made Roman dogs famous; similar cautionary notices would have been displayed all over Rome and across the wider empire. Some were undoubtedly brutish: that mosaic, from the threshold to the House of the Tragic Poet, warns us that a dangerous dog is on guard within, even though it is clearly chained up. Petronius describes a similar scene: 'There on the left as you go in . . . was a huge dog with a chain round its neck. It was painted on the wall and over it, in block capitals, was written: Beware of the Dog' (*Satyricon* 29).

We find Molossian hounds baying in Horace's tale of the town and country mice (*Satires* 2, 6), while Spartan hounds run amok in Trimalchio's dinner party (*Satyricon* 40). Lucretius describes Molossian guard dogs in his *De rerum natura* (5, 1063–72) while Trimalchio introduces his huge, chained guard dog Scylax to his dinner guests (*Satyricon* 64). The beast reappears when Trimalchio's guests try to escape, its terrifying barking sending two of them headlong into the fish pool. Meanwhile, Croesus, Trimalchio's boyfriend, has foolishly urged his obese black pet puppy, Margarita, to attack Scylax – who responds by tearing the puppy almost to bits.

Man's very best friend:

> Titus Sabinus was arrested in AD 28 on charges of treason; when he was locked up his dog stubbornly refused to leave his cell door; when Sabinus was thrown down the Steps of Sorrow, the dog sat howling over his corpse, laying by the dead man's mouth scraps of food thrown by the gathering crowd. Finally, when the body was dumped in the Tiber, the dog tried to keep it from sinking. (PLINY, *Natural History* 8, 145)

Some lucky dogs enjoyed the same burial rites as humans: 'This is the tomb of the dog, Stephanos, who perished, Whom Rhodope shed tears for and buried like a human. I am the dog Stephanos, and Rhodope set up a tomb for me.'

Other Pets

Catullus' *passer*, sparrow (or bullfinch), poems (*Carmen* 2 and 3) and a number of epigraphs and other literary references to companion animals tell us that the family pet was alive and well in ancient Rome.

Cassius Dio tells how Caracella's lion, Acinaces, shared his dinner table with him and even slept with him (79, 7, 2–3). Aelius Lampridius, one of the six authors of the *The Augustan History*, tells us that Antoninus Heliogabalus (21, 1) kept emasculated lions and leopards as pets; Ammianus Marcellinus records that Valentinian kept a pair of ferocious sows in cages near his bedroom (29, 3, 9); they went by the names Goldflake and Innocence.

Persius, Statius, Petronius and Pliny all mention magpies that kept sentinel on thresholds to greet visitors. Nero's mother, Agrippina, owned a talking pet thrush – the first of its kind at Rome. As young boys, Britannicus and Nero kept a starling and nightingales that spoke Latin and Greek; the birds practised every day, adding all the while to their vocabulary. 'Tuition' took place in a private room with a (human) teacher and nothing to disturb the intensive wrote learning ('parrot fashion'?) that was encouraged and motivated by titbits. Sometimes parrots, some of whom may have been originally kept as pets, ended up on the dinner plate, as suggested by Apicius' recipe given in the section 'Food and Feasting'. We also hear of a saluting crow and a loquacious magpie. Columella recommends keeping peacocks as pets because of their beauty, but what about the noise? He is also a devotee of geese, which make excellent guards, better even than dogs, as proven by the legend of the cackling geese that famously alerted the Romans during the 390 BC attack by the Gauls, the guard dogs disappointingly remaining silent.

Monkeys

Evidence for pet monkeys goes back to the third century BC and Plautus the comic playwright, when he refers to one in the *Miles Gloriosus*: old Periplectomonos from Ephesus commands his slaves to remove anyone found on his roof pretending to be up there to catch the monkey (160–63); in the *Mercato*, Demipho describes a dream in which he gives a nanny goat to a tame monkey to look after (229–33). A Carthaginian boy is bitten on the hand by his pet monkey in the *Poenulus* (1,073). Pliny describes the pride shown by tame monkeys for their young, which were born in the house, showing them off, encouraging people to stroke them and hugging them; indeed, sometimes hugging them too tightly and cuddling them to death.

Fish and Tricks

Tame, trained and bejewelled fish were all the rage. Cicero sneers at the people who are in transports of delight when the bearded mullets they keep in their ponds feed from their hands (*Letters to Atticus* II, I, 7). Martial (10, 30) delights in the myriad fish at balmy Formiae that swim obediently towards their master, who is enjoying some leisurely, effortless fishing: 'delicate lampreys swim up to their master; delicious mullet obey the call of the keeper, and the old carp come forth at the sound of his voice.'

Pliny tells how Antonia Minor adorned her lamprey with gold and earrings and how they were passed down as an heirloom to Claudius and then to Agrippina. Martial (4, 30, 3–7) amazes us with the anecdote that Domitian had a fish pool at Baiae populated with fish that had been given personal names, recognized the emperor and came swimming up to lick his hand when he called their names.

On mourning a moray eel:

It seems that even fishes are both tame and tractable, and when summoned can hear and are ready to accept food that is given them, like the sacred eel in the Fountain of Arethusa.

And men tell of the moray belonging to Crassus the Roman, which he had dressed up adorned with earrings and small necklaces set with jewels, just like some lovely young woman; and when Crassus called it, it would recognize his voice and come swimming up, and whatever he offered it, it would eagerly and promptly take and eat. Now when this fish died Crassus, so I am told, actually mourned for it and buried it. And on one occasion when Domitius said to him 'You fool, mourning for a dead moray!' Crassus took him up with these words: 'I mourned for a moray, but you never mourned for the three wives you buried.' (AELIAN 8, 9–10)

Looking back over centuries of the popular 'talking' nightingales Clement of Alexandria was forced to chastise those people who kept them as pets, along with parrots and curlews, rather than discharging their responsibility to look after their fellow humans. Indeed, Seneca the Younger was no less intolerant when he referred to those who 'thought nothing of raising puppies and birds and other silly pets'. Martial's menagerie of pets indicates their general popularity, and Martial's contempt for pet owners. We have a long-eared fox or lynx (*lagalopex*); a gazelle (*dorcas*); Publius' lapdog (as above); an ugly long-tailed monkey just as ugly as Comius, its owner; a mischievous Egyptian rat; a garrulous magpie, a neck-curling cold skinned serpent; and Telesilla's deceased nightingale for which she was sufficiently bereaved to erect a burial mound. To Martial, they are all just monsters (*monstra*).

MYTHOLOGY

53

The Graeae: The Oldest Triplets the World Has Ever Seen

Many of us have heard of the Three Graces, the Furies, the Sirens and the Gorgons, but Greek mythology has another set of sisters that are equally fascinating. The Graeae are a little obscure, but their story is equally enthralling and well worth wider attention.

The three sisters Graeae (or Graiai/Graiae) were born with grey hair, which stayed with them in perpetuity; they are defined by their sharing one detachable eye and one detachable tooth between the three of them. So ancient were they that any memories of their childhoods were lost in the mists of time. Hesiod, in his *Theogony* (270ff), describes the sisters as being 'fair-cheeked', while in *Prometheus Bound*, the tragedian Aeschylus has them as swan-shaped (κυκνόμορφοι) (l. 795). So, despite their antiquity they were not without a degree of beauty and gracefulness. However, what we hear less of is Aeschylus' description of them as 'siren-shaped monsters with the head and arms of old women' which perhaps explains why they are also called 'sea hags who personified the foam of the sea'. The sisters formed the chorus of a play entitled the *Phorcydes* by Aeschylus, part of his trilogy on the life of Perseus. That name derives from the fact that they were daughters of the sea-deities Ceto and Phorcys, as well as being sisters to the Gorgons, including, of course, the petrifying Medusa.

What of their individual names? Well-named they were, indicative of their evil intent: generally they epitomized, in a dark way, sisterly unity and interdependence. The shared eye symbolizes their knowledge and power, and the shared tooth their age and wisdom – all of which were central to their ability to not only foresee but hold sway over events.

Hesiod refers to only two Graeae, the 'well-clad' Pemphredo (Πεμφρηδώ, representing 'alarm') and the 'saffron-robed' Enyo ('Ενυώ, representing horror). Pseudo-Apollodorus adds the third, Deino (Δεινώ, 'dread', the pit-of-stomach anticipation of impending horror). In Aeschylus' *Prometheus Bound*, which depicts Prometheus's fate under Zeus's tyranny for gifting fire to mortals, we hear of Prometheus' encounter with the Graeae:

[Prometheus] warns Io of the perils she will face in her journey . . . crossing the surging sea until you reach the Gorgonean plains of Kisthene (Cisthene), where the Phorkides (daughters of Phorkys) dwell, ancient maids (*dênaiai korai*), three in number, shaped like swans (*kyknomorphoi*), possessing one eye amongst them and a single tooth; neither does the sun with his beams look down on them, nor ever the nightly moon. And near them are their three winged sisters, the snake-haired Gorgones loathed by mankind, whom no one of mortal kind shall look upon and still draw breath. Such is the peril that I bid you to guard against. (788ff, trans. Weir Smyth)

Perseus, son of Zeus and Danae, daughter of the king of Argos, spoiled everything for the sisters when he stole their eye while they were passing it among themselves, rendering them sightless. Perseus forced them to reveal the whereabouts of the three objects needed to kill the cursed Medusa, ransoming their shared eye for the information:

Perseus, in his mission to slay Medusa, appropriated these as leverage for the whereabouts of Medusa, and when they demanded them back, he said he would return them after they had directed him to the Nymphai (Nymphs) . . . When the Phorkides had led Perseus to the Nymphai, he returned them their tooth and eye. (PSEUDO-APOLLODORUS, *Bibliotheca* 2.37–9)

Edward Burne-Jones, *Perseus and the Graiae*, 1892, oil on canvas. This painting shows Perseus stealing the one and only eye shared by the three Graiae.

Perseus completed his mission and beheaded Medusa: '[Perseus] crept up on tiptoe, his steps soundless, and with holy hand and robber's fist caught the roving eye of Phorkys' (Phorcys') unsleeping daughter [the Graia] then lopped off the snaky swathe of Medousa' (Nonnus, *Dionysiaca* 24.270ff, trans. William Henry Denham Rouse).

The Graiai were usually depicted as old crones. Edward Burne-Jones, maximizing his artistic licence, obviously chose to ignore this in his wonderful painting *Perseus and the Graiae*. According to Aeschylus, however, they were siren-like monsters with the head and arms of old women and the bodies of swans, as noted above. Burne-Jones's picture owes much to the version of the Perseus legend that appears in William Morris's 'The Doom of King Acrisius' from the epic poem *The Earthly Paradise*:

> And at one end, upon a dais high,
> There sat the crones that had the single eye,
> Clad in blue sweeping cloak and snow-white gown;
> While o'er their backs their straight white hair hung down
> In long thin locks; dreadful their faces were,
> Carved all about with wrinkles of despair.

We might compare the Graiai with the monster bogey-woman Lamia, whom Greek writers describe as a Libyan women with removeable eyes. Ovid (*Metamorphoses* 4, 770f) tells us

> Agenorides [Perseus] told him [Kepheus (Cepheus)] of the place that lies, a stronghold safe below the mountain mass of icy Atlas; how at its approach twin sisters, the Phorcides [Graiai (Graea)], lived who shared a single eye, and how that eye by stealth and cunning, as it passed from twin to twin, his sly hand caught, and then through solitudes, remote and trackless, over rough hillsides of ruined woods he reached the Gorgones' lands.

While Nonnus in the *Dionysiaca* (24, 270f) informs that

> He [Perseus] crept up on tiptoe, keeping his footfall noiseless, and with hollowed hand and robber's fist caught the roving eye of Phorkys' unsleeping daughter [the Graia], then shore off the snaky swathe of one Medusa.

54

Philomela and Procne

Procne was married to the king of Thrace, Tereus, who had malevolent designs on her sister Philomela, whom he raped and imprisoned. When Procne discovered this she took revenge against her husband by murdering their only child, Itys. Philomela was not a woman to be crossed, and neither was her sister, Procne, both daughters of Pandion 1, king of Athens, and the naiad Zeuxippe. Philomela bore the horror of having been raped with fortitude and a determination to take revenge on her violator, revenge which itself showed considerable ingenuity in bringing him to book.

Ovid (*Metamorphoses* 6, 424–674) tells us how Procne and Tereus travelled to Athens to visit Philomela, and how Tereus became crazed with desire for his sister-in-law – a passion that culminated in her rape. A furious Philomela enraged Tereus, who cut out her tongue to silence her. Rendered mute, Philomela ingeniously wove a tapestry that narrated her story and sent it to Procne.

Procne was so incensed that she killed their son Itys in revenge. She boiled Itys and served him up as a meal for Tereus, which he ate; the coup de grâce came when the sisters presented Tereus with the severed head of his son:

> Tereus eats alone on his throne, and fills his belly with his own child. And in his ignorance shouts 'Fetch Ithys here'. Procne cannot disguise her cruel exultation, and now, eager to be, herself, the messenger of destruction, she cries 'You have him there, inside, the one you ask for.' He looks around and asks where the boy is. And Philomela springs forward, her hair wet with the dew of that frenzied murder, and hurls

the bloodstained head of Itys in his father's face. Nor was there a time when she wished more strongly to have the power of speech, and to declare her exultation in fitting words. (*Metamorphoses* 6, 619–52)

Tereus pursued the sisters wielding an axe, intending to kill them. They fled and frantically prayed to the gods to be turned into birds. The gods transformed Procne into a swallow and Philomela into a nightingale. Then the gods changed Tereus into a hoopoe. A late antiquity scholiast, Pseudo-Nonnus, names Zeus specifically as the god who put an end to the chase by transforming them all into birds (*Commentary on Gregory of Nazianzus* 39). As a bird, Procne mourned the death of Itys for the rest of her life (TZETZES, *Chiliades* 7.43). For Ovid, Procne's story serves as an origin myth for the nightingale.

55

The Unicorn

The fabulous unicorn first made its appearance on the world stage in early Mesopotamia, and is referred to in the ancient myths of India and China. As for Greek literature it is called *monokerōs* (Latin *unicornis*) by the historian Ctesias (*c.* 400 BC), who records in his *Indica* (45) that 'the Indian wild ass was the size of a horse, with a white body, purple head, and blue eyes, and on its forehead was a cubit-long [71 cm/ 28 in.] horn coloured red at the pointed tip, black in the middle, and white at the base.'

Drinking from its horn gave you protection from stomach complaints, epilepsy and poisoning. Other qualities were its fleetness of foot and being difficult to capture. Ctesias was probably describing the Indian rhinoceros. He got his information from the time he was living in Persia where he would have seen unicorns on reliefs in Persepolis, as described by John Hamilton in his *Unicorns and Other Magical Creatures* (2010).

The unicorn is nothing if not well documented in the literature. Aristotle refers to two one-horned animals, the oryx and the so-called 'Indian ass' (ἰνδικὸς ὄνος) (*On the Parts of Animals* 3, 2 and *History of Animals* 2, 1). Antigonus of Carystus in his *Compilation of Marvellous Accounts* (66), also regales us with the one-horned 'Indian ass' while the geographer Strabo (*Geography* 15, 1, 56) asserts that in the Caucasus there existed one-horned horses with stag-like heads. As might be expected Pliny the Elder (*Natural History* 8, 31; 8, 30; 11, 106) mentions the oryx and an Indian ox (perhaps a greater one-horned rhinoceros) as one-horned beasts, as well as a very fierce animal called the monoceros which has the head of the stag, the feet of the elephant, and the tail of the boar, while the rest of the body is like that of the horse; it makes a deep lowing noise, and has a single black horn, which projects from the middle of its forehead, two cubits in length.

In *On the Nature of Animals* (Περὶ Ζῴων Ἰδιότητος, *De natura animalium*), Aelian quotes Ctesias when he informs us that India has a one-horned horse (iii. 41; iv. 52), and says (xvi. 20) that the monoceros (μονόκερως) was sometimes called *cartazonos* (καρτάζωνος), which may be a form of the Arabic karkadann, meaning 'rhinoceros'.

Cosmas Indicopleustes, a merchant of Alexandria and cosmologist, certainly brings the uniform to exciting life. He lived in the sixth century and travelled to India, and gave us a description of a unicorn based on four brass figures he saw in the palace of the king of Ethiopia:

it is impossible to take this ferocious beast alive; and ... all its strength lies in its horn. When it finds itself pursued and in danger of capture, it throws itself from a precipice, and turns so adeptly in falling, that it takes all the shock on the horn, and so escapes safe and sound. (*Christian Topography* i, 7)

56
Charon: A Life Underground

We know that the Romans had a god or goddess for absolutely everything – in life and in death. From conception to the last breath there was at least one particular deity in attendance, crowding in on every aspect of life and the afterlife. Generally speaking, many pagan Romans, from the eighth-century BC foundation of their city to the gradual takeover by Christianity eight hundred years later (and beyond), believed that after death you either burned in Tartarus or lived your afterlife out in the balmy climes of Elysium. Which of the two you were consigned to depended on your conduct in life and the verdict of the underworld judges.

For the Greeks and Romans, the underworld, where you spent life after death, was just as populous as life on earth; Charon is but one example of the numerous infernal denizens you were likely to meet on your journey through what we might conveniently call heaven or hell on your own personal *katabasis* – your own *journey to the underworld*.

Charon, the unkempt and grumpy ferryman of the dead, has a long and not very illustrious history. You met him as you clamoured with hordes of other recently deceased, anxious to get over the murky underworld river, the Styx, from where we get that doom-laden adjective 'Stygian'. Conditions were far from pleasant: there were urgent crowds pressing in on you; the ferryman was churlish and repulsive; and his gloomy boat leaked. Moreover, some say you had to help with the rowing, and everyone had to have the right change ready. No obol, no ride. (The obol was the coin which unlocked your passage; six of them made a drachma. To facilitate payment at what was a very stressful time, the friends or relatives of a deceased person were careful to deposit an obol in the mouth of the corpse. Heraklides of Pontus (d. 310 BC) and the historian Ephorus *On Inventions* (mid-fourth century BC) both mention the obol in lost works.)

Charon's credentials for the job were impeccable. He was the son of sister and brother Nyx (night) and Erebus (darkness), respectively; he was the brother of Thanatos (death) and Hypnos (sleep). Nyx was born of Chaos and gave birth to Moros (doom), Ker (fate, destruction, death), as well as other negative liminal characters who included Thanatos, Hypnos, the Oneiroi (dreams), Momus (blame), Oizys (woe, pain, distress), the Moirai (Fates), Nemesis, Apate (deceit), Philotes, Geras (old age) and Eris (strife). Not much hope there from Charon's siblings to get you over the river if you didn't bring the change.

Charon's name comes from χαρωπός (charopós), 'he of the keen gaze', and reflects his piercing, laser-like eyes; Charon is also a euphemism for all-seeing doom and death.

The famous Charon episodes in Virgil's *Aeneid* 6 (298–304; 384–416) are built from a number of earlier sources that will have provided its author with a rich fund of material to work from; Charon later makes an appearance in the 'underworlds' of all four later epic poets: Lucan, Silius Italicus, Statius and Valerius Flaccus.

57
Talos: The World's First Automaton

Talos was a giant of some 30 metres (98 ft) in height forged from bronze by Hephaestus (blacksmith to the gods to protect Europa from pirates and invaders; Europa was a Phoenician princess and the mother of King Minos of Crete. Three times a day, Talos circled Crete's 262 kilometres (163 mi.) of shore in fulfilment of his guard duties. Our main source is the *Argonautica* by Apollonius of Rhodes, from which we learn that Talos had just one vein in his body, which extended from his neck to his ankle, closed up by only one bronze nail. The *Argo*, the ship that transported Jason and the Argonauts, approached Crete after obtaining the Golden Fleece. As defender of the island, Talos kept the *Argo* at bay by bombarding it with huge boulders. When boulders failed Talos would heat himself red hot and then enfold intruders in a more than warm welcoming embrace.

The death of Talos, depicted on an Athenian red-figure volute *krater*, 425–375 BC.

According to (Pseudo-)Apollodorus (*Library* 1, 9, 26), the witchy Medea slew Talos when she either drove him mad with drugs or deceived him into believing that she would make him immortal by withdrawing the nail. In the *Argonautica*, Medea hypnotized him, driving him mad with the *keres* (female death-spirits) and bewitching him so that Talos was unable to see before him a sharp crag on which he grazed his ankle, enabling her to dislodge the nail, and 'the ichor ran out of him like molten lead', exsanguinating and killing him.

58

Cerberus: Guard Dog from Hell

We have already met one of the denizens of the underworld – gloomy and grumpy Charon, your boatman for the crossing over the River Styx. If Charon never actually met Cerberus, he of the many heads, the terrifying guard dog of Hades, then he would certainly have heard him as he bellowed out his spine-chilling bark to set all comers at considerable unease and to extinguish any thoughts the freshly dead had of returning to the living world.

In the vivid *katabasis* in Virgil's *Aeneid* (Book 6) Aeneas and the Sibyl come across Cerberus and his vast bulk sprawling and filling a cave, blocking the entrance to the underworld. Cerberus is described as 'triple-throated', with 'three fierce mouths', multiple 'large backs' and serpents writhing around his neck. The Sibyl has been here before and throws Cerberus a treat, a loaf laced with soporific honey and herbs, enabling Aeneas to access the underworld. We meet the hound from hell again in Book 8, where Virgil describes Cerberus, in his bloody cave, crouching over half-gnawed bones (296–7). In Virgil's poem on agriculture and the natural world, the *Georgics*, the poet refers to Cerberus, his 'triple jaws agape', being tamed by Orpheus and his seductive lyre (4, 483).

Hesiod (*c.* eighth century BC) described the beast in his *Theogony*:

> There, further on, stands the echoing house of the chthonic god, and in front of it a fearsome hound stands guard. He is pitiless, and he has a nasty trick: those who enter, he fawns upon with his tail and both his ears, but does not let them come out again, but watches, and devours whoever he catches going out of the gates.

William Blake, *Cerberus* (first version), 1824–7, charcoal, pencil, pen and ink.
Cerberus guards the circle of Hell where gluttons are punished in Dante's
Divine Comedy (vi, 13–33).

But William Blake (*c.* 1757–1827) depicts a hellish image of
Cerberus, whose job it was to prevent the dead from escaping the
underworld, by drawing on Dante Alighieri (*c.* 1265–1321):

Cerberus, cruel monster, fierce and strange,
Though his wide threefold throat, barks as a dog
Over the multitude immersed beneath.
His eyes glare crimson, black his unctuous beard,
His belly large, and claw'd hands, with which
He tears the spirits, flays them, and their limbs
Piecemeal disparts.

(*Divine Comedy*, *Inferno*, Canto vi)

THE
MILITARY
AND
WAR

59

The Military

For much of the history of ancient Greece, somewhere an army of Greeks was doing battle with a foreign army or, much more likely, with another Greek army. Generally speaking, Athens, from the start of the Persian Wars in 490 to the Battle of Chaeronea in 338 BC, was, on average, fighting more than two years out of every three and never saw peace for a period as long as ten years.

Warfare was also an inextricable and constant part of Roman life, from the foundation of Rome in 753 BC to the eventual fall of the Roman Empire some 1,200 years later. The belligerence of the state was integral to Roman political life; Roman bellicosity shaped their economy, defined their extensive trade and characterized their society. Josephus, writing in the first century AD, stated that the Roman people emerged from the womb carrying weapons. Centuries later, F. E. Adcock, in *The Roman Art of War Under the Republic* (1940), echoed these words when he said, 'a Roman was half a soldier from the start, and he could endure a discipline which soon produced the other half.'

Cats as a Weapon of War

When Cambyses II, king of Persia, invaded Egypt in 525 BC at the Battle of Pelusium, 'Cambyses ranged before his front line dogs, sheep, cats, ibises, and whatever other animals the Egyptians hold sacred.' He did this knowing that the Egyptians honoured the cat and would do absolutely nothing to harm one. Psychological warfare at its best (POLYAENUS, *Stratagems of War* 7, 9).

The Human Telescope and Other Forms of Intelligence

Pliny tells us about the powerful human telescope – a man called Strabo blessed with prodigious long-range vision who, during the first Carthaginian War, stationed himself on the promontory of Lilybaeum so that he could see the enemy fleet coming in and out the harbour in Carthage over in North Africa, and specify the number of ships involved. This was about 160 kilometres (100 mi.) away, so Strabo provided superhuman surveillance on enemy naval activity (*Natural History* 7, 205).

Carrier pigeons were deployed by Decimus Brutus to transmit intelligence when under siege by Mark Antony in 43 BC. Harpagus was even more ingenious: 'Harpagus, in order to deliver a letter to Cyrus in secret, gutted a hare, and sewed up the letter in its belly. The bearer, equipped with hunter's nets, passed the guards on the roads without suspicion, and delivered the letter safely' (POLYAENUS, *Stratagems of War* 7, 7).

Paul-Marie Lenoir, *Cambyses II at the Battle of Pelusium*, 1872, oil on canvas. According to Polyaenus, Persian soldiers used cats – among other sacred Egyptian animals – as psychological warfare against the Egyptian army.

The Persian Army Shamed by Their Womenfolk

Going back to the womb was not an option for the flaky Persians:

> When the Persians under Cyrus were fighting against the Medes, Oebares the satrap fled from the battlefield, and all the Persians under his command followed him. The Persian women marched out all together, and met the fugitives; lifting up their skirts, they called out to the men, 'Where are you running to? Will you hide yourselves here, from where you came from?' The women's reproof struck the Persians with shame. They returned to the battle, and defeated the enemy. (POLYAENUS, *Stratagems of War* 7, 45, 2)

> When the historian Polybius and Scipio Aemilianus destroyed Carthage in 146 BC they saw man-eating lions which they crucified as a deterrent to other lions. (PLINY, *Natural History* 8, 47)

Let's drink to Postumus:

> In 216 BC a 25,000-strong army led by Lucius Postumius was annihilated by the Gauls in the Silva Litana in northern Italy. Postumius's skull was covered in gold and made into a goblet. (LIVY 23, 24)

Full-Bodied German Wine?

The battle of Aquae Sextiae in 102 BC produced a bumper wine harvest after the death of 100,000(!) Germans there:

> The people of Massalia fenced their vineyards with the bones of the dead, and the soil, after the bodies had rotted away in it and the rains had fallen all winter on it, grew so fertile and became so full of the putrefied human matter

oozing into it, that it produced a bumper harvest for many years. (PLUTARCH, *Life of Marius* 21)

Pliny the Elder, who, when he wasn't busy compiling his *Natural History*, was for his day job commander of the Misenum naval station, confirms that pouring vinegar over ships provides a modicum of protection against cyclones (*Natural History* 2, 132).

One of the world's first ghost armies: Spartacus tried to fox the Romans into believing his forces were more numerous than they actually were by tying corpses to stakes outside his camp, all bearing weapons, so that from a distance they looked like living sentries. (FRONTINUS, *Stratagems* 1, 5, 22).

According to Pliny, Julius Caesar killed huge numbers of the enemy – apparently 1,192,000 in total – in his battles, and that's not including those he killed during the civil wars. Pompey, however, easily outslaughtered him, as reported on an inscription in the Temple of Minerva in Rome:

[Pompey] completed a war career of thirty years with the routing, scattering, slaughtering or capture of 12,183,000 enemy, and with the sinking or capture of 846 ships, the surrender of 1,538 towns and forts, and the conquering of all the land from the Sea of Azov to the Red Sea. (*Natural History* 7, 97)

On Not Invading Britannia

Caligula gives us one of history's greatest military anti-climaxes:

[Caligula] drew up a line of battle on the shore of the Ocean facing Britannia, arranging his ballistas and other artillery; and when no one knew or could imagine what he was going to do, he suddenly made the troops gather shells and fill their helmets and the folds of their gowns, calling them 'spoils from the Ocean, for the Capitol and Palatine.'

As a monument to his 'victory' he erected a lofty tower, from which lights were to shine at night to guide the course of ships, as from the Pharos in Alexandria. Then, promising the soldiers a gratuity of a hundred denarii each, as if he had shown unprecedented liberality, he said, 'Go your way happy; go your way rich.' (SUETONIUS, *Caligula* 46)

Sex-Free Camping

The Latin for camp is *castra*, which is derived from *castus* (chaste) and *castrare* (to castrate). The connection comes from the fact that all sexual desire was eliminated in a military camp, as officially women and marriage were banned until the reign of Septimius Severus (r. AD 193–211).

Vegetius tells us how to catch a spy in his *Military Matters* (3, 26). Camps should always be laid out in the same way so that every soldier knows exactly where to go if the alarm sounds. Moreover, when an enemy spy has infiltrated the camp, the soldiers should all be ordered back to their tents; this leaves the spy wandering about aimlessly with nowhere to go.

60

War Crimes and Crimes Against Humanity

It is generally accepted that the three most brutal forms of execution known to antiquity were crucifixion, burning and decapitation. In 216 BC savage retribution followed in Capua when the inhabitants locked up a number of Roman citizens in the steaming, airless bath house; they died a terrible suffocating death according to Livy (23, 7). Images of the Black Hole of Calcutta spring to mind. Julius Caesar in 51 BC at Uxellodunum had the hands of the enemy cut off as a terrible and tangible warning to anyone else contemplating resistance (CAESAR, *De bello Gallico* 8, 44). In AD 78 Agricola in his campaign in northern Britannia started as he meant to go on when he massacred the Ordovices; they had had the temerity to attack one of his cavalry squadrons; he then took the island of Anglesey (TACITUS, *Agricola* 18).

In 2003 F. P. Retief reported in the *South African Medical Journal*, in an article titled 'The History and Pathology of Crucifixion', that

> In antiquity crucifixion was considered one of the most brutal and shameful modes of death. Probably originating with the Assyrians and Babylonians, it was systematically by the Persians in the 6th century BC. Alexander the Great brought it from there to the eastern Mediterranean countries in the 4th century BC, and the Phoenicians introduced it to Rome in the 3rd century BC. It was virtually never used in pre-Hellenic Greece. The Romans perfected crucifixion for 500 years until it was abolished by Constantine I in the 4th century AD.

In Roman times, we know that it was common for death on the cross to be expedited for very mundane reasons. Again, according to Retief,

> the attending Roman guards could only leave the site after the victim had died, and were known to precipitate death by means of deliberate fracturing of the tibia and/or fibula, spear stab wounds into the heart, sharp blows to the front of the chest, or a smoking fire built at the foot of the cross to asphyxiate the victim.

The Greeks were never that keen, although Herodotus describes the crucifixion of the Persian general Artayctes at around 479 BC: 'They nailed him to a plank and hung him up . . . who suffered death by crucifixion.' Alexander the Great reputedly crucified 2,000 survivors from his siege of Tyre, as well as the hapless doctor who unsuccessfully treated Alexander's friend Hephaestion.

In the war against Spartacus, Crassus revived the much-feared punishment of decimation and made crucifixion popular, and terrifying, again when he lined the road to Rome with 240 kilometres (150 mi.) of prisoners of war rotting on their crosses. Tacitus (*Annals* 2, 32, 2) tells us that there was a special place in Rome outside the Esquiline Gate for crucifixions, with an area reserved for the execution of slaves. Sometimes the victim was attached to the cross with rope, but often the more traumatic option of painful nails was used, as noted by Josephus when writing about the aftermath of the siege of Jerusalem in his *Jewish War* (5, 2): 'the soldiers out of rage and hatred, nailed those they caught, one after one way, and another after another, to the crosses, as a bit of a joke.'

Nails and other crucifixion paraphernalia were perversely much sought after as amulets with alleged medicinal qualities. To expedite the death of the victim, their legs were smashed with an iron club, a procedure called *crurifragium*. The cross itself could be of one of three shapes: either simply a vertical stake (*crux simplex*) or a stake with a cross-piece attached at the top to form a T (*crux commissa*) or just below the top (*crux immissa*). There were also crosses in the shape of the letters X and Y. The oldest surviving image of a Roman crucifixion is a graffito discovered in a taverna in Puteoli (now Pozzulio) from the time of Trajan or Hadrian. The cross is T-shaped; the inscription identifies the woman victim as Alkimila.

The only surviving skeleton of a Roman-era crucifixion was found in 1968 at Giv'at ha-Mivtar in Jerusalem, from the first century AD. These remains of one Jehohanan include a heel bone with a nail driven through it from the side, suggesting that his heels were nailed to opposite sides of the upright stake.

The intended outcome was always, of course, death – but not before hours of intensifying pain. Death occurred over a range of time from hours to days depending on method of crucifixion, the victim's health, co-existing diseases or injuries, how much time the guards had and the environment. Medical experts M. W. Maslen and P. D. Mitchell reporting research in the *Journal of the Royal Society of Medicine* in 2006 have indicated the following as possible causes of death: cardiac rupture, cardiac arrest; hypovolemic shock, acidosis asphyxia; arrhythmia; and pulmonary embolism. Sepsis, too, was common from wound infection caused by the nails or lashings, and there was always dehydration, heat stroke or being eaten alive by carrion or wild animals. Survival was possible – Josephus successfully appealed to Titus to take down three victims, and one lived – but it must have been very rare (*The Life of Flavus Josephus* 75). The Cantabrians were irrepressible; according to Strabo (*Geography* 3, 4, 18), they sang victory songs when nailed to their crosses.

Let sleeping dogs die: when the dogs guarding Rome during the 390 BC sacking by the Gauls slept on duty and some sacred geese were left to sound the warning, the dogs were nailed to crosses and crucified. The *supplicia canum* (punishment of the dogs) became an annual sacrifice in which live dogs were suspended from a fork (*furca*) or cross (*crux*) and paraded. At the same time, geese were dressed in gold and purple and similarly displayed. The failure of the watch dogs to bark was thereafter ritually punished each year (PLUTARCH, *The Fortune of the Romans* 12).

Decapitation and Other Mutilation

The severed heads of enemies were a potent weapon in wars involving the Romans. Frontinus tells how Sulla broke the siege at Preaeneste in 82 BC by sticking the heads of the enemy generals on spears and displaying them to the remaining inhabitants to shatter their morale and break their resolve (*Stratagems*, 2, 9, 3; APPIAN, *Bellum Civile* 1, 93–4). Domitius Corbulo was especially brutal while besieging Tigranocerta in AD 60: he executed the noble Vadandus, whom he had captured, and fired his head from a ballista into the enemy camp. This well-aimed human projectile landed in the middle of a meeting the enemy were holding: the meeting immediately came to a head, persuading the Tigranocertans to seek terms for surrender (FRONTINUS, *Stratagems* 2, 9, 5). Scenes 24, 72 and 57 of Trajan's Column graphically depict Dacian heads on poles; scene 147 shows the head of Decebalus, king of the Dacians. Of course, such atrocities were not exclusive to the Romans; in the same piece Frontinus tells how the Germans under Arminius in AD 9 fixed the heads of the Roman dead on spears and had them brought up to the Roman camp (*Stratagems* 2, 9, 4).

Possibly one of the military world's most ingenious interpretations of a peace treaty's terms came after the Romans' victory over Antiochus the Great, the Seleucid king, required Quintus Fabius Labeo to impound half of the king's navy. This is literally what Labeo did when he sawed all of the Seleucid ships in half and deprived the king of his entire navy (VALERIUS MAXIMUS, *Memorable Deeds and Sayings* 7, 3, 4). The following year (215 BC) Tiberius Sempronius Gracchus faced Hanno at Beneventum (Benevento). Gracchus' army consisted largely of the slaves who had joined up after Cannae – an attempt to make good the serious depletion in Roman troops. In a bid to still their restlessness, and satisfy their yearning for their promised freedom, Gracchus declared that immediate liberty would be granted to every man who brought him a Carthaginian head.

Mass decapitation followed; so intent were the slaves to deliver a head that they neglected to deal with the still-rampant living enemy who were very much in possession of their heads and all their other

The Military and War

faculties and weapons. As such the slaves were encumbered by the awkward heads they were carrying under their arms. Gracchus had to back-pedal: he ordered the slaves to leave the corpses intact, and promised freedom to all regardless – but only if the battle was won. The Carthaginians were slaughtered, with the massacre pursuing them all the way back to their camp. They lost 16,000 men to the Romans' 2,000. Gracchus kept his promise and freed the victorious slaves. Some 4,000 others, with whom he was less than pleased, were not so fortunate – he ordered that they should eat their evening meal standing up, instead of sitting down, for the rest of their service in the legions (LIVY 24, 15).

Pliny also tells us about the great-grandfather of the conspirator Lucius Sergius Catilina and his heroics in the second Punic War. He was twice captured by Hannibal and bound in chains for twenty months but escaped both times. He then had a prosthetic right arm fitted so that he could continue fighting, and twice his horse was killed beneath him (*Natural History* 7, 104–5).

Polybius describes Scipio's ruthless tactics following the siege of New Carthage in Spain in 209 BC:

> When Scipio thought that a sufficient number of troops had gone in he sent most of them, as is the Roman custom, against the inhabitants of the city with orders to kill everyone they met, but not to start pillaging until the signal was given. They do this, I think, to inspire terror, so that when towns are taken by the Romans one may often see not only the corpses of human beings, but dogs cut in half, and the dismembered limbs of other animals. (*Histories* 10, 15)

A similar revelatory eye-opener awaited Philip V and the Macedonians in the Second Macedonian War (200–196 BC) with Livy describing the Romans' merciless use of the *gladius*, the lethal short Spanish stabbing sword:

> Nothing is so uncertain or so unpredictable as the psychological reaction of a crowd. What Philip thought would

make them more ready to enter any conflict caused, instead, reluctance and fear; for his men who had seen the wounds dealt by javelins and arrows and occasionally by lances, since they were used to fighting with the Greeks and Illyrians. But when they had seen bodies chopped to pieces by the Spanish sword, arms torn off, shoulders and all, or heads separated from bodies, with the necks completely severed, or guts exposed, and the other fearful wounds, they realized in a general panic with what weapons and what men they had to fight. Fear seized the king as well, who had never met the Romans in combat. (31, 34)

Chemical and Biological Warfare

The earliest recorded use of chemical warfare in the West is from the fifth century BC, during the Peloponnesian War, when Spartans besieging an Athenian city placed a burning mixture of wood, pitch and sulphur under the walls in the hopes that the noxious smoke would drive out the increasingly incapacitated Athenians.

Solon used hellebore roots to poison the water in an aqueduct leading from the River Pleistos around 590 BC during the siege of Kirrha. Alexander the Great met with poison arrows and fire incendiaries in India at the Indus basin in the fourth century BC.

For the Romans, gas warfare emerges in the wars with the Persians. The collapsed tunnels at Dura-Europos in Syria show that during the siege of the town in the third century AD, the Sassanians used bitumen and sulphur to set it on fire. The toxic and dense clouds of choking sulphur dioxide gases killed nineteen Roman soldiers and a Sassanian.

Lucullus was confounded in the war with Mithridates in the early first century BC when the inhabitants sent bears and swarms of bees and other wild animals and pests into the tunnels under the city of Themiscyra.

The use of infected corpses – human and animal – and faeces as disease-delivering projectiles; well and other water supply contamination; gifting infected blankets and clothing; and despatching infected men and women into populations to spread disease were all relatively common in Greek and Roman warfare.

And it was not just decomposing cadavers to contend with: snake venom and blood mixed with faecal matter were also used, not least by Scythian archers, thus contaminating the enemy with *Clostridium perfringens* and *Clostridium tetani*. Here is how it was done:

> They say that they make the Scythian poison with which they smear arrows, out of the snake. Apparently, the Scythians watch for those [snakes] that have just borne young, and taking them let them rot for some days. When they think that they are completely decomposed, they pour a man's blood into a small vessel, and dig it into a dunghill, and cover it up. When this has also decomposed, they mix the part which stands on the blood, which is watery, with the juice of the snake, and so make a deadly poison. (PSEUDO ARISTOTLE, *De mirabilibus auscultationibus* 141 (845a))

Apparently, the archers had a range of around 490 metres (1,600 ft) and could launch twenty arrows every minute. Herodotus tells us how effective and elusive they were in his *Histories* (Book 4): 'None who attacks them can escape, and none can catch them if they desire not to be found.'

Ovid, in the early Roman Empire, corroborates the biocrime in his *Tristia*: 'To make wounds twice as deadly, these men [Scythians] dip in viper's venom every arrow-tip.' The Harmatelians had this down to perfection. In 326 BC, Alexander the Great and his army arrived at the fortified city of Harmatelia (probably Mansura in modern-day Pakistan), where, according to Diodorus Siculus, they faced a 'new and grave danger'. For some reason morale seemed to be running unusually high in the 3,000-strong Harmatelian camp; Alexander knew that, in the words of Quintus Curtius, the Harmatelians 'had smeared their weapons with a drug of mortal effect', of which the smallest scratch would be fatal to a man. This toxin was harvested from a particular type of viper: the deadly Russell's viper, *Daboia russelii*. The snakes were killed and left to rot in the sun so that heat soon putrified the flesh and the venom mixed with the rotting tissue. Recent herpetological research reveals that the rotting flesh of whatever prey had been digested in the snake's stomach would generate toxic bacteria, but also that vipers retain large amounts of faeces in their bodies over many months. In a dead viper, rotting excrement would add increasing loads of decomposing bacteria to the poisonous mix. A wounded man immediately went numb, suffering stabbing pains and convulsions. Then, their skin became cold and they vomited bile. Black froth spewed from the wound and green gangrene spread rapidly – a truly vile death. Even a 'mere scratch' brought the same gruesome death.

61

Women at War

Women, of course, were officially non-combatants in both ancient Greece and Rome. However, they had a direct, as well as indirect, involvement in the war machines of both civilizations; indeed, both individually and generally women were significant actors in classical military history, both as participants in war and battle – as well as agents of conflict themselves – and, just as importantly, victims of some of war's worst crimes: rape, displacement and enslavement. The following three examples show that women should be accorded their rightful place in the annals of Greek and Roman military and social history.

Pheretima

Pheretima (d. 515 BC), wife of the Greek Cyrenaean king Battus III the Lame, and the last queen of the Battiad dynasty in Cyrenaica (present-day northern Libya): she is remembered by us through a cautionary tale, told by Herodotus. When Battus (the grandfather of Pheretima's son Arcesilaus) died in 530 BC, Arcesilaus III became king but was defeated in a civil war after 518 BC and exiled to Samos, while Pheretima went to the court of King Evelthon in Salamis, Cyprus. Evelthon showered Pheretima with gifts, but would not give her an army, arguing that such a command was simply not right for a woman.

Neither Pheretima nor Arcesilaus, however, took this lying down: he recruited an army in Samos, returned with it to Cyrenaica, and regained his position by murdering and exiling his political opponents – urged on no doubt by Pheretima. When Arcesilaus left Cyrene for Barca, Pheretima ruled the city, but Arcesilaus was murdered by exiled Cyrenaeans intent on revenge.

Pheretima went hot-foot to Arysandes, the Persian governor of Egypt, to get help in avenging the death of her son; Arysandes loaned her Egypt's army and navy. She marched to Barca and demanded the surrender of those Barcaeans responsible for the murder of Arcesilaus; when the Barcaeans refused, insisting that they were all complicit, Pheretima laid siege to Barca for nine months. Amasis, her Persian commander, played a trick on the Barcaeans in which he ordered his soldiers to dig a large trench in front of the city camouflaged with wooden planks and earth; he then lured the Barcaeans out of the city with a promise of a well-rewarded armistice. They literally fell into the trap: Pheretima ordered the Barcaean wives' breasts be cut off and nailed on the city walls and enslaved the rest of the Barcaeans to the Persians.

So Pheretima avenged her son, returned to Egypt and restored the army and navy to the governor. However, while in Egypt, Pheretima had the misfortune to contract a contagious parasitic skin disease and died in late 515 BC. Herodotus tells us that she was eaten alive by worms – perhaps punishment by the gods for her butchery of the women of Barca? She lives on in the name of the worm that infested her, *Pheretima*, a genus of earthworms found mostly in New Guinea and parts of Southeast Asia.

Cleopatra II

Cleopatra II, Ptolemy VI and their brother, Ptolemy VIII, co-ruled Egypt from circa 171 to 164 BC. In 169 BC, Antiochus IV of Syria (Cleopatra's maternal uncle) invaded Egypt; Ptolemy VI Philometor joined up with Antiochus outside Alexandria. Ptolemy VI was crowned in Memphis and ruled with Cleopatra II. Cleopatra II married her other brother, Ptolemy VIII Euergetes II, in 145 BC.

Cleopatra II later led a rebellion against Ptolemy VIII in 131 BC, and drove him and Cleopatra III, her daughter with Ptolemy VI Philometor, out of Egypt. Ptolemy VIII had his son by Cleopatra II, Ptolemy Memphites, murdered and dismembered, and his head, hands and feet sent to Cleopatra II in Alexandria as a birthday present. Cleopatra II ruled Egypt from 130 to 127 BC, when she was forced to flee to Syria. Cleopatra and Ptolemy VIII settled their differences in 124 BC. After this, she ruled jointly with her brother and her daughter until 116 BC, when Ptolemy died, leaving the kingdom to Cleopatra III. Cleopatra II herself died soon after.

Fulvia Flacca Bambula

Velleius Paterculus indignantly records how Fulvia was active in the Perusine War: 'she who had nothing of the woman in her except her sex was creating general confusion by armed violence.' We have intriguing archaeological evidence from excavated sling stones showing how Octavian's troops tied obscene messages onto the stones to fire them directly at Fulvia.

> Two were intended for her cunt, even though she was in Praeneste at the time, with the unmistakeable suggestion that she was a tribade, a lesbian; Fulvia and Lucius were invited to open their arses wide to receive the penis-shaped projectiles (*glandes*): *L[ucius]A[ntonius] Calve [et] F[ulvia] culum pan[dite]*: 'Bald Lucius and Fulvia open up your arses'; 'I'm aiming for Fulvia's fanny': *Fulviae [la]ndicam pet[o]*. They in turn responded by calling Octavian a cock-sucker and wide-arsed, suggesting that he too was open to passive penetration: the ultimate insult for a free-born man: their *billets doux* read *pet[o] Octavia[ni] culum*: 'I'm going for Octavian's anus.' (VELLEIUS PATERCULUS 2, 74, 3; *CIL* XI 721)

What the innovative ballistic graffiti clearly demonstrate is that Fulvia's reputation preceded her: Octavian's soldiers knew that she was active in the war, whether she was at Perusia or not (APPIAN, *Civil Wars* 5, 3, 21; DIO 48, 10, 3).

Martial preserves for us the lascivious epigram that Octavian reputedly composed for Fulvia, another piece of Octavian propaganda designed to promote his virility and his power as a leader of men:

Because Antony is shagging Glaphyra, Fulvia has decided that my punishment will be that I shag her too. *Me fuck Fulvia?* What if Manius begged me to bugger him? Would I? I think not, if I had any sense. 'Fuck or fight', she says. Doesn't she know that my prick is dearer to me than life itself? Let the battle trumpets sound! (*Epigrams* II, 20)

62

Torture

First, some eye-watering tortures routinely carried out in the name of civilization:

> They say that the Ægyptians behave bravely when tortured. And that an Ægyptian being put to torture, will sooner die then confess the truth. As for the Indians, the wives resolutely go to the same fire with their dead husbands. The various wives of the man vie with each other as to who should burn; and she to whom the lot falls is burned with him. (AELIAN, *Miscellaneous History* 7, 18)

Scaphism

When Mithridates, whom we have met before, was naive enough to claim that he had killed Cyrus, the brother of Artaxerxes, king of Persia, he suffered the cruellest of deaths, not dissimilar to death by barbecue:

> Artaxerxes wanted all barbarians and Greeks to believe that when he was exchanging blows with his brother in the cavalry charge, he was himself wounded but personally killed Cyrus. He therefore ordered that Mithridates be put to death by the trough-torture. The trough-torture is as follows: two basins are fitted together and the convicted is placed on his back in one of them while the other is placed on top and fastened to the first so that only the head, hands, and feet are exposed while the rest of the body is covered.

The condemned is given food and if he refuses to eat, then his eyes are gauged out and he is force fed. After eating, he is forced to drink milk mixed with honey which is poured into his mouth and over his face. His head is then turned so his eye sockets always face the sun and as swarms of flies settle there, his entire face is covered by them. The consequent putrefaction caused by his faeces and urine attracted a swarm of maggots and worms which ate away at his body and insinuated itself into his innards. When the man was clearly dead, the upper skiff was removed revealing that the flesh had all been eaten away while swarms of such creatures were growing and eating all around his entrails. This is how Mithridates died after slowly wasting away for seventeen days. (CTESIAS, *Persian History* frg. 26).

It is chilling to note that a variation of this torture was visited on American soldiers during the Vietnam war.

The trough-torture was not dissimilar from the unspeakable torture that was Scaphism. The ancient Persians were among the first to deploy insects as devices of torture. The victim was initially force-fed milk and honey to bring on severe diarrhoea. Then the victim was stripped, lashed to a skiff (or a hollowed-out tree trunk) so that the head, hands and feet protruded over the sides, smeared with honey and set adrift on a stagnant pond or simply left to fry in the sun. Wasps swarmed to the honey and delivered excruciating stings, but the worst was when all manner of insects were inexorably drawn to the diarrhoea faeces swilling around in the boat. Flies would breed in the filth and then begin laying eggs in the victim's anus and increasingly gangrenous flesh. Although the misery could be prolonged by providing the victim with doses of milk and honey, the condemned would eventually succumb to sepsis from being infested with maggots.

Arbaces, a Mede who deserted to Cyrus during battle but returned to Artaxerxes' side after Cyrus was killed, was convicted by the king – not for treason and wickedness, but for cowardice and weakness

– and ordered to carry a naked prostitute on his shoulders while she straddled his neck through the marketplace for an entire day. When another man, in addition to deserting, lied about killing two enemy soldiers, Artaxerxes ordered that he be pierced with three needles through his tongue.

There is yet more from the same court. When Parysatis – the influential Persian queen and consort of Darius II (r. 423 BC–405), son of Artaxerxes – beat the king in a game of dice, for which the prize was a eunuch of their choice, she handed the eunuch over to the executioners with the order that he be flayed alive and his body transfixed sideways on three stakes while his skin was to be stretched out separately.

The Bull of Phalaris

A sadistic Perilaus crafts a bovine torture oven, the Bull of Phalaris:

A fellow countryman of mine, Perilaus, was an admirable artist, but an evil man; until now he had misjudged my character as to think that he could win me over by the invention of a new form of torture – thinking I had a love of torture. He it was who made 'the bull' and brought it to me. I no sooner set eyes on this beautiful and exquisite piece of workmanship, which lacked only movement and sound to complete the illusion than I exclaimed: 'Here is an offering fit for the God of Delphi: I must send it to him.' 'And what will you say,' said Perilaus, who stood nearby, 'when you see the ingenious mechanism inside, and learn its purpose?' He opened the back of the animal, and continued: 'When you want to punish any one, shut him up in this receptacle, apply these pipes to the nostrils of the bull, and order a fire to be kindled beneath. The occupant will shriek and roar in unremitting agony; and his cries will come to you through the pipes as the tenderest, most pathetic, most melodious of bellowings. Your victim will be punished, and you will enjoy the music.' (LUCIAN, *Phalaris* II)

A cynical Cicero tells us that the philosopher Epicurus, ever keen to see the happy side of life, would have it that a virtuous person shut up in the bull would declare: 'How pleasant this is' (*Tusculan Disputations* 2, 17).

Fatal Attraction

Nabis, ruler of Sparta from 207 to 192 BC, nailed his enemies:

> When he had exterminated most of them, he then constructed a kind of machine, if machine it may be called, which was the figure of a woman, clothed in expensive garments, and made to resemble with extraordinary fidelity his wife, Apéga. Whenever he summoned one of the citizens with a view of extorting money from him, he used first to employ a number of arguments politely expressed, pointing out the danger in which the city stood from the threatening attitude of the Achaeans, and explaining how many mercenaries he had to support for their security, and the expenses which fell upon him for the maintenance of the national religion and the needs of the State. If the listeners gave in he was satisfied; but if they ever refused to comply with his demand, he would say, 'Perhaps I cannot persuade you, but I think this lady Apéga will succeed in doing so.' Immediately the figure I have described was brought in. As soon as the man offered his hand to the supposed lady to raise her from her seat, the figure threw its arms round him and began drawing him by degrees towards its breasts. Its arms, hands, and breasts were covered in iron spikes under its clothes. When the tyrant pressed his hands on the back of the figure, and then mechanically dragged the man closer and closer to its breasts, he forced him under this torture to say anything. He destroyed many a man with this fatal attraction. (POLYBIUS, *Histories* 13, 7)

Livy describes the atrocious mutilation of the albeit treasonable and treacherous Mettius Fufetius; his remarks on the humanity of the Romans are disingenuous in the extreme:

[Tullius, the third king of Rome says to him] 'a little while ago your heart was divided between the states of Fidenae and Rome, so now you must give up your body to be torn two ways.' He then brought up two four-horse chariots, and caused Mettius to be stretched out and tied to them, after which the horses were whipped in opposite directions, and galloped off: each of the chariots carried off fragments of the mangled body where the limbs stuck to their fastenings. All eyes were turned away from so dreadful a sight. Such was the first and last punishment among the Romans of a kind that disregards the laws of humanity. In other cases we may boast that with no other nation have milder punishments been good enough. (I, 28)

Damnatio ad bestias – sentenced to death by beasts in the arena, 3rd century, floor mosaic, Amphitheatre of El Djem: 'Criminals destined for a fate without hope were nevertheless well fed in order to fatten the animals . . . a special effort had been made to bring these brave animals from abroad to serve as executioners for those condemned to death' (Apuleius, *The Golden Ass* (IV.13)).

Death was no sanctuary from torture. Fulvia Flacca Bambula (*c.* 83–43 BC) infamously pricked the decapitated Cicero's tongue with her hairpin: this was the bitter revenge she exacted for Cicero's earlier insinuation that Mark Antony, her third husband, married her only for her money (PLUTARCH, *Antony* 10, 3).

Cicero's right hand, his powerful speech-writing hand, was cut off and his head was put on public display in the Forum after his proscription in 43 BC. Fulvia is likened to a man – 'a woman in body alone' – by Velleius Paterculus, who evidently regarded her vengeful and gruesome act as unladylike and, by implication, the sort of thing only a man would or could do. This is Dio's account of the atrocity:

> Fulvia took the head into her hands before it was removed, and after abusing it spitefully and spitting upon it, set it on her knees, opened the mouth, and pulled out the tongue, which she pierced with the pins that she used for her hair, at the same time uttering many brutal jokes.

Fulvia was not the only sadist in town: Pomponia, the widow of Cicero's brother, Quintus Tullius, and sister of Atticus, was even more brutal. When Philologus, the freedman who betrayed Cicero, was brought to her, she ordered him to cut off strips of his own flesh, cook them and then eat them. At least Cicero was already dead when he was decapitated (PLUTARCH, *Life of Cicero* 49).

Tiberius was blessed with a strong left hand: 'His left hand was the more nimble and stronger, and its joints were so powerful that he could bore through a fresh, sound apple with his finger, and break the head of a boy, or even a young man, with a quick flick' (SUETONIUS, *Life of Tiberius* 68).

Epicharis was one of the leading members of the Pisonian conspiracy (AD 65) against the emperor Nero, and she bravely and cleverly outwitted Nero when he tortured her. Day one involved being put on the rack, burnt, flayed and her limbs dislocated; day two was cancelled because she committed suicide (TACITUS, *Annals* 15, 57).

Pavel Svedomsky, *Fulvia with the Head of Cicero*, 1898, oil on canvas.
Fulvia is seen gleefully and sadistically sticking pins into Cicero's tongue –
in life his biggest asset as an orator.

A desperate Sextus Condianus resorts to truly desperate measures to avoid execution by Commodus:

> Sextus Condianus, the son of Maximus, excelled all others in his natural ability and his training, when he heard that sentence of death had been pronounced on him, too, he drank the blood of a hare (he was living in Syria at the time), after which he got on a horse and deliberately fell from it; then, as he vomited the blood, which was intended to appear as to be his own, he was taken up, seemingly on the point of death, and was carried to his room. He now disappeared, while a ram's body was placed in a coffin instead of him and cremated. After this, constantly changing his appearance and clothing, he wandered about here and there. And when this story got out (for it is impossible that such matters should remain secret for very long), a search was made for him high and low. Many were punished instead of him because they resembled him and many, too, who were supposed to have shared his confidence or to have sheltered him somewhere; and still more who had probably never even seen him were

Domenico Beccafumi, *St Ignatius of Antioch Disembowelled by Trajan's Torturers*, 16th century, oil on panel.

relieved of their property. But no one knows whether he was really murdered, – though a great number of heads supposedly his were brought to Rome – or whether he made good his escape. (DIO, *Roman History* 73, 6)

Christian Persecution and Torture

The Christians obviously suffered more than their fair share of torture and death during their centuries-long persecution by the Romans. St Ignatius of Antioch is a case in point: born in Syria, Ignatius converted to Christianity, rising to become bishop of Antioch. However, in AD 107, Emperor Trajan visited Antioch and forced the Christians there to choose between death and apostasy. Ignatius would not deny Christ and thus was condemned to death in Rome in 110. This is how he described his terrible journey back to Rome: 'From Syria even to Rome I fight with wild beasts, by land and sea, by night and by day, being bound amidst ten leopards, even a company of soldiers, who only grow worse when they are kindly treated' (*Ignatius to the Romans* 5).

A few decades earlier,

> The torture and massacre of Christians gathered momentum under the emperor Nero who scapegoated the Christians for the Great Fire of Rome in AD 64 and ordered that all the Christians in Rome be arrested and tortured before executing them as a great spectacle. Some were crucified, some decapitated, some were thrown to wild animals and others were burned alive as living torches (TACITUS, *Annals* 15, 44).

Most bizarrely, the references to the 'women [who] were persecuted as Danaids and Dirce' (*1 Clement* 6.2) refer to a kind of punishment popular under Nero where the condemned women had to wear costumes of the two characters as a reenactment of their myths in the amphitheatre or arena.

SUPERSTITION
AND THE
DARK ARTS

63

Superstition

The Romans were pathologically and obsessively superstitious, and Roman religion was riven by arcane and miraculous traditions. There was a deity for virtually every action a Roman could possibly do.

The post of *flamen dialis*, chief priest to Jupiter, had many perks, but also a number of inconvenient restrictions. For example, you were not allowed to be absent from Rome for a single night, and riding a horse was also forbidden, alongside touching or talking about dogs, nanny goats, beans or ivy – and, most importantly, being naked outdoors.

The Christians took the blame for the Great Fire (July AD 64) and the people of Rome took great delight in pointing the finger of blame in their direction; they

> were convicted not so much of arson as of the more serious crime of hating the human race. When they paid the price for this universal misanthropy they were mocked in the throes of death; some were dressed in animal skins and ripped to shreds by dogs. (TACITUS, *Annals* 15, 44)

The emperor was believed to have possessed healing powers: when a blind man in Alexandria asked Vespasian to smear spit onto his eyes and another asked him to step on his withered hand, both men were miraculously cured (TACITUS, *Histories* 4, 81).

As already noted, superstition was rife and omnipresent. In a society where it was thought bad luck to have a black cat in your house or a snake slither from the roof into your yard, where it was unpropitious if you saw a statue of a god sweating blood, where such malformations as a horse born with five legs, a lamb with a pig's head and a pig with a human head, where a rampant bull skipped up three flights of stairs, a cow started a conversation, a statue laughed uncontrollably, or a horse wept steaming tears – in a world where it was luckless to sneeze near a waiter holding a tray or to sweep the floor when your guest was standing up, where it was imperative you whistle when lightning flashed – in such a world, you would expect to hear that you should cut your nails only on market days, starting with the forefinger and in complete silence but never on board a boat. In certain Italian towns, it was also illegal for women to walk through the streets carrying a spindle, symbol of womanhood as it was.

But it is important we put this into some sort of context and remember that the Romans were probably no more superstitious than many other cultures. Indeed, if we look at the old wives' tales recounted by George Orwell of a rural childhood around 1900, in his novel *Coming Up for Air* (1939), can we say with any conviction that these wives are any less rational than the Romans? Take for example:

> swimming was dangerous, climbing trees was dangerous . . .
> all animals were dangerous . . . horses bit, bats got in your
> hair, earwigs got into your ears, swans broke your leg . . . bulls
> tossed you . . . raw potatoes were deadly poison, and so were
> mushrooms unless you bought them at the grocer's . . . if
> you had a bath after a meal you died of cramp . . . and if you
> washed your hands in the water eggs were boiled in you got
> warts . . . raw onions were a cure for almost anything.

Some superstitions, of course, prevail still, 125 years after Orwell's sheltered upbringing.

The Roman state pantheon featured countless deities dedicated to every conceivable aspect of life, in both this world and, importantly, in the next. Take for example obstetrics: conception, puberty, sex, gynaecology, childbirth and the like. Fortuna Virginalis took good care of virgins, and it was to her that young girls turned and ceremoniously dedicated their togas when they reached physical and sexual maturity around the age of twelve, exchanging it for the *stola*, the garb of a *matrona*, as a mark of the transition to the safeguarding offered by Fortuna Primigenia. Diana too looked after prenuptial girls in her guise as Diana Nemorensis, named after her most celebrated shrine on the northern shore of Lake Nemi, around 30 kilometres (20 mi.) south of Rome. Ovid tells how girls enlisted her help in marriage and childbirth (*Fasti* 3, 269–72). She was also adopted by girls who died before they were married, offering their grieving parents solace with an image of their daughter happily hunting in the afterlife.

Fortuna Primigenia of Praeneste, as noted, stepped in when a girl married; she was the the goddess of mothers and childbirth,

According to the Christian apologist Arnobius, Roman *matronae* were literally taken for a ride (*inequitare*) on the 'awful phallus' of Mutunus with its 'immense shameful parts'. Other sources say that Roman brides straddled the phallus of Mutunus during preliminary wedding rites to prepare themselves for intercourse and learn not to be embarrassed by sex.

whom women shared with men in her capacity as goddess of those male attributes: manliness, material wealth and financial success. Indeed, as Augustine observes, the bridal chamber seems to have been rather overcrowded with well-intentioned divine intervention: Mutunus Tutunus, related to Priapus, was a phallic deity on whom virgins practised before consummating their marriage: Lactantius says 'brides sit on this god's organ to make the first offering of their virginity' (1, 20, 36). His temple on the Velian Hill was visited by women wearing veils, according to Festus. Both words in the god's name, Mutunus Tutunus, are slang for penis.

Sex on one's wedding night is meticulously controlled down to the very last detail:

- Virginiensis, or Cinxia, stands by to loosen the bride's girdle (*cingulum*), along with Subigus who gives up the bride to the groom.
- Prema, goddess of the sexual intercourse itself, attends, as does Inuus, or Pertunda, who helps with penetration.
- Venus provides the passion and Priapus the erection.
- Juno is the goddess in charge of women's sexual function and also has a multifunctional role in marriage: as Iterduca she is specifically responsible for leading the bride to the groom's house and, as Unxia, oversees the anointing of the bride; she is a bridesmaid, as Pronuba, and performs a midwifery function as Lucina.
- Janus paves the way for the semen to enter the vagina, leading, it is hoped, to conception, while Saturn takes care of the semen. Consevius is the god of insemination.
- Liber Pater facilitates ejaculation in men, Libera does likewise for women (sexual incontinence) – the ancients were early believers that women too ejaculated during intercourse.
- Mena (Juno) produces menstruation, which in the pregnant mother is diverted to feed the foetus. Fluonia is Juno, who keeps the nourishing blood in the womb. Vitumnus breathes life into the foetus.

- Sentinus or Sentia develop cognitive function in the newborn.

Ovid adds that women who sacrifice to Rumina – responsible for breastfeeding, as the she-wolf that suckled Romulus – do so with milk and not wine because Rumina perceptively knows that alcohol is harmful to babies (*Fasti* 1, 461–542).

The granular perinatal care continues at length. Rumina was never alone, the Roman maternity room was just as busy and crowded as the bridal suite:

- Alemona was in charge of the foetus.
- Nona and Decima ('ninth' and 'tenth') were responsible for the ninth and tenth months of gestation.
- Parca or Partula stood sentinel over the delivery: at the birth, Parca established the extent of the baby's life in her guise as a goddess of death at which point she adopted the name Morta. The *Prophecy of Parca* indicated that the child was a mortal being.
- Egeria delivered the baby. Postverta and Prosa avert breech birth, considered unlucky while Lucina is the goddess of the actual birth.

And so life begins in earnest:

- Diespiter (Jupiter) gives the infant its first squint at daylight.
- Vagitamus opens the baby's mouth to emit that first vital cry.
- Levana lifts the baby from the ground, symbolizing contact with Mother Earth.

It's not long before concerns regarding the baby's safety and its safeguarding are addressed:

- Cunina looks after the baby while in the cradle, protecting it from malevolent forces and magic.

- Statina fills the baby with energy.
- Candelifera provides the nursery light: this is kept burning to deter the spirits of darkness that would frighten the infant in the crucial first week of birth, and to deter the bogey-women – child-snatching demons such as Gello.
- The *Fata Scribunda* are invoked – the *Written Fates* – a ceremonial inscription of the child's new name. The giving of a name was as important as the birth itself: receiving a *praenomen* established the child as an individual in its own right with its own fate.
- Potina permits the child to drink, Edusa to eat; Ossipago builds strong bones, Carna healthy muscles which defend the internal organs from witches.
- Cuba helps to facilitate the child's graduation from cradle to bed.
- Paventia banishes fear from the child.
- Peta responds to its first demands.
- Agenoria endows it with an active life; Adeona helps it learn to walk.
- Iterduca and Domiduca watch over it as it makes its first tentative foray from the home and comes home again.
- Catius Pater has the power to make children sensible.
- Farinus teaches children to talk; Fabulinus provides its first words while Locutius helps it to form sentences.
- Mens provides intelligence.
- Volumnus makes the child want to do good; Numeria is there for numeracy, Camena for singing; the Muses bestow an appreciation of the arts, literature and sciences.

And so it went on with a host of spirits – or gods – attending to the person at every single stage of his or her life, and death.

64

Entombing a Vestal Virgin

The religious institution that was the Vestal Virgins remains one of the most enduring and revered in Roman history: they were one of the unshakeable foundations of official state Roman religion, influential in the all-important Roman *familia* and household and pivotal to the preservation of the Roman state itself.

In a secular context both Julius Caesar and Augustus deposited their wills with the Vestals. The fact that Vestals, as virgins, enjoyed privileges reserved for married women, matronae, and for men, highlights the ambiguity of their status, but also their vulnerability and the fragility of their reputation. Vestals received a payment on joining and a yearly stipend thereafter; as much as 2 million sesterces were paid out – twice the dowry of a rich girl; Vestals, alone of women in the Republic, could make wills and they were free to dispose of their property. They were also granted front row seats at the games. The Vestals were finally disbanded in AD 394 as a reflection of the rise of Christianity and the decline of the pagan Roman pantheon, but not before a small number had been entombed alive, the horrendous punishment penalty due to a Vestal who mislaid her virginity (*incestum*), or was suspected or falsely accused of having lost it. In Rome, *incestum* was tantamount to treason.

The religious hegemony of the Vestal virgins priesthood began in the era of the Roman monarchy: Dionysius of Halicarnassus records that the first Alba Longa Vestals were whipped to death for breaking their vows of celibacy, and that any resulting infant offspring were thrown alive into the nearest river. Alba Longa was an ancient Latin city destroyed by the Romans around 700 BC. Dionysius (3, 67) attributes the introduction of live entombment to King Tarquinius Priscus (616–576 BC) and says that his first victim was Pinaria. Opimia followed, confessing under torture. Sometimes the 'immuration' followed a whipping, as endured by Urbinia in 471 BC. Before this the punishment of choice for unchaste Vestal Virgins by King Numa Pompilius (r. 715–672 BC) was death by stoning.

That horrendous, suffocating immuration took place in a dedicated cellar under the Campus Sceleratus – the Field of the Impious probably located just south of the Porta Collina, quite close to the Servian Wall in Rome; the male partner was flogged to death in the Comitium like a slave (*sub furca*). The Comitium was the hub of the Roman judicial system so it gives some idea of just how important a trial of an errant Vestal was.

The reasoning behind entombment was that the death had to appear bloodless and it gave time for the goddess Vesta to rescue the 'Virgin' if she were innocent. Vesta never did. Plutarch ponders if entombment was decided upon because the Romans thought it somehow inappropriate that one charged with looking after Rome's eternal and highly symbolic flame should be cremated, the usual penalty, or that one so sacrosanct should be murdered. Incidentally, one of the key duties of all Vestals was keeping the flame in the temple alight so there was always one on duty at any one time. Those careless enough to allow the unthinkable were soundly whipped.

We have Plutarch to thank for his disturbing and graphic account of the solemn process where the condemned Vestal is bound and gagged, dressed as if a corpse at burial and carried to her subterranean prison in a curtained litter; she is unbound and, after a prayer, the *pontifex maximus* puts her on a ladder that leads to the small chamber below. To Plutarch, this is the most shocking spectacle in the world; when it occurs, it is always the most horrific day Rome has ever seen.

But punishment didn't come only for the cardinal sins of allowing the sacred flame to go out or surrendering one's viginity. Sexism and prejudice were sometimes brought to determine justice: in 420 BC, according to Livy, the Vestal Postumia was innocent but was tried for a sexual misdemeanour on the basis of her elegant, bright dress sense and precocious wit. Postumia was acquitted but warned by the *ponitfex maximus* to curb her sense of humour and to dress more modestly: he 'gave her warning to leave her sports, taunts and merry conceits; and in her raiment to be seene not so deft as devout, and weare her garments rather saintly than sightly'. Dionysius of Halicarnassus says that Minucia, the first plebeian Vestal, also aroused suspicion with her fashionable attire, and was arrested on the evidence of a slave. Her sense of humour, dress sense and cheery personality led to her being found guilty of unchastity and so she was buried alive in 337 BC. Her fate was as likely to have been determined more by her plebeian birth as an ill-judged dress sense. Livy matter of factly tells how in 273 BC *Sextilia, virgo Vestalis, damnata incesti viva defossa est* – 'Sextilia, a Vestal Virgin, was accused of *incestum* and buried'; Orosius adds *viva*, 'alive'. Caparronia hanged herself in 266 when accused of *incestum* (her slaves and her defiler were executed); and an anonymous Vestal was entombed in 236 BC.

65

Omens, Prodigies and Oracles

We have seen how superstition among Greeks and Romans was rife and ubiquitous. This, of course, sometimes manifested itself in omens, prodigies, oracles and miracles. And nowhere were these miraculous events more prevalent than in war.

In Lucan's *De bello civili*, Arruns and the *matrona* were called on to interpret the series of terrible omens and repellent portents that appeared in Rome as Pompey and Caesar prepared to do battle at Pharsalia: 'the tongues of brutish animals uttered human speech; and women gave birth to monstrosities both in the size and number of their limbs, and mothers were horrified by the babies they gave birth to' (1, 584f).

When Boudica marched on Camulodunum (present-day Colchester) at the head of the war-drunk Iceni, with its Temple of Claudius, a citadel symbolic of oppressive Roman rule and the focus of their subjugation, the omens were far from good for the Romans:

the statue of Victory in Camulodunum crashed to the ground, supine as if in flight; lamentations rang out, though no mortal man had uttered the words or the groan; hysterical women chorused impending doom, at night there was heard to issue from the senate-house foreign jargon mingled with laughter, and from the theatre outcries and a ghost town on the Thames was seen to be in ruins and the Channel turned blood red; shapes like bodies were washed up. (DIO CASSIUS, *Roman History* 62, 1)

Helios (sun) with signs of the zodiac, from a Byzantine manuscript
of Ptolemy's *Astronomy*, 820.

On a more mundane level: 'If a woman keeps the first tooth lost
by a child and wears it as an amulet, it will protect her from "genital discomfort" – but only if the tooth never touched the ground'
(PLINY, *Natural History* 28, 41).

The Ides of March

It should come as no surprise then that omens, prodigies and prophets
of doom swirled in profusion around the Ides of March. We have
Roman writer Julius Obsequens to thank for the precise detail surrounding supernatural events around 15 March 44 BC as published
in his *Liber de prodigiis,* an account of the wonders and portents that
occurred in Rome between 249 and 12 BC. According to Julius, things
started to get spooky at Caesar's house the night of the 14/15 March:

His wife Calpurnia dreamt that the akroterion [an architectural ornament placed on a flat pedestal called the acroter
or plinth, and mounted at the apex or corner of the pedi-
ment of a building] of the house, which had been added
in accordance with a senatorial decree, fell down. At night
when the doors of the bedroom were closed, they opened by
themselves, so that the light of the moon, which came inside,
woke Calpurnia.

But that was nothing compared to the shenanigans that took place
on the day itself:

At the games of Venus Genetrix, which Cicero performed
for his colleague, at the eleventh hour a comet appeared
from under the North Star and attracted everyone's attention . . . There were frequent earth tremors. The drydocks
and many other places were struck by lightning. A violent
whirlwind shattered the limbs and threw down a statue
which M. Cicero had placed in front of the inner sanctum
of Minerva, on the day before he went into exile in accordance with the plebiscite, and with its shoulders, arms and
head broken portended dreadful things for Cicero himself.
The bronze tablets from the temple of Fides were torn off by
a whirlwind. At the temple of Ops the doors were broken.
Trees were torn up by their roots and many buildings were
demolished. A torch in the sky seemed to be born to the
east. A star blazed conspicuously for seven days. Three suns
gleamed, and around the lowest sun a crown similar to ears
of grain in a circle gleamed out and afterwards when the
sun had been reduced to one globe the light was limpid
for months. In the temple of Castor some letters from the
names of the consuls Antony and Dolabella were shaken
out, which indicated that both of them would be exiled
from their homeland. The baying of a dog was heard during
the night in front of the home of the pontifex maximus,
[Lepidus], from these things especially as the dog was

mutilated by the others it portended scandalous disgrace to Lepidus. At Hostia a shoal of fish was left on dry land by the ebb and flow of the sea. The Po flooded and when it subsided below its banks left a large number of vipers.

Forty Marvellous Things about Water

The Florentine Paradoxographer is responsible for the riveting-sounding *Marvellous Things about Water*, which describes forty springs or rivers with amazing powers. Take the following example of a spring that can

- dye the fleeces in radiant colours of the sheep that drink from it;
- cure wounds, and if you break a stick and throw it in, it comes out joined up again;
- turn your stomach to stone if you drink from it;
- make you drunk;
- make your front teeth drop out;
- throw you back onto the bank if you swim in it.

Checking your horoscope was never going to be a good idea if you believed anything Vettius Valens said; his prognostications are a litany of doom no less, focusing on anatomy, physiology and health in general. Here is an example:

> That is what the earlier astrologers stated. The following seems more accurate in our experience: Aries is indicative of the head in general, the sensory faculties, and the eyesight. In the point now at issue, Aries causes headaches, dimming of vision, strokes, deafness, blindness, leprosy, lichenous scaliness of the skin, loss of hair, mange, baldness, stupor, festering sores, sudden attacks of panting, arthritic joints, tumours, plus whatever syndromes occur of the sensory faculties, the ears, and the teeth. (*Anthologies*, Book 2)

Miracles

Nicanor was lame; while he was sitting wide awake, a boy snatched his crutch from him and ran off. Nicanor got up and chased after him – and so was cured. (*Inscriptiones Graecae* 4, 121–2, stele 1.16)

The Egyptian goddess Isis was very popular, especially in the first century BC. No wonder, if she could guarantee immortality among her many disciples:

Standing above the sick in their sleep Isis gives them help for their diseases and works remarkable cures on those who submit themselves to her; and many who have been given up by their physicians because of the difficult nature of their illness she restores to health, while numbers who have altogether lost their sight or of some other part of their body, whenever they turn for help to this goddess, are restored to their previous condition. Furthermore, she discovered also the drug which gives immortality, by means of which she not only raised from the dead her son Horus, who had been the object of plots on the part of Titans and had been found dead under the water, giving him his soul again and made him immortal. (DIODORUS SICULUS I, 25, 6)

Lucian is, predictably, less than serious:

Cleodemus added; 'I was an unbeliever myself once – worse than you; in fact I considered it absolutely impossible to give credit to such things. I held out for a long time, but all my scruples were overcome the first time I saw the Flying Stranger; a Hyperborean, he was; I have his own word for it. There was no more to be said after that: there he was travelling through the air in broad daylight, walking on the water, or strolling through fire, perfectly at his ease!'

'What,' I exclaimed, 'you saw this Hyperborean actually flying and walking on water?' 'I did; he wore brogues, as the Hyperboreans usually do. I need not detain you with the everyday manifestations of his power: how he would make people fall in love, call up spirits, resuscitate corpses, bring down the Moon, and show you Hecate herself, as large as life.' (*The Lover of Lies* 13, 26)

66

Spells, Curses and Voodoo Dolls

The literature of Greece and Rome provides us with some considerable detail regarding the dark arts. This chapter will look at the magic dispensed by what we might call the amateur or lay practitioner of magic, or by the career magician on his or her behalf. The disaffected dedicator of a curse was for one reason or another intent on delivering life-changing catastrophe upon their victims. We will examine what forms this took, the vehicles by which it was delivered and the causes of and reasons for such dramatic and (usually) malicious activity.

One of the most fertile sources of this information comes from Egypt in the shape of the *Papyri Graecae Magicae*, or *Greek Magical Papyri*. This astonishing body of work is a veritable *vade mecum* of potions and spells, arcane occult knowledge and recipes for magical concoctions accumulated over the centuries. Committed to papyrus in the late third century AD, they are the manuals of itinerant magicians, containing magic formulae and incantations, invocations of infernal gods and daemons, deathly curses, love charms and remedies for erectile dysfunction – hellish Viagra no less.

In addition, we have the *voces magicae* and the *Ephesia Grammata*: Greek magic formulae made up of unintelligible words – mumbo jumbo – that were chanted to ward off evil, the best known being ΑΣΚΙ(ΟΝ) ΚΑΤΑΣΚΙ(ΟΝ) ΛΙΞ ΤΕΤΡΑΞ ΔΑΜΝΑΜΕΝΕΥΣ ΑΙΣΙΟΝ; and hordes of magical *ostraca*, the damning-to-hell *tabellae defixionum*, curse tablets, voodoo dolls, love philtres, amulets and phylacteries, etched with magical formulae. All of these added to the fertile fund of cabalistic and chthonic knowledge and know-how.

Space permits mention of only a few of the 1,600 or so curse tablets that have been found; *defixiones* or *katadesies*, curse tablets or binding spells, reach back as far as the early fifth century BC in the Greek colony of Selinus, Sicily, and in fourth-century Greece, notably in the Agora in Attica. By the second century AD, they had permeated the whole of the Mediterranean and beyond. One of the biggest finds of *defixiones* was at Aquae Sulis (Bath), where 130 (one written in pre-Roman Celtic) were discovered, many an angry (over-)reaction to clothes stolen while their owners were bathing: 'Docimedis has lost two gloves and requests that the thief responsible should lose his mind and eyes in the goddess' temple.'

This thief got off lightly, though, in comparison with: 'so long as someone, be he slave or free, stays silent or knows anything about it, may he be cursed in [his] blood, and eyes and every limb and even have all (his) intestines eaten away if he stole the ring or knows something about it'.

Given the geographic spread of the tablets, from Britain to Egypt, the consistency of their message is quite astonishing and illustrates clearly the uniformity of ancient hate mail throughout different lands and cultures. They reveal an enduring and popular tradition of damning and attempting to mortally or psychologically wound or destroy one's rival or (ex-)lover; traditionally, and appropriately, they were consecrated to the gods of the underworld. The chthonic recipients include Hermes or Mercury, who escorted the dead to the underworld; Hecate, of course; Hades or Pluto and his bride Persephone; and Gaia. In the more exotic empire, the tendency was more to invoke Egyptian gods such as Thoth (Hermes), Osiris and Seth. As an example of how such deities were deployed, here is a list of some of the bad and malevolent work done by Hecate with spells, as recorded in the *Greek Magical Papyri*:

III.1–164: A spell to deify a cat by drowning it and make it into a charm. Hecate is invoked with Hermes.

IV.2006–125: Necromantic spell to bind a spirit of the dead. Hecate is drawn on a flax leaf 'with three heads and six hands, holding torches in her hands, on the right side of her face having the head of a cow; and on the left side the head of a dog; and in the middle the head of a maiden with sandals bound on her feet'.

IV.2622–707: This spell 'attracts in the same hour, it sends dreams, it causes sickness, produces dream visions, removes enemies when you reverse the spell, however you wish'. The phylactery for the spell is a heart-shaped magnetite carved with 'Hecate lying about the heart, like a little crescent.'

IV.2708–84: A hymn to the full moon to secure the affections of a lover. Hecate is syncretized with Artemis, Persephone and Selene.

IV.2785–890: Another hymn with a protective charm: a lodestone carved with 'a three-faced Hecate. And let the middle face be that of a maiden wearing horns, and the left face that of a dog, and the one on the right that of a goat.'

IV.2943–66: Love spell to make a lover 'lie awake for me for all eternity'.

Predominantly a practice of the lower orders, the curses were often provoked by an unfortunate turn of events such as a commercial dispute, lawsuits, or unrequited and spurned love: they gave vent to the curser's vengeful anger, jealousy, malice and vindictiveness. Theatrical and poetical competition rivalry, influencing the outcome of athletic competitions and chariot-race rigging were all attempted through the medium of curse tablets throughout the Roman world, but mainly in North Africa and Syria, in the third and fourth centuries.

Typically, the victim's name was written on a hammered-out lead tablet, although gold, silver and marble tablets have been found; the discovery of stockpiles of blank sheets would suggest that there was a steady, ongoing trade. Animals were not immune.

The infernal consecration was duly made, inscribed and rolled up, and a nail hammered through the name; for security and ancient data protection, this was often supported by the name of the target's mother, in order to avoid mistaken identity – a calamity that would, of course, invalidate the curse and, worse, was tantamount to a missed opportunity. Magical words and symbols were added to improve the chances of success. Some tablets were enhanced with a portrait of the victim that was also pierced with nails. In tablets inspired by jilted love, a lock of the intended's hair was sometimes attached. The texts were initially anonymous, but by the Hellenistic period, a variant, known as 'vindictive prayers', appeared, which bore the name of the author.

Tomb raiding was obviously taken very seriously, as were attempts to prevent it; this stark warning was found at Agios Tychon, Cyprus: 'Anyone who does anything bad to my tomb, then the crocodile, hippopotamus, and lion will eat him.' This was nothing compared with: 'I will seize his neck like that of a goose,' 'His face will be spat at,' 'A donkey will rape him, a donkey will rape his wife' and 'He will be cooked together with the condemned.' Another, found in London and now in the British Museum, forbids the thief to urinate, defecate, speak, sleep, be well – unless and until he brings back what he has stolen to the temple of Mercury.

Many tablets (around 25 per cent of those found) display erotic magic, deployed to wreak bitter revenge on duplicitous lovers, or bind an object of desire to love and sex with the dedicator for the rest of his or her days. The following is typical: 'Bring her thigh close to his, her genitals close to his in unending intercourse for all the time of her life.' From Amathus in Cyprus, discovered in 2008: 'May your penis hurt when you make love.' Short and painfully to the point. Interestingly, it dates from the seventh century AD, demonstrating that, despite centuries of Christianity and its antipathy towards magic, old habits and sentiments die hard when it comes to love and sex.

It must be said that the vast majority of *defixiones* reveal little more than the name of the victim. However, among the remainder there is a fund of dramatic, lurid and frequently obscene detail.

The *defixio* that invokes all manner of physical and psychological calamity on the cheating victim is typical: this, also found in London, reads:

> I curse Tretia Maria and her life and mind and memory and
> liver and lungs mixed up together, and her words, thoughts
> and memory; thus may she be unable to speak what things
> are concealed, nor be able.

and:

> May burning fever seize all her limbs, kill her soul and
> her heart; O gods of the underworld, break and smash her
> bones, choke her, *arourarelyoth*, let her body be twisted and
> shattered, *phrix, phrox*.

This angry and rejected man was leaving nothing to chance. *Arourarelyoth* and *phrix, phrox* are, of course, examples of the arcane untranslatable mumbo-jumbo that often accompanied such curses.

A bitter and broken-hearted Marcus Junius Euphrosynus is equally incandescent, obviously torn between grief for a daughter and hatred towards her mother; he set up a tomb to the eight-year-old daughter, Junia, in the first century AD. On it, he very publicly curses Acte, his treacherous, tricky, hard-hearted poisoner of a shameful wife, hoping that she gets in the next life as bad as she gave in this. He considerately leaves the adulteress a nail and a rope for her neck and burning pitch to sear her evil heart.

A late second-century curse on Rufa Pulica, discovered in an urn also containing her ashes in Mentana, near Rome, lists a number of body parts: the focus on her sexual organs is somewhat prurient and suggests that illicit sex on her part was involved at some point. Ticene of Carisius suffered a similar post-mortem tirade on a tablet found at Minturnae, south of Rome; her curser wishes that everything she ever does goes wrong: his catalogue of her body parts is less sexual than Rufa's, but is weirdly systematic, running as it does, more or less, from head to toe. A man called Philo may have had something to hide when he cursed Aristo: he metaphorically ties up her hands, feet and soul, condemns her to eternal silence and wishes her tongue be bitten off. In the fourth century BC, the wife of Aristocydes curses him and his lovers, willing that he will never marry another woman ... or boy (*Deutsche Inschriften und Bilder zu den Zauberhandlungen in der Antike* (*DTA*) 78).

Over time, some tablets became more and more elaborate and sophisticated. One, a circus-competition curse from fourth-century AD Rome, features illustrations which embellish the text. It wishes an evil death on Cardelus, son of Fulgentia, within the next five days – presumably before the day of the race. Pictures include a horse-headed demon holding a whip and a chariot wheel, and the victim peering from a coffin, both transfixed with nails. Every other line is written upside down. On other curses, the name of the victim is written in reverse or jumbled up.

If Ammonion gets his way, Theodotis has little chance of escaping the clutches of this frantic and perverted paramour. What it lacks in romance it certainly makes up in comprehensiveness; all corners are covered:

> I bind you, Theodotis, daughter of Eus, to the snake's tail, the crocodile's mouth, the ram's horns, the asp's poison, the cat's whiskers, the god's appendage, so that you may never be able to have sex with another man, not be shagged or be buggered or give a blow job, nor do anything that brings you pleasure with another man, unless I alone, Ammonion, the son of Hermitaris, am that man. For I alone make this erotic binding-spell work, this one that Isis used, so that Theodotis, the daughter of Eus, may no longer be penetrated by a man other than me alone, Ammonion, the son of Hermitaris, dragged in slavery, driven crazy, taking to the air in search of Ammonion, the son of Hermitaris, and that she may rub her thigh on my thigh, her genitals to my genitals, for sex with me for the rest of her life. (*Supplementum Magicum* 38, 1990 (Egypt, second–third century AD))

For good measure this obsessive curse is complemented with a series of pictures that depict a god with a sceptre, a snake, a crocodile and a couple kissing and a penis penetrating a vagina (*Supplementum Magicum* 161).

Sarapammon (*Supplementum Magicum* 47) invokes a whole pantheon of infernal gods in his insane efforts to ensure the fidelity of Ptolemais: he asks the *daemon* Antinous to bind Ptolemais to stop her from having intercourse or from being sodomized:

> and give no pleasure to any man but me . . . and let her not eat, nor drink, nor be happy, nor go out, nor sleep with anyone but me . . . drag her by the hair and entrails until she

Nude female voodoo doll, the 'Louvre Doll', in kneeling position, bound and pierced with thirteen pins. Found in a terracotta vase with a lead tablet bearing a binding spell (*katadesmos*), Roman Egypt, 3rd–4th century AD.

does not reject me . . . submissive for her entire life, loving me, desiring me.

That tablet was found in a vase, fittingly enough in Antinoupolis, which also contained a voodoo-type clay figure of a submissive, kneeling woman, her hands tied behind her back and body pierced with needles – the 'Louvre Doll'. Love is strange.

So, some men and women were prepared to go to inordinate and obsessive lengths to bind and restrain, to guarantee the fidelity of their women and men: this voodoo doll curse (PGM 4, 296–466) is one of the most notorious and malevolent, and takes a typically prescriptive, recipe form: 'take wax or clay from a potter's wheel and form it into two figures, a male and a female . . . her arms should be tied behind her back, and she should kneel.' This is supported by some sinister instructions: inscribe magical words on her head and other parts of her body, including the genitals; stick a needle into her brain, and twelve others into other organs; tie a binding spell written on a lead plate to the figures, dedicate it to gods of the underworld and leave it at sunset near to the tomb of someone who has died violently or prematurely; invite them to rise from the dead and bring X (the object of the charm), daughter of Y, to him and make her love him. There then follows a litany of evil instructions to deprive the girl of food and drink, sexual intercourse, sleep and health – all designed to make her make love with the curser in perpetuity. Dehumanization and ritual abuse – physical, psychological and sexual subjugation – were the order of the day.

Osthanes had just the thing for any man looking to totally wreck a woman's sex life:

If the genitals of a woman are smeared with the blood of a tick from a wild black bull, she will find sex repellent, as Osthanes says, and love too, if she drinks the urine of the billy-goat, with spikenard [an aromatic plant] mixed in to disguise the disgusting taste. (PLINY, *Natural History* 28, 256)

There is more genital smearing with a lotion that, as far as fourth-century AD Akarnachthas is concerned, has everything going for it: everlasting love and exclusive sex. The spell was excavated in Egypt: the very specific recipe comprises a crow's egg, the juice of a crow's foot plant, and the bile of an electric catfish fished from the Nile; these are to be ground up with honey and smeared on his penis while chanting the following spell:

'Vagina of NN, open up and take the semen of NN and the unconquerable seed of . . . let NN love me for all of her life . . . and let her remain chaste for me, as Penelope did for Odysseus. And you vagina, remember me all my life because I am AKARNACHTHAS.' Chant these words as you work the ingredients, and whenever you anoint your genitals, and so have sex with the woman you want. She will love only you, and no one but you will fuck her. (PGM XXXVI.283–94)

The malicious objective of another papyrus (fourth century AD) aims to render the woman target sleepless until she relents:

Take the eyes out of a bat and release it alive. Take unbaked dough . . . or wax and shape a puppy dog. Put the right eye of the bat into the right eye of the puppy and the left eye of the bat into the left eye of the puppy. Take a needle and stick the magic substance into it. Prick the eyes of the puppy . . . Pray: 'I conjure you to . . . make X lose the fire in her eyes or become sleepless and have no one in mind except me . . . and love me passionately.' (PGM IV.2943–66)

Curses were not exclusively heterosexual: one from the second century AD describes a 'lesbian' curse where Heraias brings and binds the heart and soul of Sarapias. In an Egyptian curse, Sophia attempts to inflame the heart, liver and spirit of Gorgonia through a corpse demon.

It was not always fire and brimstone, however. There are occasional examples of well-intentioned love *defixiones* where a person will enlist chthonic deities to help them win the love of their life. The optimistically named Successus dedicates his wife in a bid to see his love for her requited: 'may Successa burn, let her feel herself aflame with love or desire for Successus.' Lots of fire but no brimstone here.

It is clear from these examples that the organs targeted were not coincidental. Those tablets seeking to achieve erotic restraint and binding focus on the sexual organs of the target. By the same token, tongues are often the object of binding curses intended to influence the outcomes of lawsuits. One example is fired at Selinontios, whose tongue is to be twisted until it is rendered useless (*SGD* # 99). Examples of literary evidence for this include Aristophanes' *Wasps* (946–8). Cicero, defending Titinia, describes how Curio, his adversary, completely dried up as a result of drugs and incantations (*veneficia*) delivered by Titinia (*Brutus* 217); and Ovid's old hag teaches young girls how to bind tongues with lead, thread, beans and the head of a fish (*Fasti* 2. 571–82). On a more mundane level, we have seen how it is Cicero's tongue that Fulvia gleefully cuts out from his decapitated head in revenge for his tactless remarks regarding her marriage to Mark Antony – she knew how to damage the orator most, even in death.

Competitive curses were used in a number of different scenarios: in Athens, the choral trainers and under-trainers of Theagenes were cursed (*DTA* 34) in a theatrical imprecation; a well in the Athenian Agora has given up a hex aimed at the wrestler Eutychian and other athletes (*Supplementum Magicum* 24–9). As noted, chariot races from the second century in the Roman world were a magnet for curses amid the intense fanaticism of the various factions, and the charioteers themselves; competition was at fever pitch, with betting money as well as pride at stake. Magic and cursing in competitions became so much of a problem that in AD 389, the *Theodosian Code* decreed that practitioners be exposed (9, 16, 11); Ammianus Marcellinus records three times that charioteers were prosecuted (26, 3, 3; 28, 1, 27; 29, 3, 5), and in AD 510, the great success of one, Thomas, was attributed to the use of magic – the ancient parallel to the spectre of performance-enhancing drugs today (*Variae Epistolae* 3.51, Cassiodorus) and match rigging. Attempts to compromise the fitness of athletes resulted in curses to keep them up all night and without sustenance (*Supplementum Magicum* 157).

Trade and commercial competition, then as now, brought out the worst in people, and they were not averse to resorting to sinister curses to beat the opposition. The precedent is set by a very early curse in the Hesiodic hexameter poem *Kiln*, in which aptly named demons are invoked against rival potters leaving nothing to chance. The angry dedicator invoked these demons, weapons of mass destruction: Crusher, Smasher, Unquenchable and Unbaked Pot Wrecker and Shatterer. The destruction is nothing short of total, reputational, financial and physical:

> May the entire kiln be thrown into consternation and may the potters wail at length. Just as the horse's jaw grinds, may the kiln also grind all the pots within it reducing them to fragments. Come here to me too, daughter of Helios, Circe of the many drugs cast your wild spells and damage these men and their works. Let Chiron also bring here to me all the centaurs, both those who escaped from Heracles and those who were killed. May they smash these works up, and destroy the kiln. May the potters themselves witness these terrible deeds and lament. But I will rejoice as I look upon their ill-fated handicraft. If any of them peer into the kiln, may fire scorch his whole face, so that they may all learn to treat people fairly. (*Homer Epigram 14 at Life of Homer 32 = Hesiod F302 MW*)

Disaffected potters apart, the trades involved in this magical warfare range across the whole gamut of classical commerce – from innkeepers to net makers, from brothel keepers to shield makers, from bellows makers to doctors and painters, from seamstresses to goldsmiths and flour sellers.

Voodoo dolls were deployed to bind commercial victims, too; 38 have been found. They are made from a variety of materials including lead, bronze and clay, as well as wax, wool and dough ones cited in literary sources. The typical doll demonstrated a number of characteristics that included their legs or arms twisted behind the back as if bound; impaling with nails; the extremities and/or upper torso contorted back to front; and confinement in a box or similar (coffin?). The doll might also be inscribed with the name of the victim, or found in a grave or sanctuary.

The celebrated orator Libanius is an example of a victim who fell foul of a voodoo doll. Plagued with headaches and, significantly, rendered speechless, Libanius eventually discovers the cause of an affliction that has serious consequences for him as an orator: he finds in his classroom a chameleon that had been decapitated and its mouth bunged up with one of its front legs; the head was stuffed behind its back legs; the missing forelimb equated, significantly, to the 'right arm', the invaluable gesticulating arm of a professional orator (1.243–50).

A similar outcome awaited Theophilus of Alexandria, as narrated by Sophronius in the late sixth century AD. Like curse tablets, the voodoo curse could, as Libanius found, be nullified if the guilty doll was discovered. Sophronius in the *Account of the Miracles of Saints Cyrus and John* described how Theophilus was reduced to being a tetraplegic because his so-called friends had invoked the Devil to fill all his limbs with pain. Theophilus was visited by saints in his dreams who told him to hire a fisherman to go out to sea. The fisherman duly caught a small lead-sealed box in his net. Inside was a bronze effigy of Theophilus with a nail driven though each of his limbs. As each nail was extracted, the pain and paralysis in the corresponding limb was banished.

Amulets

Amulets (*periamma, periapton, amuletum* or *remedium*) were both an important and a pervasive means of delivering magic, mainly on the health-care front. People wore them as a (distinctly unclinical) way of deflecting or curing illness and to ward off the evil eye and other unwelcome intruders on their general well-being.

Cato the Elder's folk and family medicine illustrates well the combination of the primitive amulet and *voces magicae* incantations from about 160 BC:

> If you have any kind of dislocation, it will be healed by this incantation.
> Take a green reed four or five feet long, split it down the middle, and have two men wrap it round your hips. Begin the incantation, *motas vaeta daries dardares astataries dissunapiter*, until they join. Wave a knife over them. When they have met and are touching each other, take the reed in your hand and cut it short on both right and left sides. Bind the reed-pieces to your dislocation or fracture and it will heal. Use the incantation on a daily basis, or, for a dislocation, you can use this one: *haut haut haut istasis tarsis ardannabou dannaustra*. (*De agri cultura* 160)

Valerius Maximus describes how in the reign of Tiberius, three temples were built dedicated to Febris (malaria), and that the amulets worn by the sick were brought to the temple in gratitude for their recovery. In the reign of Constantius in AD 359, the wearing of amulets was considered with such suspicion that some people protecting themselves against quartan fever were denounced and condemned to death. The Christians believed amulets to be useless, the Devil's poison indeed, even when they contained holy material.

Animals too benefitted from the insurance afforded by amulets: Grattius, an Augustan poet, ridicules the ancient habit of tying badger hair, coral and necklaces of shells and plants – all accompanied by incantations – to the collars of hunting dogs in order to ward off the evil eye.

Lotions, like amulets, could bestow invisibility; here is a recipe from the fourth century AD:

> Take some fat or one eye of a long-eared owl, a scarab's dung-ball and some sage oil. Rub them down to form a

smooth paste, smear it all over your body, and say to Helios: 'I adjure you by your great name, BORKÊ PHOIOUR IÔ ZIZIA APARXEOUCH THUTHÊ LAILAM AAAAAA IIIII ÔÔÔÔ IEÔ IEÔ IEÔ IEÔ IEÔ IEÔ IEÔ NAUNAX AIAI AEÔ AEÔ ÊAÔ.' Dilute it and say: 'Make me invisible, lord Helios, AEÔ ÔAÊ EIÊ ÊAÔ, before every person until sunset, IÔ IÔÔ PHRIX RIZÔ EÔA.' (*PGM* I.222–32)

The Evil Eye

The evil eye caused problems for anyone or anything in its range, so those who could project it were in a powerful position. Plutarch gives us some details:

> [Mestrius Florus:] For we know of people who do severe harm to children by glaring at them, compromising their development at this weak and tender stage, and corrupting. Those with sturdier and full-grown bodies are less susceptible to this. And yet Phylarchus says that the Thibians ... were deadly not just to children but also to adults. Those on the receiving end of a look, a breath, or an utterance from them shrank away and fell sick. (*Moralia* 680c–683b)

The Greeks and Romans ascribed to the evil eye a number of characteristics that include envy as the catalyst for focusing the evil eye, which, interestingly, was not confined to projection from the eye but could be emitted via speech and breath. It was damaging to fertility, and so particularly effective against children, impacting a child's future fertility and crops. It was associated with people, especially women, with double pupils (polycoria) and was often delivered by a sidelong glance. Paradoxically, it could scupper magic, so sorcerers, working as they did in a world full of envy, were especially anxious. It could ruin burgeoning love affairs but might be averted by spitting or by wearing a phallus, and in particular a phallus amulet. The skin of the hyena was also an effective weapon. The conjunction of spitting and the phallus can be seen together in an astonishing Roman mosaic depicting a phallus ejaculating into a disembodied eye (PLINY, *Natural History* 28, 256).

Apollonides describes a race of women in Scythia, the Bythiae, who had two pupils in each eye – quadrifocals. If they were angry and fixed their stare on you, you would die (DONATUS, *Hist.Med. Mirab.* 1.6).

The 'Meaningless' *Voces magicae*

The widespread use of *voces magicae* in curses and amulets is very apparent from some of the examples above from the Imperial period. They were magical words with no obvious meaning, yet their very mystery gave them, and the magic people who uttered them, considerable power. The most common *voces magicae* are the 'Ephesian letters' (*Ephesia grammata*), which look like, but are not, Greek words. Our first mention of them is a first-century AD text found near Mycenae apparently giving thanks for vengeance: 'The Ephesian vengeance (*menysis*) was sent down. Firstly Hecate harms the belongings of Megara in all things, and then Persephone reports to the gods. All these things are already so.' They are commonly used in curses, to which they added protective qualities, famously illustrated by a fragment of Menander which shows how they were used to ward off spells inflicted on newly married couples.

It would appear that many of the *voces magicae* were corruptions of the names of deities or demons derived from some language or another. One demon, Abrasax, was a cock-headed, armoured demon with snakes for legs – his Latin title was 'the Anguipede', associated with the number 365 (interestingly based on the numerical value of his name's letters and so with the Sun). Associated with this were the Charakteres, a second-century AD magical alphabet used in curses. A set of 38 of them was drawn on a pair of tablets from Apamea in Syria.

Historian of the ancient world Daniel Ogden, in an article titled 'Binding Spells', published in 1999, tells how the seven vowels held particular power and were associated with planets, angels and sounds. He also reveals that *voces magicae* would often be arranged into shapes such as squares, triangles (isosceles or right angled) or diamonds; palindromes were also quite common.

67

Witches and Witchcraft

This section describes the various qualities, characteristics and competencies of witches in ancient Greece and Rome. Not just anyone could practise witchcraft: some were born witches, it was in their DNA (the Devil's deoxyribonucleic acid); others had to learn the (witch-)craft from scratch, and others still had witchcraft imposed upon them, either through calumny or political exigency.

To be a witch in ancient times, you had to be totally unscrupulous, devoid of any morals, and prepared to work with the most objectionable of people. Witchcraft, therefore, attracted quite a lot of witches. They were, by and large, repellent creatures. In mythology, they were magical and scheming; in the real world, they were foul and repugnant, scuttling around in the deepest pits of depravity. In literature, they plumbed uncharted depths of obscene atrocity. To the Romans, though, they satisfied and responded to an obsession with superstition; so, although they were loathed, they were sometimes valued, occasionally operating at the highest level of government. Nevertheless, to most Roman men, the witch was something to be feared. The Roman woman paradigm held them as unobtrusive and subservient, looking after the home, raising the children and knitting the wool. The idea of a woman, a witch, controlling events and controlling them would have been anathema to the Roman, something to be feared, avoided at all costs, suppressed and ostracized.

Throughout history, the witch never recovered from this political, social and religious stigma, paranoia and vilification; it was the Romans who gave us the nasty, ugly, dipsomaniac witch. Ancient authors tend to agree on the stereotypical witch: she (the witch was generally a she-witch) was usually old, ugly and was sometimes drunk and over-sexed – a nymphomaniac, employing witchcraft as a means of satisfying her lust through eros magic. Witches may not always have been ugly, malevolent or alcohol dependent, but it suited Romans to stereotype them in this way: indeed, in Apuleius, we find a pretty witch in Fotis. Socially, witches were at best risible and irritating, at worst guilty of crimes against humanity. Witches were typically malicious and squalid, and they were abhorred all the more for it.

In Greece, psychiatric illness was related to demonic possession, and descriptions of witches often show them to be burdened with mental issues. In Rome, we have already noted how women with mental health problems were shunned, taunted and often spat at in public; a good example of how the Romans met superstition with superstition.

Witches were thought to be responsible for lunar eclipses: Martial describes the clashing of pots and pans in a bid to ward off their evil influence: 'when the eclipse of the moon is lashed by the Colchian magician's wheel (rhombus)'. The *rhombus* was a four-spoked magician's wheel often used to attract women: a cuckoo was attached and whipped like a top; the object of desire was then drawn by some invisible force to the wheel, and to the man. Tacitus describes how Drusus' fearful army made a clashing din and blasted their trumpets to avert an unpropitious eclipse. Pliny the Elder records that men were so unsettled by witches that they resorted to fixing a wolf's beard, good both for and against spells, to their doors to deter them. Witches and magic do not escape Juvenal's vitriolic sixth satire: women use *magici cantus* and *Thessala philtra* to vex their husbands, to drive them mad, to gaslight them, fog their brains and induce short-term memory loss.

One busy witch has left her footprint, or rather her thumb print, on history. In Rome's Piazza Euclid, the remains of a fountain dedicated to a minor goddess, Anna Perenna, have been excavated to unearth a prodigious number of voodoo dolls and lead curse tablets dating from the fourth century AD. One of the dolls has a thumbprint on it – probably a woman's, according to the local police fingerprint laboratory.

And it was not just witches who practised witchcraft. There was a lot of it going on in the wider community – particularly among the Julio-Claudians in their internecine battles to secure the succession of their sons to the imperial throne. Roman historians tell us that witches were complicit in the death of two likely heirs to the imperial throne, Germanicus and Britannicus, and in the fungal assassination – that is, death by mushroom – of one emperor, Claudius.

What were the witch's qualifications? How did she get the job? We must look now at how magic relates specifically to witches and how witches practised magic as a means to their infernal ends. Magic of one variety or another was the cornerstone of a witch's armamentarium and has been defined as 'any attempt to control the environment or the self by means that are either untested or untestable, such as charms or spells'. The virtual opposite then to empirical evidence, logic or reason. A witch had to be nothing less than a world-changer – and a life-changer, too – skilful in nighting day and daying night, eclipsing the moon, drawing it down, rolling rocks and reversing rivers, hassling the gods above, consorting with the gods below, tearing foetuses from wombs and burning babies; she had to be proficient in necromancy – and in bringing the dead back to life. Easy enough stuff for the woman qualified in dubious pharmacology and all things eschatological, the old, ugly hag adept at burying the living and communing with hell through a dead man's mouth.

In the early days of the Roman Empire, Ovid depicted a squalid specimen by the name of Tacita who performed imitative magic to 'stop hostile tongues wagging and close the mouths of enemies'. We find her tutoring three young girls in the evil arts. Having deposited three pieces of incense under the threshold of the intended victims she then binds magic threads onto lead, rolls seven black beans around in her mouth. Next she takes a fish head, the mouth of which has been sealed shut with tar and sewn up with a bronze needle, pouring some wine over it before frying it. She and the girls drink it up; she pronounces their success in silencing 'the enemy' and staggers off drunk.

All of this and more would feature on the witch's *curriculum vitae* – or should that be her *curriculum mortis?*

KNOWLEDGE OF KNOWLEDGE of the future was a key asset. The future was the future for apprentice witches. The method of choice for divining the future was through necromancy. A necromancy conducted by an old witch woman of Bessa is one of the best examples. Calasiris, a priest of Isis, and Charicleia, the heroine of the *Aethiopica* 190, a novel by Heliodorus of Emesa from the third century AD, come across the aftermath of a battle between the Persians and the Egyptians, a battlefield littered with the dying and with corpses. The only living soul is an elderly Egyptian woman mourning her dead son; she invites the couple to spend the night there, and in the course of which Charicleia witnesses a shocking scene:

> The old woman, thinking that this was a good time not to be seen or disturbed, dug a trench, then lit a fire on both sides and laid her son's body in the middle. Then, taking an earthen pot from a nearby three-footed stool, she poured honey into the trench; out of another pot she poured milk, and from the third a libation of wine. Lastly into the trench she threw a lump of dough hardened in the fire, which was formed in the shape of a man and crowned with a garland of laurel and fennel. This done, she picked up a sword which lay among the dead men's shields, and, in a Bacchic frenzy, prayed repeatedly to the moon in strange, foreign tongues. Then she cut her arm and, with a branch of laurel, sprinkled her blood on the fire; and, after doing many monstrous and bizarre things beside these, she finally bowed down to her dead son's body and whispered in his ear.
>
> She woke him up, and using her witchcraft, made him stand up suddenly. Chariclea [*sic*] looked on in terror, she trembled with horror and was utterly undone by the miraculous sight; she woke Calasiris and made him watch the spectacle. They could not be seen in their dark corner, but

they could easily see what the witch did by the light of the fire, and heard also what she said, because they were not very far away, and the old woman spoke loudly to the corpse. Her question was this: 'Would his brother, her son who was yet alive, return safely or not?' The body did not reply, but by nodding gave his mother some tenuous hope, and then fell down upon its face again. But she turned it over on its back and kept asking that question, all the more forcefully, it seemed, speaking in his ear. Sometimes she leapt, sword in hand, to the trench, sometimes to the fire, and at length she made the body stand upright again and asked the same question, compelling him to answer not by nods and motions but plainly by word of mouth.

No witch will find a better description of how to perform a necromancy and a reanimation. The corpse at first is reticent but, because his mother persists, he rebukes her for sinning against nature and breaking the all-important law relating to proper burial when she should have been busy organizing his burial. He reveals not only that his brother is dead but that she too will soon die violently because of her life outside the law, divine and secular. Before collapsing again, the corpse reveals a truth yet more terrible to his mother: her necromancy had been witnessed by both a priest 'beloved by the gods' and a young girl who has travelled to the ends of the earth looking for her lover. A happy outcome is promised for both; the old mother witch is outraged by this intrusion and, while pursuing Calasiris and Charicleia, is fatally impaled on a discarded spear.

Some witches could shape-shift, most often into a screech owl. These witches were called *strigae*, after the owls. The *strix* or *striga* was a bird of ill omen that feasted on human flesh. Some witches could also render themselves invisible. Bodysnatching, as well, was part of the witches' repertoire. In Petronius' *Satyricon*, Trimalchio tells how the recent death of his master's son attracted a coven of screeching witches; their Cappadocian slave goes out to deal with them and stabs one of them with his sword. The mourning mother then goes to her son's body only to find there a straw effigy; the witches had stolen his corpse and left the straw doll in its place. The Cappadocian – much the worse from having been touched by the evil hand of the witches – goes mad and dies soon after.

Child-hating and a facility for serial child murder were also prerequisites. We have evidence for real-world kidnapping in the shape of the three-year-old son of Iucundus, who 'was snatched by a witch's hand'. Despite their obvious grief, the parents use the tragic fate of their little boy to send a warning to other parents to 'look after their children well' lest they too suffer a similar bereavement. Ironically, the ill-named Iucundus (Happy Man) was the slave of Livia Julia (Livilla), wife of Drusus Caesar; she was executed for allegedly poisoning her husband in AD 23.

Rejuvenation and reanimation were other odious skills in the witch's tool bag. As we have seen in our discussion of Medea as a bad mother and child murderer, she was an expert in rendering the young old – with horrendous ramifications. We have also already met Erichtho, who performs what is probably one of history's most ghastly acts of reanimation.

Medea is the witch to emulate for it is she who exemplifies the gold standard in witchcraft, chthonic know-how and the satanic. Reading her opening soliloquy on her love for Jason you would get no idea of the malevolence to come. It is through Medea's potent magical herbs that Jason is able to complete some of his challenges: he pacifies the fire-breathing bulls, throws the troops born of the dragon's teeth into fatal turmoil and drugs the dragon, savage guardian of that famous fleece.

Job done, Jason and Medea marry; but Jason's first thoughts are with his father, Aeson, whose life, with his bride's help, he is anxious to extend: 'if your sorcery can achieve what I desire, take from my life some years that I should live and add them to my father's final days.' A moved Medea is shocked at the evil nature of such an impious plan but agrees to ratchet up the diabolic. If you should ever need to master the skills of rejuvenation and jugulation, Medea provides the infernal procedure through Ovid in his *Metamorphoses*. Medea transfuses him with the satanic potion and successfully restores him to a man forty years younger. Grey hair, pallid complexion, wrinkles, flabby limbs – all gone in a flash.

However, as noted, the mercurial Jason proves fickle and jilts Medea, who is then hell bent on bloody vengeance. Her first move is to murder Pelias, Jason's uncle; practising on an old sheep, which she magically transmogrifies into a lamb, the deceitful Medea then convinces Pelias's daughters that she can rejuvenate Pelias in much the same way she did the sheep, and Aeson before that. In a frightening scene that anticipates Erichtho's repellent reanimation of the civil war soldier, she fills her bubbling cauldron with placebo herbs and orders the gullible daughters to slash Pelias to pieces with swords. This they do so with some understandable reluctance; when their father resists, Medea finishes him off by sinking her knife into him and then plunging him into the cauldron. The carnage and mayhem continue when Medea flees to Corinth, kills Jason's new wife and her own children to punish him, and marries Aegeus, father of Theseus.

Medea, of course, was far from alone. Who were *the* witches to imitate and emulate? It is multi-potion (*polypharmakos*) Circe, the first 'classical' witch, a witchy kind of woman, who leads the way and provides a road map for aspirants. When Odysseus and his crew show up (in the *Odyssey* Book 10) she is there with everything any self-respecting witch can muster: magic – sympathetic and otherwise; invocations – curses and sacrifices; necromancy – the gold standard of invocations; *pharmaka* – more magic, poisons, love philtres and aphrodisiacs, potions that restore youth or are form-changing.

Circe unhelpfully magics Odysseus' crew into pigs (and then back again) at the wave of a wand and with a simple spell and a simple potion (HOMER, *Odyssey* 10, 212f). Odysseus himself is immune from all of this because Mercury, in his role as a male sorcerer, had slipped him *molu*, a dodgy kind of snowdrop with protective and mystical properties.

Immune from the porcine magic as he is, Odysseus nevertheless succumbs to Circe's physical charms and the two begin a passionate affair, during which she reveals his future for him, including Odysseus' forthcoming appointment with dead people in his necromancy. Circe has other witchy attributes: she can make herself invisible and she can fly through the air; she has the power to emasculate her lovers, as implied by Odysseus' not unreasonable insistence before he agrees to sleep with her that she does not turn him into an effeminate coward post-coitus. After a refreshing bath, Odysseus is still concerned about his men and convinces Circe that they need to be restored to their previous form; this she does, with the added bonus that they each return to the real world rejuvenated.

Circe embodies everything a witch needs to practise effectively: magical skill and magical accoutrements, mystical plants, witchcraft, erotic magic, divine intervention, rejuvenation skills and a working knowledge of eschatology. All these attributes, in the next five to six hundred years, were cultivated and developed in Greek society, literature, religion, philosophy and science. Later, it all began to insinuate itself into Roman culture and society and then to surface in Roman literature.

Pasiphaë, daughter of Helios and Perse and niece to Medea, was an active sorceress (when she was not busy having sex with a bull). She was an adept practitioner in magical herbal arts and a goddess no promiscuous man would want to cross. The fidelity charm she inflicted on Minos caused him to ejaculate serpents, scorpions and centipedes with the inevitable result that the concubine involved died a horrific death; how eye-wateringly painful this was for Minos is not recorded. Only Procris had an antidote herb that allowed her to have sex with Minos without the ineffable discharge.

As Maxwell Teitel Paule says in his *Canidia, Rome's First Witch* (2017),

> Canidia is one of the most well-attested witches in Latin literature. She has a prominent role in three of Horace's poems, and is mentioned by name in three others. Throughout Horace's Epodes and Satires she desecrates graves, kidnaps, murders, poisons, and tortures. In one poem she invades the gardens of Maecenas [Horace's literary patron], where she rips apart a lamb with her teeth and summons the dead

426

... starves a Roman child to death so she can harvest his desiccated organs, and in another she uses her spells to prevent Horace from killing himself – for the sole purpose of continuing to torment him. She is the dark anti-muse of Horace's poetry.

In *Satire* 8, Canidia and her cronies feature in Horace's turn-of-the-millennium gruesome description of a coven of witches; their evil plan is to perform a live hepatectomy so as to concoct a love potion from the liver of a terrified little boy. Canidia, Sagana, Vera and Folia are painted in equally odious and repellent terms:

- Canidia with her serpentine hair brings eggs marinaded in the blood of filthy frogs, and the teeth of a ravenous bitch dog;
- Sagana, her hair spikey like a sea urchin or a bristling boar, sprinkles water from hell;
- Veia digs the boy's grave in which he is to be buried up to his neck, tormented by an endless succession of banquets until his eyeballs melt;
- Folia, who lusts like only a man can lust.

It was believed that the tantalizing sight of unreachable food was thought to make the liver stronger and thus the potion more potent. Nevertheless, the boy retaliates with the threat of a curse, deploying his own brand of black magic: he will haunt them as a Fury from Hell.

Frogs' blood and the deployment of a human liver, however, both feature in the real world, confirming their ubiquity in the Roman *demi-monde*.

EVEN THE DEMI-GODS mock the witch. Priapus, that phallus with a face, ridicules them. He is erected as a wooden statue in a redeveloped park on the Esquiline, once a paupers' cemetery now infested by witches: to Priapus they are 'those who turn mankind's minds with their spells and potions'. They are *horrendae aspectu*, horrid to look at, as they perform a necromancy using the blood of a lamb they have just torn to shreds. The repugnant scenario comes to a premature end when Priapus breaks wind, sending the two running with hilarious consequences: Canidia's false teeth fall out, Sagana loses her wig and they both drop all their herbs and enchanted love chains.

Canidia is poison incarnate: her toxins are garlic based, that well-known potent antidote to the evil eye. No man can last out forever against a witch; Horace even concedes that Canidia's dubious 'science' actually works, acknowledges her books of spells and indulges her by asking her to draw down the stars from the skies. Her sorcery costs him: he is reduced to a sallow bag of bones: he has aged prematurely, his hair is now white and he cannot sleep; his breathing is laboured, his chest burns with pain and his head feels like it is exploding. He lists an infernal catalogue of nightmares, the terrors of magic (*terrores magici*), miracles (*miracula*), ghosts and Thessalian rites. Canidia, though, is unimpressed by this late-in-the-day endorsement and turns the tables on Horace, calling *him* a sorcerer and promising him a slow and lingering death. After all she can bring wax effigies to life, draw down the Moon, raise the dead and concoct love potions. Drawing down the Moon seems to have involved making it turn pale or red, or indeed, merely predicting the next lunar eclipse.

In real-world Rome witches and their associated magic generally were feared by the highly superstitious Romans.

Dido – Down Among the Deadmen

Virgil gives a much blacker, bleaker picture of sorcery (*Aeneid* 4, 300–301; 384–7; 450–73; 483ff.). He describes how Aeneas deserted Dido in order to get on with his god-given national responsibility to found Rome. Dido was no career witch, but her seething fury and rage at Aeneas' duplicity made her a scorned women with diabolic characteristics any professional witch would be proud to possess. Rejected by Aeneas and sidelined by his renewed focus on his mission to establish Rome, Dido 'rages, out of her mind, and rushes through the city, mad as a Bacchant'. She confronted treacherous Aeneas and promised to haunt him for eternity in a threat that is tantamount to a *defixio* (curse):

> When I'm dead and gone, when frigid death draws out the spirit from my limbs, I'll follow you all the way down into the black fires of Hell, my ghost will be all over the place; you'll pay the price, you treacherous bastard, and I'll hear about it – mark my words, the news will reach me deep down among the deadmen. (4, 584f)

Dido took the aura of a witch and created a witchy environment around herself: milk turned black on the incense-burning altars and the wine congealed into an obscene gore. *Horrendus dictu*: 'shocking to say it', but she decides to end it all. Dido recalls the warnings of the pious priests who predicted that her affair would all end in tears. Her threats are all the more poignant because it was popularly believed that one's propensity for infernal power was sharpened at death's door, particularly for suicides and others suffering an untimely end.

Virgil's audience would have appreciated and understood the power of Dido's witch-inspired threats: Rome did indeed pay the price for Aeneas' duplicity, with two near catastrophic Punic Wars; Aeneas was indeed haunted by Dido, in their icy encounter in the underworld. The Dido episode resonates uncomfortably with the political upheaval caused so recently by Cleopatra VII, a *fatale monstrum* (doom monster), the foreign queen eerily reminiscent of Dido, whose facility for global power-play and manipulation could be viewed as comparable to the unnatural, destructive skills of a sorceress. Dido's hopes to deflect Aeneas from his mission to found Rome shared the same existentialist ramifications as Cleopatra's malevolent skirmishing in the seas around Republican Rome.

Erichtho – Epic Witch

Witches were, of course, stock characters in ancient epic. Erichtho is a witch surpassing even Seneca's Medea in her repulsiveness – the satanic witch-queen of all witches. She is, literally, an epic witch. And Erichtho is just the witch for Sextus Pompey (*c.* 67–35 BC), who, racked with fear before his coming battle the following day, is anxious to know how it will turn out for him; he eschews conventional forms of divination, electing instead to deploy the ungodly, 'the mysteries of the furious enchantress'. Being in Thessaly, he is local to the world's most dreadful witches and their *herbae nocentes* (pernicious herbs).

Lucan in his *Civil War* Book 6 describes Erichtho in graphic and lurid detail: he tells how wild Erichtho communes with the dead and is expert in all things eschatological; where she goes, contagion is sure to follow; she buries the living and returns the dead back to life; she snatches burning babies from their pyres for occult research and experimentation and assaults the corpses of the dead, scooping out eyeballs and gnawing at their nails. She tears flesh from corpses crucified on crosses, harvests the black putrid congealed gore suppurating from the limbs of the decaying; she steals the meat ripped off putrefying bodies by rapacious wolves. She is a serial murderess, performing crude caesarean sections on pregnant women whenever she needs a baby for the pyre; she rips the faces off young boys; and at funerals, she opens the mouths of the dead with her teeth, bites their tongues and thereby communicates with hell.

In her horrific reanimation of the soldier, Erichtho may well have been the inspiration for Mary Shelley's *Frankenstein* some 1,750 years later: she would have been familiar with the episode through her husband, the poet Percy Bysshe Shelley, who admired Lucan.

The depraved young emperor Elagabalus seems to have been partial to child sacrifice, collecting 'children of noble birth and beautiful appearance' and employing magicians to perform daily sacrifices so that he could examine the children's internal organs and torture the victims.

John Hamilton Mortimer, *Sextus Pompeius Consulting Erichtho before the Battle of Pharsalia*, 1770s, oil on canvas. The witch Erichtho (left), the foulest of the foul, features in Lucan's *Pharsalia* (vi, 507–830), where she summons up a spirit to reveal to Sextus Pompeius the outcome of the Battle of Pharsalus. She is also mentioned by Dante in his *Divine Comedy* (*Inferno* ix 23), where Virgil tells us that he was ordered by her to endure a *catabasis* to bring back a spirit. Goethe includes her in *Faust* (Part 2, Act 2) as the first character to speak in the Classical Walpurgisnacht scene (ii.1).

Serious attempts to curb witchcraft came with Sulla's *lex Cornelia de sicariis et veneficis*, passed in 81 BC. One of the most notorious women accused of being a witch under the law was Fabia Numantina of the illustrious Fabis gens. According to Tacitus (*Annals* 4, 22), Fabia's second husband was Marcus Plautius Silvanus, the praetor in AD 24 who went on to marry a woman named Apronia, whom Tacitus adds he apparently murdered by throwing her out of a window. Soon after Apronia's murder, Fabia was 'charged with having caused her husband's insanity by magical incantations and potions', but she was acquitted.

As for Theodora (b. AD 500) and Justinian I, Procopius describes a woman who is vulgar and characterized by unquenchable lust. The couple are demons with disembodied heads that flit around the palace by night. The wife of the successful general Flavius Belisarius (*c.* AD 505–565) was the scheming Antonina. According to Procopius, '[Antonina] in her early years lived a lewd sort of a life and [she became] dissolute in character, not only having consorted much

Theatrical scene with two women consulting a witch, Roman mosaic from the Villa del Cicerone in Pompeii, 2nd century BC.

with the cheap sorcerers who surrounded her parents, but also having thus acquired the knowledge of what she needed to know' (*Secret History* I, II).

Eventually the cuckolded Belisarius arrested Antonina on evidence provided by bedchamber servants but was unable to bring himself to exact punishment – due to Antonina's skillful use of the black arts. The informants were deemed to be lying; Antonina had their tongues cut out and their bodies chopped up, and the body parts were dumped in the sea.

Man as Witch

Women did not have it all their own way when it came to witches and witchcraft. Men witches – the *magi* – were sorcerers and magicians, and there were a lot of them.

A number of men flirted with and skirted round the edges of witchery, not least some of the early Greek philosophers. Around the fifth century BC, the word *magos* started to appear describing the Persian *mages* – trained priests with the ability to perform miracles.

In Greece Orpheus was held in high regard and described as a *theios aner* (holy man); his main claim to fame was his aborted attempt to rescue Eurydice from the underworld in his famous *katabasis*.

Empedocles could heal the sick, rejuvenate the old, change the weather and summon up the dead in necromancy. For Plato, healers, sorcerers and prophets were a fact of life in Athens and had to be tolerated; they were low down in the food chain and needed to be regulated but were essentially harmless.

In the early empire, Jesus Christ appeared on the scene in a world ensconced in polytheism and emperor worship. He has been described by some as a miracle-worker, exorcising demons, healing the sick, prophesying and raising the dead – all familiar tropes of witchcraft. His miraculous birth, divine origin and his fight against the demon Satan only added to his witchy credentials, causing the Romans to vilify and vitiate such magic workers. Simon Magus was so impressed by the skilful acts of the apostles when it came to the laying on of hands and exorcism that he offered to buy those skills; any professional magician like Simon would be keen to add to his repertoire. It seems likely that there existed in Simon's day frauds who set themselves up as vendors of different kinds of magic to the susceptible and gullible.

Pliny the Elder probably spoke for many when he expressed scepticism regarding the claims of the professional magicians. He was one of the most savage critics of the *magi*, considering them to be frauds, charlatans and liars. He accuses Osthanes, a Persian *magus*, of encouraging people to drink human blood and using body parts from corpses of men who died violently in magic rites. Pliny in his *Natural History* disparages the claims of the *magi* when they assert that miscarriage can be avoided if a woman wears the white flesh of a hyena's breast in gazelle leather, along with seven hyena hairs and the genitals of a stag. Pliny, though, was prudent enough to keep his options open: magic doesn't work but it comprises 'shadows of truth', particularly the 'arts of making poisons'. Everyone, asserts Pliny, is afraid of spells.

Pliny records evidence of witchcraft among the Machyles in Africa: apart from being bisexual – that is, with one breast female the other male – they induce drought and child mortality on a prodigious scale. A less than idyllic love potion recommended by the *magi* and scorned by Pliny involved the wearing of an amulet that contained a hyena's anus.

The Pythagoreans

If you wanted to become a member of the Pythagoreans, these were some of the rules you had to live by:

1. Abstain from beans.
2. Do not pick up what has fallen.
3. Do not touch a white cock.
4. Do not break bread.
5. Do not eat meat.
6. Do not stir the fire with iron.

7. Do not eat from a whole loaf.
10. Do not eat the heart.
11. Do not walk on roads.
12. Do not let swallows share your roof.
13. When the pot is taken off the fire, do not leave the mark of it in the ashes, but stir them together.
14. Do not look in a mirror beside a light.
15. When you get out of your bedclothes, roll them together and smoothen out the impress of the body.

Pythagoras had more up his sleeve than his theorem on the hypotenuse. Here are some of his other achievements:

- Pythagoras reputedly averted plagues and controlled the weather.
- He was also said to have been seen in two cities at the same time of day.
- A white eagle allowed him to stroke it – something others would fear to attempt!
- He was greeted by a river with the words 'Hail, Pythagoras!'
- He predicted that a dead man would be found on a ship – and so it came to pass.
- He foresaw the appearance of a white bear and declared it was dead before the messenger reached him with the news.
- He bit a poisonous snake to death.

68

Werewolves and Lycanthropy

L ycanthropy, the ability to turn into a wolf, is a mythical condition, a supernatural affliction in which humans are said to
physically shapeshift into wolves. Pausanias, sceptical of this
legendary metamorphosis, says

> It is a truth universally acknowledged that many events that
> have occurred in the past, and even some that occur to-day,
> have been generally discredited because of the lies built up
> on a foundation of fact. It is said, for instance, that ever since
> the time of Lycaon a man has changed into a wolf at the sac-
> rifice to Lycaean Zeus, but that the change is not for life; if,
> when he is a wolf, he abstains from human flesh, after nine
> years he becomes a man again, but if he tastes human flesh
> he remains a beast for ever. (*Guide to Greece* 8, 2)

A number of *versipelles* (werewolves) of indeterminate sex prowl
and howl through the Greek and Latin literature. The Balts lived
in the north of Europe, around the Baltic Sea – to Herodotus they
were the Neuri, a race that seemingly enjoyed their lycanthropy.
Pausanias and Ovid tell the story of Lycaon, transformed into a
wolf for murdering a child (OVID, *Metamorphoses* 1.219–39); Virgil
described lycanthropy in the *Eclogues* (8), human beings transforming into wolves. Pliny the Elder (*Natural History* 22, 34) tells
two tales of lycanthropy: a man hung his clothes on an ash tree
and swam across a lake in Arcadia, turning himself into a wolf. The
deal was that if he refrained from attacking any human being for
nine years he could swim back across the lake and turn back into a

human. Then there is the story of a man who was turned into a wolf after eating the entrails of a child but was restored to human form ten years later.

Petronius describes an attack by a werewolf in his *Satyricon*. Nicarus, accompanied by a soldier, leaves his house by moonlight intent on visiting his mistress, Melissa; when they get to the out-of-town tombstones, the soldier strips, urinates around his pile of clothes – and promptly turns into a wolf, howls and flees into the forest; his clothes turn to stone. Nicarus reaches Melissa's house; she tells him that a wolf had just savaged her sheep and that a slave speared it through the neck. Nicarus returns home, via the stone clothes that had been replaced by a pool of blood, only to find a doctor tending the soldier for a neck wound. At this point Nicarus realizes he has been dealing with a werewolf (*Satyricon* 62).

Aëtius knows all about lycanthropy or cyanthropy (if a dog is involved): they go out at night in January and February, lurking around tombs till dawn. Symptoms include sallow complexion, vacant expression, dry, tearless and sunken eyes, dry tongue, no saliva, excessive thirst and suppurating ulcers on the legs from dog bites (*On Medicine* 6, 11). But all was not lost. Wolfsbane was something of a panacaea for anyone afflicted with wolf-like tendencies. Also known as monkshood or aconite, the plant relieves the symptoms of lycanthropy but, crucially, is not a cure. You have to drink a cup of wolfsbane potion each day for a week preceding the full moon; missing one dose alone renders the potion useless. The Romans had a zero-tolerance policy against anyone caught growing wolfsbane. Punishment was execution.

It was thought that women were particularly vulnerable to the poisonous wolfsbane, which Nicander (*fl.* 130 BC) actually calls 'woman-killer' (*Alexipharmaca* XLI). Pliny argues that 'of all poisons the quickest to act is aconite [wolfsbane], and that death occurs on the same day if the genitals of a female creature are but touched by it' (*Natural History* 27, 2 4). He adds that Marcus Caelius had accused Calpurnius Bestia (or rather, his finger) of using wolfsbane to kill his wives while they slept, presumably by applying it to the mucous membrane of the vulva.

69
Witch-Lite: The Bogeywoman
Is Coming to Get You

Witches were top of the evil tree but there was an accommodation for those who failed to make the grade, and that was being a bogeywoman, who was equally disruptive, malicious and scary: the archetypal monster under your bed.

What now seems like a feeble excuse for a form of child abuse, some Greek philosophers believed that 'of all wild things, the child is most unmanageable . . . the most unruly animal there is. That's why he has to be curbed by a great many bridles' (PLATO, *Laws* 7 808d). One of these 'bridles', which earned the support of flustered wet nurses, was the insinuation of the bogeywoman into imaginations of children in their charge. A terrifying figure like a Maurice Sendak character, reminiscent of the big bad wolves – precursors of the one that terrified Little Red Riding Hood to death – the bogeywoman feasted on naughty boys and girls, ate them alive and always had one freshly devoured and digesting in her stomach.

In ancient Greece, the queen of bogeywomen was Mormo – a petrifying donkey with the legs of a woman – variously 'a queen of the Lystraegones who had lost her own children and now vengefully murdered others', or a child-eating Corinthian. Another was Empousa, who manifested either as a cow, a donkey or a beautiful woman; Empousa could actually be a beautiful, cannibalistic child-eater. Some believe that she was Hecate in disguise (Scholion to Aristophanes, *Frogs* 293). Yet another was Gello, evil female spirit and child snatcher.

Corresponding with Mormo for the Romans was Lamia – a sexy Libyan woman whose children by Zeus were murdered by Hera; like Mormo, she too was a cannibal and exacted revenge by murdering other women's babies, eating them alive. Lamia and Empousa were sometimes described, with some justification, as *phasma* – ghosts, or nightmares.

We know that for the Romans there was a deity for every single aspect of life and death. Bogeywomen and witch deterrents were no exception:

- Cunina looks after the baby in the cradle, protecting it from malevolent forces and magic.
- Candelifera is the nursery light: this is kept burning all night to deter the spirits of darkness that might threaten the infant in the crucial first week of birth, and to banish the bogeywomen.
- Carna builds healthy muscles, protecting the internal organs from witches.

Roman experts in child psychology tried to explain away bogey-women and recommended they be avoided at all costs, along with other irrational fears such as dreams, the terrors of magic, miracles and night-time ghosts. Easier said than done if your child had spent most of his or her childhood scared half to death by a monster intent on eating them up.

70

Ghosts

'Spirits do not do as they are told and they cannot be seen
by people with freckles.'

(Pliny, *Natural History* 30.16)

Ghosts seem to have been an ever-present facet of life in Rome,
floating around in great profusion and variously called *di manes*,
Lares, *Lemures*, *umbrae*, *imagines* and *species*. These ghosts were often
malevolent. We have already encountered Empousa, Mormo and
Lamia, ghost-like spirits who frightened naughty children in their
guise as bogeywomen. It would seem from the literature that ghosts
were crowd-pleasers: Plautus wrote his *Mostellaria*, the story of a
haunted house; Pliny the Younger describes a haunted house in
great detail in a letter (*Epistles* 7, 27, 4ff); Lucian relates the exorcism
of a haunted house in his *Philopseudes* 30–31.

More seriously, Julia, wilful daughter of Julius Caesar and wife
of Pompey, died in 54 BC. In Lucan's *Civil War*, her ghost appears to
Pompey: 'Julia, an image full of horror and foreboding, appeared –
her sad face visible over the gaping earth, standing on her flaming
tomb, raging like a Fury' (1, 111–20; 3, 10ff). She ominously declares
that Hades is getting ready to receive casualties from the war. She
has received special dispensation from the kings of Hell to haunt
Pompey: her *umbra* and *manes* will be there in the battle, eerily
reminding him that 'the Civil War will make you *mine*'.

Nero arranged the murder of his mother, Agrippina, in AD 59,
appropriately near Lake Avernus in Baiae (the entrance to Hades).
Suetonius relates how Nero, fuelled by drink, paid an unhealthy
interest in his mother's corpse, thus substantiating allegations of

necrophilia and incest. Her ghost haunted him and, in a bid to rid himself of this spectre, he enlisted magicians to call up her ghost and exorcise the evil (*Nero* 34).

In Apuleius' *Metamorphoses*, a witch hired by his unfaithful wife is used to send a ghost to a cuckolded miller. The witch can either reconcile the couple or else murder him through the ghost or some other such demon. She fails in the former and angrily resorts to the latter by sending the ghost of a woman recently murdered to kill him. Dressed in rags, bare-footed, sallow, hair dishevelled, covered in ashes from her pyre and emaciated, the ghost appears to the miller. Sometime later he is found in a locked room hanging from a beam. Things get even worse when the miller's ghost then appears to his daughter, and in so doing gives her the first horrific news of his own death, revealing her stepmother's adultery, her recourse to witchcraft and how the ghost bewitched him (9, 29–31).

Phlegon of Tralles treats us to a number of ghosts, not least those of the deceased who have come back to life. They include Philinnion (*Marvels* 1), who returned to fulfil her passion for Machetes; this, of course, upset her grieving mother and father, who were cruelly punished by Philinnion for showing concern: the daughter inflicted on them another round of grief over her death(s). At this point she died anew: 'the misfortune was unbearable and the sight incredible.'

Polykritos the Aitolarch married a Lokrian woman but died four days later (*Marvels* 2). His widow gave birth to a child with two sets of genitals: the upper parts were hard and masculine, the lower softer and womanish. Local officials either deemed it an omen that presaged war between the Locrians and the Aitolians while others were all for taking the corpse out into the country and burning it. During the deliberations, Polykritos returned as a benign ghost and calmly asked for the infant to be returned to him to prevent any violence or unpleasantness. Polykritos cautioned that compliance would banish the consternation among the people, but that defiance would inflict 'irremedial calamity'. To his annoyance, the crowd vacillated, at which point Polykritos grabbed the child and tore it limb from limb and proceeded to devour it. Despite a hail of stones hurled at him, the ghost consumed all of the infant apart from its head; he then disappeared. A delegation to Delphi was being considered when the head began to speak, thus saving them a journey when it revealed the future in an oracle. The upshot was a war between the Locrians and the Acharnians in which both sides suffered terrible casualties.

A talking head also features in the story of the ghost of Publius, a Roman general deranged by divine possession (PHLEGON, *Marvels* 3, 8). Publius comes down from an oak tree he had climbed from which to address his soldiers only to be torn to bits and devoured by a wolf; just his head remained, a head that warned against it being touched and that delivered an oracle, all of which came true.

TRAVEL
AND
ARCHAEOLOGY

71

Wild Travel and Exploration

The Greek *poleis* were for the most part resource poor, so it was necessary for the Greeks to make good this deficiency through a programme of colonization, which saw Greek settlements all around the Mediterranean basis and in particular at the southern end of the Italian peninsula as well as coastal points west, where Magna Graecia developed as trading and cultural outposts.

Romans, from very early days, like other civilizations before them, had no choice but to trade with others beyond their own borders. There were cardinal reasons for this. The first is fundamental: to compensate for deficiencies in local resources, such as metals for weaponry and grain for bread. The second was to offset payments for imports by negotiating and bartering their own goods for export; the revenues from trade surplus and the associated taxes would (or should) go into the national exchequer. The third reason was to satisfy demand at home for exotic spices and food, jewellery, textiles, incense, slaves and strange animals. Trade revenues were, like militarism and expansionism, an existential issue for Rome: trade surpluses helped pay for the armies that pushed further from Rome's ever-evolving borders to enable more global trade, which helped finance more legions and the cost of occupying new territories. And so it was that on the accession of Augustus and the dawning of the Roman Empire, the Pax Romana and the relative stability it brought fostered more trade further afield, the revenues from which helped finance the administration of provinces and protectorates, at least up to the reign of Trajan (AD 98 to 117).

Herodotus describes vertically challenged natives when he relates the story of five 'proud and laddish' wild young men who set off through the Sahara to locate the source of the Nile, to 'see if they could see any farther than those who had seen the farthest':

[For] the coast is infested by wild beasts; and farther inland than the wild-beast country everything is sand, waterless and desolate . . . they travelled over the desert, towards the west, and crossed a wide desert, until after many days they saw trees growing in a plain; when they came to these and were picking the fruit of the trees, they were met by little men of less than usual stature, who took them and led them away. These Nasamonians did not speak the men's language nor did the travellers know the language of the Nasamonians. They led the men across wide marshes, after crossing which they came to a city where all the people were of a stature like that of the guides, and black. A great river ran past this city, from the west towards the rising sun; crocodiles could be seen in it. (2, 32)

Annoyingly, Herodotus does not tell us what happened next.

Around AD 130, Julia Balbilla, as court poetess and as a kind of royal correspondent, accompanied Hadrian (r. AD 117–38) and the empress Vibia Sabina (AD 83–136/7) on tours of the Nile valley. To record their visit, she inscribed on the left leg and foot of one of the Colossi of Memnon in Thebes (a monumental statue of the pharaoh Amenophis III) four epigrams in ancient Aeolic dialect – as used by Sappho some eight hundred years earlier. In so doing, Julia was following a time-honoured tradition that celebrated Memnon's amazing early morning 'singing' – an audible phenomenon emanating from fractures to the statue made by an earthquake in 27 BC. The earliest report in the literature is from the Greek historian and geographer Strabo, who said that he heard the sound during a visit in 20 BC, by which time it was already well-known. Strabo said it sounded 'like a blow', Pausanias compared it to 'the string of a lyre' breaking, but others described it as the striking of brass or whistling. Others add their comments on this phenomenon, including Tacitus, Philostratus and Juvenal.

Julia Balbilla's first three epigrams dutifully commemorate the royal visit, and the fourth, Julia's personal experience. Julia's erudition is clearly evident from these inscriptions: not only is she familiar with a long-obsolete ancient Greek dialect and metre, but she displays a working knowledge of relevant Egyptian and Greek mythology. Vibia Sabina added an inscription of her own on the instep of the left foot. The first and second epigrams tell the story of a mythical king of Aethiopia, Memnon, killed by Achilles at Troy and whom Zeus thus raised from the dead and made immortal. Balbilla is not addressing Memnon but is flattering Hadrian and Sabina.

In a similar vein, and around the same time, a Terentia was touring Egypt when she too paused to make an inscription in time-honoured tradition; she inscribed six hexameters on the Tura limestone that formed the surface of the pyramid of Cheops. It was later quarried to build part of the modern city of Cairo, but luckily, in 1335, a German tourist, Wilhelm von Boldensele, spotted it and made a copy. The lines are essentially a lament for Terentia's deceased brother, D. Terentius Gentianus, and a celebration of his career. Like Julia Balbilla's verses, it displays some erudition with its echoes of Catullus and Ovid in the second verse, reflecting their take on the death of a brother; the third verse recalls one of Horace's *Odes* (*CIG* 3 30, 2).

> I've seen the pyramids sweetest brother but you're not here,
> and grief has drained my tears – the best I can do. I carve
> out this lament, testament to our grief. So may the name
> Decimus Gentianus remain on this lofty pyramid, as priest
> and comrade, o triumphant Trajan, consul and censor.

Clement, or someone like him, is shocked by Egyptian idolatry, not least the breaking of holy wind:

> Some taught that their ox, which is called Apis, ought to be
> worshipped; others taught that the he-goat, others that cats,
> the ibis, a fish also, a serpent, onions, drains, farts, sewers, the
> limbs of irrational animals ought to be regarded as deities,

and innumerable other things, which I am ashamed even to mention. (PSEUDO-CLEMENT, *Recognitions* 5, 20)

Clement of Alexandria (AD 150–215) himself concedes that the Greeks are no better, venerating as they do 'Storks and ants in Thessaly; Weasels in Thebes; Mice in the Troad; Flies in Actium and Sheep on Samos' (*Exhortation, Protrepticus* 2, 39).

Diodorus Siculus describes the fine and fascinating inhabitants of what is today Sri Lanka, giving a new meaning to 'bilingual':

The inhabitants on this island differ greatly both in the characteristics of their bodies and in their manners from the men in our part of the inhabited world; for they are all nearly alike in the shape of their bodies and are over four cubits in height [6 foot], but the bones of the body have the ability to bend to a certain extent and then straighten out again ... There is absolutely no hair on any part of their bodies except on the head, eyebrows and eyelids, and on the chin, but the other parts of the body are so smooth that not even down can be seen on them. Their figures are also remarkably beautiful and well-proportioned. The openings of their ears are much more spacious than ours and growths have developed that serve as valves, so to speak, to close them. And they have an oddity in regard to the tongue: ... they are very versatile as to the sounds they can utter, since they imitate not only every articulate language used by man but also the varied chatterings of the birds, and, in general, they reproduce any peculiarity of sounds. And the most remarkable thing of all is that at one and the same time they can converse perfectly with two people at the same time, both answering questions and speaking relevant to the situation. (*The Library* 2, 56).

He goes on to describe their harmonious society – a very, very strange animal – and, less happily, the eugenics practised there:

They do not marry, we are told, but hold their children in common, raising the children as if they each belonged to all; they love them equally; and while the children are infants those who suckle them often change them around so that not even the mothers may know their own offspring. Consequently, since there is no rivalry among them, they never experience civil disorder and they never cease placing the highest value upon internal harmony . . . There are also animals among them, we are told, which are small in size but the object of wonder because of their bodies and the potency of their blood; for they are round in form and very similar to tortoises, but they are marked on the surface by two diagonal yellow stripes, at each end of which they have an eye and a mouth; consequently, though seeing with four eyes and using as many mouths, this creature gathers its food into one gullet, and down this it swallows its nourishment and all flows together into one stomach; similarly, its other organs and all its inner parts are single. It also has beneath it all around its body many feet, by means of which it can move in whatever direction it pleases. And the blood of this animal, they say, has a marvellous potency; for it immediately glues back on to its place any living member that has been severed; even if a hand or the like should happen to have been cut off, by the use of this blood it is glued on again, provided that the cut is fresh.

Each group of inhabitants also keeps a huge and unique bird, by means of which a test is made of the infants to learn what their spiritual disposition is: they place the children on the birds – those that can endure the flight through the air they proceed to raise, but those that are sick and panic they cast out. (*The Library* 2, 58)

Herodotus expatiates on the mind-altering personal hygiene of the Scythians:

The Scythians then take the seed of this hemp and, crawling in to their tents, throw it on the red-hot stones, where it smolders and gives off such fumes that no Greek steam bath could ever compete with. The Scythians howl with joy at the steam bath. This they do instead of bathing, for they never wash their bodies with water. (4, 75)

The Tauri were well-advised not to get too close to their king, because when he dies, his closest friends are buried with him (*The Vatican Paradoxographer* 60). Scythians were associated with cannibalism: they cut up and salted the flesh of their dead and hung it round their necks like a necklace (61). Their generosity knew no bounds, however: whenever they met a friend, they cut off a bit from the meaty ornament and gave it to him to eat.

The (nearly) law-abiding Issedones (a tribe from the Russian steppes) also wasted nothing:

When a man's father dies, all the next of kin bring sheep, kill them and cut up the flesh; they also cut up the dead father of their host, and mix all the flesh together for a feast. As for his head, they strip it bare, clean and gild it, and keep it for a sacred relic, to which they offer solemn sacrifice every year ... In other respects, these are said to be a law-abiding people. (HERODOTUS, *Histories* 4, 26)

Adding as a footnote: 'and the women have equal power with the men.'

Foreign women feature prominently in Herodotus' entertaining ethnographical excursions around the Mediterranean. Herodotus found the wider world a very strange and wondrous place. Apart from monstrous ants the size of foxes and unbelievable hippopotami, Libyan dog-headed men and headless men with eyes in their breasts, our historian found even the relatively civilized Egyptians quite amazing, not least because 'The women go to market and men stay at home and weave [the exact opposite to Greek practice]. Women even urinate standing up and men sitting down' (2, 35).

To Herodotus, the Egyptians stood the world on its head. Urine, or the wrong sort of urine, also played a big part in the cautionary tale of the adulterous wife of King Pheros:

> Pheros was a king of Egypt who went blind. After ten years the oracle at Buto said he had served his punishment and would be cured if he washed his eyes out with the urine of a woman who had never slept with any man except her husband. So he tried his wife's urine ... it didn't work, then many other women were tested until one worked and he could see again. All those women whose urine failed the test were collected together and burned. He then married the lady whose urine worked. (2, 111)

Herodotus' aim in such observations is to prove that the Greek way is the right and proper way, the only way; all barbarians, even clever barbarians like the Egyptians, had got it wrong. Some of his episodes are undoubtedly fictitious, but that matters little: his objective was to establish the contrariness of the non-Greek, the barbarian world in relation to the normative behaviour and customs of his fellow Greeks.

The Egyptians were happy to ship anything, as the *Paris Papyrus* 18b, a letter from Senpamonthes to her half-brother Pamonthes written in black ink on papyrus, shows. This parcel in fact contained the embalmed body of her mother, Senyris, with a name label round her neck. Freight had been paid to cover shipment on a boat belonging to someone called Gales. Pamonthes was able to identify the goods from the label, a pink linen shroud and from mother's name written on her stomach.

'The people of Miletus are not stupid; they just do the sort of things stupid people do.'

Aristotle, *Nicomachean Ethics*, 1151a

For the Persians, *in vino veritas*:

The Persians like their wine. No one is allowed to vomit or urinate in another's presence: this is prohibited. Moreover, it is their custom to discuss their most important matters when they are drunk; and what they approve in their drunken deliberations is put to them again the next day, when they are sober ... and if, being sober, they still approve it, they act on it, but if not, they reject it. And if they have deliberated about a matter when sober, they make a decision on it when they are drunk. (HERODOTUS, I, 133, 3)

The Gauls are even more scrupulous when it comes to decision making: 'They sentence a man to death and stab him with a dagger just above the diaphragm. They then determine the future from the way he falls, from how his limbs twitch in the throes of death and from the way his blood spurts out' (POSIDONIUS, frg. 169).

Barking? 'I have heard that there is a tribe in Ethiopia that is ruled by a dog' (AELIAN, *On Animals* 7, 40).

Care of the elderly was never a priority for the Bactrians; the Caspii pioneered a radical form of euthanasia that obviated the need for anything resembling a care home:

Those who are disabled by disease or old age are thrown alive to be devoured by dogs kept just for this purpose, and which in the local language they call 'entombers'. Outside the walls of the capital city of the Bactrians everywhere is clean, but the inside of the city is mostly littered with human bones. Something similar is related to the Caspii as well, who, when their parents have reached the age of 70 years, lock them up, and let them die of hunger. (STRABO, *Geography* II, II)

Herodotus describes the first circumnavigation of Africa:

Necos king of Egypt ... sent Phoenicians in ships, instructing them to sail [anti-clockwise around Africa] going on their return voyage past the Pillars of Heracles (Straits of Gibraltar) until they came back into the Mediterranean and so to Egypt. So the Phoenicians set out from the Red Sea and sailed the southern sea; whenever autumn came they would put in and cultivate the land in whatever part of Libya [Africa] they had reached, and there wait for the harvest; then, having gathered the crop, they sailed on, so that after two years had passed, it was in the third that they rounded the Pillars of Heracles and arrived back at Egypt. There they said (what some may believe, though I do not) that in sailing around Libya they had the sun on their right hand. (4, 42)

As the ship sailed west round the Cape of Good Hope, so the Sun of the southern hemisphere would be on its right. It was another 2,000 years before Vasco da Gama completed his circumnavigation.

72

Explorers – Gorillas or Hairy Women?

The Carthaginians, Phoenicians and Greeks and Romans were inveterate explorers, seeking out new sources of trade to compensate for their own resource deficiencies, and new markets for their own goods. Perhaps one of the most successful explorers was the sixth-century BC Carthaginian Hanno the Navigator.

Hanno embarked on a long and dangerous voyage along the African west coast as far south as modern Gabon; he was sailing into no-man's land, into lands beyond the known world. His detailed logbook (*periplus*) treats us to a vivid description of an erupting volcano, landing on a strange and mysterious island, fighting off natives, and our first known report about those cousins of ours: gorillas – or were they hairy women? That they were gorillas unfortunately seems unlikely, as they were found by Hanno on an island and gorillas cannot swim.

Here are some extracts from Hanno's account:

After four days sailing we could still see the coast by night filled with flames. In the middle was one huge flame, taller than the rest and rising to the stars which, in the light of day, appeared to be a very high mountain, which was called Chariot of the Gods.

. . .

Three days later [we arrived at] an island . . . with a lagoon, within which was another island, crowded with savages. Most of them were women with hairy bodies, whom our interpreters called 'gorillas'. Although we chased after them, we could not catch any males: they all escaped, excellent climbers as they were who defended themselves with stones. However, we did catch three women, who refused to go with those who carried them off, biting and scratching them. So we killed and flayed them and took their skins back to Carthage. We did not sail any further as we were running out of supplies. (1–18)

Hanno's account remains extant in Greek-language manuscripts, but the original version, written in the Punic language, has been lost. The Greek translation is abridged to 101 lines long and is likely derived from an original Carthaginian text. According to Brian H. Warmington in his *Carthage* (1960), the *periplus* has survived as 'the nearest we have to a specimen of Carthaginian "literature"' and is one of the few extant accounts of ancient exploration written by the explorer himself.

73

Skeletons from the Far East Found in Roman London

It's not just the remains of camels that have turned up under the ground in London. In 2016 ancient skeletons weres discovered in an old cemetery in Lant Street, Southwark. Dental enamel examinations found that the skeletons could have belonged to individuals from China who likely visited the capital between the second and fourth centuries AD. Further forensic examination by experts from Michigan State University confirmed that these two individuals were indeed Asian, and also confirmed that 'four of the 22 skulls discovered in the burial ground were of African origin.' They demonstrate just how cosmopolitan Roman Britain was, attracting people from China and other parts of the far east as slaves, prisoners of war and traders via and beyond the Silk Road.

A study led by Rebecca Redfern and colleagues examined 22 skeletons from the Lant Street cemetery by way of oxygen isotopes from the teeth, carbon and nitrogen isotopes from the bones, and the shape of the skulls, correlating those data where possible with burial evidence.

While previous archaeological work has shown the multicultural nature of the ancient city and its importance as a major trading hub, this finding in Roman London is only the second time that the bones of an individual of possibly Chinese origin have been found at a Roman site, the first being the discovery of a possibly Asian man in Vagnari, Italy.

Epilogue

So there we have it, a truly unique compilation of *miracula*, weird and wonderful stories of ancient Greece and Rome extending over 2,000 years and taking in all of the known world at the time. This is the end of a reasonably comprehensive and hitherto unpublished picture of aspects of life in ancient Greece and Rome that can only be described as being variously hilarious, plain daft, unbelievable, true, contrived and worryingly shocking: from space flight to sexual deviation, voodoo dolls, (very) bad parenting and weapons of mass destruction (the elephant).

Nevertheless, if the preceding pages have left you with a more rounded and complete picture of what has all to often conveniently been elsewhere called something like 'The Glory that was Greece' and 'The Grandeur that was Rome', then the project has been well worthwhile. Great civilizations as Greece and Rome were, they need to be known for more than their straight roads, public baths and underfloor heating. We all need to continue learning from the warts-and-all school of history, where the darker side of the past as well as the hilarious and astonishing are exposed to the full glare of publication.

I leave you by repeating what must be the last word in hedonism: 'Baths, wine, and sex corrupt our bodies; but the baths, wine, and sex are what we live for' (Epitaph for TIBERIUS CLAUDIUS SECUNDUS, *CIL* VI.15258).

Carpe diem!

FURTHER READING

Balsdon, J.P.V.D., *Life and Leisure in Ancient Rome* (London, 1969)
Beard, M., *It's a Don's Life* (London, 2009)
——, *Emperor of Rome: Ruling the Ancient Roman World* (London, 2023)
Bodel, J., *Epigraphic Evidence: Ancient History from Inscriptions* (London, 2001)
Bruce, J. Douglas, 'Human Automata in Classical Tradition and Mediaeval
    Romance', *Modern Philology*, x/4 (1913) pp. 511–26
Carcopino, J., *Daily Life in Ancient Rome: People and the City at the Height
    of Empire* (London, 1941)
Cary, Max, and Eric Herbert Warmington, *The Ancient Explorers* (London, 1929)
Chrystal, Paul, *When in Rome: Social Life in Ancient Rome* (Stroud, 2017)
——, *Reportage in Ancient Greece and Rome* (Stroud, 2019)
——, *War in Greek Mythology* (Barnsley, 2020)
——, *The Book in the Ancient World: How the Wisdom of the Ages Was Preserved*
    (Barnsley, 2024)
——, *World-Changing Women: 150 Women Who Changed the Histories of Ancient
    Egypt, Israel, Greece and Rome* (Barnsley, 2024)
——, *Rome and the Unconquered Worlds Beyond the Empire* (Barnsley, 2025)
Dersin, D., ed., *What Life Was Like When Rome Ruled the World* (Richmond, VA,
    1997)
Duckworth, Chloë N., and Andrew Wilson, *Recycling and Reuse in the Roman
    Economy* (Oxford, 2020)
Dudley, D., *Roman Society* (London, 1975)
Elliot, A., ed., *Roman Food Poems* (Totnes, 2003)
Finley, M. I., *Ancient Slavery and Modern Ideology* (Harmondsworth, 1983)
Frontisi-Ducroux, Françoise, 'Dédale et Talos: mythologie et histoire des
    techniques', *Revue Historique*, CCXLIII/2 (1970), pp. 281–96
Garland, R., *The Eye of the Beholder: Deformity and Disability in the Graeco-Roman
    World* (Bristol, 2010)
Garlick, B., ed., *Stereotypes of Women in Power* (New York, 1992)
Garnsey, P., and R. Saller, *The Early Principate: Augustus to Trajan* (Oxford, 1982)
Gowers, E., *The Loaded Table: Representations of Food in Roman Literature*
    (Oxford, 1993)
Grant, M., *Roman Cookery* (London, 2008)
Griffin, M. T., *Nero: The End of a Dynasty* (London, 2000)
Hill, H., *The Roman Middle Class in the Republican Period* (London, 1952)
Hodges, Frederick M., 'The Ideal Prepuce in Ancient Greece and Rome: Male
    Genital Aesthetics and Their Relation to "Lipodermos", Circumcision,

Foreskin Restoration, and the "Kynodesmē"', *Bulletin of the History of Medicine*, LXXV/3 (2001), pp. 375–405

Jones, P., *Vote for Caesar: How the Ancient Greeks and Romans Solved the Problems of Today* (London, 2008)

Kenney, E. J., ed., *The Cambridge History of Classical Literature: The Early Principate* (Cambridge, 1982)

Laes, Christian, ed., *Disability in Antiquity* (London, 2020)

Lewis, N., ed., *Roman Civilization Sourcebook II: The Empire* (New York, 1966)

Marcinkowski, Alexandre, 'Automates et créatures artificielles d'Héphaïstos: entre science et fiction', https://journals.openedition.org/tc/1164, accessed 8 November 2024

Matyszak, P., *Ancient Rome on Five Denarii a Day* (London, 2007)

——, *Ancient Magic: A Practitioner's Guide to the Supernatural in Greece and Rome* (London, 2019)

——, *A Walk through Ancient Rome: A Tour of the Historical Sites That Shaped the City* (London, 2024)

Mayer, Ernst, *The Ancient Middle Classes: Urban Life and Aesthetics in the Roman Empire, 100 BCE–250 CE* (London, 2014)

Mohler, S. L., 'Feminism in the Corpus Inscriptionum Latinarum', *Classical Weekly*, XXV/15 (1932), pp. 113–16

Ogden, Daniel, *Binding Spells: Curse Tablets and Voodoo Dolls in the Greek and Roman Worlds* (Philadelphia, PA, 1999)

Ogilvie. R. M., *Roman Literature and Society* (Harmondsworth, 1980)

Peachin, M., ed., *The Oxford Handbook of Social Relations in the Roman World* (Oxford, 2011)

Rawson, B., 'Family Life among the Lower Classes in Rome in the First Two Centuries of the Empire', *Classical Philology*, LXI/2 (1966), pp. 71–83

Robertson, M., 'The Death of Talos', *Journal of Hellenic Studies*, 97 (1977), pp. 158–60, esp. p. 159.

Shelton, J.-A., *As the Romans Did: A Sourcebook in Roman History* (New York, 1998)

Shopland, Norena, *A History of Women in Men's Clothes* (Barnsley, 2021)

Toner, Jerry, *Popular Culture in Ancient Rome* (Cambridge, 2009)

Veyne, P., ed., *A History of Private Life: From Pagan Rome to Byzantium* (Cambridge, MA, 1997)

Wiedemann, T.E.J., *Slavery* (Oxford, 1987)

ACKNOWLEDGEMENTS

Thanks first to Philip Matyszak for kindly agreeing to write the Foreword to this book. No book is the work of one man or woman; this one certainly is not. So my thanks go out to Dr Caitlin Green FSA, Institute of Continuing Education, University of Cambridge, for permission to quote from her 'Were There Camels in Roman Britain?' published in *Forbes Magazine* (17 November 2017).

PHOTO ACKNOWLEDGEMENTS

The author and publishers wish to express their thanks to the sources listed below for illustrative material and/or permission to reproduce it. Some locations of artworks are also given below, in the interest of brevity:

Biblioteca Apostolica Vaticana, Vatican City (Vat.gr.1291, fol. 9r): p. 398; Bibliothèque nationale de France, Paris (MS Français 2810, fol. 29v): p. 27; British Library, London (Royal MS 12 F XIII, fol. 24v): p. 333; The Cleveland Museum of Art, OH: pp. 208–9; from Heinrich Dressel, *Ricerche sul Monte Testaccio* (Rome, 1878): p. 38; Flickr: pp. 33 (Rheinischen Landesmuseum Trier; photo Carole Raddato, CC BY-SA 2.0), 42 (National Archaeological Museum, Athens; photo Tilemahos Efthimiadis, CC BY 2.0), 289 (photo Dennis Jarvis, CC BY-SA 2.0), 381 (El Djem Archaeological Museum; photo Dennis Jarvis, CC BY-SA 2.0); from Wilhelm Froehner, *La colonne Trajane d'après le surmoulage exécuté a Rome en 1861–1862* (Paris, 1872–4), vol. II: p. 314; from A. Furtwaengler and K. Reichhold, *Griechische Vasenmalerei* (Munich, 1904), photo Universitätsbibliothek Heidelberg: p. 354 (original in Museo Nazionale Jatta, Ruvo di Puglia); Houston Museum of Natural Science, TX: p. 361; Musée Carnavalet, Histoire de Paris: p. 256; Necropoli etrusche di Cerveteri e di Tarquinia: p. 258; Pereslavl-Zalessky Historical, Architectural and Art Museum: p. 383; private collection: pp. 243, 384, 431; Staatsgalerie Stuttgart: p. 346; The State Tretyakov Gallery, Moscow: p. 306; from James Stuart and Nicholas Revett, *The Antiquities of Athens and Other Places in Greece, Sicily etc.*, vol. IV (London, 1830), photo Universitätsbibliothek Heidelberg: p. 249; Tate Britain, London: pp. 183, 357; University of Pennsylvania Libraries, Philadelphia (Kislak Center for Special Collections, Rare Books and Manuscripts, Incunables, Inc B-720): p. 221; photo Dimitris Vetsikas/Pixabay: p. 311; from Gaston Vorberg, *Die Erotik der Antike in Kleinkunst und Keramik* (Munich, 1921), photo Wellcome Library, London: p. 146; The Walters Art Museum, Baltimore, MD: pp. 236, 273; Wikimedia Commons: pp. 20 (Museo Archeologico Nazionale, Naples; photo Francesco Bini (Sailko), CC BY-SA 3.0), 79 (Museo Nazionale, Ravenna; photo Rabax63, CC BY-SA 4.0), 102 (Musée du Louvre, Paris; photo BastienM, CC BY-SA 3.0), 115 (Museo Arqueológico Nacional, Madrid; photo Marie-Lan Nguyen (Jastrow), CC BY 2.5), 149 (Musée du Louvre, Paris; photo Marie-Lan Nguyen (Jastrow), CC BY 3.0), 161 (Museo Archeologico Nazionale, Naples; photo Marie-Lan Nguyen (Jastrow), CC BY 2.5), 223 (Altes Museum, Staatliche Museen zu Berlin; photo Dosseman, CC BY-SA 4.0), 268 (Musée du Louvre, Paris; photo Marie-Lan Nguyen (Jastrow), CC BY 3.0), 284 (photo Francesco Bini (Sailko), CC BY 3.0), 287 (Museo Archeologico Nazionale, Naples; photo ArchaiOptix, CC BY-SA 4.0), 328 (El Djem Archaeological Museum;

INDEX

Page numbers in *italics* refer to illustrations